logics of
TELEVISION

Logics of Television: Essays in Cultural Criticism
is Volume 11 in the series

THEORIES OF CONTEMPORARY CULTURE
Center for Twentieth Century Studies
University of Wisconsin–Milwaukee

General Editor, KATHLEEN WOODWARD

logics of
TELEVISION
essays in cultural criticism

EDITED BY

Patricia Mellencamp

INDIANA UNIVERSITY PRESS
Bloomington and Indianapolis

BFI PUBLISHING, London

First published in the United States of America by
Indiana University Press
10th and Morton Streets
Bloomington, Indiana
and
Published in Great Britain by
The British Film Institute
21 Stephen Street
London W1P 1PL

The paper used in this publication meets the minimum requirements of
American National Standard for Information Sciences—Permanence of
Paper for Printed Library Materials, ANSI Z39.48-1984.
⊗™

Manufactured in the United States of America

Library of Congress Cataloging-in-Publication Data

Logics of television : essays in cultural criticism / edited by
   Patricia Mellencamp.
      p.   cm. — (Theories of contemporary culture ; v. 11)
   Includes bibliographical references.
      ISBN 0-253-33617-1 (alk. paper). — ISBN 0-253-20582-4 (pbk. : alk. paper)
      1. Television broadcasting—Social aspects.   2. Television
   broadcasting—United States.   I. Mellencamp, Patricia.   II. Series.
   PN1992.6.L64   1990
   302.23'45'0973—dc20   89-46004
                                                                  CIP

British Library Cataloguing in Publication Data

Logics of television: essays in cultural criticism - (Theories of contemporary culture v.2)
   1. Television services. Social aspects
   I. Mellencamp, Patricia   II. Series
   302.2345

   ISBN 0-85170-278-3

   2 3 4 5   94 93 92

CONTENTS

Acknowledgments

This volume and a year's worth of research on television resulted from a collaboration with Kathleen Woodward, Director of the Center for Twentieth Century Studies. At the Center, 1987/88 was referred to as "the year of television." All of our theories were beautifully put into practice by Carol Tennessen, Program and Publications Coordinator, and Jean Lile, Office Manager. During the year, Patrice Petro, a fellow at the Center, provided consultation along with intellectual energy.

The research was orchestrated around a series of intensive seminars called "Television and . . . Talk, Psychoanalysis, Postmodernism, Vietnam, Audience, Genre, Law, Body," with invited speakers who represented a wide array of approaches to television. In addition to the Center fellows who formed the nucleus of our audience—Roswitha Mueller, Rob Danielson, Barry Brummett, Arthur Seeger, Andrew Martin, Andrew Tolson, Peter Madsen, Joe Milicia, and Daniel Perkins—we invited regional scholars to become associate research fellows. This lively and impressive gang of inventive TV academics was composed of Mimi White, James Schwoch, Pam Falkenberg, and James Collins. I am deeply indebted to them for their participation, which clearly upped the ante of the debates, encouraging participants to think harder. I want to acknowledge the contribution of Modern Studies graduate students, particularly Sonja Rein, Aine O'Brien, and Connie Balides, and Henry Jenkins from Madison, in addition to Center graduate project assistants Ed Schelb and Linda Geimer.

The list of speakers in these sessions of productive television scholarship, in addition to papers by the associates and fellows, included Sandy Flitterman-Lewis, Maureen Turim, Chris Straayer, Rick Altman, Julie D'Acci, John Carlos Rowe, Susan Jeffords, Don Le Duc, Robert Allen, David Marc, and Bob Thompson, along with the crew of *60 Minutes* which left Mimi White's and my talks on the cutting room floor, thereby missing a big opportunity to include women's voices. A television issue of *Discourse*, co-edited by Woodward, Mueller, and Petro, suggests some of the exciting range of this research.

The presence of Meaghan Morris from Australia during the fall semester and the research and TV pedagogy of John Caughie in the spring enhanced the year to the nth degree. We consider these exemplary scholars, like Stephen Heath, to forever be Milwaukee regulars; in fact, Morris has already returned.

The international conference, the scene that set the stage for this volume, took place from April 12 through April 15, 1988, at the Center for Twentieth Century Studies; speakers not represented by essays in this volume include Lidia Curti (Italy), Michèle Mattelart (France), Jane Feuer, Ondina Fachel Leal (Brazil), James Collins, Andrew Tolson (Scotland), Mimi White,

Pamela Falkenberg, James Schwoch, Richard Campbell, Hilary Radner, Carole-Anne Tyler, Connie Balides, Laura Goostree, Glenn Hendler, Ana Lopez, Brian Nienhaus, Thomas Streeter, William Uricchio, Simon Frith (Scotland), and Patrice Petro; our energetic discussants included Brian Winston, John Fiske, Hans Gumbrecht (Germany), Dana Polan, and Robert Deming. Needless to say, given the caliber of scholars, it was a lively and sometimes contestatory event of which this book is only a partial and idiosyncratic record.

I am grateful to the National Endowment for the Arts, which funded the segments of the event called "Guerrilla TV and Feminist Video," particularly because we refused to change the title of the proposal to a less threatening one. Artists participating in these programs included Deedee Halleck, Doug Hall, Chip Lord, Annie Goldson, and Judith Barry. April 16 and 17 consisted of a video festival curated by Cecelia Condit and Rob Danielson; all of this video was technologically orchestrated, to perfection, by Rob Yeo. With Danielson's coordination, for two weeks prior to the event, Paper Tiger tapes were broadcast on cable access; the following Saturday, the Paper Tiger conference extravaganza, a production orchestrated by Danielson with the MATA staff and UWM-video students, was broadcast live. It is another record of this event. For his patience and attention to detail, I thank Thomas Piontek for his assistance in copy-editing the manuscript, Suzy Michaels and Barbara Obremski for their careful typing, and David Crane for indexing.

For exclusions and oversights either at the conference or regarding this volume, I express my regrets of unintentionality.

PATRICIA MELLENCAMP

logics of
TELEVISION

PROLOGUE

Patricia Mellencamp

This is not a proper introduction but rather a collection of impressions which begin and end with personal scenes across a generational divide. In the 50s, after the Monday night broadcast of "*I Love Lucy*" and with "Hound Dog" blaring from the radio, I drove to McDonald's, then a new teenage drive-in hangout, for a cheap hamburger, fries, and shake. To adolescent Elvis imitators with their hair slicked back, I gushed about Elvis's first appearance on the Ed Sullivan show *Toast of the Town*. Today not only can I watch Lucy cavort daily at 10:30 in the morning, or see her in primetime playing a seventy-year-old bag lady, watch my bootlegged tape of Elvis's 50s TV stints, or say "Charge it to the King" with an Elvis Presley charge card, but I can have an Egg McMuffin, Chicken McNuggets, or upscale shrimp salad in a neat, international, family oasis rather than greaser/hot rod milieu. Or, I can drive in and through. (Not a day goes by without a reference to Presley in the media.)

Along with taking 50s teenage culture into middle age, the postmodern will to power and desire for capital gains (called diversification) appears on its designer surface to complicate the modernized virtues of specialization. The rapidly expanding and profitable service industries are dividing and multiplying labor into discrete, timed units. Local *centralization* (all-service garages or department stores) is shifting to national *dispersion* (local franchises of international monopolies for fast services like Midas Muffler or McDonald's, which takes a 12% commission, unlike Subway, which gets 8%). Franchise culture (ironically, franchise means liberty or freedom from restriction or servitude), uniform down to the pickle, is trademark culture— a minutely disciplined culture (which has also taken Taylorism and Fordism into leisure along with "professionalizing" the family). The guarantee is that the Big Mac will be *exactly* the same in Moscow as in Washington. To purchase something in the USSR entails standing in three separate lines to complete three separate transactions—ordering, paying, and picking up. What will shock the Soviet sense of temporality will be not product uniformity, so prevalent already in consumer choices, but rather the speed achieved with the system of incremental labor descended from Taylor's

1917 schema of timed "scientific management" *without,* however, its monetary incentives. For me, who as a child of Cold War paranoia and foreign policies of defensive containment lived in Wisconsin when Senator Joseph McCarthy was wielding his list of "known Communists," standing some thirty years later in Red Square was to experience disbelief and wonder. Seeing a Big Mac in Moscow is as logical and incongruent as Kuleshov's editing experiments.

Within the US television industry, a similar imaginary shift from centralization to internationalization has emerged—from *network* television (an amalgam of the local and the national with regional differences, including accents, now vanishing, as are locally owned retail department stores) to *syndication* and *national cable channels* or superstations which specialize in weather, prayer, shopping, movies, sports, news, medicine, and more recently, genres or styles. These services are picked up by local cable franchises such as Viacom or Warner, which are national monopolies competing for markets, or cities. (Countries and perhaps even continents will soon follow; for example, plans are complete for a European news cable channel that will operate over and above national boundaries, transmitting versions of the same news in various languages.) When a five-minute segment like the weather (the weather is the most watched and hence most profitable segment of news on local stations; thus it is placed in the middle of the program to prevent channel switching) turns into a national all-day channel, TV behaves overtly like the service industry it is.

Along with the presumed if not self-proclaimed diversity, pluralism, and freedom of choice signaled by this new electronic/satellite constellation, this liberated economics of broadcasting (broadcasting denotatively means disbandment, decentralization, and hence is accurate for television, but is now termed "narrowcasting") can also be read as standardization and specialization (the twin principles of industrial, monopoly capitalism). This is centrism in clever and evanescent disguise as intangible dispersion, occupying narrower bands of the spectrum but mimicking the networks just the same—like Elvis, the return of David Sarnoff as Ted Turner or Rupert Murdoch. Under the uniformity of local franchises, we are being rapidly disenfranchised of differences.

As Raymond Williams pointed out years ago, national transmission (and real estate—by stations in major cities) and clear, private reception (and the sale of TV sets or "consumer durables"), not content or product, have always been network, corporate concerns resembling what "video guerrillas," in their critique of network or "beast television" as product culture, hailed in the mid-1960s as "process" culture. Although public debates and journalistic plaints centered on products and effects (we were relieved to learn in December, 1988, that the millions of studies suggesting or demonstrating the harmful effects of TV on our children were absolutely wrong, that TV has no detrimental effects and might even be a learning stimulus), program was, to a degree, a secondary concern of the networks.

Albeit by regulatory decree which declared TV a service, not a product, networks jobbed out production to independent producers/creators like Desi Arnaz and Lucille Ball, who retained ownership of tangible, filmed commodities which could be transported around the world. The more rapid internationalization of television via the immediacy of satellites on a *global* allocation of an electromagnetic spectrum never imagined as nationally determined, replicates this emphasis on transmission. This is a revision of the noble, primitive dream of a global electronic community fostered in the 60s by McLuhan, Michael Shamberg, Nam June Paik, Gene Young-blood, and other video visionaries.

However, the recent deregulation of international TV markets, permitting the televising of programs produced in the US, and the 1988 Writers' Guild strike for profit-sharing or "points" (opposed by the producers with the tricky claim that the money at stake was only minor, which is indeed true for the conglomerates who own the studios) demonstrated the mind-boggling profits from the sale of TV series for national syndication and to international markets; TV series are and always have been very hot properties. They are not owned by the networks as are soaps (and *60 Minutes* and other varieties of news), which remained on the air during the strike. While the scholarly analysis of TV representation is unfashionable if not disdained, series are circulating internationally, out of context, with a re-alignment of an economic superstructure. The new media barons—modeled on the Rupert Murdoch empire which in the US can outmaneuver federal courts and the FCC—function trans- or supranationally, unrestrained, exempt from ordinary law or due process.

John Berger's assessment in 1972 of the replacement of political choice by a polynomial begetting of new and improved products—their dizzying reiteration, an endogamy of the same as innovative—is right on the money. The difference is packaging. Tylenol sells "pain relief" as an aside: in the beginning, there were tablets, then capsules, then caplets. Today there are "new extra strength *gel caps*, not capsules. It's not a capsule, it's better," says spokeswoman Susan Sullivan, the serious, presumably smart, former star of *Falcon Crest*. (Jay Leno scales his verbal register of incredulity: A *gel cap*?) Amidst all this infinitesimal *differentiation*, the political concept of *differences*, along with meaningful choices, is arduous to maintain.

What is operative is the old structure of vertically integrated and horizontally divaricated monopolies, *divested* into competitive packaging, a re-fracted more *as* the difference we identify—the perplexity of choosing among Burger King, Wendy's, and McDonald's, acclaimed as different and thus built on the same corner of the "strip shopping" agglutination surrounding shopping malls. Like burgers, the packaging of television has been redesigned and recalibrated. There is infinitely more television, available on seventy channels, for twenty-four hours per day. However, in contrast to the quantum leap of theoretical physics which overthrew geometry along with Newton's laws of motion, this is often more of the same, including the appeal to the new paradox of local, mass, subcultural (Taco Bell) audiences. Such localized diversity is illustrated by the proliferation of culture/art and politics magazines. The national scope of magazines divided and multiplied into *East* and *West*; *New York* magazine, then *Chicago* and *Los Angeles* branched out and were followed by *Milwaukee* magazine, which subdivided into *Art Muscle,* the *Shepherd Express,* and the soon-to-appear Milwaukee version of the *Village Voice.* TV cable access—local, unpolished, and unpredictable—might promise more of the glossy same.

At the same time, the differences, albeit incremental and annihilated under the pressure of trend, are critical. While *Milwaukee* shares a glitzy, celebrity fascination with *New York,* it is not New York. Paper Tiger TV, working (and networking) in and with local public-access facilities and groups, has used the reluctant bribes of cable corporations: The payoff for the city-wide contract is a free studio, equipment, training, and a cable channel available to anyone. Paper Tiger is not PBS or a rarefied art video scene; rather, in its structure, method, and videotapes, it critiques our mediated institutions, including television, all the while enacting an artistic, intellectual, and economic model of collaborative work which has revitalized the early 1970s goals of *Guerrilla TV* and added women and race to the agenda.

Given commercial TV's (1) reliance on parody, an internal referentiality to itself and the forms, styles, and characters of other media, (2) enunciation along a spectrum of live/recorded, direct/indirect address, the presence of audiences and laugh tracks, (3) recycling of old and familiar formats, genres, and stars as programming techniques (*Roseanne* is a return of *Lucy,* with a feminist, working-class, stand-up-comedy twist), (4) representation of motherhood, marriage, and the family home, (5) dominance of white male characters on the news in particular but also in entertainment, and (6) representation of women and race—given all this, TV history (or what Walter Benjamin might call "a tiger's leap into fashion") is remarkably consistent, or better, fashionable. For example, when women and their issues are "in style" as they were in the early 1970s, we will, as with padded shoulders in 1988, see them on television. Women's "lib" was both joke and story on the old *Bob Newhart*; in 1986 feminism is introduced into *LA Law* as issue or shocking event, then turned into gossip or scandal—transformed into crazy idiosyncrasy and hence contained like all the "strong," single professional women who were coupled to (im)perfect mates with amazing speed.

However, the figures charting a severe decline in the representation of blacks and other minorities are very disturbing. From 1970 to 1980, (1) whites enhanced their overall domination, (2) blacks had a representation of only 6 to 8 percent, and (3) other minorities were virtually excluded from portrayal.[1] The study concludes that the black female has become almost invisible, and appearances by other minorities have dropped in representation, while white women have increased their representation.

The percentage of major roles for whites, both male and female, has increased, while those for blacks of both sexes have decreased. Granted that these figures are pre-Cosby (never mind their methodological limitations), these findings replicate a report from 1969 to 1974: white males were overrepresented, females underrepresented, and minority females almost invisible (p. 285). This tradeoff, of (equivocal) gains for white women and losses for women of color, is a disconcerting turn of events.

On the other hand, television is an oasis for white women when it is compared to the 1988 configuration of US cinema—with its predominance of male buddy movies as Christmas specials, the trend toward male regression in movies like *Big* and *Sea of Love,* and the dominance of male stars, particularly when serious issues were at stake—the stock market, the Vietnam war, or civil rights (*Mississippi Burning*)—and with professional women as monsters (*Fatal Attraction*), mothers as resigned martyrs (*The Good Mother*), or bimbos and bombshells (*Sea of Love, Black Rain*). On television we find *Murphy Brown* who is independent, tough, beautiful, funny, and professionally superior. *Roseanne* does not play to or for men or represent the imaginary blissful, labor-free joys of motherhood; more radically, she is fat. *Annie MacGuire* talks about politics (and has been canceled). Although it is difficult to imagine Candice Bergen or Mary Tyler Moore as 60s protestors, both of their 1988 characters claim an activist past—Murphy's Tom Hayden-like ex-husband appeared; their mutual instant lust was all that remained of their radical past. Annie and Murphy both attended the 1968 political conventions as protestors. Bergen as Murphy states her forty-year age, while Moore as Annie takes care of her aging parents, and Barr as Roseanne complains about her children, her husband, and her overwork.

Thus, it is a serious oversight, which functions as a prohibition, to ignore the subject of representation in television (other than in its moment of subcultural reception), claiming, as do many critics, that it is an "unmanageable" subject or that its significance is lost amidst the sway of flow. Equally delimited is a narrow notion of "text" that ignores enunciation, address, in short, the audience, or its context and conditions of production—history and the industry. The specific mechanisms, techniques, and economics of exclusion and containment, the textual absences and contradictions that promulgate and cover up racism, sexism, and ageism, are not insignificant. In an era of mass diversity of sameness, it is critical to identify differences and unravel the operations of contradiction rather than focusing on the manufacture of indifference.

Thus, this book is obliquely and directly concerned with representation not as a discrete, delimited, ontological object which can be "deconstructed" like a book or film (although retaining the option of deciphering specificity) but as a *question,* considering ways in which we can begin to think about "representing television" as it is inextricably bound up with audiences and industry, and with libidinal and economic systems (and the politics) of production, transmission, and reception. For example, Eileen Meehan's essay on the ratings system can be read as the industry's historical representation of an imaginary audience, simultaneously pitched to, and skewed for, advertisers and networks. Lynn Spigel's analysis of the advertising campaign that introduced television into US homes considers the means by which the television industry, particularly manufacturers of TV sets, represented its product as an "opportunity" for the nuclear family and in particular women to reconfigure and redecorate domestic space. Jane Gaines's history of the legal shift from copyright law to trademark cases (with legal interpretations swerving from consumer protection to defense of corporate property) documents a cultural shift in the very terms and legal conditions of representation—a move positively or negatively labeled "postmodernism." The theoretical swirl around "Baudrillard," addressed in detail here by Meaghan Morris and Stephen Heath, is a debate about the status of representation which is unwittingly predicated on television as its model. The place of the real or the true in relation to simulation is at issue in William Boddy's analysis of the responses of the television industry and critics to the quiz show scandals of the 50s—a position of industrial cynicism (much like the position of the raters).

In addition, critical to the context of this book is the awareness for film scholars of the misfit that occurs when the intricate methods of film analysis, including psychoanalytic constructs of desire and disavowal, are superimposed on TV. The first realization of the difference between film and TV is often centered around arguments regarding the difficulty in defining or locating the "TV text," the dilemma of finding the locus for research. Stage two involves questioning the intellectual's relationship to the theoretical object, to television as a material artifact.

During an international conference on television in April, 1988 (the forum in which the majority of these essays were initially presented), this scholastic disputation became more heated, momentarily dividing around the issue of pluralism (with an emphasis on the audience, and a move away from representation, with a celebratory stance toward television and the people capable of subversive readings, with these intellectuals positing themselves as liking or respecting television) versus a Marxist critique of "pluralism" and its concomitant notion of "popular pleasure." At moments it seemed that an old-fashioned lefty condemnation of television as instrumentally manipulative was being revived and enacted. The old debate of whether television was a good or bad object circulated here, and a certain tedium settled in during arguments about whether the "people" were clever deconstructors or not. In the US, these divisions are currently, and arbitrarily, represented by those who focus on the audience as the critical object of study, and those who view the audience as one relay within the textual and industrial process of television.

The question of the relation of the intellectual to TV emerges in these essays as a methodological issue. The scholar's relation to and involvement with the objects under study becomes an issue of enunciation which inscribes the author's historical relation to the texts. John Caughie, for example, suggests that "[a] television criticism which can identify with itself may avoid speaking for experiences it isn't having." Morris points to the gap in variants of cultural studies between "the cultural student and the culture studied." Although not the theoretical focus of his argument, the figure of the intellectual circulates throughout Boddy's paper in the form of Charles Van Doren, one of the rare scholars turned star on television, and, ironically, TV's biggest scandal. By 1961, "cultural democracy," or giving the people what they want, had become the networks' reply to their critics, an answer to deception and simulation, a virtual *raison d'être,* and a tautological one at that. Meehan meticulously dissects the evidence, the basis for this claim by the networks and scholars to television as pure democracy: the audience, historically constructed and traded as a commodity by the raters, its accuracy and existence as the democratically plural argued through statistical science and technology. Meehan unravels this corporate practice and logic, and argues that the networks use the false premise of cultural democracy against critics, labeling them elitists and thus squelching opposition. That this rhetorical syllogism, involving a sleight of its major premise, is repeated in academia is not without interest. That the raters' audience is not representative is Meehan's premise and clearly documented conclusion.

Also at stake in the conference was "theory," and the value of "theorizing" television. For some of us, the notion of "text" partakes of audience *and* representation without the mutual exclusivity claimed by many scholars. And, this theorization of the text is not contextless. It includes the economic conditions of production, although within television studies (particularly with those approaches derived from "the Birmingham School" and transposed in "cultural studies"), the moment of consumption or reception is the valued focus of research.

Morris, in a paper initially delivered while she was teaching in Milwaukee, directly addresses issues of this debate, along with the status of representation in the work of Baudrillard and Michel de Certeau—her critique being defined by feminism. Echoes of these issues, particularly constructs of Baudrillard, reverberate in a very different way in Heath's concluding essay, which marks out the terrain of "representing television." Heath's location of representation within economic determinants and political treatises is demonstrated in Meehan's history of the rating system passed on from the 20s to the present.

Andrew Ross (in)directly engages issues of postmodernism in relation to *Max Headroom,* with (political) economics a clear subtext, specifically the Cola Wars. The economics of the legal shift from copyright law to trademark law, which Gaines charts via court cases, along with her analysis of various *Superman* texts, provides a basis for rethinking postmodernism and is a legal explanation for what I call "franchise culture." Lynne Joyrich assesses the place of the female spectator or consumer within postmodernism and television scholarship, and, with a nod to Baudrillard, detects what is called "hypermasculinity" in critical texts. Spigel sketches a historical consumer—the audience addressed by women's magazines of the 50s urging the buying and installation of TV sets as a solution to family/home dilemmas.

The necessity of analyzing the TV text is posed as an issue of value, perhaps even aesthetics, by Charlotte Brunsdon, who maps a brief intellectual history of British scholarship on television which leads to the contemporary focus on the audience. Here she centers on representation. From the context of Scotland, displaced into Milwaukee where he taught, Caughie addresses the theoretical tourist/scholar's dilemma (recalling Baudrillard and Disneyland, Barthes and Japan, Raymond Williams and San Francisco as disparate examples of traveling academics), deriving a model of irony from his cultural displacement and from television. Traveling fast within the central city by car (unlike de Certeau's or Benjamin's pedestrian), and familiar with the landscape, Margaret Morse employs and updates Bakhtin's notion of the chronotope—specifically freeways and malls as analogue models for television and its experience. Her reading of Walter Benjamin is elaborated by Mary Ann Doane's and my essays in relation to TV time and catastrophe. Temporality is also a concern of Heath, and catastrophe is related as a "theoretical" anecdote of cultural difference by Morris.

Central to many papers is a historical logic of contradiction. Gaines points to both trademark and copyright law encouraging and standing against a monopoly of culture. The takeover of trademark law, with its emphasis on source, origin, and sponsorship as opposed to authorship, and with the character detached from the work, snugly fits the development and marketing of television, a shift which begins in the post–World War II period. Spigel, working with materials from the postwar period, documents the contradiction of ad campaigns which depicted TV as simultaneously disrupting and unifying "the family circle." Boddy describes the network circling of the wagons around the quiz show scandals in the 1950s. I locate my theory of contradiction and the postmodern catastrophic imagination in the same time frame, specifically the postwar nuclear tests. I submit that contradiction is TV's *overt*, defining logic, hence the book's title.

Perhaps taken together, these essays suggest that a more satisfying model of postmodernism (a term which doesn't fit some of these authors comfortably, suggesting that it either is out of style or perhaps is wearing out) could be argued from the point of view of popular culture rather than art. The late 40s might be a more apt starting point for an exploration of postmodernism. Similarly we might shift our focus—and perhaps our theories—to include methods of mass production, distribution, and reception, including standardization and specialization and their economic and electronic variants. In many ways, British cultural studies and US postmodernism, mutually left positions, echo each other—one placed firmly in the audience of mass culture, the other in the representation of art. The reverberation of a cross-cultural collision or collaboration might just result in a third term, a more satisfying entity which could consider representation along with its audience, neither at the expense of the other (which is what the raters and networks argue).

Within the general terrain of postmodernism, Ross analyzes *Max Headroom* as both a critique of TV and a paradoxical but predictable enactment of containment. Against "liberal" readings, he argues that audiences might have enjoyed the truancy of Max more than his militancy. Joyrich posits a postmodern feminist critique of "hypermasculinity," while Gaines, in her "disjunctively ironic" examples of two Superman commodity experiences, suggests that perhaps the 80s are not so terribly different from the 40s, that for actants within mass cultural experiences, postmodernism might be old hat rather than high fashion.

As I stated earlier, overlapping with the lofty question of the intellectual's relation to television is the more mundane terrain of method—how should we look at television and how should we contextualize it? Methodology is the organizing principle for the arrangement of these essays, more an arbitrary than an orderly principle. Thus, placed first is Morris's general overview of the state of cultural studies and cultural critique. She suggests how academics might proceed, what questions might be asked, and how our projects might be framed—operating through a method of cultural sites as rhomboid intersections of textual practices, mediated by theories, and carefully negotiated by the writer (Morris gives us anecdotes as allegories rather than as personal experience). Similarly, Caughie asks more specifically how we should study television as a cultural object without losing sight of its national contexts. He argues for local (rather than universal) theory which respects cultural difference, seen, as with Morris and Australia, from his context, Scotland. Methodology is the terrain of Brunsdon's history, which is also set within the context of specific debates around a dominant model of audience studies. The often covert differences among our theories, which circulate out of contexts that specify if not overdetermine our arguments, begin to emerge. In 1988 cultural differences yield insights as critical as sexual difference did for feminist film theory.

Historiographic approaches to television follow in the cross-media analysis of Spigel and the more traditional study by Boddy, which largely draws on journalism in the trade magazines. Meehan's economic analysis, like Gaines's, is informed by an ideological materialist critique. Both essays elucidate the contradictions of late capitalism—whether corporate or legal. As Gaines writes, "the recurring dilemma is whether law asserts itself as material base or disengaged superstructure." Ross echoes Caughie's call for "disjunctive irony," in an essay written with what Caughie notices is itself an attribute of television, its presumption of a "street-wise smartness," an "ironic knowingness," like, perhaps, the anarchy of the computer hacker. Postmodernism is a given, as it is for Joyrich, who draws on television scholarship.

The next three essays assume that cultural criticism is the way to think about television. (That the *theoretical* models developed for film are not directly applicable is an assumption loudly declared by their absence.) Morse uses a model of nonspace, while Doane and I, in divergent ways, employ a system of time. Television becomes emblematic of larger cultural issues for Doane, centering on information. While Morse's essay is to a degree dependent on the experience of Los Angeles, mine is derived from my experience of anxiety, TV, and domesticity. The last pages are given to Heath, who returns to previous issues—including representation, cultural studies, and democratic pluralism—taking them into theory and pedagogy.

It is the revelation of *academic* differences that is the most invigorating aspect of the recent cultural study of television. For this research, I asked participants to take intellectual risks, to refuse either scholastic caution or repetition of old formulas. Some essays included in this book represent that kind of adventurous labor in which the process of thought is almost palpable. The stakes in these debates in television studies are significant, given television's rearrangement of everyday life, politics, culture, our imaginaries, and national borders, given its forty years of marketing which began in the US amidst Cold War policies, and given the current dispersal of the networks and audience decline coincident with the end of the Cold War (its conclusion declared by the 1988 televised coverage of Reagan in Red Square surrounded by smiling Soviet citizens). Without models, methods, or intellectual tactics, we cannot effectively critique television but only end up repeating arguments which, unwittingly, overlap with network positions, for example, the relationship between "giving the audience what it wants" and the celebration of "popular pleasure."

As with television (and history), what is absent from this research and from this book is also important. While I consider this collection to represent an extremely high stratum of inventive thought about television, providing invaluable and creative models for studying other cultural artifacts in addition to television, I anticipate negative criticisms, including its emphasis on US network television. While it is presumed as axiomatic that television massively addresses women (for Adrienne Rich, this is bad; for others, it is good), the terms of that enunciation have not been specified, or theorized; if they had been, the liberated containment of women that is the result would certainly raise a few eyebrows. In fact, even without deep thought or analysis, the raw data are unsettling. Women still are underrepresented on television (with three male characters to every two females as the best assessment).

Also absent is any analysis of the representation of race—a scholastic oversight resembling the move of the Democratic party against the vice-presidential candidacy of Jesse Jackson in 1988 (illustrating that TV is about differentiation, not difference). A crucial question of our present is the politics of colonialism or benign inclusion and/or exclusion. The "special" commercials inserted during the coverage of the Olympics, glaringly presented as "exceptional" just like the black athletes who *represented* the US, pointed to TV's resolute exclusion of blacks and other minorities during their "regularly scheduled programming." Momentarily linked, for the world to see, were the concepts of "Olympic," "Nation," and "Racial Balance/Harmony." (Significantly, commercials and programs since January, 1989, are beginning to include images of African-Americans; and NBC premiered its soap opera *Generations* in March, 1989, structured, as the aesthetic ads state, around "black and white.")

Another absence is the lack of a critique of current manifestations of "familialism." More than anything else, US television—in its commercials and its programs and its overriding enunciation—appeals to an ideology of familialism (and happy cleanliness), to a myth of the middle-class, happy family reproduced in sitcoms, local news staffs, the *Today* show, a nuclear family which is in fact splitting in this society, creating a new class of the female poor at the same time that it is reconstituting itself in newly married couples and what might become a new baby boom. Like working women in real life, including professional women, numerous female characters and performers on television are pregnant. Daycare has become a political and Republican issue on television. Even the coverage of catastrophe is transformed into personal family dramas of loss and separation. Think of the December, 1988, airplane crash in Scotland with the US college students returning home for Christmas among the victims, Baby Jessica's rescue, John-John saluting his father's coffin, and Christa MacAuliffe's parents watching the *Challenger* explosion.

More predictable is the lack of emphasis on alternative video practice. I structured the conference on "Television: Representation/Audience/Industry" to lead to and conclude with sessions devoted to alternative video culture. The theoretical move of the three-day format was deliberate—from commercial representation, through audience, to industry, and then to alternative politics, economics, and representations. These latter sessions included Doug Hall, Chip Lord, Judith Barry, and Annie Goldson (and their work in video), and Deedee Halleck with clips from Paper Tiger productions. For an alternative account of the conference, see Paper Tiger's local TV production at MATA in which several speakers participated in their own parody (including Morse, Caughie, Goldson, and Hilary Radner), and which is notable for Halleck's crazy and clever rendering of the "theory weather."

Some of us involved in film studies for more than a decade have shifted our attention to include television, which is set within the larger terrain of cultural studies. Given that cinema does not divide easily into art versus mass culture, that its economic determinations and structures have been taken as critical, and that the conventions of classical narrative function within contradictions and industrial practices, this interdisciplinary move is logical. For many film scholars, postmodernism was very familiar. An

early harbinger of this shift to cultural criticism was Roland Barthes's
"Change the Object Itself" (in *Image-Music-Text*), a short revision of his
earlier essay on myth. Barthes writes that our "operational concepts would
no longer be sign, signifier, signified, and connotation but citation, reference, and stereotype." Rather than separating signifier from signified, a
step which any student now regularly performs, we should work on the
sign, "widening the historical field." The critic must ask: "What are the
articulations, the displacements, which make up the mythological tissue of
a mass consumer society?" In a culture of signs "endlessly deferring their
foundation," the direction "of combat is not that of critical decipherment
but of evaluation." The critic's task must be "to change the object itself, to
produce a new object, point of departure." For many intellectuals historically leery of entertaining machines of pleasure, TV is just too banal an
object. Or, when faced with television, their response is akin to Jack Gould's
comment (quoted by Boddy) that after one episode of a quiz show or a
Western, he had nothing else to say. The aim of this book is "to change
the object itself," transforming TV into a theoretical object.

While the generational divide in many ways structures the relation of
the intellectual to television and in fact has much to do with TV's enunciative strategies, generational difference has worked to my benefit. My
commitment to thinking about television came about for one very specific
reason, and I am intellectually indebted to that delightful circumstance of
my life. I have two intelligent, independent children who watched television
critically and parodically, and who loved Shakespeare, calculus, and chem-
istry at the same time. It all began in the early 70s with *Speed Racer*, amidst
a liberal context of civil rights protests, debates about the Vietnam War and
violence, that resulted in most academics forbidding their children to watch
television or play with toy guns and soldiers. (The old "effects" arguments,
with statistics wielded by philosophers and semioticians in heated debates,
determined TV censorship by intellectuals and parents. Equally operative
was the always/already disavowal of the intelligentsia: "But *I* don't watch
[have a] television [set].")

When I would walk into the den and condescendingly trash that aggressive program, *Speed Racer*, the favorite (or whatever happened to be
on), Rob and Dae would point out the knee-jerkiness of my predictable
and irritating response, largely based on lack of any knowledge of television. I appreciated TV, automatically, in a glance, when I cooked, ironed,
or performed other domestic tasks, and watched it gratefully whenever I
was single-parent tired. Gradually, I developed a critical rather than dismissive attitude toward television. And, because watching TV (and studying
all those episodes of Lucy) made me anxious, I was finally led to Freud's
texts on anxiety. Rob and Dae are now at college, with no time for television,
while I edit this book and watch the delayed 1988 TV season, fortunately
not perversely awaiting, as I did last year at the same time, catastrophes

to use as examples for my project. The new season is a massive return to sitcoms. I wonder. Is this the 80s? Or the 50s?

NOTES

1. John Seggar, Jeffrey Hafen, and Helena Hannonen-Gladden, "Television's Portrayals of Minorities and Women in Drama and Comedy Drama 1971–1980," *Journal of Broadcasting* 25.3 (Summer 1981):281.

BANALITY IN
CULTURAL STUDIES

Meaghan Morris

This paper takes a rather circuitous route to get to the point. I'm not sure that banality can have a point, any more than cultural studies can properly constitute its theoretical object. My argument *does* have a point, but one that takes the form of pursuing an aim rather than reaching a conclusion. Quite simply, I wanted to come to terms with my own irritation about two developments in recent cultural studies.

One was Jean Baudrillard's revival of the term "banality" to frame a theory of media. It is an interesting theory that establishes a tension between everyday life and catastrophic events, banality and "fatality"—using television as a metonym of the problems that result. Yet why should such a classically dismissive term as "banality" appear to establish, yet again, a frame of reference for discussing popular culture?

The other development has occurred in the quite different context that John Fiske calls "British Cultural Studies,"[1] and is much more difficult to specify. Judith Williamson, however, has bluntly described something that also bothers me: "left-wing academics . . . picking out strands of 'subversion' in every piece of pop culture from Street Style to Soap Opera."[2] In this kind of analysis of everyday life, it seems to be *criticism* that actively strives to achieve "banality," rather than investing it negatively in the object of study.

These developments are not *a priori* related, let alone opposed (as, say, pessimistic and optimistic approaches to popular culture). They also involve different kinds of events. "Baudrillard" is an author, British Cultural Studies is a complex historical and political movement as well as a library of texts. But irritation may create relations where none need necessarily exist. To attempt to do so is the real point of this paper.

I want to begin with a couple of anecdotes about banality, fatality, and television. But since storytelling itself is a popular practice that varies from culture to culture, I shall again define my terms. My impression is that American culture easily encourages people to assume that a first-person anecdote is primarily oriented toward the emotive and conative functions, in Jakobson's terms, of communication: that is, toward speaker-expressive and addressee-connective activity, or an I/you axis in discourse. However, I take anecdotes, or yarns, to be primarily referential. They are oriented futuristically towards the construction of a precise, local, and *social* discursive context, of which the anecdote then functions as a *mise en abyme*. That is to say, anecdotes for me are not expressions of personal experience but allegorical expositions of a model of the way the world can be said to be working. So anecdotes need not be true stories, but they must be functional in a given exchange.

My first anecdote is a fable of origin.

TV came rather late to Australia: 1956 in the cities, later still in the country regions where the distance between towns was immense for the technology of that time. So it was in the early 1960s that in a remote mountain village—where few sounds disturbed the peace except for the mist rolling down to the valley, the murmur of the wireless, the laugh of the kookaburra, the call of the bellbird, the humming of chainsaws and lawnmowers, and the occasional rustle of a snake in the grass—the pervasive silence was shattered by the voice of Lucille Ball.

In the memory of many Australians, television came as Lucy, and Lucy *was* television. There's a joke in *Crocodile Dundee* where the last white frontiersman (Paul Hogan) is making first contact with modernity in his New York hotel, and he's introduced to the TV set. But he already knows TV: "I saw that twenty years ago at so-and-so's place." He sees the title, *"I Love Lucy,"* and says, "Yeah, that's what I saw." It's a throwaway line that at one level works as a formal definition of the "media-recycle" genre of the film itself. But in terms of the dense cultural punning that characterizes the film, it's also, for Australians, a very precise historical joke. Hogan was himself one of the first major Australian TV stars, finding instant stardom in the late 1960s by faking his way onto a talent-quest show, and then abusing the judges. Subsequently, he took on the Marlboro Man in a massive cigarette-advertising battle that lasted long enough to convert the slogan of Hogan's commercials ("Anyhow, have a Winfield") into a proverb inscrutable to foreigners. So Hogan's persona already incarnates a populist myth of indigenous Australian response to Lucy as synecdoche of all American media culture.

But in the beginning was Lucy, and I think she is singled out in memory—since obviously it was not the only program available—because of the impact of her voice. The introduction of TV in Australia led not only to the usual debates about the restructuring of family life and domestic space, and to predictable fears that the Australian "accent" in language and culture might be abolished, but also to a specific local version of anxiety about the effects of TV on children. In "Situation Comedy, Feminism, and Freud: Discourses of Gracie and Lucy," Patricia Mellencamp discusses the spectacle

of female comedians in the American 1950s "being out of control via language (Gracie) or body (Lucy)."[3] In my memory, Lucy herself combines
both functions. Lucy was heard by many Australians as a screaming hys-
teric: as "voice," she was "seen" to be a woman out of control in both
language *and* body. So there was concern that Lucy-television would, by
some mimesis or contagion of the voice, metabolically transform Australian
children from the cheeky little larrikins we were expected to be into ragingly
hyperactive little psychopaths.

My own memory of this lived theoretical debate goes something like this.
My mother and I loved Lucy, my father loathed "that noise." So once a
week, there would be a small domestic catastrophe, which soon became
routinized, repetitive, banal. I'd turn Lucy on, my father would start grum-
bling, Mum would be washing dishes in the next room, ask me to raise the
volume, I'd do it, Dad would start yelling, Mum would yell back, I'd creep
closer to the screen to hear, until finally Lucy couldn't make herself heard,
and I'd retire in disgust to my bedroom, to the second-best of reading a
novel. On one of the rare occasions when all this noise had led to a serious
quarrel, I went up later as the timid little voice of reason, asking my father
why, since it was only half an hour, did *he* make such a lot of noise. He
said that the American voices (never then heard "live" in our small town)
reminded him of the Pacific war. And that surely, after all these years,
there were some things that, in the quiet of his own home, a man had a
right to try to forget.

Looking back from the contradictions of the present, I can define from
this story a contradiction which persists in different forms today. On the
one hand, Lucy had a galvanizing and emancipating effect because of her
loquacity and her relentless tonal insistence. Especially for Australian
women and children, in a society where women were talkative with each
other and laconic with men, men were laconic with each other and catatonic
with women, and children were seen but not heard. Lucy was one of the
first signs of a growing sense that women making a lot of noise did not
need to be confined to the haremlike rituals of morning and afternoon tea
or the washing up. On the other hand, my father's response appears, ret-
rospectively, as prescient as well as understandable. The coming of Lucy,
and of American TV, was among the first explicit announcements to a
general public still vaguely imagining itself as having been "British" that
Australia was now (as it had, in fact, been anyway since 1942) hooked into
the media network of a different war machine.

My second anecdote follows logically from that, but is set in another
world. Ten years later, after a whole cultural revolution in Australia and
another war with the Americans in Asia, I saw a TV catastrophe one banal
Christmas Eve. There we were in Sydney, couch-potatoing away, when the
evening was shattered by that sentence which takes different forms in different cultures but is still perhaps the one sentence always capable of reminding people everywhere within reach of TV of a common and

vulnerable humanity—"We interrupt this transmission for a special news flash."

Usually on hearing that, you get an adrenaline rush, you freeze, you wait to hear what's happened, then the mechanisms of bodily habituation to crisis take over to see you through the time ahead. This occasion was alarmingly different. The announcer actually stammered: "Er . . . um . . . something's happened to Darwin." Darwin is the capital of Australia's far north. Most Australians know nothing about it, and live thousands of miles away. It takes days to get into by land or sea, and in a well-entrenched national imaginary it is the "gateway" to Asia, and in its remoteness and "vulnerability," the likely port of a conventional invasion. This has usually been a racist nightmare about the "yellow peril" sweeping down, but it does also have a basis in flat-map logic. There's no one south of Australia but penguins.

So people panicked, and waited anxiously for details. But the catastrophe was that there was *no information.* Now, this was not catastrophe *on* TV— like the explosion of the space shuttle *Challenger*—but a catastrophe of and *for* TV. There were no pictures, no reports, just *silence*—which had long ceased to be coded as paradisal, as it was in my fable of origin, but was now the very definition of a state of total emergency. The announcer's stammer was devastating. He had lost control of all the mechanisms for assuring credibility;[4] his palpable personal distress had exposed us, unbelievably, to something like a *truth.* When those of us who could sleep woke up the next day to find everyday life going on as usual, we realized it couldn't have been World War III. But it took another twenty-four hours for "true" news to be reestablished, and to reassure us that Darwin had merely been wiped out by a cyclone. Whereupon we went into the "natural disaster" genre of TV living, and banality, except for the victims, resumed. But in the aftermath, a question surfaced. Why had such a cyclone-sensitive city not been forewarned? It was a very big cyclone—someone should have seen it coming.

Two rumors did the rounds. One was an oral rumor, or a folk legend. The cyclone took Darwin by surprise because it was a Russian weather warfare experiment that had either gone wrong or—in the more menacing variant—actually found its target. The other rumor made its way into writing in the odd newspaper. There had been foreknowledge: indeed, even after the cyclone there was a functioning radio tower and an airstrip which might have sent news out straight away. But these belonged to an American military installation near Darwin, which was not supposed to be there. And in the embarrassment of realizing the scale of the disaster to come, someone somewhere had made a decision to say nothing in the hope of averting discovery. If this was true, "they" needn't have worried. The story was never, to my knowledge, pursued further. We didn't really care. If there had been such an installation, it wasn't newsworthy; true or false, it wasn't catastrophic; true or false, it merged with the routine stories of conspiracy and paranoia in urban everyday life; and, true or false, it was—compared with the Darwin fatality count and the human interest stories to be had from cyclone survivors—just too banal to be of interest.

My anecdotes are also banal, in that they mark out a televisual contradiction which is overfamiliar as both a theoretical dilemma and an everyday experience. It is the contradiction between one's pleasure, fascination, thrill, and sense of "life," even birth, in popular culture and the deathly shadows of war, invasion, emergency, crisis, and terror that perpetually haunt the networks. Sometimes there seems to be nothing more to say about that "contradiction," in theory, yet as a phase of collective experience it does keep coming back around. So I want to use these two anecdotes now to frame a comparison between the late work of Baudrillard and some aspects of "British" (or Anglo-Australian) cultural studies—two theoretical projects that have had something to say about the problem. I begin with Baudrillard, because "banality" is a working concept in his lexicon, whereas it is not a significant term for the cultural studies that today increasingly cite him.

In Baudrillard's terms, my anecdotes marked out a historical shift between a period of concern about TV's effects on the real—which is thereby assumed to be distinct from its representation (the *Lucy* moment)—and a time in which TV *generates* the real to the extent that any interruption in its processes of doing so is experienced as more catastrophic in the lounge room than a "real" catastrophe elsewhere. So I have simply defined a shift between a regime of production and a regime of simulation. This would also correspond to a shift between a more or less real Cold War ethos, where American military presence in your country could be construed as friendly or hostile, but you thought you should have a choice, and that the choice mattered; and a pure war (or, simulated chronic cold war) ethos, in which Russian cyclones or American missiles are completely interchangeable in a local imaginary of terror, and the choice between them is meaningless.

This analysis could be generated from Baudrillard's major thesis in *L'échange symbolique et la mort* (1976). The later Baudrillard would have little further interest in my story about Lucy's voice and domestic squabbles in an Australian country town, but might still be mildly amused by the story of a city disappearing for thirty-six hours because of a breakdown in communications. However, where I would want to say that this event was for participants a real, if mediated, experience of catastrophe, he could say that it was just a final flicker of real reality. With the subsequent installation of a global surveillance regime through the satellization of the world, the disappearance of Darwin could never occur again.

So Baudrillard would collapse the "contradiction" that I want to maintain: and he would make each polar term of my stories (the everyday and the catastrophic, the exhilarating and the frightful, the emancipatory and the

terroristic) invade and contaminate its other in a process of mutual exac-
erbation. This is a viral, rather than an atomic, model of crisis in everyday
life. If, for Andreas Huyssen, modernism as an adversary culture constitutes itself in an "anxiety of contamination" by its Other (mass culture),[5]
the Baudrillardian text on (or of) mass culture is constituted by perpetually
intensifying the contamination of one of any two terms by its other.

So like all pairs of terms in Baudrillard's work, the values "banality" and
"fatality" chase each other around his pages following the rule of dyadic
reversibility. Any one term can be hyperbolically intensified until it turns
into its opposite. Superbanality, for example, becomes fatal, and a super-
fatality would be banal. It's a very simple but, when well done, dizzying
logico-semantic game which makes Baudrillard's books very easy to understand, but any one term most difficult to define. A complication in this
case is that "banality" and "fatality" chase each other around two books,
De la séduction (1979) and *Les stratégies fatales* (1983).

One way to elucidate such a system is to imagine a distinction between
two sets of two terms—for example, "fatal charm" and "banal seduction."
Fatal charm can be seductive in the old sense of an irresistible force, exerted
by someone who desires nothing except to play the game in order to capture
and to immolate the desire of the other. That's what's fatal about it. Banal
seduction, on the other hand, does involve desire: desire for, perhaps, an
immovable object to overcome. That's what's fatal for it. Baudrillard's next
move is to claim that both of these strategies are finished. The only irresistible force today is that of the moving *object* as it flees and evades the
subject. This is the "force" of the sex-object, of the silent zombie-masses,
and of femininity (not necessarily detached by Baudrillard from real
women, but certainly detached from feminists).

This structure is, I think, a "fatal" travesty, or a "seduction" of the terms
of Althusserian epistemology and *its* theory of moving objects. In *Les stratégies fatales*, the travesty is rewritten in terms of a theory of global catastrophe. The human species has passed the dead point of history: we are living
out the ecstasy of permanent catastrophe, which slows down as it becomes
more and more intense (*une catastrophe au ralenti*, slow-motion, or slowing-
motion catastrophe), until the supereventfulness of the event approaches
the uneventfulness of absolute inertia, and we begin to live everyday catastrophe as an endless dead point, or a perpetual freeze frame.

This is the kind of general scenario produced in Baudrillard's work by
the logic of mutual contamination. However, an examination of the local
occurrences of the terms "banal" and "fatal" in both books suggests that
"banality" is associated, quite clearly and conventionally, with negative aspects of media—overrepresentation, excessive visibility, information ov-
erload, an obscene plenitude of images, a gross platitudinousness of the
all-pervasive present.

On the other hand, and even though there is strictly no past and no
future in Baudrillard's system, he uses "fatality" as both a nostalgic and a

futuristic term for invoking a classical critical value, *discrimination* (redefined as a senseless but still rule-governed principle of selectiveness). "Fatality" is nostalgic in the sense that it invokes in the text, for the present, an "aristocratic" ideal of maintaining an elite, arbitrary, and avowedly artificial order. It is futuristic because Baudrillard suggests that in an age of over-load, rampant banality, and catastrophe (which have become at this stage equivalents of each other), the last Pascalian wager may be to bet on the return, in the present, of what can only be a simulacrum of the past. When fatal charm can simulate seducing banal seduction, you have a fatal strategy. The animating myth of this return is to be, in opposition to critical philosophies of Difference (which have now become identical), a myth of *Fatum*—that is, Destiny.

So read in one sense, Baudrillard's theory merely calls for an aesthetic order (fatality) to deal with mass cultural anarchy (banality). What makes his appeal more charming than most other tirades about the decay of standards is that it can be read in the opposite sense. The "order" being called for is radically decadent, superbanal. However, there is a point at which the play stops.

In one of Baudrillard's anecdotes (an enunciative *mise en abyme* of his theory), set in some vague courtly context with the ambience of a mid-eighteenth-century French epistolary novel, a man is trying to seduce a woman. She asks, "Which part of me do you find most seductive?" He replies, "Your eyes." Next day, he receives an envelope. Inside, instead of the letter, he finds a bloody eye. Analyzing his own fable, Baudrillard points out that in the obviousness, the literalness of her gesture, the woman has purloined the place of her seducer.

The man is the banal seducer. She, the fatal seducer, sets him a trap with her question as he moves to entrap her. In the platitudinous logic of court-liness, he can only reply "Your eyes"—rather than naming some more vital organ which she might not have been able to post—since the eye is the window of the soul. Baudrillard concludes that the woman's literalness is fatal to the man's banal figuration: she loses an eye, but he loses *face*. He can never again "cast an eye" on another woman without thinking literally of the bloody eye that replaced the letter. So Baudrillard's final resolution of the play between banality and fatality is this: a banal theory assumes, like the platitudinous seducer, that the subject is more powerful than the object. A fatal theory knows, like the woman, that the object is always *worse* than the subject ("*je ne suis pas belle, je suis pire . . .* ").

Nonetheless, in making the pun "she loses an eye, but he loses face," Baudrillard in fact enunciatively reoccupies the place of control of meaning by *de*-literalizing the woman's gesture, and returning it to figuration. Only the pun makes the story work as a fable of seduction, by draining the "blood" from the eye. Without it, we would merely be reading a horror story (or a feminist moral tale). So it follows that Baudrillard's figuration is, in fact, "fatal" to the woman's literality, and to a literal feminist reading of her story that might presumably ensue. In the process, the privilege of "knowing" the significance of the woman's fatal-banal gesture is securely restored to metalanguage, and to the subject of exegesis.

Recent cultural studies offers something completely different. It speaks not of restoring discrimination but of encouraging cultural democracy. It respects difference and sees mass culture not as a vast banality machine but as raw material made available for a variety of popular practices.

In saying "it," I am treating a range of quite different texts and arguments as a single entity. This is always imprecise, polemically "unifying," and unfair to any individual item. But sometimes, when distractedly reading magazines such as *New Socialist* or *Marxism Today* from the last couple of years, flipping through *Cultural Studies,* or scanning the pop-theory pile in the bookstore, I get the feeling that somewhere in some English publisher's vault there is a master disk from which thousands of versions of the same article about pleasure, resistance, and the politics of consumption are being run off under different names with minor variations. Americans and Australians are recycling this basic pop-theory article, too: with the perhaps major variation that English pop theory still derives at least nominally from a Left popul*ism* attempting to salvage a sense of life from the catastrophe of Thatcherism. Once cut free from that context, as commodities always are, and recycled in quite different political cultures, the vestigial *critical* force of that populism tends to disappear or mutate.

This imaginary pop-theory article might respond to my television anecdotes by bracketing the bits about war and death as a sign of paranoia about popular culture, by pointing out that it's a mistake to confuse conditions of production with the subsequent effects of images, and by noting that with TV one may always be "ambivalent." It would certainly stress, with the Lucy story, the subversive pleasure of the female spectators. (My father could perhaps represent an Enlightenment paternalism of reason trying to make everything cohere in a model of social totality.) With the Darwin story, it would insist on the creativity of the consumer/spectator, and maybe have us distractedly zapping from channel to channel during the catastrophe instead of being passively hooked into the screen, and then resisting the war machine with our local legends and readings. The article would then restate, using a mix of different materials as illustration, the enabling theses of contemporary cultural studies.

In order to move away now from reliance on imaginary bad objects, I'll refer to an excellent real article which gives a summary of these theses— Mica Nava's "Consumerism and Its Contradictions." Among the enabling theses—and they *have* been enabling—are these: consumers are not "cultural dopes" but active, critical users of mass culture; consumption practices cannot be derived from or reduced to a mirror of production; consumer practice is "far more than just economic activity: it is also about dreams and consolation, communication and confrontation, image and identity. Like sexuality, it consists of a multiplicity of fragmented and contradictory discourses."[6]

I'm not now concerned to contest these theses. For the moment, I'll buy the lot. What I'm interested in is first, the sheer proliferation of the restatements, and second, the emergence in some of them of a *restrictive definition* of the ideal knowing subject of cultural studies.

John Fiske's historical account in "British Cultural Studies and Television" produces one such restatement and restriction. The social terrain of the beginning of his article is occupied by a version of the awesomely complex Althusserian subject-in-ideology, and by a summary of Gramsci on hegemony. Blending these produces a notion of subjectivity as a dynamic field, in which all sorts of permutations are possible at different moments in an endless process of production, contestation, and reproduction of social identities. By the end of the article, the field has been vastly simplified: there are "the dominant classes" (exerting hegemonic force) and "the people" (making their own meanings and constructing their own culture "within, and sometimes against," the culture provided for them) (286).

Cultural studies for Fiske aims to understand and encourage cultural democracy. One way of understanding the *demos* is *"ethnography"*—finding out what the people say and think about their culture. But the methods cited are "voxpop" techniques common to journalism and empirical sociology—interviewing, collecting background, analyzing statements made spontaneously by, or solicited from, informants. So the choice of the term "ethnography" for these practices emphasizes a possible "ethnic" gap between the cultural student and the culture studied. The "understanding" and "encouraging" subject may share some aspects of that culture, but *in the process of interrogation and analysis* is momentarily located outside it. "The people" is a voice, or a *figure of* a voice, cited in a discourse of exegesis. For example, Fiske cites "Lucy," a fourteen year old fan of Madonna ("She's tarty and seductive . . . but it looks alright when she does it, you know, what I mean . . . "); and then goes on to translate, and diagnose, what she means: "Lucy's problems probably stem from her recognition that marriage is a patriarchal institution and, as such, is threatened by Madonna's sexuality" (273).

If this is again a process of embedding in metadiscourse a sample of raw female speech, it is also a perfectly honest approach for any academic analyst of culture to take. It differs from a discourse that simply appeals to "experience" to validate and universalize its own conclusions. However, such honesty should also require some analysis of the analyst's own institutional and "disciplinary" position—perhaps some recognition, too, of the double play of transference. (Lucy tells him her pleasure in Madonna: but what is his pleasure in Lucy's?) This kind of recognition is rarely made in populist polemics. What takes its place is first, a citing of popular voices (the informants), an act of translation and commentary, and then a play

of *identification* between the knowing subject of cultural studies and a collective subject, "the people."

In Fiske's text, however, "the people" have no necessary defining characteristics—except an indomitable capacity to "negotiate" readings, generate new interpretations, and remake the materials of culture. This is also,
of course, the function of cultural studies itself (and in Fiske's version, the
study does include a "semiotic analysis of the text" to explore *how* meanings
are made [272]). So against the hegemonic force of the dominant classes,
"the people" in fact represent the most creative energies and functions of
critical reading. In the end they are not simply the cultural student's object
of study and his native informants. The people are also the textually del-
egated, allegorical emblem of the critic's own activity. Their *ethnos* may be
constructed as other, but it is used as the ethnographer's mask.

Once "the people" are both a source of authority for a text and a figure
of its own critical activity, the populist enterprise is not only circular but
(like most empirical sociology) narcissistic in structure. Theorizing the problems that ensue is one way—in my view, an important way—to break out
of the circuit of repetition. Another is to project elsewhere a misunderstanding or discouraging Other figure (often that feminist or Marxist Echo,
the blast from the past) to necessitate and enable more repetition.

The opening chapter of Iain Chambers's *Popular Culture* provides an
example of this, as well as a definition of what counts as "popular" knowledge that is considerably more restrictive than John Fiske's. Chambers argues that in looking at popular culture, we should not subject individual
signs and single texts to the "contemplative stare of official culture." Instead, it is a practice of "distracted reception" that really characterizes the
subject of "popular epistemology." For Chambers, this distraction has consequences for the practice of writing. Writing can imitate popular culture
(life) by, for example, "writing through quotations," and refusing to "explain . . . references fully." To explain would be to reimpose the contemplative stare and adopt the authority of the "academic mind."[7]

Chambers's argument emerges from an interpretation of the history of
subcultural practices, especially in music. I've argued elsewhere my disa-
greement with his attempt to use that history to generalize about popular
culture in The Present.[8] Here, I want to suggest that an image of the subject
of pop epistemology as casual and "distracted" obliquely entails a revival
of the figure that Andreas Huyssen, Tania Modleski, and Patrice Petro
have described in various contexts as "mass culture as woman."[9] Petro, in
particular, further points out that the contemplation/distraction opposition
is historically implicated in the construction of the "female spectator" as
site, and target, of a theorization of modernity by male intellectuals in
Weimar.[10]

There are many versions of a "distraction" model available in cultural
studies today: there are housewives phasing in and out of TV or flipping
through magazines in laundromats as well as pop intellectuals playing with

quotes. In Chambers's text, which is barely concerned with women at all, distraction is not presented as a female characteristic. Yet today's recycling of Weimar's distraction nonetheless has the "contours," in Petro's phrase, of a familiar female stereotype—distracted, absent-minded, insouciant, vague, flighty, skimming from image to image. The rush of associations runs irresistibly toward a figure of mass culture not as woman but, more specifically, as bimbo.

In the texts Petro analyzes, "contemplation" (of distraction in the cinema) is assumed to be the prerogative of male intellectual audiences. In pop epistemology, a complication is introduced via the procedures of projection and identification that Elaine Showalter describes in "Critical Cross-Dressing."[11] The knowing subject of popular epistemology no longer contemplates "mass culture" as bimbo, but takes on the assumed mass cultural characteristics in the writing of his own text. Since the object of projection and identification in post-subcultural theory tends to be black music and "style" rather than the European (and literary) feminine, we find an actantial hero of knowledge emerging in the form of the *white male theorist* as bimbo.

However, I think the problem with the notion of pop epistemology is not really, in this case, a vestigial antifeminism in the concept of distraction. The problem is that in antiacademic pop-theory writing (much of which, like Chambers's book, circulates as textbooks with exam and essay topics at the end of each chapter), a stylistic enactment of the "popular" as *essentially* distracted, scanning the surface, and short on attention span, performs a retrieval, at the level of *enunciative* practice, of the thesis of "cultural dopes." In the critique of which—going right back to the early work of Stuart Hall, not to mention Raymond Williams—the project of cultural studies effectively and rightly began.

One could claim that this interpretation is possible only if one continues to assume that the academic traditions of "contemplation" really do define intelligence, and that to be "distracted" can therefore only mean being dopey. I would reply that as long as we accept to restate the alternatives in those terms, that is precisely the assumption we continue to recycle. No matter which of the terms we validate, the contemplation/distraction, academic/popular oppositions can serve only to limit and distort the possibilities of popular practice. Furthermore, I think that this return to the postulate of cultural dopism in the *practice* of writing may be one reason why pop theory is now generating over and over again the same article. If a cultural dopism is being enunciatively performed (and valorized) in a discourse that tries to contest it, then the argument in fact *cannot* move on, but can only retrieve its point of departure as "banality" (a word pop theorists don't normally use) in the negative sense.

For the thesis of cultural studies as Fiske and Chambers present it runs perilously close to this kind of formulation: people in modern mediatized societies are complex and contradictory, mass cultural texts are complex and contradictory, therefore people using them produce complex and contradictory culture. To add that this popular culture has critical and resistant elements is tautological—unless one (or a predicated someone, that Other who needs to be told) has a concept of culture so rudimentary that it excludes criticism and resistance from the practice of everyday life.

Given the different values ascribed to mass culture in Baudrillard's work and in pop theory, it is tempting to make a distracted contrast between them in terms of elitism and populism. However, they are not symmetrical opposites.

Cultural studies posits a "popular" subject "supposed to know" in a certain manner, which the subject of populist theory then claims to understand (Fiske) or mimic (Chambers). Baudrillard's elitism, however, is not an elitism of a knowing subject of theory but an elitism of the *object*—which is forever, and actively, evasive. There is a hint of "distraction" here, an echo between the problematics of woman and literalness and mass culture as bimbo which deserves further contemplation. A final twist is that for Baudrillard, the worst (that is, most effective) elitism of the object can be called, precisely, "theory." Theory is understood as an objectified and objectifying (never "objective") force strategically engaged in an ever more intense process of commodification. Like "distraction" it is distinguished by the rapidity of its *flight*, rather than by a concentrated pursuit.

However, it is remarkable, given the differences between them and the crisis-ridden society that each in its own way addresses, that neither of the projects I've discussed leaves much place for an unequivocally pained, unambivalently discontented, or momentarily *aggressive* subject. It isn't just negligence. There is an active process going on in both of discrediting—by direct dismissal (Baudrillard) or covert inscription as Other (cultural studies)—the voices of grumpy feminists and cranky leftists ("Frankfurt School" can do duty for both). To discredit such voices is, as I understand it, one of the immediate political functions of the current boom in cultural studies (as distinct from the intentionality of projects invested by it). To discredit a voice is something very different from displacing an analysis which has become outdated, or revising a strategy which no longer serves its purpose. It is to character-ize a fictive position from which anything said can be dismissed as already heard.

Baudrillard's hostility to the discourses of political radicalism is perfectly clear and brilliantly played out. It is a little too aggressive to accuse cultural studies of playing much the same game. Cultural studies is a humane and optimistic discourse, trying to derive its values from materials and conditions already available to people. On the other hand, it can become an apologetic "yes, *but* . . . " discourse that most often proceeds *from* admitting class, racial, and sexual oppressions *to* finding the inevitable saving grace—when its theoretical presuppositions should require it at least to do both simultaneously, even "dialectically." And in practice the "but . . . "—that is to say, the argumentative rhetoric—has been increasingly addressing not the hegemonic force of the "dominant classes" but other critical theories (vulgar feminism, the Frankfurt School) inscribed as misunderstanding popular culture.[12]

Both discourses share a tendency toward reductionism—political as well as theoretical. To simplify matters myself, I'd say that where the fatal strategies of Baudrillard keep returning us to his famous Black Hole—a scenario that is so grim, obsessive, and, in its enunciative strategies, maniacally overcoherent that instead of speaking, a woman must *tear out her eye* to be heard—the voxpop style of cultural studies is on the contrary offering us the sanitized world of a deodorant commercial where there's always a way to redemption. There's something sad about that, because cultural studies emerged from a real attempt to give voice to much grittier experiences of class, race, and gender.

Yet the sense of frustration that some of us who would inscribe our own work as cultural studies feel with the terms of present debate can be disabling. If one is equally uneasy about fatalistic theory on the one hand and about cheerily "making the best of things" on the other, then it is a poor solution to consent to confine oneself to (and in) the dour position of rebuking both.

In *The Practice of Everyday Life,* Michel de Certeau provides a more positive approach to the politics of theorizing popular culture, and to the particular problems I have discussed.[13] One of the pleasures of this text for me is the range of moods that it admits to a field of study which—surprisingly, since "everyday life" is at issue—often seems to be occupied only by cheerleaders and prophets of doom. So from it I shall borrow—in a contemplative rather than a distracted spirit—two quotations to modify the sharp oppositions I've created, before discussing his work in more detail.

The first quotation is in fact from Jacques Sojcher's *La Démarche poétique.* De Certeau cites Sojcher after arguing for a double process of mobilizing the "weighty apparatus" of theories of ordinary language to analyze everyday practices, *and* seeking to restore to those practices their logical and cultural legitimacy. He then uses the Sojcher quotation to insist that in this kind of research, everyday practices will "alternately exacerbate *and disrupt* our logics. Its regrets are like those of the poet, and like him, it struggles against oblivion." So I will use his quotation in turn as a response to the terrifying and unrelenting coherence of Baudrillard's fatal strategies. Sojcher:

And I forgot the elements of chance introduced by circumstances, calm or haste, sun or cold, dawn or dusk, the taste of strawberries or abandonment, the half-understood message, the front page of newspapers, the voice on the telephone, the most anodyne conversation, the most anonymous man or woman, everything that speaks, makes noise, passes by, touches us lightly, meets us head on. (xvi)

The second quotation comes from a discussion of "Freud and the Ordinary Man," and the difficult problems that arise when "elitist writing uses the 'vulgar' [or, I would add, the 'feminine'] speaker as a disguise for a metalanguage about itself." For de Certeau, a recognition that the "ordinary" and the "popular" can act as a mask in analytical discourse does *not* imply that the study of popular culture is impossible except as recuperation. Instead, it demands that we show *how* the ordinary introduces itself into analytical techniques, and this requires a displacement in the institutional practice of knowledge:

> Far from arbitrarily assuming the privilege of speaking in the name of the ordinary (it cannot *be* spoken), or claiming to be in that general place (that would be a false "mysticism"), or, worse, offering up a hagiographic everydayness for its edifying value, it is a matter of restoring historicity to the movement which leads analytical procedures back to their frontiers, to the point where they are changed, indeed disturbed, by the ironic and mad banality that speaks in "Everyman" in the sixteenth century, and that has returned in the final stages of Freud's knowledge. . . . (5)

In this way, he suggests, the ordinary "can reorganize the place from which discourse is produced." I think that this includes being very careful about our enunciative and "anecdotal" strategies—more careful than much cultural studies has been in its mimesis of a popular voice—and their relation to the institutional *places* we may occupy as we speak.

In spirit, de Certeau's work is much more in sympathy with the *bricoleur* impulse of cultural studies than with apocalyptic thinking. The motto of his book could be the sentence "People have to make do with what they have" (18). Its French title is *Arts de faire:* arts of making, arts of doing, arts of making do. Its project, however, is not a theory of popular culture but "a science of singularity": a science of the relationship that links "everyday pursuits to particular circumstances." So the study of how people use mass media, for example, is defined not in opposition *to* "high" or "elite" cultural analysis, but in connection *with* a general study of *activities*—cooking, walking, reading, talking, shopping. A basic operation in the "science" is an incessant movement between what de Certeau calls "polemological" and "utopian" spaces of making do (15–18): a movement which involves, as my quotations may suggest, both a poetics and a politics of practice.[14]

The basic assumption of a polemological space is summed up by a quotation from a Maghrebian syndicalist at Billancourt: "They always fuck us over." This is a sentence that seems inadmissible in contemporary cultural studies: it defines a space of struggle, and mendacity ("the strong always win, and words always deceive"). For the peasants of the Pernambuco region of Brazil, in de Certeau's main example, it is a socioeconomic space of innumerable conflicts in which the rich and the police are constantly victorious. But at the same time and in the same place, a utopian space is reproduced in the popular legends of *miracles* that circulate and intensify as repression becomes more absolute and apparently successful. De Certeau mentions the story of Frei Damiao, the charismatic hero of the region.

I would cite, as a parable of both kinds of space, a television anecdote about the Sydney Birthday Cake Scandal. In 1988, governments in Australia spent lavish sums of money on bicentenary celebrations. But it was really the bicentenary of Sydney as the original penal colony. In 1988 "Australia" was in fact only eighty-seven years old, and so the event was widely understood to be a costly effort at simulating, rather than celebrating, a unified national history. It promoted as our fable of origin not the federation of the colonies and the beginnings of independence (1901) but the invasion of Aboriginal Australia by the British penal system—and the catastrophe that, for Aborigines, ensued.

A benevolent Sydney real-estate baron proposed to build a giant birthday cake above an expressway tunnel in the most famous social wastage-and-devastation zone of the city, so we could know we were having a party. The project was unveiled on a TV current affairs show, and there was an uproar—not only from exponents of good taste against kitsch. The network switchboards were jammed by people pointing out that, above the area that belongs to junkies, runaways, homeless people, and the child as well as adult prostitution trade, a giant cake would invoke a late eighteenth-century voice quite different from that of our first prison governor saying, "Here we are in Botany Bay." It would be Marie Antoinette saying, "Let them eat cake." There was nothing casual or distracted about *that* voxpop observation.

The baron then proposed a public competition, again via TV, to find an alternative design. There were lots of proposals: a few of us wanted to build Kafka's writing machine from "In the Penal Colony." Others proposed an echidna, a water tower, a hypodermic, or a giant condom. The winner was a suburban rotary clothesline: Australia's major contribution to twentieth-century technology, and thus something of a symbol for the current decline in our economy. But in the end, the general verdict was that we'd rather make do with the cake. As one person said in a voxpop segment, "At least with the cake, the truth about the party is all now out in the open." So had the cake been built, it would have been, after all that polemological narrativity, a wildly utopian popular monument.

No monument materialized, and the story died down. However, it reappeared in a different form when an extravagant birthday party was duly held on January 26, 1988. Two and a half million people converged on a few square kilometers of harbor foreshore on a glorious summer's day to watch the ships, to splash about, to eat and drink and fall asleep in the sun during speeches. The largest gathering of Aboriginal people since the original Invasion Day was also held, to protest the proceedings. The party ended with a fabulous display of fireworks, choreographed to music progressing "historically" from the eighteenth century to the present. The climax was "Power and the Passion," a famous song by Midnight Oil (Australia's favorite polemological rock band), which is utterly scathing about public as well as "popular" chauvinist culture in urban white Australia. Only those watching the celebrations on TV were able to hear it and to admire the fireworks dancing to its tune. The day after, a slogan surfaced in the streets and on the walls of the city and in press cartoons: "Let them eat fireworks."

For de Certeau, a polemological analysis is entailed by "the relation of procedures to the fields of force in which they act" (xvii). It maps the terrain and the strategies of what he loosely calls "established powers" (in opposition not to the "powerless" but to the nonestablished, to powers and possibilities not in stable possession of a singular *place* of their own). This analysis is an accompaniment, and not an alternative or a rival, to utopian tactics and stories. Polemological and utopian spaces are distinct, but in proximity: they are "alongside" each other, not in contradiction.

These terms need clarification, since it is not just a matter of opposing major to minor, strong to weak, and romantically validating the latter. A strategy is "the calculus of force-relationships which becomes possible when a subject of will and power (a proprietor, an enterprise, a city, a scientific institution) can be isolated from an 'environment' " (xix). Strategy presupposes a place of its own, one circumscribed as "proper," and so predicates an exterior, an "outside," an excluded Other (and technologies to manage this relationship). Tactics, however, are localized ways of using what is made available—materials, opportunities, time and space for action—by the strategy of the other, and in "his" place. They depend on arts of *timing*, a seizing of propitious moments, rather than on arts of colonizing space.[15] They use "the place of the other," in a mode of *insinuation*—like the street slogans in my example, of course, but more exactly like the mysterious appearance of "Power and the Passion" in the festive choreography of State.

The "miracle" created by the appearance of this heretical song did not necessarily derive, unlike the graffiti, from a deliberate act of debunking—although it's nice to think it did. While Midnight Oil's public image in Australia is unambiguously political, it is just possible that for the ceremony planners, the reference may have been more like Ronald Reagan's "Born in the USA": a usage crucially inattentive to detail, but functional, and not inaccurate, in mobilizing parts of a resonant myth of how Sydney feels as a *place*. But the intention didn't matter: the flash of hilarity and encouragement the song gave viewers otherwise mortified by the Invasion festival would be, in de Certeau's terms, a product of *their* "tactical" use of the show, their insinuation of polemical significance into the place of programmed pleasure.

It is in this sense of popular practice as a fleeting appropriation, one which diverts the purposive rationality of an established power, that de Certeau's theory associates consumer "reading" with oral culture, and with the survival skills of colonized people: like dancers, travelers, poachers, and short-term tenants, or "voices" in written texts, "they move about . . . passing lightly through the field of the other" (131). In this movement, polemological space is created by an "analysis of facts": not facts as objectively validated by a regime of place, but facts produced by *experience* of another place, and time spent on the other's terrain. Polemological analysis in this sense accords no legitimacy to "facts." "They always fuck us over" may be a fact but not a law: utopian spaces deny the immutability and authority of facts, and together both spaces refuse the fatality (the *fatum*, "what has been spoken," destiny decreed) of an established order.

This general definition of popular culture as a *way of operating*—rather than as a set of contents, a marketing category, a reflected expression of social position, or even a "terrain" of struggle—is at once in affinity with the thematics of recent cultural studies and also, I think, inflected away from some of its problems.

Like most theories of popular culture today, it does not use "folk," "primitive" or "indigenous" cultures as a lost origin or ideal model for considering "mass" cultural experience. Unlike some of those theories, it does not thereby cease to think connections between them. Global structures of power and forces of occupation (rationalizing time and establishing place) do not drop out of the analytical field. On the contrary, imperialism and its knowledges—ethnology, travel writing, "communications"—*establish* a field in which analysis of popular culture becomes a tactical way of operating.

De Certeau shares with many others a taste for "reading" as privileged metaphor of a *modus operandi*. However, the reading he theorizes is not a figure of "writerly" freedom, subjective mastery, interpretive control, or caprice. To read is to "wander through an imposed system" (169)—a text, a city street, a supermarket, a State festivity. It is not a passive activity, but it is not independent of the system it uses. Nor does the figure of reading assert the primacy of a scriptural model for understanding popular culture. To read is not to write and rewrite but to travel: reading borrows, without establishing a "place" of its own. As a schooled activity, reading happens at the point where "*social* stratification (class relationships) and *poetic* operations (the practitioner's construction of a text) intersect." So a reader's autonomy would depend on a transformation of the social relationships that overdetermine her relation to texts. But in order not to be another normative imposition, any "politics" of reading would also have to be articulated on an analysis of poetic practices already in operation.

In this framework, popular culture does not provide a space of exemption from socioeconomic constraints, although it may circulate stories of exemption denying the fatality of socioeconomic systems. At the same time, it is not idealized as a reservoir or counterplace for inversions of "propriety" (distraction vs. contemplation, for example). As a way of operating, the practice of everyday life has no place, no borders, no hierarchy of materials forbidden or privileged for use: "Barthes reads Proust in Stendhal's text: the viewer reads the landscape of his childhood in the evening news" (xxi).

De Certeau's insistence on the movement *between* polemological and utopian practices of making do makes it possible to say that if cultural studies is losing its polemological edge—its capacity to articulate loss, despair, disillusion, anger, and thus to learn from failure—Baudrillard's work has not lost its utopianism but has rather produced too much *convergence* between polemological and (nightmare) utopian spaces: his stories are negative miracles, working only to intensify the fatality of his "facts."

Yet de Certeau's formulations draw heavily on a distinction between having and not having a place (and on a "fleeting appropriation" of Derrida's critique of *le propre*) which can in turn pose difficulties for feminists, or indeed anyone today for whom "a room of one's own" is a utopian aspiration rather than a securely established premise, and for whom a stint of "short-term tenancy" in someone else's place seems less like denying fatality, and more like one's usual fate.

There are serious problems here (and not only for a feminist appropriation of de Certeau's work). Another is the way that any rhetoric of otherness may slide, by association or analogy between historically "othered" terms, toward assimilating its figures of displacement in an ever-expanding exoticism: peasants in Brazil, Maghrebian workers in Billancourt, Barthes in the library, and television viewers in Sydney can come into equivalence in a paradigm of *exempla* of desirably transient practice. And the political question of "positioning" in relation to "practice" in cultural studies is clearly not eliminated by a rhetorical shift from "having" words to "doing" words, from values of propriety to modes of operativity—or from territorializing to technicist frames of reference.

The Practice of Everyday Life doesn't eliminate or avoid these problems, although its solutions may not satisfy feminists. It deals with them through a historical critique of the "logics" of cultural analysis, the objects of study they constitute, and the limits they construct and confront. I need to refer briefly to this critique in order to consider the relation between place, storytelling, and a politics of "banality" in his theory.

There is an insistent "we" structuring de Certeau's discourse, which is not a humanist universal but an (otherwise undifferentiated) marker of a class position in knowledge. It locates the text's project (and the writer and reader of cultural analysis) in a "place"—the scholarly enterprise, the research institution. Whether or not de Certeau's reader is prepared to go along with his tenured (masculine) "we," its placing works to interrupt rather than facilitate any slide toward exoticism. It also creates intervals, or spaces, of polemological reflection on that utopia for analysis, the nonplace of the other. For as Wlad Godzich points out in a foreword to de Certeau's collection of essays *Heterologies*, his "other" "is not a magical or a

transcendental entity; it is the discourse's mode of relation to its own historicity in the moment of its utterance."[16]

In the quotations with which I began my discussion of *The Practice of
Everyday Life,* the "regrets" of research involve a moment of remembering
"the element of chance introduced by circumstances . . . everything that
speaks, makes noises, passes by, touches us lightly, meets us head on." Since
these fugitive encounters with the other are also the very object of analysis,
remembering entails not only a poetics of regret but also a history of forgetting, a "struggle against oblivion." If the taste of strawberries or abandonment can "alternately exacerbate and disrupt our logics," it is not
because of some essential inadequacy of "thought" (analysis) in relation to
"feeling" (the popular), as Iain Chambers's mind/body dualism implies;
nor is it because of a tantalizing gap in *being* founding the subject's pursuit
of its objects (that famous "lack" still assumed, if parodied, by Baudrillard's
theory of fatality). It is, rather, that what may transform analytical procedures at their frontiers is precisely a "banality" of which the repression
has constituted *historically* an enabling, even empowering, condition for the
study of popular culture.

This is a large thesis, which rests on several distinct arguments.[17] I can
mention only two, in drastically simplified form. One is a historical account
of how French scholarly interest in popular culture emerged during the
nineteenth century from projects to destroy or "police" it, and how this
primary "murder" inflects procedures still used today: for example, that
play of identification which leads cultural historians into writing, in the
name of the "popular," other-effacing forms of intellectual autobiogra-
phy.[18] The second argument takes the form of an allegory of the relationship between European writing and "orality" since the seventeenth
century.[19] It combines a history of a socioeconomic and technological space
("the scriptural economy") with an interpretation of the emergence of modern disciplines, and of the birth-in-death of "the other." The work of
Charles Nisard (*Histoire des livres populaires,* 1954) is the focus for the first
account, and Defoe's *Robinson Crusoe* (1719) is read as an inaugural text
for the second.

They are linked by a claim that the scriptural economy entailed for intellectuals a "double isolation" from the "people" (in opposition to the
"bourgeoisie") and from the "*voice*" (in opposition to the "written"): "Hence
the conviction that far, too far away from economic and administrative
powers, 'the People speaks' " (131–32). This new "voxpop" (my term, not
his) becomes both an object of nostalgic longing and a source of disturbance.
Thus Robinson Crusoe, master of the island, the white page, the blank
space (*espace propre*) of production and progress, finds his scriptural empire
haunted by the "crack" or the "smudge" of Man Friday's footprint on the
sand—a "silent marking" of the text by what *will* intervene *as voice* ("a
marking of language by the body") in the field of writing (154–55).[20] With
the figure of Man Friday appears a new and long-lasting form of alterity

defined *in relation to* writing: he is the other who must either cry out (a "wild" outbreak requiring treatment) or make his body the vehicle of the dominant language—becoming "his master's voice," his ventriloquist's dummy, his mask in enunciation.

If this is a large thesis, it is also today a familiar one, not least with respect to its form. Defining the "other" (with whatever value we invest in this term in different contexts) as the repressed-and-returning in discourse has become one of the moves most tried and trusted to (re)generate writing, remotivate scriptural enterprise, inscribe signs, maybe myths, of critical difference. De Certeau admits as much, describing the "problematics of repression" as a type of ideological criticism that doesn't change the workings of a system but endows the critic with an appearance of distance from it (41). However, his own emphasis is on "restoring historicity" in order to think the critic's *involvement* in the system, and thus the operations that may reorganize his place.

If the other figures mythically as "voice" in the scriptural economy, the voice in turn discursively figures in the primary form of quotation—a mark or trace of the other. Two ways of quoting have historically defined this voice: quotation as *pretext*, using oral "relics" to fabricate texts, and quotation-*reminiscence*, marking "the fragmented and unexpected return . . . of oral relationships that are structuring but repressed by the written" (156). De Certeau gives the first an eighteenth-century name, "the *science of fables*"; the second he calls "returns and turns of voices" ("*retours et tours de voix*"), or "sounds of the body."

The science of fables involves all "learned" hermeneutics of speech—ethnology, psychiatry, pedagogy, and political or historiographical procedures which try to "introduce the 'voice of the people' into the authorized language." As "heterologies," or "sciences of the different," their common characteristic is to try to *write* the voice, transforming it into readable products. In the process, the position of the other (the primitive, the child, the mad, the popular, the feminine . . .) is defined not only as a "fable," identical with "what speaks" (*fari*), but as a fable that "does not know" what it says. The technique enabling this positioning of the other (and thus the dominance of scriptural labor over the "fable" it cites) is *translation:* the oral is transcribed as writing, a model is constructed to read the fable as a system, and a meaning is produced. John Fiske's "ethnographic" fable of Lucy's response to Madonna provides a step-by-step example of this procedure.[21]

The "sounds of the body" marked in language by quotation-reminiscence are invoked by de Certeau in terms strongly reminiscent of a thematics of Woman—resonances, rhythms, wounds, pleasures, "solitary erections" (the *inaccessibility* of the voice, says de Certeau, makes "people" write), fragmentary cries and whispers, "aphasic enunciation"—"everything that speaks, makes noise, passes by, touches us lightly, meets us head on." Necessarily more difficult to describe than the science of fables, these returns and turns of voices are suggested, rather than represented, by examples:

opera (a "space for voices" that emerged at the same time as the scriptural economy), *Nathalie Granger,* Marguerite Duras's "film of voices," but also the stammers, voice-gaps, vague rhythms, unexpectedly moving or memorable turns of phrase that mark our most mundane activities and haunt our everyday prose (162–63).

Perhaps these are the sounds that are banished from Baudrillard's story of the eye—or rather by the "scriptural labor" of his subsequent exegesis. Baudrillard finds a triumph of *literalness* in the woman's substitution of an eye for the letter. So, in the manner of the science of fables, he specifies a meaning for the fable that suits the antifemin*ist* discourse for which it acts as a pretext. However, he does this not by trying to "write" the woman's voice (body) but, on the contrary, by rephrasing an extremist bodily gesture as an urbane triumph of writing.

But we could say instead that a rejection of *writing* is the primary reversal on which the story of the eye depends. The "translation" of the letter as body is precisely a refusal of "literal-ness." The woman sends the eye as commentary (metadiscourse): as Baudrillard notes, her gesture cites and mocks the seducer's courtly platitude. But the "blood" in the envelope is also a reminder of the gap between the rhetorical promise of seduction and its material consequences, in this social code, for women.

In the epistolary novels to which Baudrillard's fable refers (see, for example, *Les lettres de la Marquise de M*** au Comte de R****, by Crébillon fils), the usual outcome is death, often by suicide, for the female co(r)respondent. So the eye sliding out of the envelope cheats death, as well as cheating the seducer of his pleasures. He loses face, but she merely gives him the eye. And it cheats on literary narrative; the eye in this fable is the mark of a high-speed, fast-forward reader who tears to the end of the story without submitting to the rituals of "writing." Something in this fable—perhaps a shudder—leaps from a woman to man in the circuit reserved for the letter, but it doesn't take the form of a pun. It has a historically resonant *eloquence* to which Baudrillard's discourse, even as it tells the story, remains resolutely deaf.

It is crucial to say, however, that in de Certeau's framework both of the major forms of quoting are understood positively as capable (when their history is not forgotten and the position of the "scribe" not denied) of leaving ways for the other to speak. It is precisely this capacity which makes possible a feminist reading of Fiske's and Baudrillard's stories, and which can enable feminist cultural criticism to resist, in turn, its own enclosure as a self-perpetuating, self-reiterating academic practice.

The science of fables uses voices to proliferate discourse: in the detour through difference, quotation alters the voice that it desires and fails to reproduce, but is also altered by it. However, unlike an exoticism which multiplies anecdotes of the same, a "heterological" science will try to admit the alteration provoked by difference. Its reflexivity is not reinvested in a narcissistic economy of pleasure, but works to transform the conditions that make its practices possible, and the positioning of the other these entail.

Quotation-reminiscence "lets voices out": rather than generating discourse, the sounds of the body interrupt it from an "other" scene. As "letting out," this kind of quotation seems to be involuntary: memories rush from that nonplace conveniently cast beyond the citing subject's "domain" of responsibility. However, it is in a *"labor"* of reminiscence that the body's sounds can interrupt discourse not only in the mode of event but as practice. De Certeau sees this "struggle against oblivion" in philosophies which (like Deleuze and Guattari's *Anti-Oedipus*, Lyotard's *Libidinal Economy*) strive to create "auditory space"; and in the "reversal" that has taken psychoanalysis from a "science of dreams" toward "the experience of what speaking voices *change* in the dark grotto of the bodies that hear them" (162, emphasis mine).

So while both of these "ways of quoting" belong to the strategy of the institution, and define the scholarly place, each therefore can be borrowed by tactical operations that—like the recognition of alterity, the labor of reminiscence—change analytical procedures by "returning" them to their limits, and insinuating the ordinary into "established scientific fields." The event of this change is what de Certeau calls "banality": the arrival at a *common* "place," which is not (as it may be for populism) an initial state of grace, and not (as it is in Baudrillard) an indiscriminate, inchoate condition, but on the contrary, the outcome of a practice, something that "comes into being" at the end of a trajectory. This is the banality that speaks in *Everyman*, and in the late work of Freud—where the ordinary is no longer the object of analysis but the *place* from which discourse is produced.

It is at this final point, however, that my reading can fellow-travel no further, and parts company with de Certeau's "we."

A feminist critique of *The Practice of Everyday Life* would find ample material to work with. De Certeau's Muse—the silent other to whom his writing would strive to give voice—is unmistakably The Ordinary Man.[22]

My problem here, however, is specifically with the characteristics of the *scholarly* "place" of enunciation from which the notion of banality is constructed, and for which it can work as a myth of transformation. For to invoke with de Certeau an "ironic and mad banality" that can insinuate itself into our techniques, and reorganize the place from which discourse is produced, is immediately to posit an awkward position for "scholarly" subjects for whom *Everyman* might not serve as well as *"I Love Lucy"* as a fable of origin, or indeed as a myth of "voice." For me as a feminist, as a distracted media baby, and also, to some extent, as an Australian, the reference to *Everyman* (and, for that matter, to Freud) is rather a reminder of the problems of disengaging my own thinking from patriarchal (and Eurocentric) cultural norms.

The analytical scene for de Certeau occurs in a highly specialized, professional place. Yet in contrast to most real academic institutions today, it is not already *occupied* (rather than nomadically "crossed") by the sexual, racial, ethnic, and popular differences that it constitutes as "other." Nor is it squarely *founded*, rather than "disrupted," by the ordinary experience encountered at its frontiers. It is a place of knowledge secured, in fact, by precisely those historic exclusions which have made it so difficult to imagine or *admit* the possibility of a scholarship "proper" to the other's "own" experience—except in the form of an error (essentialism), or apocalyptic fantasy (rupture, revolution). Construed from de Certeau's "here," the other as narrator, rather than object, of scholarly discourse remains, as a general rule, a promising myth of the future, a fable of changes to come.

In other words: in this place, the citing of alterity and the analytical labor of reminiscence promise something like the practice of a "writing cure" for the latter-day Robinson Crusoe.

This is a "fate" all the more awkward for me to assume in that for de Certeau, "place," "the proper," and even "closure" are not always necessarily *bad values*, but modes of spatial and narrative organization everywhere at work in everyday social life. It is the primary function of any *story*, for example, to found a place, or create a field that authorizes practical actions (125). So there is no suggestion in his work that those who have been most intimately marked in history by Man Friday's Alternative (the cry, the impersonation) should not now, in writing their stories, thereby lay claim to a place. The utopian deferral of an "other" narration in de Certeau's theory occurs, like the apotheosis of banality as the Ordinary *Man*, because the "place" of the other may never coincide with that of any subject of a discourse (nor, of course, the subject's with that of an actual speaker). To dream otherwise is a "false mysticism"—longing for Presence, denial of History, nostalgia for God.

Unfortunately, since the other here is also "the discourse's mode of relation to *its own* historicity in the moment of its utterance" (emphasis mine), this argument encourages us to conclude that scholarly knowledge in the present must continue to be written, and transformed, from Crusoe's place. In practice, of course, de Certeau drew no such conclusion, writing that "the history of women, of blacks, of Jews, of cultural minorities, *etc.*" (my emphasis) puts into question "the subject-producer" of history and *therefore* "the particularity of the place where discourse is produced."[23] But the "*etc.*" points to a problem with the rhetoric of otherness that lingers when the epistemology that sustained it is apparently revised. "Etc." is Man Friday's footprint: a unifying myth of a *common* otherness—Black, Primitive, Woman, Child, People, "Voice," Banality—deriving its value only from its function as negation (polemological challenge, utopian hope) for that same singular writing subject of historical production.

I am skeptical that a theory grounded on (rather than tactically using) the category of otherness can ever end up anywhere else.[24] However, in the context of cultural studies, the immediate practical disadvantage of this construction of analysis is to reinscribe *alienation* from everyday life as a constitutive rather than contingent feature of the scholar's enunciative place. An old pathos of separation creeps back in here, of which the polarities (elite/popular, special/general, singular/"banal") mark not only the semantic organization of de Certeau's discourse but the narrative thrust of his text. The main line of *The Practice of Everyday Life* moves from its beginnings in "A Common Place: Ordinary Language" to "The Unnamable," a meditation on that absolute other, ultimate frontier, and final banality, Death.

Rather than venturing any further on to that forbidding theoretical terrain, I shall shift the scene of my own analysis to a more congenial place.

One of the enduring lounge-room "institutions" of Australian TV is Bill Collins, host of an ancient show that was once *The Golden Years of Hollywood*, but is now just a time-slot for *Movies*. A former teacher, Collins has spent twenty years using his "place" to define what counts on television as knowledge of cinema history. He now has many competitors and probably not much power, but for years he had a monopoly—years when there were no old films in theaters, no video chains, and no systematic study of media in schools. So it is no exaggeration to say that Collins was one of the founders of Australian screen education.

His pedagogy has changed little with time. Collins is a trivia expert, respectful rather than mocking in his relentless pursuit of the detail. His address to the audience is avuncular, his construction of film auratic. Never raucous or unkind, rarely "critical," his scholarship is a perpetual effusion of an undemanding love. Usually placed in a "home study" decor with posters, magazines, and books, Collins represents knowledge as a universally accessible domestic hobby. It is from his enthusiasms, rather than any formal training (which in this "place" is rather despised), that his authority derives. His "history" is a labyrinthine network of minuscule anecdotes: its grand theme is less the rise and fall of famous careers than the ebb and flow of fortune in the lives of the humbler figures near the bottom of the credits, or toward the edge of the frame. His own image expounds his theme: plump, owlish, chronically middle-aged, unpretentiously dressed, Collins has one eccentricity, a voice just a little bit pompous and prissy.

While I was working on this essay, he showed two films that seemed chosen to stimulate my thinking. Both were fables about "proper" places (malign in one case, benign in the other) and a principle of fatality at work in everyday life.

David Green's *The Guardian* (1984) could have been subtitled *Man Friday's Revenge*. Martin Sheen plays the white husband and father worried about the security of his apartment block, invaded by junkies from the street. After a murder and a rape inside, he persuades the other residents to hire a guardian (Louis Gossett, Jr.). Tough, streetwise, and black, the solitary

"John" moves in and makes the place his own. A sinister conflict emerges. Sheen wants a flexible frontier: residents inside, desperados outside, ordinary peaceful neighbors moving in and out as before. Gossett demands strict closure, total control: he bashes visitors, kills intruders, and polices not only the building but the residents' everyday lives.

At last, the sleeping liberal awakens in the would-be white vigilante. Too late: charging off into the night to tackle Gossett *chez lui*, Sheen falls afoul of a ghetto gang. Pulverized by terror, he is saved at last by Gossett—to suffer the ignominy of his own abject gratitude for the guardian's greater violence. Back at the ranch, the two men lock gazes in the final scene of the film: black guardian standing triumphantly inside, undisputed master of the place; white resident creeping furtively outside, insecure and afraid between the zones of home and street—in each of which he will henceforth be but a tenant without authority.

The structural reversal is complete, the moral ambiguity of the moment absolute. Was Sheen's first mistake to accept violence by inviting Gossett in, or was it to deny the implications of this action and, by dithering, lose control? Either way, *The Guardian* dramatizes with white-and-black simplicity a problem besetting any thematics of place primarily articulated by binary oppositions between "haves" and "have-nots," self and other, propriety and mobility. In such a schema, the drifter's desire is colonized as the settler's worst nightmare.[25] The *other*'s desire for a place can be represented only in terms of a choice between the *status quo* (critique of property, romance of dispossession) or as a violent reversal of roles that intensifies the prevailing structuration of powers. Totalitarian violence is in the end the true successor to Sheen's liberal paranoia—and it is the only image that the film can admit of what "a room of one's own" for the (black) urban poor might mean.

If *The Practice of Everyday Life* provides a sophisticated attempt to undermine the fatality of this kind of system by introducing nonsymmetry to its terms—theorizing difference rather than contradiction between them, refusing to assign *a priori* a negative value to either side—it nevertheless leaves us stranded when it comes to developing, rather than arriving at, the critical practice of a feminism (for example) already situated *both* by knowledge and social experience of insecurity and dispossession, *and* by a politics of exercising established institutional powers. Similarly, this aspect of de Certeau's work may not be of much help with the problems of an emerging cultural criticism which is equally—though not indifferently—"at home" in a number of sometimes conflicting social sites (academy, media, community group as well as "home" and "street"), moving between them with an agility which may well owe more to imperatives derived from technological changes, and from shifts in employment patterns, than it does to transient desire.

Bill Collins introduced *The Guardian* with a promise that it would unsettle anybody who lived in an apartment. Screening Alfred Hitchcock's *The Trouble with Harry* (1955) for the first time on TV, he saved his lesson till last.

The Trouble with Harry provided the perfect counterpart to the pure polemological message ("they always fuck us over") of *The Guardian*. Subtle, elusive, hilariously amoral in its utopian treatment of death, it also promised a perfect ending for my essay. For in this film, one day in a quiet mountain village—where few sounds disturb the silence except for the drifting of autumn leaves, the bird song in the valley, the honking of an antique car horn, the popping of a shotgun, the call of an excited child, and the occasional rustle of a rabbit in the grass—the pervasive calm is shattered by the appearance of a corpse.

Harry is a strange body, in more ways than one. He is a foreigner to the valley: the curious insignificance of his death, the incongruity of his presence there, is established by repeated shots of his feet sticking up as he sprawls headfirst down the hillside. But as the locals begin to arrive, it seems that there may be more trouble in paradise than the mere apparition of Harry. One by one, the adults respond with astounding banality: they talk of blueberry muffins, coffee, elderberry wine, lemonade; a reader trips on the corpse and ignores it, going straight on with his book; a tramp steals Harry's shoes; an artist sketches the scene. The initial suspect, watching from the bushes, mutters: "Next thing you know they'll be televising the whole thing!"

As the mystery of these responses begins to be dispelled, another takes its place. The inhabitants of this tiny village barely know each other, and coexist in an anomic isolation far exceeding small-town discretion. This may be a not-quite-innocent paradise, but it isn't really a *place*; a utopia, but not a community. But when the truth of Harry's death starts to emerge from a casual chat about destiny, new relationships swiftly develop. During the ensuing narrative play between deception and detection, the corpse shifts repeatedly between temporary homes—in the ground, on the hillside, in the bathtub. Only when the full story has been told does Harry find his proper location (where he was in the beginning) and identity (as a banal victim of a fatal heart attack); couples are formed, first names exchanged, histories shared, community established; and, when the founding of a place is complete, "the trouble with Harry is over."

Grasping something like this in my first viewing, thrilling in an allegorical sensitivity to each phrase, every scene, that echoes *The Practice of Everyday Life,* I resolved to do a reading of the film—forgetting that to retrieve a given theory of popular culture from a text framed as an *exemplum* of both would be to produce, at the end of my trajectory, precisely the kind of "banality" I was setting out to question.

I did not long enjoy the contemplation of my intention. "Did you notice," asked Bill Collins in his meditative moment, "how everyone in this film seems to *want* to feel guilty?" "*That's not the point!*" I told the television, ready with my counterthesis. "Well," declared that irritating voice, "there's a Ph.D. in that!"

In a fascinating essay on the figure of the speaking voice in the work of Rousseau and Plato, Michèle Le Doeuff points out that this voice (indefinite, uncertain, irrational in its effects, *"celle dont on aurait pu penser qu'elle était la banalité même"*) may function in philosophy not only as an emblem of the other but, therefore, as an instrument of demarcation whereby a theory can speak obliquely not of voices but of philosophy itself—its limits, its failures, and its problems of legitimacy.[26]

I suspect that in cultural studies, its function is rather the opposite. Parasitic on philosophy as cultural studies has been, it is perhaps today the discipline most at odds with the historic, self-legitimating dream of philosophical autonomy analyzed by Le Doeuff in *L'imaginaire philosophique*. Careless about its own epistemological grounding, its theoretical integrity, and its difference from "other" discourses, cultural studies has been more concerned (and, I think, rightly so) with analyzing and achieving political effects. It may be for this reason, then, and along with the historical determinations that de Certeau describes, that the "banality" of the speaking voice becomes in cultural studies a way of *suspending* the question of legitimation, and all the problems that question entails.

"Banality," after all, is one of the group of words—including "trivial" and "mundane"—whose modern history inscribes the disintegration of old European ideals about the common people, the common place, the common culture. In medieval French, the "banal" fields, mills, and ovens were those used communally. It is only in the late eighteenth century (and within the "scriptural economy") that these words begin to acquire their modern sense of the trite, the platitudinous, the unoriginal.

So if banality is an irritant that repeatedly returns to trouble cultural theory, it is because the very concept is part of the modern history of taste, value, and critique of judgment that constitutes the polemical field within which cultural studies now takes issue with classical aesthetics. "Banality" as mythic signifier is thus always a mask for questions of value, of value judgment, and "discrimination"—especially in the sense of how we distinguish and evaluate *problems* (rather than cultural "products"), legitimate our priorities, and defend our choice of what matters.

This is a debate which has barely begun, and which is all the more complex in that the professional protocols inherited by cultural studies from established disciplines—sociology, literary criticism, philosophy—may well be either irrelevant or contentious. If I find myself, for example, in the contradictory position of wanting polemically to reject Baudrillard's use of "banality" as a framing *aesthetic* concept to discuss mass media, yet go on to complain myself of a syllogistic "banality" in British cultural studies, the dilemma can arise because the repertoire of critical strategies available to people wanting to theorize the discriminations that they make in relation to their experience of popular culture—without needing to defend the validity of that experience, still less that of culture *as a whole*—is still extraordinarily depleted.

And there is an extra twist to the history of banality. In the Oxford version of this history, it has a double heritage in, on the one hand, old English, *bannan*—to summon, or to curse—and a Germanic *bannan:* to proclaim *under penalty.* So banality is related to banishing, and also to wedding *bans.* In other words, it is a figure inscribing power in an act of *enunciation.* In medieval times it could mean two things besides "common place." It could mean to issue an edict or a summons (usually to war). That was the enunciative privilege of the feudal lord. Or it could mean to proclaim under orders: to line the streets, and cheer, in the manner required by the call *"un ban pour le vanqueur!"* To obediently voice a rhythmic applause is the "banal" enunciative duty of the common people, the popular chorus.

This two-sided historical function of banality—lordly pronouncement, mimetic popular performance—is not yet banished from the practice of theorizing the popular today. It's very hard, perhaps impossible, not to make the invoked "voice" of the popular perform itself obediently in just that medieval way in our writing. However, when the voice of that which academic discourses—including cultural studies—constitute *as* popular begins in turn to theorize its speech, then you have an interesting possibility. That theorization may well go round by way of the procedures that Homi Bhabha has theorized as "colonial mimicry," for example, but may also come around eventually in a different, and as yet utopian, mode of enunciative practice.[27] However, I think that this can happen only if the complexity of social experience investing our "place" as intellectuals today— including the proliferation of different places in and between which we may learn and teach and write—becomes a presupposition of, and not an anecdotal adjunct to, our practice.

For this reason, I think that feminists have to work quite hard in cultural studies *not* to become subjects of banality in that old double sense: not to formulate edicts and proclamations, yet to keep theorizing, not to become supermimics in the Baudrillardian sense of becoming, by reversal, the same as that which is mimicked, yet to refuse to subside either into silence or into a posture of reified difference. Through some such effort, pained and disgruntled subjects, who are also joyous and inventive practitioners, can begin to articulate our critique of everyday life.

NOTES

1. John Fiske, "British Cultural Studies and Television," in *Channels of Discourse: Television and Contemporary Criticism,* ed. Robert C. Allen (Chapel Hill: University of North Carolina Press, 1987), pp. 254–89.

2. Judith Williamson, "The Problems of Being *Popular,*" *New Socialist* Sept. 1986:14–15.

3. Patricia Mellencamp, "Situation Comedy, Feminism, and Freud: Discourses of Gracie and Lucy," in *Studies in Entertainment: Critical Approaches to Mass Culture,* ed. Tania Modleski (Bloomington: Indiana University Press, 1986), pp. 80–95.

4. Cf. Margaret Morse, "The Television News Personality and Credibility: Reflections on the News in Transition," in *Studies in Entertainment,* pp. 55–79.

5. Andreas Huyssen, *After the Great Divide: Modernism, Mass Culture, Postmodernism* (Bloomington: Indiana University Press, 1986), p. vii.

6. Mica Nava, "Consumerism and Its Contradictions," *Cultural Studies* 1.2 (May 1987):204–210. The phrase "cultural dopes" is from Stuart Hall, "Notes on Deconstructing 'the Popular,' " in *People's History and Socialist Theory,* ed. Raphael Samuel (London: Routledge & Kegan Paul, 1981), pp. 227–39.

7. Iain Chambers, *Popular Culture: The Metropolitan Experience* (New York: Methuen, 1986), pp. 12–13.

8. Meaghan Morris, "At *Henry Parkes* Motel," *Cultural Studies* 2.1 (1988):1–47.

9. Andreas Huyssen, "Mass Culture as Woman: Modernism's Other," in *After the Great Divide,* pp. 44–62; Tania Modleski, "Femininity as Mas(s)querade: A Feminist Approach to Mass Culture," in *High Theory/Low Culture,* ed. Colin MacCabe (Manchester: Manchester University Press, 1986), pp. 37–52; Patrice Petro, "Mass Culture and the Feminine: The 'Place' of Television in Film Studies," *Cinema Journal* 25.3 (Spring 1986):5–21.

10. Patrice Petro, "Modernity and Mass Culture in Weimar: Contours of a Discourse on Sexuality in Early Theories of Perception and Representation," *New German Critique* 40 (Winter 1987):115–46.

11. Elaine Showalter, "Critical Cross-Dressing: Male Feminists and the Woman of the Year," in *Men in Feminism,* ed. Alice Jardine and Paul Smith (New York: Methuen, 1987), pp. 116–32.

12. This sectarianism may be partly a result of the notions of "negotiated," "resistant," and "oppositional" *readings* that still play such a large part in our analyses. In the end, the aim of analysis becomes to generate one of these, thus repeatedly proving it possible to do so. Since there is little point in regenerating a "dominant" reading of a text (the features of which are usually presupposed by the social theory that frames the reading in the first place), the figure of a misguided but onside Other is necessary as a structural support to justify the exercise and guarantee the "difference" of the reading.

13. Michel de Certeau, *The Practice of Everyday Life,* trans. Steven F. Rendall (Berkeley: University of California Press, 1984), p. xvi.

14. A space for de Certeau is the product of, as well as a potential arena for, a practice. Cf. *The Practice of Everyday Life,* Part III, "Spatial Practices."

15. I have tried to develop this notion of timing further in relation to the public use of live television in "Panorama: The Live, The Dead, and The Living," in *Island in the Stream: Myths of Place in Australian Cultural Criticism,* ed. Paul Foss (Sydney: Pluto, 1988).

16. Michel de Certeau, *Heterologies: Discourse on the Other,* trans. Brian Massumi (Manchester: Manchester University Press, 1986), p. xx.

17. It is unfortunate that de Certeau's theoretical essays remain better known in English than his work as a historian, and so are read in isolation from it. For background to the following discussion, cf. Michel de Certeau, *La possession de Loudun* (Paris: Julliard-Gallimard, 1970); *L'absent de l'histoire* (Paris: Mame, 1973); *La culture au pluriel* (Paris: 10–18, 1974); *L'écriture de l'histoire* (Paris: Gallimard, 1975); and with D. Julia and J. Revel, *Une politique de las langue, La Révolution française et les patois* (Paris: Gallimard, 1975).

18. Michel de Certeau, Dominique Julia, and Jacques Revel, "The Beauty of the Dead: Nisard," in *Heterologies*, pp. 119–36.

19. Michel de Certeau, *The Practice of Everyday Life*, Part IV, "Uses of Language."

20. De Certeau restricts the use of a writing/orality opposition in several important ways. First, there can be no *quest* for this voice "that has been simultaneously colonized and mythified" (132). There is no origin, authenticity, or spontaneity of presence to be found in a mythic voxpop, and no "pure" voice independent either of the scriptural systems that it inhabits or of the ways of "hearing"/receiving by which it is codified.

Second, "writing" and "orality" should not be construed as terms that *always* found a metaphysical opposition, the recurrence of which analysis can perpetually retrace. If "writing" and "orality" can function now as imaginary unities, they do so as a result of reciprocal distinctions made "within successive and interconnected historical configurations," from which they cannot be isolated (133). (Cf. *L'écriture de l'histoire*, Part III, "Systèmes de sens: l'écrit et l'oral.")

Third, the orality in question is one *changed* by three or four centuries of Western fashioning. It cannot be "heard" except as insinuation in the text of the scriptural economy. In Defoe's "theoretical fiction," Man Friday's footprint is not another local trace of an eternal illusion of presence. It represents the emergence of something *novel* in Defoe's text, outlining "a *form* of alterity in relation to writing that will also impose its identity on the voice . . ." (155).

21. In this perspective, "pop epistemology" works in a slightly different way. It "writes the voice" by effacing scriptural labor, as well as the translation that makes "distraction" readable, thus producing a fable of the coincidence of its own writing with "what speaks" in popular culture. The problem here is not that the "materiality" of writing is effaced but that the relationship of this practice to the disciplinary history from which it emerges (and which it claims to contest) is simply ignored.

22. Certainly, he is a Man now marked as Woman, Child, or Savage (and the text is sensitive to the problem of assimilating any one of these terms to the bodies of people they have been used to represent). However, de Certeau's history of this marking presupposes the indifference of the primary figure.

23. *Heterologies*, pp. 217.

24. For a different view, cf. Elizabeth Grosz, "The 'People of the Book': Representation and Alterity in Emmanuel Levinas," *Art & Text* 26 (Sept.–Nov. 1987):32–40.

25. An extreme case is Jean Duvignaud, "Esquisse pour le nomade," in *Cause commune: Nomades et vagabonds* (Paris: 10–18, 1975), pp. 13–40.

26. Michèle Le Doeuff, "La philosophie dans le gosier," in *L'imaginaire philosophique* (Paris: Payot, 1980), pp. 171–79. Translation by Colin Gordon forthcoming (London: The Athlone Press).

27. Homi K. Bhabha, "Of Mimicry and Man: The Ambivalence of Colonial Discourse," *October* 28 (Spring 1984):125–33.

PLAYING AT BEING AMERICAN

Games and Tactics

John Caughie

Playing at being American. There's a kind of impudence here that pulls in two directions:

First: there's a conscious and deliberate echo of Venturi's *Learning from Las Vegas*;[1] the sense of an objectification, from the outside, of a mental landscape which has a special status in the cultural imaginary. But whereas Venturi may appeal to the democracy of the vernacular, my sense of this objectification is that what it in fact does is to confer on the observer a token of superiority, the "distant distinction" which Pierre Bourdieu sees as the distinguishing, aesthetically "ennobling" mark of the owner of cultural capital. "Nothing," says Bourdieu, "is more distinctive, more distinguished, than the capacity to confer aesthetic status on objects that are banal, or even 'common.' "[2] In the context of a "media imperialism" which has America as its center, this impudent objectification of an imaginary America which can be played at and with, claims such a distinction, seeking to reverse the current of imperialism. The empire strikes back at its center, the "colonized unconscious" *knows* its colonizer, the periphery creates the core as *its* other, the subaltern attempts speech. The rhetorical "tactic,"[3] then, is one of empowerment.

Second: if sarcasm is indeed the lowest form of wit, it may be because it's the last resort of the powerless. The cheekiness of the "Kynic," which Peter Sloterdijk[4] traces in the heirs of Diogenes as a defense against the cynical reason of a decaying Enlightenment, offers a certain satisfaction—rudeness rather than rationality as the rebuttal of idealism, farting in the face of the Platonic dialogue[5]—but the carnival of fools happens only under license, and it's business as usual next day. Impudence may confirm rather than subvert the "normal" relations of power. So the insubordination of playing at being American may, in fact, be nothing more than a licensed game, one of the permitted games of subordination.

Tactics of empowerment and games of subordination: a play of subjectivity and identification reminiscent of the oscillations of women's identification discussed by Laura Mulvey in her afterthoughts on "Visual Pleasure and Narrative Cinema"[6] or, perhaps more exactly, with the process of "double identification"—subject and object, seer and seen, both inextricably at once—argued by Teresa de Lauretis in *Alice Doesn't.*[7] I want to suggest that this play of subjectivity, oscillation or doubling, with all the sometimes pleasurable, sometimes painful contortions which either process involves, is a more adequate way of understanding the "colonized unconscious" than the simple and singular positioning which theories of media imperialism usually allow.

ANECDOTE: LOCAL KNOWLEDGE

Imagine, if you will: a remote village, high in the Spanish Pyrenees; on one side of the single unpaved street, a cluster of buildings, on the other side, fields; in the fields, women and men, scything, forking over the hay, raking with wooden rakes; in the very center of the village an open cow barn; immediately beside the cow barn, a cantina, bead-curtained and stone-floored; inside the cantina, a woman behind the bar, a girl (could she be barefoot?) sweeping the floor, and a television set. It is 11 A.M. on Wednesday 23 July, 1987, and the television is on.

We (mountain-walking, non-Spanish-speaking "enlightened tourists") drink Coke and glance at the television. It is twenty minutes before either of us realizes that the person we are glancing at is indeed Joan Collins, and that this is indeed *Dynasty*, almost more realistic in Spanish, the melodramatic legitimized as foreign, other, operatic. The cultural anomaly—outside, there are cows in the main street, inside, the world of *Dynasty*—isn't enough to hold our interest for long, but our moves to leave are met with some kind of anxiety. By this time, half the population of the village seems to have congregated to watch television; there is anticipation of something big about to happen which we, particularly, should be witness to, and so we stay—politely. *Dynasty* finishes, and on comes, sure enough, to communal delight and recognition, the English Royal Wedding: Fergie and Andrew (Nancy Reagan, Princess Di as bit players), along with all the pageantry and the celebration of English nationhood and identity, which makes us, in our "distant distinction" (and our Scottishness), seek out otherness and difference in the first place.

The story is nothing special. Most of us probably have a version of it. It's the kind of story that we bring back in our luggage and drop into conversation to illustrate the thesis of cultural homogenization: there is no difference, the media have made it all the same out there. But if it's to be circulated as anything other than a cute epiphany, its meaning cannot be self-evident.

First, there's an appropriateness in these particular programs which gives some specificity to the kinds of marketable images which the US and UK now sell, images which come to define them in the international imaginary, and which secure their places in the international image markets. *Dynasty* (with *Dallas*—the two, "Dallas n' Dynasty," as Richard Collins points out,[8] become shorthand, a codeword for the moral panic generated by the American penetration of the European psyche and the European markets) surely both celebrates and castigates advanced capitalist structures and relationships, offering desires and their punishments in the same movement, short-circuiting guilt, giving us things to wish for and rewarding us with confirmations of our own superiority because we don't have them: a playful mode, available to more than one reading. The Royal Wedding (an episode in a continuing series) marks out with wonderful precision what it is that Britain can still sell easily on the image market: the past, tradition, the spectacle of national pageantry, the costume dramas of a simpler class hierarchy, the nostalgia for a lost aristocracy: *Brideshead Revisited, The Jewel in the Crown, Upstairs, Downstairs,* "Masterpiece Theater"—even the soap operas—*Eastenders*—for all their qualities of recognition and familiarity in the home market, enter the US market as a mild nostalgia for a lost community. So if Britain and America are indeed the exporters in the international dream market, they may be marketing dreams which are dreamed in quite diverse ways, a fantasy of the other as quaint, perhaps, rather than as compelling object of desire.

Second, and consequently, is *Dynasty,* dubbed into Spanish, watched by Spanish men and women in a Spanish village, still, only and simply, an American text (with all that textuality has come to mean)? Is the English Royal Wedding *celebrated* in Catalonia, the most fiercely independent region in mainland Europe outside the Basque territory? How can it mean the same thing in Spain, with that country's intensely contradictory history of monarchism and republicanism, as it does in the shires of Southern England, which may contain, albeit in isolated pockets, the only audience that is decoding it "correctly" in the way it was encoded?

The seduction of the thesis of homogenization and the eradication of cultural difference is hard to resist, and can continually be supported by empirical data on ownership and distribution. But at the level of theory (and experience), it seems continually to fall back on the belief in the passively receptive, "duped" consumer, the always obedient subject jumping into line at the call of interpellation. If we revise that view in favor of a more complex and various view of reading relations for the theorized domestic subject (female or male; audience, viewer, reader), we're clearly going to have to rethink it for the "colonized" subject as well.

A depressingly familiar scenario, then: the "enlightened tourist" seeking to penetrate the other without penetrating its otherness; in search of the virgin unknown, and constantly disappointed by its loss of innocence. This is the twist that makes travelers' tales, and it's founded on the same old paternalism: the owner of cultural capital laments the corruption of the other, who knows no better, despite our warnings, than to want to own the goods too.

The question of locality seems to me to have a particular urgency for television. It's increasingly accepted that theory and critique become most material when they are localized rather than universalized. For any film and television theory which has been attentive to feminism, the universal, neutered subject (the "it" that always concealed a "he") must give way to a subjectivity located within specific and "local" formations of gender and sexuality. I want to suggest that one of the localities from which theories can be materialized is the embarrassingly persistent category of the nation.

Now, clearly, nationalism has not had a particularly good press in the twentieth century; so it's important to say that the nation I'm talking about has less to do with the "nation state" of nineteenth-century nationalism, a legal and political "ego" presumed to function as a concrete subject, and more to do with the "imagined community" which Benedict Anderson describes,[9] this "imagining" qualifying in complex ways, rather than simply disqualifying, its subjectivity. (Parenthetically, the condensing image for me of this "imagining" is the road signs, encountered when driving through Arizona, that mark out tribal land—"Entering the Navajo Nation," "Leaving the Hopi Nation": a nationhood apparent less in its legal or economic status, which may be formal, and even derisory, than by the affective, subjective, and political aspiration which transforms as well as transcends its physical landscape.) The nationality in which I'm interested, then, and from which I speak (Scotland—in relation to the US a periphery on the edge of a periphery, a community which has often suffered from too much imagining), is never given, never already has pride of place, but is uncertain, tentative, wary of its own double edges.

Clearly also, even this tentative, marginalized nationality as locality cannot smoothly be expropriated from feminism as locality. Although nationalism conceived in this way seems to resonate in important ways with feminist theory and experience (the pressure to smile complicitly at our own humiliation, the marketing of the images of our own subjection, landscape as body, excessive identification—national dress and the tourist trade—"double identification" and the masquerade—precisely "playing at being American"), the relation to power remains different, the identification more abstract, the options—to play or not to play—more open.

Nevertheless, despite the dangers, it's this subjectivity, with those resonances, that is the context here for a way of thinking the subjectivity of television from a local perspective. Much television writing, while it is sensitive (sometimes) to systems of gender, is strikingly insensitive to the specificities of national systems, an insensitivity which drags it toward universal theories and descriptions of television that ignore the extent to which viewing is formed within particular national histories and localized broadcasting systems. Paradoxically, this universality is most apparent in those rhetorical celebrations of television as the quintessence of postmodernity which, while proclaiming the end of grand narratives and universal theories, simultaneously universalize a local, national experience—the US experience—as the essence of television, thus marginalizing all other experiences, and confusing the effect of a particular commercial arrangement with an inevitability of nature. For the record, I would argue that British television, and much European television, is still rooted in modernity, the concept and practice of public-service broadcasting part of an unbroken tradition of "good works" dating from the administration of capitalism in the latter part of the nineteenth century. While that tradition is clearly under threat from the readministration of capitalism and the redistribution of power in global markets, nevertheless the scenario of magical transformation—the marvelous vanishing act of deregulation: now you see "quality," now you don't—in both its optimistic and its pessimistic variants seems naive. More likely is a scenario in which transformation is uneven and diverse, continually modified by local conditions, local demands, expectations, resistances, and compromises, the future still bearing the residual traces of the way it always was. This diversity and local specificity seems important, not as a point of national pride, or nationalist pique, but as a challenge to notions of the in-difference of an essentialized and universal television.

So: playing at being American. In general terms, the question of how US television and the discourses which surround it figure in the empire of signs and representations and critical and theoretical practices that constitute television and our various relationships to it inside and outside America is clearly very important. I'm interested, generally, in the assumptions that ground the commonsense notion of the colonization of the unconscious or the imaginary, a notion which informs quite persistent national anxieties about the seductiveness of American popular entertainment, and about the dependency on US production within the schedules of popular television. These anxieties surface at a number of levels from the genuinely political to the cynically populist. I'm interested in this from a Scottish or British or possibly European context, and have no real sense or experience of what it might mean in the context of the more specialized forms of economic and mental subjection involved in the exploitation of so-called Third World markets. But here, in this essay, at a more particular and fundamental level, I'm interested in the extent to which the desire to locate television within local perspectives complicates assumptions and theoretical formulations about reception and representation and interpellation and identification in quite significant ways.

DETOUR: DISCOVERING AMERICA

As a slight detour, in the context of an American conference and an American publication, it may be useful to continue the objectification of the American experience as other, and to identify, very loosely, some of the local variants of watching television in America which strike me with the enlightening force of anthropological surprise. To characterize the specificity, or, for me, the difference, of watching television in America (as opposed to watching American television—which one can do anywhere), I want to offer three fairly basic, obvious, banal observations. They have to do not with program style or content but with the structure of viewing. They are consciously naive snapshots which may crystallize my "tourist" sense of the radical otherness, from a habituated British perspective, not simply of American television conceived as programs but of the American "televisual" conceived as an experience of watching and viewing, and switching on and switching off and switching over, and spending time.

First, and most obvious, the technologies of plurality. Even without peripheral technologies, there is a plurality of choice which is still (and the temporality of the "still" has to be emphasized) unknown in Britain. This is so obvious that it barely needs comment, except to suggest that this plurality breaks down the pattern of channeled or even programmed viewing. While there is still the anticipation of favorite programs, or favorite clusters on particular evenings, for many of us and for much of the time the televisual in America seems to be a relatively unstructured activity, zapping more satisfying than planning. Much more characteristically, I think, than in Britain, the American televisual is contingent.

Second, the organization of time. In some sense cutting against the contingency, in another sense reinforcing it, I am struck by the regularity of the network schedules, by the clarity of temporal definition given to primetime, by the ease of cross-over in a temporal system in which each program begins and ends on the hour or half-hour, by the starkness of choice when like is scheduled against like—not just "Do I want to see a cop show or a sitcom?" but "Which cop show?" "Which sitcom?" There is no space here to consider the extent to which this conflation of time and genre and the resulting competition within generic boundaries may account for the continual inventiveness and self-reflexive fluidity of US popular genres—an inventiveness which compares favorably with the repetition, stability, and even stasis of British generic conventions. Here, I am simply interested in the difference which American scheduling makes to the structuring of my time, particularly my primetime. It had never seemed odd before that a program such as *Dallas,* shown in Britain on BBC, should begin at 8:10 P.M. (because without commercials it lasts only fifty minutes), thus creating a ten-minute gap of "dead-time" between the end of a domestic soap opera on one channel and the beginning of *Dallas* on another. (Nor did it seem unusual that a film which lasted an hour and forty minutes in the cinema would also last an hour and forty minutes on television.) The specific nature of "flow" produced by the staggered scheduling of British television, with built-in resistance to clean channel cross-over—the risk of "dead-time"— seems to me to encourage a residual degree of channel loyalty (or inertia— it's easier to stay than to switch) quite uncharacteristic of US television flow.

And the relative absence of like-against-like scheduling organizes the movement from program to program in what seems like more structured, rational choices. The regularity of American television time, the opposition of like against like, dissolves my loyalties and draws me to the jumpy, nervy, mosaic gratifications of sampling. There's no need to insist on the generality of my secret practices and domestic rituals: the point is in the differences.

Third, and most important, the breaks and interruptions. For all the preparation that one receives from conventional wisdom about the annoyance of the commercial interruptions on American television, their effect still catches me a little unprepared. It is much less the regularity of the interruption, or the wonderful blatancy of their placement, more the specific way they interrupt, their effect on (or, more exactly, in) the text. In Britain, commercials interrupt programs, but in parentheses: a logo or a caption—*St. Elsewhere,* or "End of Part 1"—signals the suspension and resumption of the program, bracketing our disengagement, demarcating the adjustments in the form of our attention. On American television, Cagney looks out of frame, and the answering reverse-field is a commercial for Mack trucks. The space of the commercial is continuous from the space of the fiction: a split second of cognitive dissonance, but, for the unhabituated viewer, enough for a lurch in attention, a hiccup in the mental logic. Added to this, on the local stations, there are the breaks just before the final coda, or the station announcements over the credits, or station identification superimposed on the image. At one level, these are simply irritations of commercialism. At another level, though, they can be read symptomatically as little contests between commercial logic—the need to deliver audiences to advertisers—and narrative logic—the need to hold audiences in identification. What is so striking to someone raised in the protective shelter of public service is the visibility of the contest. I *experience* the effect which I had always known in theory: a quite radical destabilizing of the text as an autonomous and logical fictional space complete within its own boundaries. For a still "foreign" viewer, the experience of watching American television is never simply the experience of watching programs as texts in any classical sense, but is always also the experience of reading the specific forms of instability of an interrupted and interruptible space.

Part of the force for me of these banal reflections comes from the experience of teaching a television course, using largely British material, for American undergraduate students, and finding my assumptions about what television is and what the experience of viewing is in tension, albeit productive tension, with assumptions structured by a radically different economy of viewing and the televisual. There is a real risk in the theorizing and, particularly, in the teaching of television of opening up a gap between the television which is taught and theorized and the television which is experienced. Teaching seeks out the ordering regularities of theory. A television is constructed which is teachable, but may not be recognizable.

But another part of the force of this different watching is that of an estrangement effect, a seeing "as if for the first time," in which television viewing appears as a specific procedure, necessarily learned in response to specific textual practices. Each of my banal reflections crystallizes (for me) a specific uncertainty around the television text, the particular "strangeness" of American television giving that uncertainty a peculiar sharpness. Nothing theoretically new in the problem of textuality—except the force of experience, which opens the suspicion that a television theory which has still to find its own way of understanding textuality is not yet adequate to the difference of the television text, and the particular forms of its uncertainty and instability.

In theory and in criticism, what I'm suggesting as the instability of the television text, the blurring of its boundaries, the erosion of its integrity and its autonomy, are features completely familiar to poststructuralist and postmodernist criticism, not at all specific to television. The integrity of the autonomous text exists, at the theoretical level, only in formalist nostalgia (although in theoretical and critical practice the yearning for an isolation ward for critical cases still seems quite frequently to have material effects). All I want to suggest here is that the systematic qualifications and interruptions and erosions of the text-as-program, the text-as-unitary, build contingency into the structure of viewing in a way which faces the securities of the theoretical landscape with quite hard-edged problems. It may not be enough to qualify or even reverse the terms in order to accommodate television, sailing on a different part of the ocean of discourse but steering by the same stars; it may be that the metaphors which frame our theoretical discourse have to be checked for their continuing adequacy. I've suggested elsewhere,[10] in the context of theories of popular culture, that the economic metaphor, rooted in a nineteenth-century industrial economy, often brings with it a discourse of struggle which can be both romantic and virile, creating a romance of titanic forces. In its duality of production and consumption, it stabilizes the system, one term always already valued over the other, allowing a pendulum swing of critical values, but still swinging along the same axis. Here, in the context of thinking about television, I want to suggest that the spatial metaphor also—distance, positionality; a metaphor which can also be used to stabilize relationships in a diagrammatic geography—is, at the very least, up for review.

The spatial metaphor of position has been foundational for much film theory, either implicitly or explicitly. It allowed us to think not only positions but opposition, not only identification but distance, founding not only a textual economy but a politics of textuality: a kind of political geography whose orientation can be detected in the fact that while distance has been constantly recharted—detachment, distraction, passionate detachment, relaxed detachment, decentering—we seemed always to come back to the same old home port of identification, the wrong place to be. Politically, identification was passive, on the side of the consumer, where distance was

active, on the side of production, and the simple pleasures of consumption
were rejected in favor of the romance of radical resistance.

In his book *Horizons of Assent: Modernism, Postmodernism, and the Ironic
Imagination*,[11] Alan Wilde distinguishes, very provisionally—"an ad hoc
short-hand," he calls it, "deliberately 'inadequate' "[12]—three divisions of
what he calls the "ironic imagination": "mediate irony," "disjunctive irony,"
and "suspensive irony." "Mediate irony" is the mode of satire, essentially,
Wilde argues, a premodernist mode. It "imagines a world lapsed from a
recoverable norm."[13] "Disjunctive irony" Wilde associates with the heroic
agonism of the high modernists, fashioning meaning out of the fragments.
"The ironist confronts a world that appears inherently disconnected and
fragmented. . . . Disjunctive irony both recognizes the disconnections and
seems to control them."[14] Finally, perhaps most appropriate for a consideration of television, is "suspensive irony," which Wilde associates with
postmodernity:

> Suspensive irony . . . with its yet more radical vision of multiplicity, randomness,
> contingency, and even absurdity, abandons the quest for paradise altogether—
> the world in all its disorder is simply (or not so simply) accepted. . . . Ambiguity
> and paradox give way to quandary, to a low-keyed engagement with a world of
> perplexities and uncertainties, in which one can hope, at best, to achieve what
> Forster calls "the smaller pleasures of life," and Stanley Ilkin, its "small satis-
> factions."[15]

The interest of Wilde's work in the present context is not simply to
discover three more terms we can happily instrumentalize for television
studies, inaugurating debates on whether *St. Elsewhere* was disjunctive or
suspensive, or discovering the mediate irony in *Family Ties*. Wilde himself
is careful to insist that he is not constructing a teleology or even a rigid
critical taxonomy, but that each of the ironic modes may be present in any
text or any author in particular but shifting configurations and hierarchies.
The classifications are intended to enjoy, he says, "a strictly performative
function as discriminating and temporary instruments . . . , a 'truly empirical' sounding of the movements and sinuosities within the concrete
appearances of single or grouped phenomena."[16]

In the context of the development of television studies, what I find attractive in Wilde's "sounding" of irony (while reserving judgment on the
"assent" of some of his conclusions) is not simply the flexibility which he
produces, but rather the extent to which his formulation of the "ironic
imagination" echoes Peter Brooks in his formulation of an earlier "melodramatic imagination,"[17] offering a way of thinking *together* a historical
consciousness in which subjects do their imagining *and* a set of determinate
textual conditions and practices. Thus it's possible to argue that some kind
of ironic imagination, an ironic "suspensiveness" perhaps, or what Sloterdijk calls "enlightened false consciousness,"[18] is something we increasingly

bring to television, an ironic sensibility already formed outside the space of television, a function of our local histories of modernity and postmodernity, within or against which television always has to play; and, at the same time, to argue that the specific practices and procedures of television—the de-textualizing which it performs on its texts, the snaps in consciousness, the distractions, the physical rather than metaphorical spatial configurations of our rooms, the dipping in and out—provide very particular material and textual conditions for the production and play of an ironic imagination.

The irony which I'm talking about, then, has very little to do with authorial or institutional intention, and more with historical and textual condition. Such a concept of irony offers a way of thinking about dissociation and engagement as simultaneous or, at least, temporally connected activities, a knowing play in the "movements and sinuosities" of television, outside the spatial metaphor in which texts assign us to a position. In the sense in which Michel de Certeau elaborates the terms, it allows us to think of viewing practices and relations as "procedures" rather than as places.[19] It allows us, that is, to think of the possibility of negotiating two (or more) "conditions" at once (in such a way that the metaphor of boundaried place becomes inadequate), of holding subjectivities in suspension or disjunction, of knowing but agreeing not to know, of a play of irony, of playing at being. . . .

This attention to irony, then, whether it be to ironic forms of attention as a principle of modern or postmodern readership or viewership, or to forms of television address which constitute the conditions of ironic suspensiveness, is intended simply to open up within theory and criticism a more complicated, shifting, and sensitive way of thinking about how we might be relating to the appeals of television than is offered by the metaphors of place and position. It is emphatically not intended as a new methodology which can instrumentally be "applied" to television; nor am I suggesting that irony is a property of the television text, or that every television text is ironic, or that every television moment is a moment of play; nor, finally, am I suggesting that irony is an exclusive property of the televisual, although I am suggesting that the specific conditions of television produce the possibility of more ironic forms of attention than the conditions of, say, the cinematic. Less intensely fascinating in its hold than cinema, television seems to insist continually on an attention to viewing as mental activity and "knowingness" (almost a "street-wise" smartness), rather than to the obedience of interpellation or the affect of the "always already."

The implications of an attentiveness to this ironic imagination might be traced in distinct ways in analysis, and in theory and criticism. At the level of analysis, the question can be asked: If an ironic imagination is a characteristic mode for television, is there a way of identifying a characteristic figure within the routines of television rhetoric which supports it and puts it into play? I am thinking of the various ways in which the point-of-view shot has been used to figure out notions of cinematic identification. As a possible line of inquiry, if the point-of-view shot (which for various historical and practical reasons is relatively weak in television) is a foundational figure for cinematic identification, could it be that the reaction shot forms an equivalent figure for the ironic suspensiveness of television? As it has been argued, the point-of-view shot centers knowledge within the narrative space by identifying the look of the spectator with the look of a character. The reaction shot, as it is characteristically used in television, disperses knowledge, frequently registering it on the faces of a multiplicity of characters whose function may only be to intensify the event, to charge it with the emotional excess which Jane Feuer identifies in primetime melodrama,[20] but without the centered identification of the point-of-view shot: reaction without identification. Soap opera and melodrama may represent privileged instances here, but at the same time, a similar process can be detected in the cutaways to audience or panelists in studio discussions, game shows, or talk shows, or to spectators or managers in television sport. There isn't space here to develop the point, but in that gap between reaction and narrative identification may lie one of the ways in which irony is figured within the specific textual practices of television.

At the level of theory and criticism, it seems endemic to television writing that whereas film theory is marked by a sense of people trying to come to terms with their own, almost perverse, fascination—what Paul Willemen calls "cinephilia"[21]—television theory always seems to be written by people who can see the seduction but are not seduced. The critic's fascination with the audience in television writing may be due, at least in part, to a lack of fascination with the texts. An effect of this is that television viewers always risk being constructed as the determinate or indeterminate "other," reified as an object of investigation or special attention in roughly the same abstract, and even cynical, way in which election campaigns construct the housewife, the farmer, or the consumer. One of the things that attract me about the concept of an ironic play, of a kind of suspensiveness of knowing and not knowing, being and not being, is that it seems to identify the most characteristic way in which I respond to television, the "small pleasure" that I use television for. Even if this is simply the superior and privileged response of the intellectual, the owner of cultural capital, it is at least worth acknowledging. A television criticism which can identify with itself may avoid speaking for experiences it isn't having.

The argument, then, is that television produces the conditions of an ironic knowingness, at least as a possibility, which may escape the obedience of interpellation or cultural colonialism and may offer a way of thinking subjectivity free of subjection. It gives a way of thinking identities as plays of cognition and miscognition, which can account for the pleasures of playing at being, for example, American, without the paternalistic disapproval that goes with the assumption that it is bad for the natives. Most of all, it opens identity to diversity, and escapes the notion of cultural identity as a fixed volume for which, if something comes in from the outside, something from the inside must inevitably go out. But if it does all this, it does not do it in that utopia of guaranteed resistance which assumes the progressiveness of naturally oppositional readers who will get it right in the end. It does it, rather, within the terms hung in suspension at the beginning of this essay: tactics of empowerment, games of subordination, with neither term fixed in advance.

For this continual return to suspensiveness is, in every sense, double-edged. With one edge, it opens closed systems and dispenses with guarantees; with the other, it lays waste solid ground and exposes ideals, objectives, and aspirations to a sceptical or cynical paralysis. It echoes those familiar terms of postmodernity—ambivalence, indeterminacy, paradox—which challenge the accustomed systems of rationality that founded "enlightened" theory and politics. This challenge is common to much of contemporary cultural and social studies. But for a television studies which is still looking for a definition, however indefinite, and which, imbricated in every way with contemporaneity, cannot avoid the implications of the analysis of postmodernity, the "quandary" seems to represent a particularly numbing critical impasse.

The terms of the impasse can be indicated very schematically: value, politics, the text. What are the terms of decidability by which we can argue for or against values when indecidability is the rule of the game? How do we measure progressiveness without the certainty of the linear narrative of progress? And, underpinning all this, what is the television text anyway? Within the impasse may lie a certain discomfort in television studies on the part of the radical/popular/academic intellectual (for whom impasse and crisis are, of course, terms of self-dramatization). For many of us, formed historically in theory and ideology critique, in a political commitment to popular culture, and in a belief in our special (and "subversive") place at the cutting edge of the liberal academy, television, and particularly the television text, without the proper sanctification of a theory, may still be an unworthy object, the clarion call to "take television seriously" still a little desperate. The result is a series of displacements. The privileged objects of much television studies—the audience, the institutions, the market—are effective ways of displacing the theoretical problems of values, politics, and texts onto empirically testable bodies. Which is not at all to devalue such studies, but simply to remind ourselves that the question of television's textuality—untestable, uncertain, repressed—will keep returning.

The attempt to rediscover irony may be to contribute as much to the problem as to the solution. In its suspensiveness, or disjunction, its play of being and knowing, its ability to go either way, the ironic imagination may simply play out the amused quandary which dissolves held positions of value, principle, or politics. Attractive because it holds open the possibility of a "difference" which can play with an objectified dominance without being subjected to it, suspensiveness may also conceal the smile of an in-difference to which nothing much matters anymore.

In trying to bring irony—as a term of analysis, theory, and criticism—into some kind of conjunction with nationality—as a term of culture and identity—I'm trying to ground the one in the other precisely as a way out of that quandary of in-difference. Irony not as a universal theory but as a various and local "tactic"; nationality not as an always already but as a set of aspirations. If irony is a useful concept, even if only to hold at the back of the mind, it is not because it offers a guarantee of the resistance which John Fiske discovers everywhere in television viewing,[22] or even the ro-mance of the guerrilla tactics of counterproduction and refunctioning which de Certeau finds in "consumer practices."[23] It is not a universal category, and its inflection depends on local conditions. The claims to use-fulness would be much more modest. Simply, irony seems to me to offer a neglected aesthetic category which might bring together textual practices which could be identified by analysis, the peculiar disidentificatory *dispositif* of television as discursive practice, and a possible historically formed dis-position of locally constituted audiences. It recognizes distance, but also the "incorrect" "small satisfactions" of being superior *and* being the dupe. As an experiential category, it seems to me to avoid the well-meaning cy-nicism of the audience as the intellectual's other, and implicates the critic in his/her own discourse as a material, rather than a transcendent, subject.

But what if playing at being American is the only game in town? Is there anything else we can play at being? The return, again, of the national question. The essay comes to seem somewhat perverse and awkward in its desire to hold on, till the very end, to that conjunction of irony and locality, an aesthetics and a cultural politics. Clearly, as an aesthetic category, ironic suspensiveness has very little to say about the economic and ideological power of the American film and television industries in the international television market. Almost to the contrary, the ironic imagination, as a mere playing at being, might seem to dissolve the importance of that dominance as a cultural issue. But the very difficulty of the conjunction seems to me to be important, setting up a number of resistances between the two terms. Irony, in the sense in which I would use it, approaches viewing as a pro-cedure rather than a place, giving a name to the play of identity and dis-tinction—sometimes pleasurable, sometimes contorted; sometimes conscious, sometimes unconscious; sometimes resistant, often compro-mised—of subject and object, seer and scene. The insistence on the na-tional, or the local in any of its forms, prefers, if only as a possibility, difference and diversity to indifference and mere plurality. The continual return to locality, whether it be of nation, race, class, gender, or generation, resists the easy rationality of a general category or a universal theory. It is conscious of a less systematic specificity, to be determined by local readings of texts and conditions and histories and objectives, and it proposes a politics which is not guaranteed by textuality or by natural resistance but is open to historical conditions. For television, these conditions are, in their turn, enmeshed in the expectations, aspirations, and possibilities produced by particular histories of broadcasting and by particular legal, commercial, and political arrangements of regulation and deregulation.

One of the things which make television writing so difficult, particularly at an international level, is precisely the absence of an "international standard," of the sort that Hollywood's "classical cinema" has provided for writing about film. In that absence, general statements are always vulnerable to local and empirical knowledges and experiences. But since these are the conditions, it may be as well to find ways of coping with them. In her essay "Feminism and Critical Theory," Gayatri Spivak takes certain American feminists to task for their attitude to history: "As long as [they] understand 'history' as a positivistic empiricism that scorns 'theory' and therefore remains ignorant of its own, the 'Third World' as its object of study will remain constituted by those hegemonic First World intellectual practices."[24] It seems to me that there is something for television studies in that warning, in its insistence on the need for empirical and local understandings of histories and practices, dispositions and *dispositifs*, which poses the resistance to imperial theory.

NOTES

1. Robert Venturi et al., *Learning from Las Vegas* (Cambridge: MIT Press, 1972).
2. Pierre Bourdieu, *Distinction: A Social Critique of the Judgement of Taste* (Cambridge: Harvard University Press, 1984), p. 5.
3. For the distinction between "tactics" and "strategies," see Michel de Certeau, *The Practice of Everyday Life* (Berkeley: University of California Press, 1984), pp. 34–39.
4. Peter Sloterdijk, *Critique of Cynical Reason* (Minneapolis: University of Minnesota Press, 1987), particularly chapter 5, "In Search of Lost 'Cheekiness.' "
5. Ibid., p. 101.
6. Laura Mulvey, "Afterthoughts on 'Visual Pleasure and Narrative Cinema' inspired by *Duel in the Sun*," *Framework* 15/16/17 (1981).
7. Teresa de Lauretis, *Alice Doesn't: Feminism, Semiotics, Cinema* (Bloomington: Indiana University Press, 1984), particularly chapter 5, "Desire in Narrative."
8. Richard Collins, "Wall-to-Wall *Dallas*? The US-UK Trade in Television," *Screen* 27:3–4 (May–Aug. 1986).
9. Benedict Anderson, *Imagined Communities: Reflections on the Origin and Spread of Nationalism* (London: Verso, 1983).
10. See John Caughie, "Popular Culture: Notes and Revisions," in Colin MacCabe, ed., *High Theory/Low Culture*, (Manchester: Manchester University Press, 1986), pp. 161–62.
11. Alan Wilde, *Horizons of Assent: Modernism, Postmodernism, and the Ironic Imagination* (Baltimore: Johns Hopkins University Press, 1981).
12. Ibid., p. 9.
13. Ibid., pp. 9–10.

14. Ibid., p. 10.

15. Ibid.

16. Ibid., p. 9.

17. See Peter Brooks, *The Melodramatic Imagination: Balzac, Henry James, Melodrama, and the Mode of Excess* (New Haven, Conn.: Yale University Press, 1976).

18. Sloterdijk, pp. 5–6.

19. De Certeau, see particularly pp. 34ff.

20. See Jane Feuer, "Melodrama, Serial Form, and Television Today," *Screen* 25.1 (Jan.–Feb. 1984).

21. Paul Willemen, "The Desire for Cinema: An Edinburgh Retrospective," *Framework* 19 (1982).

22. See John Fiske, *Television Culture* (London: Methuen, 1987).

23. De Certeau, see particularly pp. xiiff.

24. Gayatri Chakrovorty Spivak, *In Other Worlds: Essays in Cultural Politics* (London: Methuen, 1987), pp. 81–82.

TELEVISION

Aesthetics and Audiences

Charlotte Brunsdon

What is good television? This has not been a very fashionable question for television scholars in the UK.[1] I want to think about some of the answers that have been given to this question, and to query its continuing banishment. In this process, I will make a series of observations about the progressive valuation of the television audience(s) over the television text (however conceptualized) since the mid-70s. I am not arguing that the emphasis of television studies should be evaluative rather than analytic, but I am suggesting that there is something rather odd about the fascination with what "real" (i.e., other, nonacademic) people think about television when it is combined with a principled refusal to reveal what academics think about it.

This paper emerges from attempts to think through some of my own past practice—I do not hold myself exempt from these criticisms. Also, the focus of my remarks is on Britain. Apart from Janice Radway's work on the readers of romance fiction (which is in any case not about television), the long-term Katz and Liebes *Dallas* project[2] (which comes from a very different tradition), and the work of the Tübingen Soap Opera Project, I am not in a position to comment on any US ethnographic audience work.[3]

We can start by outlining two traditional ways in which television has been seen to be good in Britain, both of which minimize its role or presence. The first draws its legitimation from other, already validated art forms: theatre, literature, music. Television (by implication, not itself good) becomes worthy when it brings to a wider audience already legitimated high- and middlebrow culture. In this mode (the contradictions of which I shall discuss later), television can be good as a potentially democratic, or socially extensive, transmitter.

The other mode of legitimation, or set of discourses within which television is allowed to be good, poses a privileged relation to "the real." Although this mode does reference specific qualities of broadcast media, the qualities concerned—those facilitating the transmission of reports of live events—are precisely read as self-negating. Thus sports, public events, current affairs, and wildlife programs are "good television" if we seem to get unmediated access to the real world, and are not distracted by thinking about television *as television.*

The other term constructed in opposition to "good television" is not bad television; it is referred to as popular or commercial television, and its origin in Britain is usually, casually, dated to 1955 and the start of commercial broadcasting. This bad television, which is where we find soap operas and game shows, has another name—and that is "American series." In reciprocal moves, US ideas of British culturalness are confirmed by the broadcasting of imported British programs to the small audiences of PBS, while American vulgarity is confirmed to Brits by the popularity of *Dallas, Dynasty,* and imported game show formats. Dick Hebdige has discussed the subcultural significance of the American, and particularly of the discriminations made about design details such as streamlining among British working-class youth in the 1950s.[4] Ien Ang has pointed to the significant anti-American element in what she refers to as the "ideology of mass culture."[5] There are two points here. One is about the positive value, the appropriateability of American mass culture—the way in which it has historically at certain points provided an escape route, a domain of cultural expression, for those excluded from legitimate national culture. The other—in some ways the same point differently inflected—is about the derogatory meaning, within legitimate cultural discourse, of "American," particularly when coupled with "television."

So we have "good television," so far, constructed across a range of oppositions which condense colonial histories, the organizing and financing of broadcasting institutions, and the relegitimation of already legitimate artistic practices. That is to say, the dominant and conventional way of answering the question "What is good television?" is to slip television, unnoticeably, transparently, into the already existing aesthetic and social hierarchies. (And it is, of course, because of this that television scholars within the culturalist tradition have eschewed judgment, but that is to open up another trail which I don't want to pursue at present.) This leaves out a lot of television and, perhaps more significant, denies a great deal of the pleasure that people get from watching and talking about television. This other television, which is endlessly produced and reproduced in the popular press—but precisely as news and gossip; there is no such thing as an EXCLUSIVE critical insight—reemerges within legitimate cultural discourse in the use of metaphors of addiction, and in features such as "Schlockwatch" in the new *Listener.* In this series, well-known personalities from within the high cultural field comment, usually in an unspeakably patronizing manner, on a popular television program they watch. The title of the feature says it all. Only within a frame which designates the program as "schlock" can there be a discussion of it. Indeed, it is only within this frame that viewing can be admitted. To put this another way, only when somebody you wouldn't expect (for example, Paul Theroux) watches a genre program, *Coronation Street,* is the program interesting.[6] And what is seen as interesting is precisely how the author gets on with the not-good program.

However, there is something else going on here which illuminates another way in which television exists in relation to/is constructed by/constructs the aesthetic field. This something else is the newsworthiness of certain categories of persons watching television at all. So we have a double structure of distinction. First, we have the way in which, in British critical discourse about television, good television is constructed through reference to that which is other than television—already existing and validated art forms or "the real." Second, and here it is pertinent to remember Bourdieu's argument that the aesthetic gaze is constructed in and through an opposition to the naïve gaze, we have the way in which, in much contemporary cultural discourse, television is *the* object of the naive gaze *against which* the aesthetic gaze is constructed.[7] Television secures the distinction of all nontelevisual cultural forms. At this deep level, there can be no answer to the question "What is good television?" because it is founded on an oxymoron. Thus bad cinema or theatre is designated soap opera, while video art barely makes it to the Arts pages of newspapers.[8] (And it is here that we can find the source of the contradictoriness of the "transmitter" model of good television. Is the "Ode to Joy" or "I Heard It through the Grapevine" quite the same to the connoisseur if everybody sings along?)

This constitution of television as the bad cultural object creates a critical abyss when we try to shift the gaze, to look at television, not through it to the Real or High Art. To echo a formulation which has a different political and historical resonance to my own project, there is almost no elaborated discourse of quality, judgment, and value which is specific to television and which is not derived from production practices or professional ideologies.[9] That is, if we forget "Art Television" for the moment, what are the terms we can use to talk critically about that other television, terms which neither collapse pleasure and quality into each other, nor constitute quality as the ghost of class, gender, and national privilege? Can it be done, and should we, in this relativizing age, wish to do it?

The third answer to the question of what is good television takes a sideways step away from the question, and says: forget these value judgments, let's look at what the people watch. I want to suggest that this sideways step is beginning to have the effect of merely inverting existing aesthetic hierarchy (the popular is good), leaving the power relations in place.

Can we have a television aesthetic, and do we want one? There are two main problems in thinking about a television aesthetic. The first, which I do not address substantially but which informs the endeavor of this paper, is part of the broader problem of popular aesthetics in general, and particularly popular aesthetics of mass cultural commodity production. This is to do with the suitability of the noun "aesthetics," encrusted as it is with the meanings of high culture, in collocation with the adjective "popular." Here, some of the work done on popular music by people such as Simon Frith and Dick Hebdige, or on fashion by Angela McRobbie, may be more useful than some of the existing ideological explications of popular television.[10] The second problem, which is superficially more specific to television, has to do with the phenomenon of the rapidly disappearing television text. Or, to put it another way, how do we constitute the television text as an object of study?

Horace Newcomb, writing in 1974, argued for the use of criteria of intimacy, continuity, and history in a television aesthetic, as well as for the importance of soap opera in the development of television drama.[11] Intimacy and continuity do seem important elements in characterizing what is specific to television in certain textual modes. They are also, of course, characteristic of certain ways of watching television. The challenge of an adequate television aesthetic (if this is indeed what we should wish to call it) is not only that it must take a position on the relationship(s) between what we might call the institutional and the program components of televisual discourse, but that it must also address extremely variable and diverse ways of watching television.

By the former, I mean to indicate the critical and analytical importance granted to what we might temporarily call the television-ness of television, which can be taken as the dominant focus for analysis, as opposed to the more traditional concentration on single programs. The classical site within British cultural theory for discussion of how the television text can be constituted as an object of study is the late Raymond Williams's formulation of "flow," taken up by John Caughie in analysis of "the world" of television, and John Ellis with the notion of the segment.[12] In the US, "the viewing-strip" was proposed as the relevant unit by Newcomb and Hirsch in their 1983 essay.[13] These attempts to theorize how we may both grasp the *continuousness* of television and integrate the *experience* of viewing into analysis can, I think, be most usefully supplemented by the deployment of the notion of "mode of address," which allows us to specify, at a formal level, the way in which the television text is always constructed as continuously there *for someone*. The differing identities posed in these interpellations (child, citizen, hobby enthusiast, consumer, etc.) and the overlapping and contradictory ways in which we are called to watch form one of many sites for further research.[14] An insistence on the analytic importance of these moments—continuousness and mode of address—gives some access to the inscription of television's institutional basis in its formal operations.

The difficulty of defining or constituting the television text is accentuated by the privacy of television usage and the absence of an academy concerned to regulate both the production and consumption of television.[15] These factors tend to privilege the perception of diverse modes of engagement with the television text as a specific and defining feature of television viewing. There are two problems with this view. As Paddy Scannell has argued, this is surely a feature of broadcast media rather than television as such.[16] Second, we should not forget that people have always engaged variously with all cultural texts. Many books bought are not read, many paintings in art galleries not looked at; much music used as background—but the institutions of high culture, the academy, the museum, patronage, the auction room, have historically codified, both explicitly and implicitly, the proper mode of engagement with the text—be it a (sublime) mountain view or a lyric poem. Although many people may not engage in these proper ways, critical and aesthetic discussion is usually conducted on the assumption— or negotiation—of this type of engagement. This is not to polemicize for and against particular ways of watching television. It is to point out that although the historical research of writers such as William Boddy and Lynn Spigel shows us that there was originally considerable uncertainty about how to understand the place of television in the home, the institutions of television are primarily concerned with maximizing audiences and revenue, not with the codifying of proper ways to watch.[17]

An aesthetic of television would thus, in some ways, have to be an anti-aesthetic to be adequate to its object and the practices constituting it. Engaging with the popular, the domestic, and the functional, it undercuts the very constitution of classical aesthetic judgment.

The difficulty which I have outlined above of constituting the television text as an object of study is compounded by a series of critical shifts since the 1960s, which I now want to sketch before returning to these problems. I am thus arguing that there are qualities of television as a medium (and these can be qualities of usage, rather than essential qualities) which predispose one to abandon text for audience, and that this tendency has been much facilitated by a range of different, but obviously related, critical trajectories. The audience has come to dominance in Britain in five main ways: (1) through the changing paradigms in literary studies, (2) through the growth of cultural, and particularly subcultural, studies, (3) through particular logics in the development of film and television studies, (4) through the increasingly fashionable theorization of postmodernity, and (5) through the impact of feminist methodologies on academic discourse. I will deal with these five areas more and less schematically.

The modes of dispersal of the television text: I wish here to examine what has happened to the television text as an object of study in recent years. I want to trace, very schematically, the different ways in which the television text as an object of study has been under assault, and to argue for the importance of retaining the notion of text as an analytic category.

Literary studies, and my next category, cultural studies, I want only to reference. Catherine Belsey's 1980 *Critical Practice* (and indeed, to a certain extent, the Methuen *New Accents* list), Terry Eagleton's 1982 *Literary Theory*, and Raymonds Williams's 1981 and 1983 accounts of the crisis in Cambridge English provide, in their shared references (which is not to equate their arguments), a patterning of the transformation of English and literary studies since the 1960s.[18] For our purposes, what is most significant is not so much the assault on the canon as the elevation of the act of reading, over the text, as the point of meaning production. The ascendancy of (different) theories of reading and reception has contributed to a radical devaluation of the notion of the text.

Ethnographic sociology and the study of subcultures, perhaps best exemplified by the 1975 Centre for Contemporary Cultural Studies' *Resistance through Rituals,* Paul Willis's 1977 *Learning to Labour,* and Hebdige's 1979 *Subculture: The Meaning of Style,* also worked to validate the role of the cultural consumer in the construction of meaning. The apparent, obvious or intended meanings of a whole series of commodities were revealed as transformed within subcultural practice.[19]

In relation to film and television studies, I want to make my points through observations of trends at the two International Television Studies Conferences held in London in 1984 and 1986.[20] There are, of course, always ongoing debates in particular intellectual fields, which sometimes gel into apparently obvious sets of issues and concerns at particular historical moments in the academy. There are also always more and less fashionable and attractive areas for research. Although not the only shift in parameters of debate, there was, between the 1984 and 1986 conferences, a clear move in interest from what is happening on the screen to what is happening in front of it—from text to audience.

This is not in any way to underestimate the amount of research that has already been conducted into the behavior and readings of the audience, both in Britain/Europe and in the United States. It is to suggest that the 1986 conference provides a convenient, if arbitrary, way of marking the entry of new and different interests into audience research. The 1984 conference took place just at the very end of a period of ten years or so of British culturalist analyses of popular film and television texts.

These analyses had, in the main, what one could call a political motivation. For a range of quite complexly articulated reasons, including the (semi-) institutionalization of film and television studies within the academy, the rightward shift in the British political scene, the aging of the generation radicalized in 1968, not to mention the institutional convenience of textual analysis, we had in Britain the burgeoning of academic analyses of popular texts which sought to discredit both the left-pessimist despair over and the high cultural dismissal of mass and popular cultures. From the mid-70s onwards, "progressive" academics in these fields became increasingly involved in the production of what could be termed "the redemptive reading." Film noir, 50s color melodrama, and television programs such as *The Sweeney, Coronation Street,* and *Crossroads* were among the texts addressed.[21]

The point about the "redemptive reading" is that it is not a simple populist embrace of the entertainment forms of late capitalism. The purely populist moment—although of course there has always been a straight-forwardly populist strain contributing to the arguments for this sort of work—comes at the end of this period roughly contemporary with the shift to the audience which I am describing, and, in popular cultural terms, with Madonna's rise to stardom. The redemptive reading is not populist in that it starts with an acceptance of the uncongenial politics of whatever cultural text—for it is primarily a political reading—and then finds, at the least, incoherences and contradiction, and at the most fully articulated, subtexts of revolt. Partly because of the centrality of Hollywood to the constitution of Film Studies as a discipline, it is here that this form of critical practice is at its most sophisticated and elaborated. The notorious category "e" of *Cahiers du Cinéma* ("films which seem at first sight to belong firmly within the ideology and to be completely under its sway, but which turn out to be so only in an ambiguous manner")[22] is of course a category of reception ("If one reads the film obliquely, looking for symptoms . . . "), unlike all the other categories in their influential 1969 taxonomy. The famous account of *Young Mr. Lincoln* reveals what was at stake for cinephiles when ideological correctness became the principal critical criterion. The loved object, Hollywood cinema, which would have had to be jettisoned under the regime of the "right on," could be retrieved if its textual (here standing for ideological) coherence could be demonstrated to be only apparent.[23]

The redemptive reading frequently meets with a certain scepticism, a doubt that *real* readers really read like that. The 1984 ITSC marked a suitable final appearance for the dominance of this type of textual analysis—the theoretical position had now to be supported by research into how nonacademic readers read. In the 1984 ITSC, the conference strand that was bulging at the seams was that of "textual analysis." In 1986, submissions to this area were radically reduced, and there was increased evidence of qualitative audience research. This "new" audience work, which comes partly from the necessity of testing the type of textual hypotheses referred to above, and is often influenced by the ascendancy of reception theory in literary studies, met, often in ignorance, the older, more quantitative traditions of mass communications research. As Jane Feuer observed in her 1986 paper, the television text has been displaced by the text of audience—a much more various and diverse text—and the enormous conceptual and methodological problems entailed.[24]

We are beginning to see a whole new body of research into how people view television, and this research functions to further disperse the text as an analytic category. We can now, following the work of, for example, Peter Collett, Ann Gray, Dorothy Hobson, and David Morley (to take British examples), only argue that people watch television in extremely heterogeneous ways. People watch alone, with intimates, with strangers. They watch while they're doing something else, even when they're in another room. The notion of "flow," made less harmonious through practices such as channel zapping, has to be supplemented by the major variable of audience-presence-for-the-text. But how can we theorize this in a way which allows us to do more than accumulate an ethnography of particular practices?

With the "everything is everything else" of "postmodernity," we have also lost any innocent notion of what might constitute the television text through a recognition of the proliferation, across different media, of potential textual sites. At one level, this is a phenomenon of marketing and product licensing, and of the international character of image markets, to paraphrase Mattelart et al.,[25] at another, of the deep penetration of television into our daily lives. Thus we can buy videos of early episodes of *Coronation Street*, read novels based on any of the soaps, overhear and join in conversations about soap characters, and read about predicted narrative events in newspapers.[26] Again, what is posed for us is the question of how we organize our perception of these issues rather than the self-evident, textual destruction that some have found.

Tony Bennett and Janet Woollacott have done exemplary work on what they call "the Bond phenomenon," in which they examine the many moments, textual existences, and transformations of James Bond. They set out "to demonstrate, in a practical way rather than just theoretically, that 'the text itself' is an inconceivable object."[27] Their achievement, I think, is to prove not that the text itself is an inconceivable object, but that the choice of what is recognized as constituting "a" text, consciously or not, is a political as well as a critical matter. It is around this issue that the contemporary struggles to dominate the critical field will be fought.

Literary analysis has as one of its specialisms the identification of reference and allusion. Modernism was partly modern in its use of quotation and the assumed knowledge of other texts. But the intertextuality of television is in some ways more radical, without the central, organizing drive of the author or, as I have argued earlier, the specific hierarchies of form given by an established aesthetic. This quality, the promiscuous and nearly parodic self-referentiality of television, is not quite specific to television in a way that could define the medium. It is a quality—along with others also attributable to television—seen as characteristic of a postmodern era.[28] The recognition of television and video as major agents of our understanding of contemporary time and space, indeed, along with the computer, of the transformation of these categories in everyday life, is essential, and potentially more useful than the analysis of single programs as if they were poems. But I'm not sure that this perception requires that we throw up our hands and say, "But it's all so ephemeral/such pastiche/without reference/depthless/intertextual that there's nothing to analyze."

The final trajectory through which we can trace a dispersal of the text has its origins in feminist critical initiatives. This is of particular relevance because women have historically figured as preferred objects (I use the term advisedly) of audience research. Women soap opera viewers and listeners have proven particularly attractive to both commercial and academic researchers in ways that are relevant here.

If we accept that soap opera is in some ways the paradigmatic television genre (domestic, continuous, contemporary, episodic, repetitive, fragmented, and aural), we have also to ask why it has received until recently so little serious critical attention. Soap opera has been neglected except, ironically, in terms of the investigation of its effects on audiences, because it has not been considered textually worthy. We find, in the massive research on the "effects" of soap viewing, the repeated pathologizing of the audience. Robert Allen puts this nicely when he writes of soap opera viewers not being granted the capacity for aesthetic distance from the text.[29] Dorothy Hobson in particular has also argued for the key significance of the social status of soap opera fans in determining the aesthetic status of the form.[30] Feminist criticism has taken an interesting path in relation to the genre.

Firstly, in a relatively short period, feminist criticism has moved from its initial repudiation of women's genres to the analysis and defense of traditionally feminine forms such as soap opera, melodrama, and romance.[31] This process, as I have argued at more length elsewhere, has necessarily involved the attempt to analyze, and enter imaginatively into, the pleasures of these forms for their audiences.[32] Sometimes motivated by a desire to defend the audience and its pleasures, sometimes concerned principally to use cultural texts as sites where the constitution of contemporary femininities can be analyzed, this work necessarily demands the investigation of the responses of audiences/readers/viewers to the relevant texts. Thus, much of the new audience research to which I have already referred has been specifically concerned with "feminine" texts, female audiences, and feminist methodologies.

It is the notion of feminist methodology which points to the other important element contributed by feminist criticism. This is the use of autobiographical data and the validation of the use of "I" in academic discourse. I am, of course, simplifying and generalizing to make my point—the "I" also enters academic discourse through other routes, and the exploration of subjectivities constituted in subordination has been essential to groups other than women and fragments the simple gender category. Here, however, the point is that the particular value set on the recounting and exploration of personal experience within second-wave feminism, and the recognition of the extremely contradictory nature of experience and identity, have worked to construct autobiographical data as "proper" data.[33] Because the definition of feminist methodologies frequently involves particular political understandings of the way in which the researcher herself inhabits the gender category "woman," we have in much feminist research a certain fluidity of pronouns, a blurring of the separation of the object and the subject of research. This blurring is also a feature of some sociologies; what I wish to do here is to point to the peculiar force that the first-person pronoun has in some feminist discourse.

This "I" of some feminist discourse is a rather complicated affair in terms

of to and for whom it speaks. Sometimes we have the simple use of autobiographical data, which are not explicitly articulated with either the
assumed or researched experiences of "other women." Sometimes we have
an "I, the researcher" who sees herself as part of a larger category "we
women," *on whose behalf, for whose good,* and *to whom* she will, at different
moments and simultaneously, speak. There will thus be the validation of
autobiographical material and a feminine "I" over and above any unitary
and inherent meaning of the text, but the status and identity for this reader/
writer validated over the text fluctuate.

The point could be seen as a paradoxical one, in that feminist intervention in a particular academic field turns out to reproduce exactly the existing structure or patterning of the field. The traditional approach to soap
opera within media research was to focus on audience rather than text.
Although differently motivated, and ascribing different moral qualities to
the two terms, text and audience, feminist research, also, has moved from
the "bad" text to the "good" audience.

To conclude: I am not trying to argue for the reinstatement of what we
might call the pre-audience text. Through the different routes which I
have tried to outline, I think we can see some of the reasons for the growth
in ethnographic and qualitative audience research. These include the fundamental transformations of adjacent, and often formative, intellectual
fields. The discrediting of a simple cross/tick political aesthetic of popular
texts—as if that is all they merit—was overdue. The investigation of the
activities of viewers reveals the variety of contexts and modes of viewing
which prevent the television text ever being, in any way, a simple, self-
evident object for analysis. Similarly, we have to accept the potentially infinite number/flow of textual sites. Together, I think these recognitions
begin to lead us to the postmodern haven of insignificance, and I would,
in this context, characterize the pursuit of the audience as a search for
authenticity, for an anchoring moment in a sea of signification. Just like
television, academics are obsessed with "real people."

So firstly, I want to argue that, difficult as it may be, we have to retain
a notion of the television text. That is, *without* the guarantees of common
sense, or the authority of a political teleology, and *with* the recognition of
the potentially infinite proliferation of textual sites, and the agency of the
always already social reader, in a range of contexts, it is still necessary—
and possible—to construct a televisual object of study—and judgment.

Here, I think we can most usefully learn from the practices of television
itself. The broadcast world is structured through regularity and repetition.
Time-shift video recording alters the viewer's position in relation to this
regularity and repetition, but I'm not sure that it fundamentally transforms
the broadcast structure of the day and week. Although it is tempting to
start with a distinction between viewing alone and viewing with others (and

recent research suggests that this might be particularly important in relation to understanding women's pleasures), the primary distinction seems to be between modes of viewing which are repeated on a regular basis and uncommon or unfamiliar modes of viewing (which thus incorporates the solitary/in company distinction).[34]

The need to specify context and mode of viewing in any textual discussion, and the awareness that these factors may be more determining of the experience of a text than any textual feature, do not, in and of themselves, either eliminate the text as a meaningful category or render all texts the same. I may normally watch *Brookside* with one other person, and indeed prefer watching it in this familiar way, but I can still recognize the program when alone or with a large group doing something else. The fact that the text is only and always realized in historically and contextually situated practices of reading does not demand that we collapse these categories into each other.

Secondly, I do want to raise questions about the overall political shape or weighting of this concentration on what we might call the post-1960s audience. Although frequently informed by a desire to investigate, rather than judge, other people's pleasures, this very avoidance of judgment seems somehow to recreate the old patterns of aesthetic domination and subordination, and to pathologize the audience. Because issues of judgment are never brought out into the open, but always kept, as it were, under the seminar table, criteria involved can never be interrogated. It is for this reason that I wish to retain/construct the analytic category of the television text, for if we dissolve this category into the audience, we further inhibit the development of a useful television criticism and a television aesthetic. This is difficult enough without collapsing bad programs into bad audiences. I do not wish to argue that television studies should be devoted to discriminating between "good" and "bad" programs, but I do want to insist that most academics involved in television studies are using qualitative criteria, however expressed or repressed, and that the constitution of the criteria involved should be the subject of explicit debate. To return to Bourdieu. Only the inheritors of legitimate culture, researching other people's pleasures, pleasures they may well share, can afford to keep quiet about the good and bad of television. They—we—through years of training have access to a very wide range of cultural production. Watching television *and* reading books about postmodernism is different from watching television and reading tabloid newspapers, even if everybody concerned watched the same television.

What we find, very frequently, in audience data is that the audience is making the best of a bad job. The problem of always working with what people are, of necessity, watching is that we don't really ever address that something else—what people might like to watch (and I don't mean to imply that these other desires simply exist without an object, but that is another paper). The recognition of the creativity and competences of the audience must, I think, be mobilized back into relation to the television text and the demands that are made on program makers for a diverse and plural programming which is adequate to the needs, desires, and pleasures of these audiences. Otherwise, however well intentioned, our work reproduces and elaborates the dominant paradigm in which the popular is the devalued term. Having started with "What is good television?" I would like to finish with "What are we going to do about bad television?" Nothing, if we're not prepared to admit it exists.

NOTES

An earlier draft of this paper was first presented to the Blaubeuren symposium, "Re-thinking the Television Audience," held at the University of Tübingen in February 1987. My thanks to the organizers, Hans Borchers, Gabriele Kreutzner, Ellen Seiter, and Eva-Maria Warth.

1. The following have addressed these issues: John Caughie, "On the Offensive: Television and Values," in *Television and Schooling*, ed. David Lusted and Phillip Drummond (London: BFI and the Institute of Education, 1985), pp. 53–66; and "Television Criticism: 'A Discourse in Search of an Object,'" *Screen* 25.4–5 (July–October 1984):109–120; Judith Williamson, "The Problems of Being Popular," *New Socialist* 41 (September 1986):14–15.

2. Janice Radway, *Reading the Romance* (Chapel Hill: University of North Carolina Press, 1984). There are many accounts of the *Dallas* project available, for example: Katz and Liebes, "Mutual Aid in the Decoding of *Dallas:* Preliminary Notes from a Cross-Cultural Study," in *Television in Transition*, ed. Phillip Drummond and Richard Paterson (London: BFI, 1985), pp. 187–98; E. Seiter et al., "Don't Treat Us Like We're So Stupid and Naive," "Re-thinking the Television Audience," symposium at the University of Tübingen, Tübingen, West Germany, Feb. 1987.

3. This is, in Britain, inextricable from the image of BBC and ITV. Laurie Taylor and Bob Mullan provide some interesting insights on channel image in *Uninvited Guests* (London: Chatto, 1986), pp. 114–15. David Buckingham also discusses the issue in terms of the *Jewel in the Crown/Thornbirds* controversy in *Public Secret: EastEnders and Its Audience* (London: BFI, 1987).

4. Dick Hebdige, "Towards a Cartography of Taste," *BLOCK* 4 (1981):39–56.

5. Ien Ang, *Watching Dallas: Soap Opera and the Melodramatic Imagination*, trans. Della Couling (London: Methuen, 1985).

6. *The Listener*, which used to be a magazine dealing only with BBC broadcasts, has since March 1988 also dealt with the output of the commercial companies. Paul Theroux, "*Coronation Street*," *The Listener* 31 March 1988.

7. Pierre Bourdieu, *Distinction*, trans. Richard Nice (London: Routledge, 1984).

8. The problems of the legitimation of video art as an art form are to some extent explored in John Hanhardt's collection *Video Culture* (New York: Visual Studies Workshop Press, 1987). See also Michael O'Pray's polemical "Shows, Schisms, and Modernisms," *Monthly Film Bulletin* 55, 649 (Feb. 1988):57–59.

9. The following provide useful surveys of television criticism in Britain and the US: Mike Poole, "The Cult of the Generalist: British Television Criticism 1936–83," *Screen* 25.2 (Mar.Apr. 1984):41–61; John Caughie, "Television Criticism: 'A Discourse in Search of an Object,'" *Screen* 25.4–5 (July–Oct. 1984):109–120; Horace Newcomb, "American Television Criticism 1970–1985," *Critical Studies in Communication* 3 (1986):217–28.

10. Simon Frith, *Music for Pleasure* (Cambridge: Polity, 1988); Dick Hebdige, *Hiding in the Light* (London: Routledge/Comedia, 1988); Angela McRobbie, ed., *Zoot Suits and Second-hand Dresses* (London: MacMillan, 1989).

11. Horace Newcomb, *TV: the Most Popular Art* (New York: Anchor Doubleday, 1974), particularly chapter 10. Robert Allen has argued that Newcomb is over-dependent on British television to exemplify his point. This would be significant in the context of my argument because of the way in which the art/entertainment axis is inscribed over British/American television. Robert C. Allen, *Speaking of Soap Operas* (Chapel Hill: University of North Carolina Press, 1985), pp. 222–23. See also chapter 4.

12. Raymond Williams, *Television: Technology and Cultural Form* (London: Fontana, 1974); John Ellis, *Visible Fictions* (London: Routledge, 1982); John Caughie, "The 'World' of Television," in *History, Production, Memory*, special issue of *Edinburgh Film Festival Magazine*, ed. Claire Johnston (1977), pp. 72–83.

13. Horace Newcomb and Paul Hirsch, "Television as a Cultural Forum," *Quarterly Review of Film Studies* (Summer 1983), reprinted in *Television: The Critical View*, ed. Horace Newcomb (New York: Oxford University Press, 1987).

14. The 1982 British Film Institute Summer School course "Who Does Television Think You Are?" coordinated by David Lusted and held at Stirling University, attempted to work through some of the issues involved in conceptualizing television through notions of mode of address.

15. I don't want to underestimate the role of industry spectaculars, Emmy nights, etc., but in Britain, at least, these are radically separate from any type of endorsement of television as "legitimate" culture—that one can, for example, gain instruction in at universities. The more practice- and industry-oriented courses in broadcast media at North American universities may make generalization about this point quite improper.

16. Paddy Scannell, "Radio Times: The Temporal Arrangements of Broadcasting in the Modern World," International Television Studies Conference, London, 1986. See also Simon Frith's discussion of the making of BBC light entertainment, "The Pleasures of the Hearth," in *Formations of Pleasure* (London: Routledge, 1983), pp. 101–123.

17. William Boddy, " 'The Shining Centre of the Home': Ontologies of Television in the 'Golden Age,' " in *Television in Transition*. Lynn Spigel, "Ambiguity and Hesitation: Discourses on Television and the Housewife in Women's Home Magazines, 1948–1955," International Television Studies Conference, London, 1986.

18. Catherine Belsey, *Critical Practice* (London: Methuen, 1980); Terry Eagleton, *Literary Theory* (Oxford: Basil Blackwell, 1983); Raymond Williams, *Writing in Society* (London: Verso, n.d.).

19. *Working Papers in Cultural Studies* 7–8 (1975), reprinted as *Resistance through Rituals* (London: Hutchinson and the Centre for Contemporary Cultural Studies, 1976); Paul Willis, *Learning to Labour* (Farnborough: Saxon, 1977); Dick Hebdige, *Subculture: The Meaning of Style* (London: Methuen 1979).

20. I was a member of the organizing committee of the 1986 ITSC, and a discussant in 1984.

21. E. Ann Kaplan, ed., *Women in Film Noir* (London: BFI, 1978); Geoffrey Nowell-Smith, "Minnelli and Melodrama," *Screen* 18.2 (Summer 1977):113–18; *Screen Education* 20 (Autumn 1976) (special issue on *The Sweeney*); BFI Television Monograph 13 *Coronation Street*, ed. Richard Dyer et al. (London: BFI, 1981).

22. Jean-Louis Comolli and Jean Narboni, "Cinema/Ideology/Criticism," *Cahiers du Cinéma* 216 (Oct. 1969), reprinted in translation in *Movies and Methods I*, ed. Bill Nichols (Berkeley: University of California Press, 1976), pp. 22–30.

23. "Young Mr. Lincoln," *Cahiers du Cinéma* 223 (1970), reprinted in translation in *Movies and Methods I*, pp. 493–529.

24. Jane Feuer, "Reading Dynasty: Television and Reception Theory," International Television Studies Conference, London, 1986.

25. A. Mattelart, X. Delcourt, and M. Mattelart, *International Image Markets* (London: Comedia, 1984).

26. Rosalind Brunt, "Street Credibility," *Marxism Today* (Dec. 1983):38–39.

27. Tony Bennett and Janet Woollacott, *Bond and Beyond: The Political Career of a Popular Hero* (Basingstoke: Macmillan, 1987), p. 7.

28. Fredric Jameson, "Postmodernism, or, The Cultural Logic of Late Capitalism," *New Left Review* 196 (July-Aug. 1984):53–92. See also Lawrence Grossberg, "The In-difference of Television," *Screen* 28.2 (Spring 1987):28–45.

29. Allen, *Speaking of Soap Operas*, pp. 28–29. Allen also provides an extensive bibliography.

30. Dorothy Hobson, *Crossroads: The Drama of a Soap Opera* (London: Methuen, 1982).

31. A restricted set of references here would include Ellen Seiter, "The Role of the Woman Reader: Eco's Narrative Theory and Soap Operas," *Tabloid 6* (1981); Hobson, *Crossroads*; Brunsdon, "*Crossroads:* Notes on Soap Opera," *Screen* 22.4 (1981):32–37; R. Dyer et al., *Coronation Street*; Ang, *Watching Dallas*; Christine Gledhill, ed., *Home Is Where the Heart Is: Studies in Melodrama and the Women's Picture* (London: BFI, 1987); Radway, *Reading the Romance*; Jean Radford, ed., *The Progress of Romance* (London: Routledge, 1986).

32. Brunsdon, "Women Watching Television," *MedieKultur* 4 (Nov. 1986):100–112.

33. See, for example, Rosalind Coward and Jo Spence, "Body Talk," in *Photography Politics: Two*, ed. Patricia Holland et al. (London: Comedia 1986), pp. 24–39. See also Sarah McCarthy's "Autobiographies," pp. 134–41 in the same volume.

34. Ann Gray, "Behind Closed Doors: Video Recorders in the Home," in *Boxed In: Women and Television*, ed. Helen Baehr and Gillian Dyer (London: Pandora, 1987); D. G. Morley, *Family Television* (London: Comedia, 1986).

TELEVISION IN THE FAMILY CIRCLE

The Popular Reception of a New Medium

Lynn Spigel

In Nicholas Ray's *Rebel without a Cause* (1955) there is a melodramatic moment in which family members are unable to patch together the rift among them. The son, Jim, returns home after the famous sequence in which he races his car to the edge of a cliff, only to witness the death of his competitor. Jim looks at his father asleep in front of the TV set, and then he lies down on a sofa. From Jim's upside-down point of view on the sofa, the camera cuts to his shrewish mother who appears at the top of the stairwell. In a 180-degree spin, the camera flip-flops on the image of the mother, mimicking the way Jim sees her descending the stairs. This stylized shot jolts us out of the illusionary realism of the scene, a disruption that continues as the camera reveals a television screen emitting a menacing blue static. As the camera lingers on the TV set, Jim confesses his guilt. Moments later, when Jim's mother demands that he not go to the police, Jim begs his henpecked father to take his side. Finally, with seemingly murderous intentions, Jim chokes him. The camera pans across the TV set, its static heightening the sense of family discord. With its "bad reception," the TV serves as a rhetorical figure for the loss of communication among family members. In fact, as Jim's father had admitted early in the scene, he was not even aware of his son's whereabouts during this fateful night, but instead had learned of the incident through the TV newscast.

As this classic scene illustrates, the television set in postwar years became a central figure in representations of family relationships. The introduction of the machine into the home meant that family members needed to come to terms with the presence of a communication medium which might transform older modes of family interaction. The popular media published reports and advice from social critics and social scientists who were studying the effects of television on family relationships. The media also published pictorial representations of domestic space which showed people how television might—or might not—fit into their own homes. Most significant, like the scene from *Rebel without a Cause*, these media discourses were organized around ideas of family harmony and discord.

Indeed, contradictions between unity and division formed a central trope in representations of television during the period of its installation. Television was the great family minstrel which promised to bring Mom, Dad, and the kids together; but at the same time, it was something that had to be carefully controlled to harmonize with the separate gender roles and social functions of individual family members. This meant that the contradiction between unity and division was not a simple binary opposition; it was not a matter of either/or but rather both at once. Television was supposed to bring the family together but still allow for social and sexual divisions in the home. In fact, the ability to maintain a balance between these two ideals was a central tension at work in popular discourses on television and the family.

This essay concentrates on the way in which popular media of the postwar era represented family relationships in the home equipped with television. It looks at the household spaces occupied by the family watching television and focuses upon the sexual and social differences suggested for the reception and enjoyment of TV programs. How was television made into a domestic object, and how was its mode of use defined? How was TV shown to affect family members, and what was its impact upon their daily activities in the home? In answering these questions, I look at popular magazines and print advertisements produced from the years 1948–55, a period when more than half of all US homes installed a television set and when television became a dominant mass medium. I especially examine middle-class women's home magazines which included articles, cartoons, illustrations, and ads that represented TV and domestic life.[1] Rather than simply promoting television, the media deliberated TV's place in the family circle. These magazines and their advertisements showed readers how to glean pleasure from television as a family medium, but they also warned of TV's displeasing effects, specifically its disruption of conventional family dynamics.

This ambivalent response reminds us that technological innovation is not simply brought about by big business and its promotional campaigns. While it is true that television was controlled by large corporations, the public's fascination with TV was not determined by the sales effort alone. Instead, this fascination was rooted in modern US culture at large. As other historians have shown, since the end of the nineteenth century our culture has had a long-standing obsession with communications technology and its impact on American life. The telegraph, telephone, movies, and radio were all viewed with a mixture of utopian hope and dystopian fear. For example, while some promised that radio would bring about a democratic society through its peculiar ability to link the world via invisible ethers, others warned that it was a supernatural force which needed to be carefully controlled.[2] Popular discourses on television were thus a product of the modern imagination, a part of the history of ideas about communications technology.

This is especially important to keep in mind when considering consumer magazines and their advertisements. A popular assumption in advertising history and theory is that ads are the voice of big industry, a voice which instills consumer fantasies into the minds of the masses. This often leads to a mind-management theory of mass media which sees the public as passive recipients of consumer persuasion. From my point of view, advertising is not one voice but rather is composed of multiple voices. Advertising adopts the voice of an imaginary consumer—it must try to speak from his or her point of view—even if that position is at odds with the immediate goals of the sales effort.

Advertisers do not simply promote ideas and values in the sense of "product propaganda"; rather they follow certain *discursive rules* which are part of the wider media context. Since the nineteenth century, women's magazines had been a site for women's discourse, albeit in a mass-produced form. Advertisers placed their consumer messages in this site in order to appeal to potential female consumers (who they assumed were responsible for about 80% of family purchasing decisions), often adjusting their sales messages to fit with the concerns of the magazines. They typically acknowledged the problems which television might bring to the family, and they promoted their television sets as solutions to these problems.

The media discourses I explore provide a clue to an imaginary popular culture—that is, they tell us what various media assumed about the public's concerns and desires. However, as Roland Marchand has argued in the case of advertising, the mass media are often distanced from the people to whom they speak, and their assumptions about the public can be quite off the mark—even with the aid of market research.[3] Thus, popular representations of television do not directly reflect the public's response to television. Instead, they begin to reveal a general set of discursive rules which were formed for thinking about TV in this early period. These magazines provided a media context through which people (here, especially middle-class women) might make sense of television and its relationship to family life.

THE FAMILY UNITED

In 1954 *McCall's* magazine coined the term "togetherness." The appearance of this term between the covers of a women's magazine is significant not only because it shows the importance attached to family unity during the postwar years, but also because it is symptomatic of discourses aimed at the housewife. Home magazines primarily discussed family life in language organized around spatial imagery of proximity, distance, isolation, and integration. In fact, the spatial organization of the home was presented as a set of scientific laws through which family relationships could be calculated and controlled. Topics ranging from child rearing to sexuality were discussed in spatial terms, and solutions to domestic problems were overwhelmingly spatial: if you are nervous, make yourself a quiet sitting corner far away from the central living area of the home. If your child is cranky, let him play in the yard. If your husband is bored at the office, turn your garage into a workshop where he'll recall the joys of his boyhood. It was primarily within the context of this spatial problematic that television was discussed. The central question addressed was: *"Where should you put the television set?"*

By 1951 the TV set occupied almost every represented territory in the family home. It appeared in the basement, living room, bedroom, kitchen, fun room, converted garage, music room, TV room, and a host of multipurpose rooms including a guest-child-TV room, a sitting-sleeping room, and a living-dining room. Not only the room but the exact location in the room had to be considered for its possible use as a TV "zone."

The magazines included television as a staple home fixture before most Americans could even receive a TV signal, much less consider purchasing the expensive item. These media discourses did not so much reflect social reality; instead, they preceded it. The home magazines helped to construct television as a household object, one which belonged in the family space. More surprising, however, in the span of roughly four years, television itself became *the* central figure in images of the American home; it became the cultural symbol par excellence of family life.

Television, it was said, would bring the family ever closer, an expression which, in itself a spatial metaphor, was continually repeated in a wide range of popular media—not only women's magazines but also general magazines, men's magazines, and on the airwaves. In its capacity as a unifying agent, television fit well with the more general postwar hopes for a return to domestic values. It was seen as a kind of household cement which promised to reassemble the splintered lives of families who had been separated during the war. It was also meant to reinforce the new suburban family unit which had left most of its extended family behind in the city.

The emergence of the term "family room" in the postwar period is a perfect example of the importance attached to organizing household spaces around ideals of family togetherness. First coined in George Nelson and Henry Wright's *Tomorrow's House: A Complete Guide for the Home Builder* (1946), the family room encapsulated a popular ideal throughout the period. Nelson and Wright, who alternatively called the family room "the room without a name," suggested the possible social functions of this household space:

> Could the room without a name be evidence of a growing desire to provide a framework within which the members of a family will be better equipped to enjoy each other on the basis of mutual respect and affection? Might it thus indicate a deep-seated urge to reassert the validity of the family by providing

a better design for living? We should very much like to think so, and if there is any truth in this assumption, our search for a name is ended—we should simply call it the "family room."[4]

Such notions of domestic cohesion were integral to the design for living put forward in the home magazines which popularized the family room in the years to come. Given a place here, the television set would provide family entertainment. In 1950, *Better Homes and Gardens* literally merged TV with the family room, telling readers to design a new double-purpose area, the "family-television room."[5]

But one needn't build a new room in order to bring the family together around the television set. Barring the finances for remodeling costs, living rooms, kitchens, and dining rooms would do just as well. What was needed was a particular attitude, a sense of closeness which permeated the room. Photographs, particularly in advertisements, graphically depicted the idea of the family circle with television viewers grouped around the TV set in semicircle patterns.

As Roland Marchand has suggested with respect to advertising in the 1920s and 1930s, the family circle was a prominent pictorial strategy for the promotion of household goods. The scenes always suggested that all family members were present; and since they were often shot in soft focus, or contained dreamy mists, there was a romantic haze around the family unit. According to Marchand, this visual cliché recalled Victorian notions about domestic havens, implying that the home was secure and stable. The ads suggested a democratic model of family life, one in which all members shared in consumer decisions—although, as Marchand suggests, to some extent the father remained a dominant figure in the pictorial composition. In this romanticized imagery, modern fixtures were easily assimilated into the family space:

> The products of modern technology, including radios and phonographs, were comfortably accommodated within the hallowed circle. Whatever pressures and complexities modernity might bring, these images implied, the family at home would preserve an undaunted harmony and security. In an age of anxieties about family relationships and centrifugal social forces, this visual cliché was no social mirror; rather it was a reassuring pictorial convention.[6]

Much like advertisements for the radio and phonograph, television ads made ample use of this reassuring pictorial convention—especially in the years immediately following the war when advertisers were in the midst of their reconversion campaigns, channeling the country back from the personal sacrifices and domestic upheavals of World War II to a peacetime economy based on consumerism and family values. The ads suggested that television would serve as a catalyst for the return to a world of domestic love and affection—a world which must have been quite different from the actual experiences of returning GIs and their new families in the chaotic time of readjustment to civilian life.

The returning soldiers and their wives underwent an abrupt shift in social and cultural experiences. Horror stories of shell-shocked men circulated in the psychiatric journals. Even for those lucky enough to escape the scars of battle, popular media such as film noir showed angst-ridden, sexually unstable men, scarred psychologically and unable to relate to the familial ideals and bureaucratic realities of postwar life (the husband-killing insurance agent Walter Ness in *Double Indemnity* is a classic example). Sociological studies such as William H. Whyte's *The Organization Man* (1957) presented chilling visions of middle-class white-collar workers who were transformed into powerless conformists as the country was taken over by nameless, faceless corporations.[7]

Meanwhile, women were given a highly constraining solution to the changing roles of gender and sexual identity. Although middle- and working-class women had been encouraged by popular media to enter traditionally male occupations during the war, they were now told to return to their homes where they could have babies and make color-coordinated meals.[8] Ferdinand Lundberg and Marynia Farnham's *Modern Woman: The Lost Sex* (1947) gave professional/psychological status to this housewife image, claiming that the essential function of women was that of caretaker, mother, and sexual partner.[9] Even if people found the new domestic ideal seductive, the housing shortage, coupled with the baby boom of 1946, made domestic bliss an expensive and often unattainable luxury. Indeed, perhaps for this reason, the housewife image might have had the unplanned, paradoxical effect of sending married women into the labor force in order to obtain the money necessary to live the ideal (whereas before the war single women accounted for the majority of female workers, the number of married women workers skyrocketed during the 1950s, so that by 1960 they constituted about 60% of the total female labor force).[10]

The sharp discrepancies between wartime and postwar life resulted in a set of ideological and social contradictions concerning the construction of gender and the family unit. The pictorial convention of the family circle might well have been intended to serve the "therapeutic" function which both Marchand and T. J. Jackson Lears have ascribed to advertising in general. These illustrations of domestic bliss and consumer prosperity presented a soothing alternative to the tensions of postwar life.[11] The government building policies and mortgage loans of the 1950s sanctioned the materialization of these advertising images by giving white middle-class families a chance to buy into the "good life" of ranch-style cottages and consumer durables. But both the advertising images and the homes themselves were built on the shaky foundations of social upheaval and cultural conflict which never were completely resolved. The family circle ads, like suburbia itself, were only a temporary consumer solution to a set of complicated political, economic, and social problems.

In the case of television, the family circle ads almost always showed the product in the center of the family group. While soft-focus mists were sometimes used, the manufacturers' claims for picture clarity and good reception seem to have necessitated the use of sharp focus and high contrast which better connoted these product attributes. The product-as-center motif not only suggested the familial qualities of the new appliance, but it also implied a mode of use: the ads suggested that TV should be watched by a family audience.

A 1951 ad for Crosley's "family theatre television" is a particularly striking example. As is typical in these kinds of ads, the copy details the technical qualities of the set, but the accompanying illustration gives familial meanings to the modern technology. The picture in this case is composed as a *mise en abyme*; in the center of the page a large drawing of the outer frame of a TV screen contains a sharp-focus photograph of a family watching television. Family members are dispersed on sofas on three sides of a room, while a little boy, with arms stretched out in the air, sits in the middle of the room. All eyes are glued to the television set which appears in the center lower portion of the TV frame, in fact barely visible to the reader. The actual Crosley TV console is depicted in minuscule dimensions on the lower margin of the page. According to the logic of this composition, the central fascination for the reader is not the actual product but rather its ability to bring the family together around it. The ad's *mise en abyme* structure suggests the idea that Crosley TV literally contains the domestic scene, thereby promising not just a TV set but an ideal reflection of the family, joined together by the new commodity.[12]

Such advertisements appeared in a general climate of postwar expectations about television. Numerous Americans saw television as a vehicle for the revival of domestic virtues. In his book of 1956, *The Age of Television*, Leo Bogart presented a summary of audience research on television and claimed that social scientific surveys "agree completely that television has had the effect of keeping the family at home more than formerly. . . ."[13] One respondent from a Southern California survey boasted that his family "now stays home all the time and watches the same programs. [We] turn it on at 3 p.m. and watch until 10 p.m. We never go anywhere."[14]

Moreover, studies indicated that people believed TV strengthened family ties. A 1949 survey of an eastern city found that long-term TV owners expressed "an awareness of an enhanced family solidarity."[15] A 1951 study of Atlanta families produced similar findings. One respondent admitted that "it keeps us together more," and another commented, "it makes a closer family circle." Some women even saw television as a cure for marital problems. One housewife confided: "My husband and I get along a lot better. We don't argue so much. It's wonderful for couples who have been married ten years or more. . . . Before television, my husband would come in and go to bed. Now we spend some time together."[16]

Television was also seen as a remedy for problem children. In the 1950s, juvenile delinquency was a constant topic of public debate. Women's magazines and child psychologists such as Dr. Benjamin Spock, whose *Common Sense Book of Baby and Childcare* had sold a million copies by 1951, gave an endless stream of advice to mothers on ways to prevent their children from becoming antisocial and emotionally impaired. Not only was child-rearing literature big business in America, but the state had taken a special interest in the topic of disturbed youth when the Senate Subcommittee on Juvenile Delinquency opened its hearings in 1954. Against this backdrop, audience research showed that parents believed TV would keep their children off the streets. One mother, responding to a 1955 *Better Homes and Gardens* readership survey, suggested one reason for keeping up with the Joneses. She said, "It [TV] keeps the children home. Not that we have had that problem too much, but we could see it coming because nearly everyone had a set before we weakened."[17]

TROUBLE IN PARADISE

While television rapidly came to signify domestic values, the attempts to domesticate the machine belied a set of grave anxieties. Even if TV was often said to bring the family together in the home, popular media also expressed tensions about its role in domestic affairs. Television's inclusion in the home was dependent upon its ability to rid itself of what *House Beautiful* called its "unfamiliar aspect."[18]

At a time when household modernization was a key concern, women's magazines continually examined the relationship between the family and the machine. The magazines were undecided on this subject, at times accepting, at times rejecting the effects of mechanization. On the one hand, they offered their female readers technological fantasy worlds which promised to reduce the time and energy devoted to household chores. Dream kitchens, which had been displayed by women's magazines since the 1920s, resembled Technicolor spectacles found on the cinema screen, only here the bold primary colors depicted a woman's Shangri-la of electric gadgets and sleek linoleum surfaces.

Just in case this pictorial display of technological commodity fetishism was not enough, the magazines didactically reminded their readers of the need to be "up to date." In 1951 *House Beautiful* included a quiz entitled "How Contemporary Is Your Life?" Most of the fifty-eight questions had to do with the degree to which the home was equipped with "modern" appliances, and the magazine warned that if "you score less than forty . . . you are depriving yourself of too many contemporary advantages." Owning a television set was a must, according to this modernity exam.[19]

Whereas in the prewar and war years a fully mechanized household would have been presented in the popular press as a futuristic fantasy, in the postwar years it appeared that tomorrow had arrived. Living without an array of machines meant that you were anachronistic, unable to keep up with the more progressive Joneses. Still, this rampant consumerism and its attendant "machine aesthetic" had a dark underside from which the new household technologies and mechanized lifestyles appeared in a much less flattering light.

By the postwar years, ambivalence toward technology was well established in US culture. As other cultural historians have shown, by the second half of the nineteenth century, US thinkers embraced the new industrial order, but they also feared the devastating consequences of economic depression, urban crime, and labor strikes. The ambivalent response to technology grew stronger in the twentieth century. By the time of the World's Fairs of the 1930s, Americans represented technology in highly hyperbolic and contradictory ways. As Warren Susman has argued, at the same time that Americans were celebrating the technological future in the "Land of Tomorrow" at the New York World's Fair, Gallup polls revealed that most people believed technological development caused the unemployment of the Great Depression.[20]

The home magazines of the postwar era adopted this ambivalence toward machines, scrutinizing each step forward in household technology for its possible side effects. *House Beautiful,* the same magazine which tested its readers on their modernity quotients, just as often warned of the dismal future in store for the residents of the mechanized household. In 1951, the magazine asked if the "houses we live in . . . accustom us . . . to feel more at home in surroundings where everything suggests only machines . . . that do as they are told and could never have known either joy or desire." And if so, there is an overwhelming threat that "man is nothing but a machine . . . [who] can be 'conditioned' to do and to want whatever his masters decide."[21] This threat of the "machine man," couched in the rhetoric of behavioralism, gave rise to a host of statements on the relationship between television and the family. Would the television set become the master and the family its willing subject? The adage of the day became "Don't let the television set dominate you!"

The idea of "technology out of control" was constantly repeated as the language of horror and science fiction invaded discussions of everyday life. The television set was often likened to a new breed of man-made monster who, like Frankenstein before it, threatened to wreak havoc on the family. *American Mercury* called television the "Giant in the Living Room," describing it as a kind of supernatural child, a bad seed, whose actions might turn against its master at any moment. The essay proclaimed, "the giant . . . has arrived. He was a mere pip-squeak yesterday, and didn't even exist the day before, but like a genie released from a magic bottle in *The Arabian Nights,* he now looms big as life over our heads. Let us therefore try and circle round him and see if he will step on us, or make us sick and happy, or just what."[22] As such statements suggest, television posed the intimidating possibility that private citizens in their own homes might be rendered powerless in the face of a new and curious machine.

The threatening aspects of television technology might have been related to TV's use during World War II. Television, like radio before it, was a valued technology during wartime, serving as both a surveillance and a reconnaissance weapon. To some degree, the public was aware of this because television's aircraft and military applications were discussed in literature of the thirties and during wartime.[23] TV's function as a powerful weapon continued to engage the public's imagination in the postwar years and was often discussed in such men's magazines as *Popular Science*.[24]

Television's associations with World War II and its apocalyptic aftermath sharply contradicted the images of TV and domestic bliss that were put forward after the war. It seems plausible that television's military applications created doubts about its ability to enter the home.[25] In fact, television's effect on culture was sometimes discussed in the context of warfare and atomic weaponry. Words such as "invasion" and "battle" were often employed in criticisms of the new medium. A popular assumption was that television would cause cancer by transmitting waves of radiation. Later, in 1961, when FCC Commissioner Newton Minow chided the TV industry in his famous "Vast Wasteland" speech, he used the imagery of atomic warfare to suggest the powerful effects that TV might have on the public. He claimed:

> Ours has been called the jet age, the atomic age, the space age. It is also, I submit, the television age. And just as history will decide whether the leaders of today's world employed the atom to destroy the world or to rebuild it for mankind's benefit, so will history decide whether today's broadcasters employed their powerful voice to enrich the people or debase them.[26]

Although popular discourses suggested that TV technology was out of control, they also provided soothing antidotes to this fear of machines. In 1953, the Zenith Corporation found a way to master the beast, promising consumers, "We keep them [TV sets] in a cage until they're right for you." A large photograph at the top of the page showed a zoo cage which contained a Zenith scientist testing the inner components of the receiver. On the bottom of the page was the finely constructed Kensington console model, artfully integrated into a living room setting. As this ad so well suggests, the unfamiliar technology could be domesticated by turning the set into glamorous furniture.[27]

Another popular strategy was anthropomorphism. In 1951 *House Beautiful* declared, "Television has become a family member."[28] The magazines variously described TV as a "newborn baby," a "family friend," a "nurse," a "teacher," and a "family pet." Advertisers particularly drew on the image of the faithful dog—a symbol which had proven particularly useful since the turn of the century when RCA/Victrola used the picture of a fox terrier, with ears perked up, listening to "his master's voice." As the domesticated animal, TV obeyed its owner and became a benevolent playmate for children. A 1952 ad for Emerson shows a typical scenario. The immanent petlike quality of the television set emanates from the screen where a child and her poodle are pictured.[29]

Even if anthropomorphism helped to relieve the tensions about television technology, the media continued to express doubts. The idea of "technology out of control" was turned around and reformulated. Now it was viewers who had lost control of themselves. Considering television's negative effects on the family, Bogart claimed that "the bulk of the disadvantages listed by the TV owners reflect their inability to control themselves once the set has been installed in the house."[30] At least at the level of popular discourse, Bogart's suggestions are particularly accurate.

More than any other group, this discourse on human control was aimed at children. Here, TV was no longer simply a source of domestic unity and benevolent socialization. Instead, it had potent effects which needed to be understood and properly managed.[31] Most typically, television was said to cause passive and addictive behavior which in turn would disrupt good habits of nutrition, hygiene, social behavior, and education. A cartoon in a 1950 issue of *Ladies' Home Journal* suggests a typical scenario. The magazine showed a little girl slumped on an ottoman and suffering from a new disease called "telebugeye." The caption describes the child as a "pale, weak, stupid looking creature" who grew "bugeyed" from watching television for too long.[32]

As the popular wisdom often suggested, the child's passive addiction to television might itself lead to the opposite effect of increased aggression. These discussions followed in the wake of critical and social scientific theories of the 1930s and 1940s which suggested that mass media injected ideas and behavior into passive individuals. Adopting this "hypodermic model" of media effects, the magazines circulated horror stories about youngsters who imitated TV violence. In 1955, *Newsweek* reported on young Frank Stretch, an eleven-year-old who had become so entranced by a TV western that "with one shot of his trusty BB gun [he] demolished both villain and picture tube."[33] In reaction to the popular furor, as early as 1950 the Television Broadcasters' Association hired a public-relations firm to write pro-television press releases which suggested the more positive types of programming that TV had to offer.[34]

While scholarship has centered around the reform movements concerning children's television, little has been said about the popular media's advice to parents on how to control TV's effect on their children. What I find particularly interesting is the degree to which such discussions engaged questions concerning parental authority. In a time when juvenile delinquency and problem children were a central concern, television opened up a whole array of disciplinary measures that parents might exert over their youngsters.

Indeed, the bulk of discussions about children and television were offered in the context of mastery. If the machine could control the child, then so could the parent. Here the language of common sense provided some reassurance by reminding parents that it was they, after all, who were in command. As TV critic Jack Gould wrote in 1949, "It takes a human hand to turn on a television set."[35] But for parents who needed a bit more than just the soothing words of a popular sage, the media ushered in specialists from a wide range of fields: child psychologists, educators, psychiatrists, and broadcasters recommended ways to keep the problem child in line.

In 1950 *Better Homes and Gardens* wrote, "Because he had seen the results of . . . viewing—facial tics, overstimulation, neglect of practicing, outdoor play . . . homework—Van R. Brokhane, who produces education FM programs for New York City schools, decided to establish a system of control." Brokhane's control system was typical; it took the form of a careful management of time and space. "The Brokhanes put their receiver in the downstairs playroom where it could not entice their teen-age daughter away from her homework." And "then they outlined a schedule—their daughter could watch TV before dinner, but not afterward, on school nights."[36]

The publication of B. F. Skinner's *Walden Two* in 1948 precipitated a popular embrace of behavioralist psychology in the fifties. The women's home magazines discussed ways to control children's behavior through positive reinforcement, and television found its way into the behavioralist technique. In 1955, *Better Homes and Gardens* reported: "After performing the routine of dressing, [and] tidying up his room . . . Steve knows he can . . . joy of joys—watch his favorite morning TV show. His attitude is now so good he has even volunteered . . . to set the table for breakfast and help his little sister dress."[37] Thus discipline was conceived not only in the negative sense but also in the positive, "prosocial" terms suggested by behavior modification.

Expert advice also borrowed principles from psychoanalysis and typically engaged in a kind of therapeutic interrogation of family dynamics. Here television was not so much the cause of aberrant deeds as it was a symptom of deep-rooted problems in the home. As *Better Homes and Gardens* advised in 1950, "If your boy or girl throws a tantrum when you call him away from the set, don't blame television. Tantrums are a sign that tension already exists in a family."[38]

The paradox of this expert advice on television and children was that the experts—rather than the parents—took on the authoritative role. To borrow Jacques Donzelot's phrase, this expert advice amounted to a "policing of families" by public institutions.[39] By the turn of the century in the US, doctors, lawyers, clergymen, educators, industrialists, architects, and feminists had all claimed a stake in the management of domestic affairs.

One of the central conduits for disciplined domesticity was the new mass-circulation women's magazines which functioned in part as a site for reform discourses on the family. During the Progressive Era and especially in the 1920s, the public control of domestic life was regularized and refined as public agencies began to "administer" private life. In the 1920s, the secretary of commerce, Herbert Hoover, became a housing crusader. His policies encouraged a proliferation of government administrations as well as civic centers which disseminated advice on subjects ranging from building to child rearing. Hoover, in conjunction with private industry and civic groups, thought that the public agencies would help stabilize social and economic turmoil by ensuring a proper home life for all Americans. Women's magazines were closely linked to Hoover's campaigns, most obviously when Mrs. William Brown Meloney, editor of the *Delineator,* asked him to serve as president of Better Homes in America, a voluntary organization which by 1930 had 7,279 branches across the nation.[40] More generally, women's magazines were inundated with advice from professionals and industrialists who saw themselves as the custodians of everyday life.

Television appears to have been an ideal vehicle through which to regulate the family. As in the above example, TV was typically figured as a sign of larger family problems which needed to be explored by outside authorities. In this sense, it served to support the social regulation of family life. It made parents more dependent upon knowledge produced by public institutions and thus placed parents in a weakened position. In 1951, an article in *House Beautiful* complained about this loss of parental dominion, claiming:

> It seems that raising a child correctly these days is infinitely more difficult than it was 30 years ago when no one ever heard of Drs. Kinsey and Gessell, and a man named Freud was discussed only in women's beauty parlors. . . .
> 20 or 30 years ago when there weren't so many authorities on everything in America, the papas and mamas of the nation had a whole lot easier going with Junior than we have today with the authorities.

The author connected his loss of parental power directly to television, recalling the time when his little boy began to strike the TV with a large stick. Unable to decide for himself how to punish his son, the author opted for the lenient approach suggested by the expert, Dr. Spock. Unfortunately, the author recounted, "the next day Derek rammed his shovel through the TV screen [and] the set promptly blew up."[41]

In part, anxieties about parental control had to do with the fact that television was heavily promoted to families with children. During the fifties, manufacturers and retailers discovered that children were a lucrative consumer market for the sale of household commodities, including television. Numerous surveys indicated that families with children tended to buy TV sets more than childless couples did. Basing their appeals on the data, manufacturers and retailers formulated strategies by which to pull parents' purse strings. In 1950, the American Television Dealers and Manufacturers ran nationwide newspaper ads that played on parental guilt. The headline read, "Your daughter won't ever tell you the humiliation she's felt in begging those precious hours of television from a neighbor." Forlorn children were pictured on top of the layout, and parents were shown how television could raise their youngsters' spirits. This particular case is especially interesting because it shows that there are limits to which advertisers can go before a certain amount of sales resistance takes place. Outraged by the ad, parents, educators, and clergymen complained to their newspapers about its manipulative tone. In addition, the Family Service Association of America called it a "cruel pressure to apply against millions of parents" who could not afford TV sets.[42]

Just as TV advertisements bestowed a new kind of power onto child consumers, TV programs seemed to disrupt conventional power dynamics between child and adult. Popular media complained that the television image had usurped the authority previously held by parents. As TV critic John Crosby complained, "You tell little Oscar to trot off to bed, and you will probably find yourself embroiled in argument. But if Milton Berle tells him to go to bed, off he goes."[43] Here as elsewhere, television particularly threatened to depose the father. TV was depicted as the new patriarch, a machine which had robbed men of their dominion in the home.

TV critics (most of whom were male) lashed out at the appearance of bumbling fathers on the new family sit-coms. The forum for such criticism was not the women's magazines but more typically the general weeklies and news magazines which were popular with male as well as female readers. In 1944, *Time* magazine claimed, "In television's stable of 35 home-life comedies, it is a rare show that treats Father as anything more than the mouse of the house—a bumbling, well-meaning idiot who is putty in the hands of his wife and family."[44]

The kind of criticism directed at television and its bumbling fathers had its roots in a well-established tradition of mass-culture criticism based on categories of sexual difference. As film and literary scholars have observed, culture critics have often paired mass media with patriarchal assumptions about femininity. Mass amusements are typically thought to encourage passivity and are represented in terms of penetration, consumption, and escape. As Andreas Huyssen has argued, this link between women and mass culture has served since the nineteenth century to valorize the dichotomy between "low" and "high" art (or modernism). Mass culture, Huyssen claims, "is somehow associated with women while real, authentic culture remains the prerogative of men."[45] The case of broadcasting is especially interesting in this regard because the threat of feminization was particularly aimed at men. Broadcasting quite literally was shown to disrupt the normative structures of patriarchal (high) culture and to turn "real men" into passive homebodies.

The "feminizing" aspects of broadcast technology were a central concern during radio's installation in the twenties. Radio hams of the early 1900s were popularized in the press and in fiction as virile heros who saved damsels in distress with the aid of wireless technology (a popular example was the "Radio Boys," Bob and Joe, who used wireless to track down criminals and save the innocent).[46] But as Catherine Covert has argued, once radio became a domestic medium, men lost their place as active agents. Now they were shown to sit passively, listening to a one-way communication system.[47]

In the early 1940s, the connection between radio technology and emasculation came to a dramatic pitch when Philip Wylie wrote his bitter attack on US women, *Generation of Vipers*. In this widely read book, Wylie maintained that American society was suffering from an ailment he called "momism." US women, according to Wylie, had become overbearing, domineering mothers who turned their sons and husbands into weak-kneed fools. The book was replete with imagery of apocalypse through technology, imagery which Wylie tied to the figure of the woman. As he saw it, an unholy alliance between women and big business had turned the world into an industrial nightmare. Corporations such as Alcoa and General Electric had created a new female "sloth" by supplying women with machines which deprived them of their "social usefulness." Meanwhile, claimed Wylie, women had become "Cinderellas"—greedy consumers who "raped the men, not sexually, but morally. . . . "[48]

In his most bitter chapter, entitled "Common Women," Wylie argued that women had somehow gained control of the airwaves. He suggested that they had made radio listening into a passive activity which threatened manhood and, in fact, civilization. As Wylie wrote, "The radio is mom's final tool, for it stamps everyone who listens to it with the matriarchal brand. . . . Just as Goebbels has revealed what can be done with such a mass stamping of the public psyche in his nation, so our land is a living representation of the same fact worked out in matriarchal sentimentality, goo, slop, hidden cruelty, and the foreshadow of national death. . . . "[49] In the 1955 annotated edition, Wylie updated these fears, claiming that television would soon take the place of radio and turn men into female-dominated dupes. Women, he wrote, "will not rest until every electronic moment has been bought to sell suds and every bought program censored to the last decibel and syllable according to her self-adulation—along with that (to the degree the mom-indoctrinated pops are permitted access to the dials) of her desexed, de-souled, de-cerebrated mate."[50] The mixture of misogyny and "telephobia" which ran through this passage was clearly hyperbolic; still, the basic idea was repeated in more sober representations of everyday life during the postwar period.

Indeed, the paranoid connections which Wylie drew between corporate technocracies, women, and broadcasting would continue to be drawn in the 1950s when large bureaucracies increasingly controlled the lives of middle-class men. Television was often shown to rob men of their powers, making them into passive, helpless women, or even children. Unlike the male spectator of the classical cinema, who has been represented in terms of mastery and control over the scene, television in these popular accounts was shown to take away authority over the image. It threatened to make men into female spectators.

Here, one popular theme had to do with Dad's inability to control TV technology. In a 1952 episode of "*I Love Lucy*" entitled "The Courtroom," Ricky Ricardo shows his friends, Fred and Ethel Mertz, how to operate their brand-new TV set. Bragging of his technical know-how, Ricky takes two wires from the back of the TV set. But when the wires connect, the set goes up in smoke along with Ricky's masculine pride. Enraged by the destruction of their new console, the Mertzes march upstairs to the Ricardo apartment where Fred retaliates by kicking in the picture tube of Lucy and Ricky's TV set.

Finally, the Mertzes take the Ricardos to court, where we are given yet another example of male incompetence. This time the bumbling man turns out to be the judge—the ultimate patriarchal authority—who is also emasculated by TV technology. Attempting to reenact the crime, the judge brings his TV out from his chambers. Convinced that he's an authority on television technology, he believes that he can connect the wires without causing the disastrous results that Ricky did. The last laugh, of course, is on the judge who winds up destroying his own TV set.

A related theme was that of the man's inability to control his passion for mindless TV entertainment. Against his better judgment, the father would succumb to television and become childlike. The first episode of *The Honeymooners*, entitled "TV or Not TV" (1955), revolved around this dilemma. In the opening scene, Alice Kramden begs her husband, Ralph, for a TV set. After buying it, Ralph and his friend Ed Norton are turned into passive viewers. Ralph sits before the set with a smorgasbord of snacks which he deliberately places within his reach so that he needn't move a muscle while watching his program. Norton's regressive state becomes the center of the comedic situation as he is turned into a child viewer addicted to a sci-fi serial. Wearing a club-member space helmet, Norton tunes into his favorite TV host, Captain Video.

In an episode of *The Adventures of Ozzie and Harriet* ("An Evening with Hamlet," ca. 1953), this form of technological emasculation was tied directly to the father's parental authority, and by extension to the traditions of patriarchal culture. The episode opens at the breakfast table as the young son, Ricky, sadly announces that the television set is broken. As was the case in many postwar households, the father in this home is unable to fix the complicated technology himself. Instead, the family is dependent upon a new cultural hero, the TV repairman. Ozzie uses this occasion to assert his parental authority by finding family amusements which compete with television for the boys' attention. His idea of family fun recalls Victorian modes of domestic recreation—specifically, dramatic reading. But his sons are less than pleased. As Ricky says in a subsequent scene, "Hey Mom, that television man didn't get here yet . . . now we're stuck with that darn Shakespeare."

This episode goes on to highlight the competition for cultural authority between fathers and television by objectifying the problem in the form of two supporting characters. While the Nelsons recite *Hamlet,* two men visit the family home. The first is a wandering bard who mysteriously appears at the Nelson door and joins the family recital. The bard, who looks like he is part of an Elizabethan theater troupe, evokes associations of high art and cultural refinement. The second visitor, a TV repairman, represents the new electronic mass-produced culture. He is presented as an unrefined blue-collar worker who is good with machines but otherwise inept. A conversation between Ozzie and the repairman succinctly suggests this point:

> REPAIRMAN: Oh, a play, huh, I used to be interested in dramatics myself.
> OZZIE: Oh, an actor.
> REPAIRMAN: No, a wrestler.

As this scene so clearly demonstrates, television not only competes with the father at home but also disturbs the central values of patriarchal culture by replacing the old authorities with a new and degraded form of art.

A HOUSE DIVIDED

In a home where patriarchal authority was undermined, television threatened to drive a wedge between family members. This kind of reasoning was put forward by TV critics such as Goodman Ace, who wrote a satiric essay on the subject in 1953, "A Man's Television Set Is His Castle." The irony of this title was quickly apparent as Ace drew a rather unromantic picture of his life with television:

> The big television networks, fighting as they do for the elusive high rating, are little concerned with the crumbling of a man's home. Programs are indiscriminately placed in direct opposition one to the other, regardless of domestic consequence.
> That she [his wife] likes Ann Sothern and I much prefer Wally Cox opposite Miss Sothern is of little import to the executive vice presidents in charge of programming. . . .

The critic concluded with a tip for the prospective TV consumer: "Don't be misled by advertisements announcing the large 24-inch screens. Buy two 12-inch screens. And don't think of it as losing your eyesight but rather as gaining a wife."[51]

Harmony gave way to a system of differences in which domestic space and family members in domestic space were divided along sexual and social lines. Here, the ideal of family togetherness was achieved through the seemingly contradictory principle of separation; private rooms devoted to individual family members ensured peaceful relationships among residents. Thus, the social division of space was not simply the inverse of family unity; rather, it was a point on a continuum which stressed ideals of domestic cohesion. Even the family room itself was conceived in these terms. In fact, when coining the phrase, Nelson and Wright claimed, "By frankly developing a room which is 'entirely public' . . . privacy is made possible. Because there's an 'extra room,' the other living space can really be enjoyed in peace and quiet."[52]

The ideology of divided space was based on Victorian aesthetics of housing design and corresponding social distinctions entailed by family life. The middle-class homes of Victorian America embodied the conflicting urge for family unity and division within their architectural layout. Since the homes were often quite spacious, it was possible to have rooms devoted to intimate family gatherings (such as the back parlor) and social occasions (such as the front parlor) as well as rooms wholly given over to separate family members. This allowed the Victorians to experience private, familial, and social life within conventionalized and highly formalized settings so that residents and guests would often know what kind of social situation to expect by the household space they occupied at any particular moment.

In the early decades of the twentieth century, the size of homes shrank because of the added expenses of plumbing and electrical fixtures. The number and kinds of rooms in the family home were thus sacrificed for the inclusion of advanced technology. In addition, the ideology which accompanied the rigid hierarchies of space was somewhat altered. Progressive housing reformers, architects, and feminists all stressed comfort over the Victorian ideals of formality and social ritual. For both economic and ideological reasons, then, the social hierarchies of family life were less distinctly a part of architectural design. In the bungalows of the 1910s, for example, the exclusion of the front parlor meant that both family and social occasions took place in one space, now commonly referred to as the living room.

By the 1950s, the typical four-and-one-half-room dwellings of middle-class suburbia were clearly not large enough to support entirely the Victorian ideals of socio/spatial hierarchies. Still, popular home manuals of the postwar period put a premium on keeping these spatial distinctions in order. They presented their readers with a model of space derived in part from the Victorian experience.

The act of watching television came to be a central concern in this discourse on divided space, as the magazines showed readers rambling homes with special rooms designed exclusively for watching TV. Television sets were placed in children's playrooms or bedrooms, away from the central spaces of the home. In 1951, *House Beautiful* had even more elaborate plans. A fun room built adjacent to the home and equipped with television gave a teenage daughter a "place for her friends." For the parents it meant "peace of mind because teenagers are away from [the] house but still at home."[53]

It seems likely that most readers in their cramped suburban homes did not follow these suggestions. A 1954 national survey showed that 85% of the respondents kept their sets in the living room, so that the space for TV was the central, common living area in the home.[54] Perhaps recognizing the practical realities of their readers, the magazines suggested ways to maintain the aesthetics of divided spaces in the small home. While it might not have been possible to have a room of one's own for television viewing, there were alternative methods by which to approximate the ideal.

Rooms could be designed in such a way that they functioned both as viewing areas and as centers for other activities. In this sense, television fit into a more general functionalist discourse in which household spaces were supposed to be made "multi-purposeful." In 1951 *Better Homes and Gardens* spoke of a "recreation area of the living room" which was "put to good use as the small fry enjoy a television show."[55] At other times such areas were referred to specifically as "television areas." While in many cases the television area was marked off by furniture arrangements or architectural structures such as alcoves, at other times the sign of division was concretized in an object form—the room divider.

Given their ability to separate viewers from nonviewers, it is not surprising that room divider companies used the idea of television and family squabbles within their advertisements. In a 1955 ad for Modernfold doors, Mother sits at one end of a room, while her child and the TV set are separated off by a folding wall. Suggesting itself as an object of dispute, the television set supports the call for the room divider—here stated as "that tiresome game of 'Who gets the living room.' " Moreover, since room dividers like this one were typically collapsible, they were the perfect negotiation between ideals of unity and division. They allowed parents to be apart from their children, but the "fold-back" walls also provided easy access to family togetherness.[56]

The socio-sexual division of space was often presented in advertisements for television sets. In 1955, GE used this division as a vehicle for promoting the sale of a second set. A cooking program on a portable set in the kitchen gave Mother and Daughter a baking lesson, while Father watched football on the living room console. Accompanying the illustration was a caption which read, "when Dad wants to watch the game . . . Mom and Sis, the cooking show . . . there's too much traffic for one TV to handle."[57]

But the depiction of divided families wasn't simply a clever marketing strategy; rather, it was a well-entrenched pictorial convention. Indeed, by 1952, advertisements in the home magazines increasingly depicted family members enjoying TV alone or else in subgroups. At least in the case of these ads, it appears that the cultural meanings which were circulated about television changed somewhat over the course of the early years of installation. While television was primarily shown to be an integrating activity in the first few years of diffusion, in the 1950s it came to be equally (or perhaps even more) associated with social differences and segregation among family members.[58]

It is important, however, to remember that the contradiction between family unity and division was just that—a contradiction, a site of ideological tension, and not just a clear-cut set of opposing choices. In this light, we might understand a number of advertisements which attempted to negotiate these tensions by evoking ideas of unity and division at the same time.

These ads pictured family members watching television in private, but the image on the TV screen contained a kind of surrogate family. A 1953 ad for Sentinel TV shows husband and wife gently embracing as they watch their brand-new television set on Christmas Eve. The pleasure entailed by watching TV is associated with the couple's romantic life more than it is associated with their parental duties. However, the televised image contains two children, apparently singing Christmas carols. Thus, the ad shows that parents can enjoy a romantic night of television apart from their own children. But it still sustains the central importance of the family scene because it literally *re-presents* the absent children by making them into an image on the screen. Moreover, the ad attaches a certain amount of guilt to the couple's intimate night of TV, their use of television as a medium for romantic rather than familial enjoyment. The idea of guilty pleasure is suggested by the inclusion in the ad of two "real" children who appear to be voyeurs, clandestinely looking onto the scene of their parents' pleasure. Dressed in pajamas, the youngsters peek out from a corner of the room, apparently sneaking out of bed to take a look at the new TV while the grown-ups remain unaware of their presence.[59]

The tensions between opposing ideals of unity and division were also expressed in material form. Manufacturers offered strange TV gizmos which allowed families to be alone and together at the same time. In 1954, *Popular Science* displayed a new device which let parents tune out the set while their children watched. As the magazine explained, "NOBODY IS BOTHERED if the children want to see a rootin'-tootin' Western when Dad and Mother want to read, write or talk. Earphones let the youngsters hear every shot, but the silence is wonderful." The accompanying photograph captures the sense of divided attention among family members. It represents a middle-class domestic setting in which parents and children sit in chairs dispersed throughout the room in such a way that no two people appear to acknowledge their mutual presence in the space. Three adults, located at the remote corners of the room, appear to be absorbed in reading materials and undisturbed by the television set. (In fact, the father is distanced from the entire scene of television; since he is off-frame in the composition, we see only the lower portion of his body.) Two children with earphones appear in the center of the composition and sit in front of a television set which is situated in the background. Long running wires are attached to the children's earphones and connected to an audio box located on a table in the center of the foreground. The wires dominate and even seem to tie together the central space of the composition. On the one hand, then, the scene evokes a sense of social isolation as registered in the portrayal of the human figures attending to separate media interests. On the other hand, the compositional importance of the connecting wires suggests the idea of social integration or, quite literally, "family ties" which bind separate family members together.[60]

DuMont had an even better idea with its "Duoscope" TV. This elaborate construction was composed of two receivers housed in a TV cabinet, with two chassis, two control panels, two picture tubes, and a common screen that were mounted at right angles. Through polarization and the super-imposition of two TV images, the set allowed two viewers to watch different programs at the same time. Thus, as the article suggested, a husband and wife equipped with polarized glasses were able to watch TV together but still retain their private pleasures.[61]

While the Duoscope never caught on, the basic problematic of unity and division continued. The attempt to balance ideals of family harmony and social difference often led to bizarre solutions, but it also resulted in everyday viewing patterns which were presented as functional and normal procedures for using television. Popular discourses tried to tame the beast, suggesting ways to maintain traditional modes of family behavior and still allow for social change. They devised intricate plans for resistance and accommodation to the new machine, and in so doing they helped construct a new cultural form.

The relationship between culture and communications technology is a dialogical one. As Warren Susman has suggested, communications technologies are shaped by the way the culture thinks about them, and in turn can give rise to cultural change. While the dialogue between mass culture and the public is never direct, these popular magazines do help to reveal a set of discursive rules which were constructed for thinking about TV in the period of its installation. By examining popular discourses, we might thus begin to account for the ways we use and think about television in our own everyday lives.

NOTES

1. This article is based on the examination of four of the leading women's home magazines from the postwar years, *American Home, Better Homes and Gardens, Ladies' Home Journal,* and *House Beautiful.* I examined every issue of these publications from 1948 to 1955. All four magazines emphasized discussions of homemaking (the first three focus primarily on interior decor and home economics, whereas *Ladies' Home Journal*—often referred to as a women's service magazine—deals with a wider array of women's issues). The editorial and advertising texts were addressed to a middle-class (and often upper-middle-class) female reader. Readership reports indicate that middle-class women were the most faithful audience—although as early as the 1920s

the magazines had a significant lower-class constituency. See Alfred Politz Research, *The Audiences of Nine Magazines: Their Size and Characteristics—A National Study* (New York: Cowles Magazines, 1955), p. 17; and W. Lloyd Warner and Paul S. Lunt, *The Social Life of a Modern Community* (New Haven: Yale University Press, 1941), pp. 398–405. (As a caveat, I'll add that industry-sponsored readership reports often overreported the number of upscale readers in order to attract advertisers.)

For purposes of comparison by gender and class, I analyzed a sample of other magazines including the general weeklies, the popular men's magazines *Esquire* and *Popular Science*, and the women's magazine *Good Housekeeping*, which was addressed to a less affluent female readership. The home magazines and general weeklies included by far the greatest number of ads for television. This seems to suggest, at least from the advertiser's point of view, that TV sets were both a gender- and class-specific item. Television was aimed at a female and family consumer, but it was rarely promoted to the predominantly male readers of *Esquire* and *Popular Science*. In addition, television was almost never advertised in the less upscale woman's magazine *Good Housekeeping*. For more on the evidence used in this study, see my "Installing the Television Set: The Social Construction of Television's Place in the American Home, 1948–55," diss., University of California, Los Angeles, 1988.

2. For an interesting discussion of the cultural response to radio, see Catherine L. Covert, " 'We May Hear Too Much': American Sensibility and the Response to Radio, 1919–1924," in *Mass Media between the Wars: Perceptions of Cultural Tension, 1918–1941*, ed. Catherine L. Covert and John D. Stevens (Syracuse: Syracuse University Press, 1984), pp. 199–220.

3. Roland Marchand, *Advertising the American Dream: Making Way for Modernity, 1920–1940* (Berkeley: University of California Press, 1985), especially chaps. 1 and 2.

4. George Nelson and Henry Wright, *Tomorrow's House: A Complete Guide For the Home Builder* (New York: Simon, 1946), p. 80.

5. *Better Homes and Gardens* 28 (Aug. 1950):45.

6. Marchand, pp. 248–54.

7. William H. Whyte, *The Organization Man* (Garden City, N.Y.: Doubleday, 1957).

8. As Maureen Honey shows in her study of women's magazine fiction during the war, the Office of War Information gave suggestions to the magazine editors on ways to encourage married middle-class women to work. Honey points out, however, that the magazines suggested wartime work for women was temporary— to be discarded when the GIs returned. Despite this, many women did not want to leave their jobs when the men came home. See *Creating Rosie the Riveter: Class, Gender, and Propaganda during WWII* (Amherst: University of Massachusetts Press, 1984).

9. Ferdinand Lundberg and Marynia F. Farnham, *Modern Woman: The Lost Sex* (New York: Harper, 1947). As William Chafe has claimed, the essentialists were challenged by resistant voices (mainly women sociologists and anthropologists) who argued that gender was an effect of social conditioning. See his "The Debate on Woman's Place," in *The American Woman: Her Changing Social, Economic, and Political Roles, 1920–1970* (New York: Oxford University Press, 1972), chap. 9. However, the prevailing media presented a picture of women as housewives and mothers. While popular discourses did at times express discontent with that role, they nevertheless assumed that it was the woman's proper place, and thus they typically discussed female dissatisfaction as a "woman's problem" rather than a political issue.

10. These work-force estimations are based on Rochelle Gatlin, *American Women since 1945* (Jackson: University of Mississippi Press, 1987), p. 25.

11. Marchand, pp. 335–59; and T. J. Jackson Lears, "From Salvation to Self-realization: Advertising and the Therapeutic Roots of Consumer Culture, 1880–1930," in *The Culture of Consumption: Critical Essays in American History, 1880–1980*

(New York: Pantheon, 1983), pp. 1–38. Although I do believe these ads were intended to function therapeutically, I am not suggesting they actually did. In fact, they might have caused increased anxieties and feelings of inadequacy for the many families who could not afford the products which promised to bring domestic bliss.

12. *American Home* 44 (Oct. 1950):25. For other examples of the family circle/product-as-center motif, see *House Beautiful* 91 (Nov. 1949):1; *Ladies' Home Journal* (Oct. 1948):115; *House Beautiful* 91 (Feb. 1949):1.

13. Leo Bogart, *The Age of Television: A Study of Viewing Habits and the Impact of Television on American Life* (1956; New York: Ungar, 1958), p. 101. As a cautionary note, I would suggest that in his attempt to present a global, synthetic picture of the TV audience, Bogart often smooths over the contradictions in the studies he presents. This attempt at global synthesis goes hand in hand with Bogart's view that the TV audience is a homogeneous mass and that TV further erases distinctions. He writes, "The levelling of social differences is part of the standardization of tastes and interests to which the mass media give expression, and to which they also contribute. The ubiquitous TV antenna is a symbol of people seeking—and getting—the identical message" (5). Through this logic of mass mentalities, Bogart often oversimplifies the heterogeneity of audience responses in the studies he presents.

14. Edward C. McDonaugh, "Television and the Family," *Sociology and Social Research* 40:4 (Mar.Apr. 1956):117.

15. John W. Riley et al., "Some Observations of the Social Effects of Television," *Public Opinion Quarterly* 13.2 (Summer 1949):232.

16. Raymond Stuart, cited in Bogart, p. 100.

17. Ann Usher, "TV . . . Good or Bad for Your Children?" *Better Homes and Gardens* 33 (Oct. 1955):209.

18. "Television Has Become a Member of the Family," *House Beautiful* 93 (Sept. 1951):118.

19. *House Beautiful* 97 (Jan. 1955):39–43, 84.

20. Warren I. Susman, "Culture and Communications," in *Culture as History: The Transformation of American Society in the Twentieth Century* (1973; New York: Pantheon, 1984), p. 268.

21. Joseph Wood Krutch, "Have You Caught On Yet . . . ," *House Beautiful* 93 (Nov. 1951):221.

22. Calder Willingham, "Television Giant in the Living Room," *American Mercury* 74 (Feb. 1952):117.

23. For discussions of this, see Jeanne Allen, "The Social Matrix of Television: Invention in the United States," in *Regarding Television*, ed. E. Ann Kaplan (Los Angeles: University Publications of America, 1983), p. 113; and Robert Davis, "Response to Innovation: A Study of Popular Argument about New Mass Media," diss., University of Iowa, 1965, pp. 100–101.

24. See, for example, Bill Reiche, "Television Is the Navy's School Teacher," *Popular Mechanics* 90 (Nov. 1948):125–27, 270, 272; Devon Francis, "TV Takes Over Test Pilot's Job," *Popular Science* 158 (Mar. 1951):144–148; "Dismantling Bombs by TV," *Science Digest* 35 (Jan. 1954), inside cover.

25. Elsewhere I discuss this military association with reference to popular fears about television's status as a surveillance mechanism. See my dissertation, chap. 7, or my article "Installing the Television Set: Popular Discourses on Television and Domestic Space, 1948–55," *Camera Obscura* 16 (Aug. 1988):11–47.

26. Newton Minow, "The Vast Wasteland," Address to the 39th Annual Convention of the National Broadcasters, Washington, 9 May 1961.

27. *Look* 21 Apr. 1953:18.

28. "Television Has Become a Family Member," p. 66.

29. *Better Homes and Gardens* 30 (Dec. 1952):133.

30. Bogart, p. 97

31. This concern with media effects on children was part of a larger history. For example, controversies about these influences were launched by middle-class reformers during the Progressive Era. By the 1930s reform arguments had gained particular strength, with film and radio as prime targets of public scrutiny. In the 1950s, this concern with broadcasting was transferred to television—most strikingly in 1955 when the Kefauver investigation held special hearings on television's effect on children. For more on this, see Davis, especially pp. 163–71, 209–216, and 233–53.

32. *Ladies' Home Journal* 67 (Apr. 1950):237. For a similar cartoon see *Ladies' Home Journal* 72 (Dec. 1955):164.

33. "Bang! You're Dead," *Newsweek* 21 Mar. 1955:35.

34. Edward M. Brecher, "TV, Your Children, and Your Grandchildren," *Consumer Reports* 15 (May 1950):231.

35. Jack Gould, "What Is Television Doing to Us?" *New York Times Magazine* 12 June 1949: 7.

36. Dorothy Diamond and Frances Tenenbaum, "Should You Tear 'em Away from TV?" *Better Homes and Gardens* 29 (Sept. 1950):56.

37. *Better Homes and Gardens* 33 (Mar. 1955):173.

38. Diamond and Tenenbaum, p. 239.

39. Jacques Donzelot, *The Policing of Families* (New York: Pantheon, 1979). Donzelot discusses the history of the public regulation of the family in France.

40. For a detailed discussion see Gwendolyn Wright, *Building the Dream: A Social History of Housing in America* (New York: Pantheon, 1981), p. 197.

41. Lloyd Shearer, "The Parental Dilemma," *House Beautiful* 93 (Oct. 1951):220, 222.

42. "Television Tempest," *Newsweek* 27 Nov. 1950:62.

43. John Crosby, "Parents Arise! You Have Nothing to Lose but Your Sanity," in *Out of the Blue! A Book about Radio and Television* (New York: Simon, 1952), p. 115.

44. "Daddy with a Difference," *Time* 17 May 1954:83. For additional examples see Eleanor Harris, "They Always Get Their Man," *Colliers* 25 Nov. 1950:34; "The Great Competitor," *Time* 14 Dec. 1953:62; "Perpetual Honeymoon," *Time* 22 Mar. 1954:82.

45. Andreas Huyssen, "Mass Culture as Woman: Modernism's Other," in *Studies in Entertainment: Critical Approaches to Mass Culture,* ed. Tania Modleski (Bloomington: Indiana University Press, 1986), p. 191.

46. Susan J. Douglas discusses this in "Amateur Operators and American Broadcasting: Shaping the Future of Radio," in *Imagining Tomorrow: History, Technology, and the American Future,* ed. Joseph J. Corn (Cambridge, Mass.: MIT Press, 1986), pp. 46–47.

47. Covert, p. 205.

48. Philip Wylie, *Generation of Vipers* (1942; New York: Holt, 1955), pp. 199–200.

49. Ibid., pp. 214–15.

50. Ibid., pp. 213–14.

51. Goodman Ace, "A Man's TV Set Is His Castle," *The Saturday Review* (Apr. 1953). Reprinted in his *The Book of Little Knowledge: More Than You Want to Know about Television* (New York: Simon, 1955), pp. 165–67.

52. Nelson and Wright, p. 76.

53. *House Beautiful* 93 (Oct. 1951):168.

54. Alfred Politz Research, *National Survey of Radio and Television Sets Associated with U.S. Households* (New York: The Advertising Research Foundation, 1954).

55. *Better Homes and Gardens* 29 (Nov. 1951):263.

56. *American Home* 54 (Sept. 1955):17.

57. *Better Homes and Gardens* 33 (Oct. 1955):139.

58. For ads which depicted divided families, see, for example, *Better Homes and Gardens* 31 (Nov. 1953):40; *Better Homes and Gardens* 30 (Dec. 1952):30; *American Home* 46 (Nov. 1951):10.

59. *American Home* 51 (Dec. 1953):84.

60. Phil Hinter, "Television As You Like It," *Popular Science* 164 (May 1954):216–18. A similar device was marketed by Philco.

61. "Two-Headed TV Set Displays Different Shows at Once," *Popular Science* 164 (Mar. 1954):156.

THE SEVEN DWARFS AND THE MONEY GRUBBERS

The Public Relations Crisis of US Television in the Late 1950s

William Boddy

Two otherwise unrelated cover stories in the national newsweeklies in 1987 conjured up the traumatic events in the US television industry of the late 1950s. With the characteristic mixture of fascination, facetiousness, and moralism with which the television game show is often discussed, *Newsweek*'s cover article ("Game Shows: America's Obsession—TV Cashes In") offered readers a sidebar entitled "Whatever Happened to Charles Van Doren?" where it recounted the fortunes of the starring figure in American television's most infamous scandal, the rigging of several prime-time quiz programs in the late 1950s. The authors concluded their account of the scandal with the following:

> from the perspective of a more cynical, or at least less gullible, age, the reaction to the quiz shenanigans seems almost quaintly overwrought. A grand jury issued subpoenas, a congressional committee opened hearings. Virtually every executive connected with a quiz show was fired and blacklisted. All the big giveaways were yanked from prime time—and a nation turned its lonely eyes to Matt Dillon.[1]

Time magazine's cover story, "What Ever Happened to Ethics," cataloging the contemporary missteps of Wall Street brokers, television evangelists, and Reagan advisers, located the quiz show scandals in a similar context: "America has been through these orgies of moral self-flagellation before. Sometimes the diagnosis was far more dire than the disease. Intellectuals reacted to the TV quiz-show scandals of the late 1950s with an outrage that now seems comically disproportionate to the offense. . . . "[2]

These casual, if perhaps representative, recent references to the 1950s quiz show scandals pay witness to the trauma the episode occasioned, even while confessing puzzlement at the "orgies" of "overwrought" public reaction. Unpacking some of the wider context and stakes in the scandals may restore some substance to television's past, in danger of being relegated to the merely quaint or comic.

Viewed as the response to revelations of misconduct in a specific program genre, public reaction to the quiz program fraud does indeed seem hyperbolic. Veteran New York TV critic John Crosby wrote at the time:

> The moral squalor of the quiz mess reaches clear through the whole industry. . . . The heavy hand of the advertiser suffocates truth, corrupts men and women. . . . The worst crumbs in the business are now in the saddle and the best and the most idealistic and creative men in the business either can't get work or they quit in disgust and go on to better things.[3]

In the *Nation,* blacklisted screenwriter Dalton Trumbo denounced "the arrogant greed of men who have appropriated the free air and turned it into a witch's bazaar of howling peddlers hawking trash." The quiz show scandal, according to Trumbo, "reveals the future which there has been projected for us—a future boldly rigged for the naked worship of things and self, animated by a materialism so primitive that it is incapable of developing either philosophical or moral objective: a future of true godlessness, of corruption absolute."[4] Meanwhile, the *New Republic* scorned the government regulators of the television industry, the Federal Communications Commission (FCC), as "the Seven Dwarfs" who "parcel it [the airwaves] out free to money grubbers."[5] Among many religious leaders who commented upon the scandals was Rabbi Maurice N. Eisendrath, the president of the Union of American Hebrew Congregations, who told the *Chicago Sun Times:* "I am less concerned about the scandals in television than I am with the fact that American television itself is a national scandal. The moral lapses of Charles Van Doren and others like him are of minor significance compared to the moral bankruptcy of television itself."[6] Responding to questions about the scandal at two national press conferences, President Eisenhower called the quiz show fraud "a terrible thing to do to the American people" and ordered his attorney general to prepare a report on television practices.[7]

Public statements from many within the television industry at the same time shared the alarmist, even apocalyptic, tone of broadcast critics in response to what one industry executive called the quiz "holocaust." One commentator in the trade press worried that the scandal would taint the entire television advertising medium, and a Hearst magazine executive warned: "television viewers are consumers, and disbelief is a disease that spreads rapidly. And already there is evidence that the taint attached to the entertainment phase of television has begun to contaminate advertising in all media." In a speech in March 1960, CBS executive Richard Salant worried: "We are going to pay for these mistakes for a long time, and we are paying for them now. All sorts of dissatisfactions about television crystallize as a result of these miserable events." CBS network president Frank Stanton told the Academy of Television Arts and Sciences in December 1959: "The quiz show scandals triggered the explosion of pent-up discontents with television with large segments of the American people that go far beyond phoney and deceitful practices and include everything from irritating commercials to program content."[8]

Some of the perplexity of present-day commentators about the reactions to the 1950s quiz show scandals may be due to the way in which the scandals did indeed crystallize pent-up general discontent and critical disillusionment with commercial television. Thus it may be helpful to examine more closely the manner in which the rise and fall of the prime-time quiz show related to larger issues in US television of the 1950s.

The first of the prime-time network quiz programs, *The $64,000 Question*, began as a summer replacement show in June 1955; by August it was enormously popular. *Fortune* called the show "a hit unparalleled in the annals of television," and within months the program was receiving a 50 rating and an 85 share nationally, with one October broadcast earning a 97 share in the New York City market. The program's producers received 10,000–20,000 applications each week from those wishing to appear on the show.[9]

Without the expenses of professional writers, location shooting, or professional actors, the programs' low budgets and short-term contract commitments made them especially appealing for single sponsorship by advertisers. The sponsor of *The $64,000 Question*, Revlon cosmetics, paid its producers, Entertainment Productions, Inc. (EPI), only $15,000 in production fees and $10,000 in prize money each week. Meanwhile the popular success of the program made Revlon the stuff of advertising industry legend: *Printer's Ink* called the company's experience the "most amazing sales success in the history of the cosmetics industry." A 1956 *Fortune* article, "Revlon's Jackpot," commented: "It is no reflection on the quality of Revlon's merchandise to suggest that one could, apparently, sell an outright facial corrosive in quantity if the program were hawking it." In 1955–56, company sales increased 70 percent, and profits jumped 130 percent; the price of Revlon's stock, introduced on Wall Street in December 1955, rose from twelve dollars to thirty dollars a share in its first three months.[10]

The success of *The $64,000 Question* quickly inspired other prime-time quiz programs and set off a fierce bidding contest among the three networks for the original show following its one-year licensed run on CBS, in what *Variety* called "the most extravagant power play in TV's annals." Most successful among the new programs was NBC's *Twenty-One,* produced by Barry-Enright Productions for Pharmaceuticals, Inc., manufacturers of Geritol and other patent medicines. At the height of the genre's popularity in 1958, there were twenty-four network quiz shows in prime time, representing an estimated $100 million in production and time charges; quiz programs constituted 18 percent of NBC's overall schedule. There were spin-offs of the popular quiz programs in Brazil, Mexico, Great Britain, Italy, and Sweden. The producer of *The $64,000 Question,* Louis Cowan, became a CBS executive in August 1955 and head of the network in 1958; in May 1957, NBC announced the purchase of *Twenty-One* and four other quiz shows from Barry-Enright for $2.2 million in a deal that guaranteed the producers $100,000 a year and 50 percent of the show's profits after the purchase price was recouped.[11]

Not every prime-time quiz show was rigged, and not every contestant on tainted programs was coached, but such practices were widespread among the most popular programs. Indeed, it seems surprising that such elaborate manipulation of purported contests of skill or chance could have remained a secret as long as it did. Contestant contracts for *Big Surprise* stipulated that winners had no claim to the amounts they "won"; instead, winnings received were to be determined solely by the producers. On a number of programs, successful contestants negotiated their actual winnings, usually much less than the announced amounts. Some contestants extracted better settlements by threatening to go public with the fraud. When a standby contestant stumbled across winning contestant Marie Winn's prompt book on *Dotto* and shared it with the losing contestant, he extracted $4,000 for the loser and $1,500 for himself from the producers in exchange for their silence. Mechanical devices which determined prize amounts were rigged to prevent large payoffs on CBS's *Dotto*; on other shows, stakes and tie matches were manipulated to keep prize budgets under specified limits. The outcomes of children's spelling contests were controlled by quizzing favored contestants only upon words they had spelled correctly in lengthy "pre-tests"; some of the favored adult contestants were handled the same way.

At other times, producers went further, coaching contestants when to deliberately miss questions, as well as when and how to stammer, pause, and remove perspiration ("Pat, don't wipe"). Eleven-year-old Patti Duke was appearing on Broadway in *The Miracle Worker* when she won $32,000 on one rigged program; when her agent discovered her struggling to memorize the coached answers, he supplied her with pencil and paper and took 15 percent of her "winnings." Production staffers on *Treasure Hunt* placed members of the studio audience on the program in exchange for kickbacks of half of their prize money. A Pennsylvania department store owner paid the producers $10,000 under the table to get one of his employees on *The $64,000 Challenge* for publicity purposes. On some programs, producers faced direct pressure from sponsors to remove "undesirable" champions or guarantee the longevity of particular contestants. In the case of *The $64,000 Question* and *The $64,000 Challenge*, Revlon executive vice-president Martin Revson met with the producers each week, deciding the future of specific contestants with rating charts and press clippings, at one point simply telling the producers to "have more losers."[12]

Although the scandal culminated in the fall of 1959, rumors of fraud had circulated for years within the industry and, to an extent, in the popular press. In March 1957 *Twenty-One* contestant Herbert Stempel, after obediently taking a fall against Charles Van Doren, threatened to expose his own long experience of coaching under producers Barry and Enright. Promised money and a job by the two producers, Stempel signed a false retraction of his charges. In 1957, both *Time* and *Look* published articles on the allegations of rigging, reassuring readers that despite rumors, the quiz shows were generally honest. The first public sign that the trade rumors might have substance was the abrupt cancellation of *Dotto* in August 1958. Sponsor Colgate-Palmolive and the networks released a terse announcement which offered no reason for the show's termination. After the full scandal emerged, New York television reporters and critics recalled their earlier skepticism about the program's integrity and described investigative stories which were killed by newspaper editors and lawyers. Barry and Enright sued two New York papers for libel for reporting the Stempel charges against *Twenty-One*. One critic told of forwarding the complaints of fraud to the FCC in 1958 to no effect.[13]

The unmasking of fraud was largely the work of a Manhattan grand jury which began its investigation in August 1958, hearing testimony from Stempel, who retracted his earlier, false retraction of fraud, as well as from another *Twenty-One* contestant, James Snodgrass. Snodgrass had been coached before each of his appearances except his last, and had written out the prepared questions and answers in a self-addressed letter postmarked *before* his weekly appearances. Most of the other witnesses (including Charles Van Doren) called before the grand jury were less forthcoming about their involvement in the fraud. The New York district attorney who led the investigation estimated that of 150 witnesses, 50 were truthful. Lawyers for Barry and Enright coached witnesses in false testimony (they called it "preparing the witness") and advised others to leave town to avoid testifying. Declining to indict any individuals, the grand jury completed its report, or presentment, in June 1959; however, the judge, in an unusual move, ordered the presentment sealed. By this time, committees of both houses of Congress announced plans for public hearings on the quiz scandals for the fall of 1959. The grand jury presentment was released to the committees' staffs, and the growing public interest in the scandals focused on hearings before a House of Representatives committee chaired by Congressman Oren Harris, and particularly on the spectacular public confession of Charles Van Doren in early November. President Eisenhower commented on the affair in two national press conferences and ordered his attorney general to prepare a report on problems in the television industry; the report was delivered to the president and reprinted in full in the *New York Times* on January 1, 1960.[14]

If this is a chronology of the unfolding of the scandal, it remains to address the breadth and passion of the reactions from both within and without the industry. One clue to the intensity of the response lies in the relation of the quiz shows to larger debates over programming in the 1950s. Perhaps surprisingly, the quiz shows were initially well received by some critics who found affinities between them and the aesthetic values of "Golden Age" drama programming. The 1955–56 season was seen by many in the industry as a watershed, pitting the sponsorship and programming ideas of NBC's Pat Weaver against the new Hollywood telefilm strategies of ABC. George Wolf, TV columnist for *Advertising Agency Magazine*, called it "the most heralded year in the brief history of the medium" and promised that "the 1955–56 season would be head and shoulders above anything yet seen in the medium." Wolf wrote that Weaver's ambitious plans for the live expanded-length network "spectacular" and for "magazine advertising," which Weaver argued would strengthen the network's enlightened hand in programming matters, had "officially been accepted by the opposition." Wolf also noted that prominent New York television critics Jack Gould and John Crosby, "astute observers of the television scene who call them as they see them untempered by commercial or corporate considerations, see in the new programming pattern the strengthening of the entire television medium." Crosby had recently described the prospect of a two-hour live network spectacular every night in prime time, and in congressional testimony, Weaver had forecast the three-hour network spectacular.[15]

In this context of critical optimism, *The $64,000 Question* was seen as congruent with the promised elevation of prime-time programming. Gould lauded the program as evidence of the "voice of the people" and chided the networks for not using real-people programming earlier: "Television complains continually that it doesn't know where its material will come from next. . . . Yet, meanwhile it overlooks the bottomless reservoir of intelligent people." A September 1955 article in *Advertising Agency Magazine*, "Ordinary Folks—Heroes of TV Programming," elaborated the affinities between the quiz programs and the prestigious live dramas of the "Golden Age," quoting an NBC official explaining the appeal of "ordinary people":

> Stick with them, and be honest about it, and you'll do all right. . . . Take a look at what's big and what's lasted in television. Groucho—talking to ordinary people. Godfrey—very folksy. *Too* folksy sometimes. *This Is Your Life, Truth or Consequences, People Are Funny, Person to Person, What's My Line*; *The $64,000 Question*—no frills, no glamor, just people! Even when it comes to that television staple, drama, you can't go too far wrong if you eschew the chi-chi and play it

honestly. Take *Marty* . . . just the life and hard times of a Bronx butcher, that's all.[16]

The surprising association of quiz programs with prestige live drama via notions of honesty, authenticity, and populism suggests the contradictory pressures on producers and sponsors. While the quiz shows were represented as uncontrolled and unpredictable contests between nonactors, producers were sensitive to their affinities with traditional dramatic forms. In November 1955, Revlon's advertising director discussed the popularity of *The $64,000 Question:*

> I think it will last. I say that primarily because *The $64,000 Question* is not a true quiz show. It has a variety of elements that I believe will make it survive. There are two elements that are extremely important . . . interesting people and suspense. . . . They're the elements responsible for the success of a good book, a good play or a good motion picture.[17]

Likewise, a 1957 *Broadcasting* article on the popularity of the quiz show, "Making Money by Giving It Away," warned that "a quiz program can't just give money away and do nothing else. They must have the attributes of any successful TV program, the main factor being sustained personality interest." As the scandal began to unravel in the fall of 1958, a similar rationale was invoked by one advertising executive who displaced responsibility for the fraud onto the audience:

> The program producers are pushed into this sort of thing in a way. The viewer actually demands a quiz contestant who is lively and has a certain degree of personality. The viewer wants him to be on the show as long as possible without being told why he is on the show so long. To give the viewer what he wants, therefore, the producer has to set up some kind of controls.[18]

The use of spectacle, suspense, and sympathetic protagonists in these ostensible contests of knowledge formed the commercial imperative and dramatic principles of the quiz show rigging. Not only were outcomes fixed, but each narrative advance was controlled: pauses, hesitations, and order of answers for each contestant were arranged. So too were the frequently prolonged series of tie matches by which a popular rivalry was extended.

Producers paid a great deal of attention to the dramatic elements of the shows. *Mise en scène* was often highly theatricalized; in the case of *The $64,000 Question*, contestants were placed in glass isolation booths (without air conditioning) resembling large chess pieces, surrounded by a darkened set with their faces eerily lighted from below. Each show used rituals of secrecy and security whose procedures were reiterated in elaborate detail: bank officers whose companies' vaults safeguarded questions were introduced; armed guards brought in sealed questions and hovered in the wings;

and professors from prestigious universities were credited with verifying information. *The $64,000 Question* featured a prominent oversize Diebolt vault (actually made of cardboard and the result of a $30,000 surreptitious fee paid by the manufacturer to the producer, unbeknownst to the show's official sponsor).[19] Some programs employed split screens to juxtapose battling contestants and superimposed dollar amounts of possible winnings over close-ups of anxious contestant faces. *The $64,000 Question* typically began with urgent tight shots of the spouses of winning contestants from the previous week as contestants pondered whether to risk all to continue.

A constant challenge for the producer-as-dramaturge was the danger of the unpopular winner. Diane Lawson, a free-lance recruiter of contestants for several quiz producers, explained the dilemma: "People tend to change like Jekyll into Hyde the minute they win twenty-five bucks. They go kind of nuts with that kind of carrot in front of 'em. They win something and boom! All the things you picked them for go out the window. All they're thinking about is the damned money."[20] Her lament about the inconsistency of the real-people protagonists was echoed by many advertising agency executives and program producers.

One common dramatic technique in *The $64,000 Question* and other quiz shows was casting against type (what one producer called "our policy of paradoxes on the show"), which tested a contestant against an incongruous body of knowledge, for example, Joyce Brothers on boxing or an eleven-year-old on modern physics. Individuals with distinctive backgrounds were recruited; a white-haired woman from Idaho was introduced on *Twenty-One* with this whispered voice-over: "She has a law degree. She is a retired major in the U.S. Army. She is now the director of the National Association of Business and Professional Women. When visiting in the Orient, she was captured by Chinese bandits."[21]

An extension of such creative casting was pitting stereotypical characters against one another to heighten dramatic conflict; as one blunt advertising agency memo put it: "Let the farmer become champion and find a good city slicker to compete against him in some other contest." The most successful oppositional casting was *Twenty-One*'s pitting of the slender, patrician WASP and Columbia University graduate student Charles Van Doren (his father was a Pulitzer Prize–winning poet, his mother an editor of the *Nation*, and his uncle a Pulitzer Prize–winning biographer) against Herbert Stempel, a "struggling" CCNY student from Brooklyn. *Broadcasting* reported the sales of the sponsor's Geritol (for "tired blood") up 40 percent in the twelve weeks surrounding Van Doren's appearances and the sales of Sominex (for "safe, natural-like sleep") up 69 percent. The producers arranged for several tie matches between Van Doren and Stempel before Stempel was told to deliberately incorrectly identify the Academy Award–winning picture of 1955—*Marty*. Stempel later revealed that after ordering a bad haircut for the new contestant, the program's producer selected an ill-fitting, discarded suit from Stempel's closet the night before Stempel's first appearance on the show. Furthermore, despite Stempel's marriage to the daughter of a Queens factory owner, *Twenty-One*'s producer-host, Jack Barry, told Stempel on the program, "I know how badly you need the money." After Stempel won a match, Barry, with unintended irony, told him in a slip of the tongue: "I know everyone congratulates me for the brilliant showing you made."[22]

The popular quiz programs of the 1950s also point to public ambivalence toward class, the role of intellectuals, and popular culture. Educators were especially popular as contestants; a Brooklyn school teacher appeared on *The $64,000 Challenge* in 1958 and told the host that his salary was $400 a month. The host responded incredulously: "After eighteen years of study, they pay you only $400 a *month*?" "That's correct," the teacher replied. The host: "It may be correct, but I don't think it's right, really. I won't get up on my soapbox, but see me after the show and we'll campaign together."[23]

The disingenuously apologetic "campaign" on behalf of US educators was most evident in the case of the genre's most popular hero, Charles Van Doren. As the champion for several months on *Twenty-One*, the soft-spoken graduate student received 2,000 letters a week, including 500 marriage proposals. He was promoted to assistant professor at Columbia and signed a $50,000 annual contract to make regular appearances on NBC's *Today* show to discuss poetry and other literary topics. One of *Twenty-One*'s producers boasted to the press: "He's the modern equivalent of the Renaissance man . . . he's what every woman wants her husband to be like." Van Doren's quiz show success landed him on the cover of *Time* magazine, which revealed that "he has never bothered to own a TV set" and wrote: "Just by being himself, he has enabled a giveaway show, the crassest of lowbrow entertainment, to whip up a doting mass audience for a new kind of TV idol—of all things, an egghead." Law school dean and broadcast researcher Roscoe Barrow explained to a Kiwanis Club audience in 1960: "The successful contestants were viewed as intellectuals or eggheads who had found an area in which they could be heroes, and it was satisfying to have intellectual heroes for a change."

If Van Doren's reign was spectacular, so too was his fall; after lying about the fraud to the press, the New York grand jury, and congressional investigators for more than a year, and evading a congressional subpoena for several days, he chose a packed House of Representatives chamber for his public confession. A repentant Van Doren told the committee: "I was able to convince myself that it did not matter what I was doing because it was having such a good effect on the national attitude toward teachers, education and the intellectual life." While most committee members offered testimonials to Van Doren's belated honesty, *Broadcasting* wrote of his appearance: "The television quiz era ended officially last Monday when its symbol took off his respected mask and showed the world a cheat." In the *New York Times*, Hans J. Morgenthau wrote that a "mendacious professor . . . is like the physician who, pledged to heal, maims and kills."[24]

The implicit model of knowledge constructed by the quiz programs is related to wider ideologies of knowledge and realism in popular television. John Tulloch has argued in *Screen Education* that British quiz programs operate to reinforce traditional nonfiction television's positivist epistemology as well as a rigidly hierarchical educational system. In the US quiz shows of the 1950s, knowledge represented the accumulation of discrete facts, atomized and offered unproblematically within a priori categories and levels of difficulty, presided over by the authority of college professors, bank presidents, and armed guards; the model of knowledge precluded reflection, explanation, or the activity of thought. Wendell Brogan, writing in the *New Republic* in 1955, attributed some of the appeal of the quiz programs to "an old Yankee spelling bee respect for the ability to answer questions of straight fact in non-controversial areas." *Commonweal* discussed Van Doren's popularity in 1957:

> It has been said that the TV quizzes, and Charles Van Doren particularly, have fostered a new respect for learning in this country. We fear not. With all respect for Mr. Van Doren, who is a highly intelligent and cultivated man, his performances have nothing to do with learning or with thought. Americans have always venerated the fact, and the quiz show has merely underlined this aspect of our culture.[25]

Stempel, compelled to respond with an answer he knew to be incorrect, responded to the producer's subsequent public defense of rigging on the grounds of the shows's "educational value": the knowledge displayed on *Twenty-One* was, according to Stempel, "esoteric garbage. A feedback system, a parrot system of throwing out a lot of irrelevant facts. Knowledge, unless it is correlated, has no meaning."[26]

The House committee hearings on the scandals were the most widely covered hearings of the congressional session and the most spectacular public hearings since the Army-McCarthy hearings of the early 1950s. Compounding the reactions to the scandals and the public denunciations of television was a coincidental series of business scandals in the industry. A New York City grand jury and congressional committees began investigations of commercial bribery—payola and plugola—in radio and television, discovering what one congressional report called "a situation that bordered on racketeering." In unrelated court proceedings, it was revealed that in February 1959, telefilm producer Hal Roach, Jr., and his partners, the new owners of the Mutual Radio Network, were paid $750,000 by the Dominican Republic dictator, Rafael Trujillo, in exchange for a year's worth of favorable network news coverage of the dictator. In 1958 an FCC commissioner, Richard Mack, resigned after admitting that he had accepted bribes in a station licensing case; and after several incidents involving expense-account padding, acceptance of industry gratuities, and illegal ex parte contacts, FCC Chairman John C. Doerfer resigned in March 1960.[27]

Adding to what Frank Stanton called the "pent-up discontents" triggered by the revelation of the rigged quiz shows were growing complaints over the death of what was already being called television's "Golden Age" of live drama. The 1955–56 season, hailed then as the beginning of a new age of "pure television" live dramas and spectaculars, appeared by the end of the decade to be the beginning of the quick death of such programming in favor of continuing-character telefilm series produced in Hollywood. The 1955–56 season marked a high point in scheduling instability, and the proportion of live prime-time programming fell from 50 percent to 30 percent the following year. The number of live anthology dramas on all three networks fell from fourteen in 1955–56, to seven in 1956–57, to only one in 1959–60.[28] The virtual extinction of the market for live television drama stirred bitter complaints from many of TV's most prominent writers. The national chairman of the Writers Guild of America, David Davidson, told the FCC in 1960: "Never in history have so many writers been paid so much for writing so badly." Television writer and critic Erik Barnouw summarized the mood of television writers when he told the commission: "I don't remember any time in the last twenty-five years when writers in general in the broadcast field have been as bitter or as disillusioned as they are at the present moment. . . . "[29]

The disappearance of live anthology drama often meant a perceived decline in the power and status of TV critics as well. John Crosby confessed in 1958: "After the first show, I don't know what to say about a western or a quiz show, and I don't know anybody else who does either."[30] Many prominent television critics echoed the writers' complaints about the direction of prime-time programming, complaints which found occasional echo from within the industry in 1957–58, when network television faced a national economic recession, apparent in the slow growth of advertising revenues, a near-saturation level of set ownership, and a plateau in audience viewership.

By 1959, however, the television industry was in healthier shape: pretax profits surged more than 30 percent; the network leader, CBS, celebrated its best year; and average station profit levels rose from 11.4 percent to 14.3 percent of sales. As *Broadcasting* wryly noted: "Broadcasters can cope with the great ethical and moral issues of the times without having also to worry about unusual economic troubles." A January 1960 article in *Television Age*, "TV Future Bright," noted: "In television the financial picture must be considered a rosy one. . . . As 1960 begins, television has reason to feel confidence in its future. In spite of the unfavorable publicity from the quiz scandals and the payola investigations, viewing continues at a very high scale." Looking ahead to the next decade, *Television Age* reported strong confidence among major television advertisers, equipment manufacturers, and networks: "The opinion seems unanimous—the future for America is a bright one, and television will have the most important of roles in fulfilling that future."[31]

Even the individual sponsors who supported and often controlled the tainted quiz programs seemed unscathed by the scandals; an article in *Sales Management,* "The Sponsor: More to Be Pitied Than Censured," reassured television advertisers that "it seems extremely unlikely that the sponsor's products will suffer in any direct fashion." In "Hardly a Scratch in TV's Image," *Broadcasting* revealed a public opinion survey containing the "startling result" of television's undisturbed public popularity, despite the quiz show scandals. The article quoted one respondent: "My only regret is that I didn't have a chance to get on one of the shows before they were discovered rigged."[32]

The quiz show scandals, breaking when the industry was enjoying renewed prosperity in the face of rising creative and critical complaints, probably had the effect of hardening industry defensiveness toward public criticism of any kind. One direct effect was a $600,000 public-relations campaign directed by the National Association of Broadcasters' new Television Information Office. The organization commissioned a survey of public attitudes toward the industry, placed advertisements in "highbrow" magazines highlighting cultural and public-service programming on television, and generally "helped put the quiz scandal storm in perspective," according to *Broadcasting.* An article in *Printer's Ink,* "TV Goes after the Intellectuals—but Gently," explained that the organization "has been concentrating on reaching the so-called intellectual audience" via sponsored research, public information, and print advertising. *Business Week* noted: "One thing the whole industry agrees on: the new Television Information Office, designed to create a greater public image of the industry, certainly has its work cut out."[33]

Some common claims by historians about the impact of the quiz show scandals on the structure of the television economy may be exaggerated. The decline of single sponsorship in favor of multiple sponsors for each program, the shift of prime-time program production from New York to Hollywood, and the control of program licensing and scheduling by the networks are developments which predate and overshadow the public calamities of the quiz shows, already anachronisms in their mode of production in the second half of the 1950s. The shows were broadcast live from New York when this practice was giving way to Hollywood-produced film programs; they were generally controlled directly by single sponsors when network licensing and participating sponsorship were becoming the rule. However, the scandals did provide a reformist gloss on long-running network efforts to wrest control of program procurement and scheduling from sponsors and advertising agencies. Because most of the shows implicated in the scandal were licensed by individual sponsors, network leaders claimed ignorance, even victimization, in the fraud. NBC president Robert Kintner told the Office of Network Study: "We were merely taken in by a small group of deceitful people," and claimed before the House Commerce Committee that "NBC was just as much a victim of the quiz show frauds as was the public."[34]

Behind some of the hyperbole in the critics' reaction was not only a widespread cynicism about network protestations of innocence, but also the end of a decade-long faith in the television networks as defenders of free expression, minority programming, and quality drama. Gould concluded that "their plea that they were 'deceived' along with everyone else is not persuasive." Independent producer David Susskind told the FCC in 1960 that the networks "used the national horror at the quiz show scandals as the excuse for establishing complete and absolute control of the programming. . . . "[35] The policies and behavior of the networks in the late 1950s clearly undermined the earlier view of them as special friends of television reformers. By the end of the decade, any hope in the networks as protectors of creative freedom or program balance seemed woefully naive.

With the exception of Louis Cowan's ungracefully handled resignation at CBS, the industry managed to contain the damage of the quiz show scandals, limiting it to lower-ranked personnel and peripheral practices of the business. Broadcast critic Charles Siepmann commented sarcastically on the various investigations of the television quiz programs:

> That a Committee of the Congress and the entire press should, of late, have found the moral jungle of broadcasting a rich game preserve and happy hunting ground is no matter of surprise to anyone acquainted with the industry. One might, though, question the genuine concern for the public interest of either group on this safari as one observes the particular wildlife on which they seem to have chosen to concentrate fire. The bag, to date, seems to comprise a large number of frightened rabbits, not a few skunks, and innumerable rats. But the big game seems, by some odd coincidence, to have escaped as targets of the noisy gunfire—if in fact this was ever aimed in their direction.[36]

Of the twenty-three persons indicted for perjury in the quiz show scandal, all but one were contestants.

Television critics responded bitterly to the lack of subsequent reform. As the public revelations began in October 1959, Gould associated the fraud with "the final phoniness of a troubled decade," commercial censorship of programming, an exodus of TV writers, and "the spreading virus of materialism" represented by "the awesome competitive pressures that everyone in the business feels." Despite this, Gould argued that "the quiz show scandals . . . may prove to be a blessing in disguise. Television no longer can afford not to care." One year later, however, he wrote bitterly: "The answer of TV to the supposed crisis has been just business as usual. The volume of tripe has grown." Eighteen months after the first revelations, television columnist Harriet Van Horne confessed: "Boy, was I a fool to believe the pious declarations made by the networks. I thought they'd have the decency to make amends for the lives they shattered with their sordid schemes that even involved children. The most disgraceful part of the whole thing is that the top executives learned absolutely nothing. . . . "[37]

In November 1960 *Variety's* television editor, George Rosen, wrote that "an exciting medium is going down the drain. . . . " At the end of the 1960–61 season, he wrote that "uninspired trivia . . . reduced the present season to a new low level of mediocrity. . . . "[38]

The extensive public hearings also highlighted a new set of industry attitudes toward television critics and the public responsibilities of commercial television. The scandals cemented industry responses to a half-decade of increasing critical attacks on the medium. The television industry, under the strengthened leadership of the three networks, offered new public definitions of its programming responsibilities, its creative workers, and its audience. The new positions mark the end point of a trajectory which began in the mid-1950s, and one dramatically opposed to that offered by writers and critics of the "Golden Age." NBC president Robert Sarnoff told the press in 1960: "I'm not sure I know what it is that has to be reformed. I don't think anyone has proved that bad television is harmful." His father, David Sarnoff, chairman of NBC's parent corporation, RCA, told Crosby: "We're in the same position of a plumber laying a pipe. We're not responsible for what goes through the pipe."[39]

Responding to critics, ABC president Leonard Goldenson asked the FCC in 1960: "Can we legislate taste? Can we make it a criminal offense to be mediocre? Shall we set up a commissar of culture?" A network and advertising executive, Max Wylie, remarked blandly: "There is nothing wrong with mediocrity if you are mediocre. Mediocrity is exactly right. Most television critics never take this into account." Robert Sarnoff complained, "If we listened to the eggheads, we'd be out of business in six months." In March 1959, Sarnoff told a convention of the National Association of Broadcasters that the critics' complaints of program mediocrity represented a more serious phenomenon: "We must understand that it is a minority distaste for programs chosen by the majority that has triggered the slogan of mediocrity—and we must label this slogan for what it really is, a failure to respect freedom of taste, an effort of the few to impose tastes upon the many."[40]

Not only were critics cultural elitists, but they also portrayed antidemocratic tendencies, at least according to Goldenson, who told the Office of Network Study in 1960: "Since we are a medium of mass communication, it seems to me that we should primarily be concerned with majority programming. What puzzles me a great deal about the critics of TV is their persistent attack on the fundamental concept of the vote of majority. . . . " *Variety* quoted a TV station owner's warning of "autocrats who would set up a cultural tyranny within the framework of democracy": "The attack may be expected to be sounded more frequently in the future. It has the appeal of championing plain folk versus the intellectual snobs who take a patronizing view, allegedly, toward what they call the tastes of the 'masses.' "[41]

Thus, the lasting changes brought about by the uproar over the quiz show scandals were not legal or regulatory reforms, which the broadcast industry was able to frustrate in Congress and at the Federal Communications Commission; neither were they structural or economic change within the industry. Rather, the scandals and the television industry's counterattack signaled a dramatic and lasting shift in the debates over the public-service responsibilites of broadcasters and in the expectations and prestige of creative workers in the industry. After the quiz scandal had ebbed from public attention, Gould wrote: "The scandal caused no lasting loss in audience size, or general acceptability of the medium. . . . In many ways the peril of TV is greater since the scandal. An industry that so simply survived a storm of such huge proportions is going to be less inclined than ever to see merit in proposed changes. The status quo has been undeniably hardened."[42] The growing cynicism indicated an increasing recognition that the problems of programming and public interest were embedded in the structure of commercial broadcasting itself. A veteran broadcast critic, Charles Siepmann, told the FCC in 1960 that the previous twenty-five years had seen "a significant and disastrous sea change" in industry perception and performance of public service responsibilities in broadcasting.[43] Many critics saw the quiz show fraud as a symptom of widespread sponsor interference in program matters; Barnouw told the commission that "the question is whether such decisions should be put to them in the first place. The real question is whether we can afford to have our culture and artistic life become a byproduct of advertising. My answer is that we can't."[44]

Many in the industry were equally blunt in response to such complaints; Max Enelow, the director of advertising for Philco, told *Advertising Age* in December 1959: "All the moralizing and preaching . . . won't convince the advertiser that he should pay the same millions for a ten rating that he does for a thirty, not as long as we have a system of commercial sponsorship. And what's more, all the laws and regulations that Congress and the FCC may pass won't do it either." The advertising executive explained that while

the airlanes belong to the people of the United States . . . the people have decided to sell those airlanes to the advertisers of the United States for commercial purposes. . . . Don't blame the advertiser for using every legitimate means to get full value for the millions he invests. . . . [If] this produces dull, sterile, imitative programming, don't blame the sponsors, blame the system.[45]

The quiz show scandals provoked a new and more polarized relationship between the television industry and its various critics, and an end to the hope, or illusion, of many for significant reform of US television within existing commercial and regulatory structures. The stalemated antipathy between commercial television and US intellectuals is perhaps the most lasting legacy of the quiz scandals, one which persists even in today's "cynical, or at least less gullible, age."

NOTES

1. Harry F. Waters with Michael A. Lerner, "Game Shows: America's Obsession—TV Cashes In," *Newsweek* 9 Feb. 1987:64–65; as history, this commentary is somewhat careless: it is at least an exaggeration to argue that more than a handful of prominent executive careers were permanently derailed by the scandals, and Matt Dillon's *Gunsmoke* had been on the air since 1955 and was already the number one program in 1957–58, the height of the quiz program's popularity.

2. Walter Shapiro, "What Ever Happened to Ethics," *Time* 25 May 1987:14.

3. Quoted in "He Who Throws Stones," *Broadcasting* 15 Feb. 1960:166.

4. Dalton Trumbo, "Hail Blythe Spirit! . . . ," *Nation* 24 Oct. 1959:245.

5. "TRB," *New Republic* 19 Oct. 1959:2.

6. *Chicago Sun Times* 29 Jan. 1960.

7. For accounts of President Eisenhower's news conferences of October 22 and November 4, 1959, see *Broadcasting* 25 Oct. 1959 and 9 Nov. 1959.

8. For the holocaust reference, see "Quiz Scandal Shows Broadcaster Must Control Output: Petersmeyer," *Advertising Age* 9 Nov. 1959:2; for the fears of taint and contagion, see "Quiz Shows Pose Big Money Questions to Ad Men, and the Answers Affect All TV," *Printer's Ink* 5 Sept. 1958:9, and "TV Quiz Doubts Threaten All Ads, Deens Tells 4As," *Advertising Age* 23 Nov. 1959:34; speech by Richard Salant, 15 Mar. 1960, copy in file 12-VI-A Broadcast Pioneers Library; quoted in James L. Baughman, *Television's Guardians: The FCC and the Politics of Programming, 1958–67* (Knoxville: University of Tennessee Press, 1985), p. 31; speech by Frank Stanton to the Academy of Television Arts and Sciences, p. 1, collection of the Television Information Office; for elaboration of industry fears of viewer dissatisfaction, see John P. Cunningham, " 'Creeping Mediocrity' Bringing Boredom to TV: It's Advertiser's Worry, Cunningham Warns," *Advertising Age* 2 Dec. 1957:65–67; William N. McPhee, "Working Paper: Suggested Research on the Potentialities of Television for CBS," quoted in NBC, *Television and Modern Marketing* Nov. 1960, collection of NBC Research Library, and "Videotown Ten Years Later," *Sponsor* 7 Dec. 1957:35, 43.

9. Daniel Seligman, "Revlon's Jackpot," *Fortune* Apr. 1956:239 (Seligman's article contains a very interesting profile of the company's leadership and marketing strategies as they related to television); Dick Bruner, "Networks Woo Revlon for *The $64,000 Question*," *Printer's Ink* 30 Oct. 1955:45; "*Printer's Ink* Shoots Some 64,000 Questions at Revlon: Interview with George T. Abrams," *Printer's Ink* 18 Nov. 1955:24; Kent Anderson, *Television Fraud: The History and Implications of the Quiz Show Scandals* (Westport, Conn.: Greenwood Press, 1978), p. 9. While Anderson's book contains a thorough chronology of the quiz show scandals, the present essay examines their significance in the context of broader issues: the 1950s industry and its critical and trade discourses.

10. "Some 64,000 Questions at Revlon," p. 24; "Revlon's Jackpot," pp. 136, 137.

11. "Networks Woo Revlon for *The $64,000 Question*," p. 45; *Variety* is quoted in "Revlon's Jackpot," p. 239; Anderson, pp. 34, 104; also see "Quiz Shows Stalked by Mr. DA," *Broadcasting* 1 Sept. 1958:42, for the estimate of time and production costs. The British-ITV version of *Twenty-One*, also controlled by Barry-Enright, was introduced in July 1958. It achieved high ratings but was dropped after charges of contestant coaching (later supported in a three-month official inquiry) on the part of the producers designed "to make the show more interesting." See "Rigging Charges Hit 'Twenty-One' in London," *Advertising Age* 10 Nov. 1958:2; "Probe Upholds Charge British '21' Was Rigged," *Advertising Age* 2 Mar. 1959:44. NBC's

purchase price of the Barry-Enright shows was never recouped as the scandal caused the programs to be pulled from the network's schedule.

12. "House Fans TV Quiz Ashes to Life," *Broadcasting* 12 Oct. 1959:82. The suspicions of one New York television columnist were aroused when the public-relations firm for *Twenty-One* told him that a planned profile of one contestant would keep another week. The contracts for EPI shows prohibited contestants from disclosing to the press their experiences in preparing for the program; see "TV Critics Say Libel Laws Delayed Quiz Show Expose," *Editor and Publisher* 17 Oct. 1959:13; "Crackdown on TV Programs? Quiz Hearing Rouses Talk of New Control," *Broadcasting* 12 Oct. 1959:27. Unhappy with the disparity in payoffs, the *Dotto* contestant went public with the incident anyway; see Weinberg, pp. 4–6; "A Sad Ending to the Quiz Era," *Broadcasting* 9 Nov. 1959:42; Peter Flint, "TV Quiz Kickback Laid to Two on Show," *New York Times* 9 July 1960:1; Paul Healy and Robert Thompson, "64G Sponsor Asked for Fix, Sez the Fixer," *New York Daily News* 4 Nov. 1959:3; "Quiz Scandal Spotlight May Alter Basic Structure of TV Advertising," *Advertising Age* 9 Nov. 1959:8, for an account of how the Revson meetings operated and of the department store plugola.

13. "Libel Laws Delayed Quiz Show Expose," p. 13; "Quiz Biz Starts New York Legal Fiz," *Editor and Publisher* 6 Sept. 1959:47, 56.

14. This chronology is summarized in the attorney general's report. William P. Rogers, *Report to the President by the Attorney General on Deceptive Practices in the Broadcast Industry*, reprinted in the *New York Times* 1 Jan. 1960:10; also see "House Fans TV Quiz Ashes to Life," p. 82. In October 1960 the grand jury heard testimony that lawyers for the quiz show producers urged perjury before the grand jury. See Dan Forst, "TV Grand Jury May Cite Lawyers," *New York Post* 18 Oct. 1960:5; and " 'Jury' Eyes Role of Lawyers in TV Quiz Probe," *New York Journal-American* 19 Oct. 1960.

15. Jack Gould, *New York Times* 10 Aug. 1955:51; George Wolf, "Exciting News for TV Clients," *Advertising Agency Magazine* 29 Apr. 1955:20; George Wolf, "New TV Programming Pattern," *Advertising Agency Magazine* 24 June 1955:27.

16. George Wolf, "Ordinary Folks, Heroes of TV Programming," *Advertising Agency Magazine* 2 Sept. 1955:23. The next month Wolf scorned ABC's Hollywood telefilm program strategy, noting that "critics and audiences seemed unimpressed with *Warner Bros. Presents* and *MGM Parade.*" George Wolf, "TV Program Outlook Bright As New Big Season Opens," *Advertising Agency Magazine* 28 Oct. 1957:22.

17. "Some 64,000 Questions at Revlon," p. 25.

18. "Making Money by Giving It Away," p. 31; "Quiz Shows Pose Big Money Questions to Ad Men," p. 10.

19. Jack O'Brian and Ralph Mahoney, "Purchased TV 'Plugs' at $30,000," *New York Journal-American* 15 Nov. 1959:1, 4.

20. "The People Getters," *Time* 25 Aug. 1958:65.

21. "64G Sponsor Asked for Fix, Sez the Fixer," p. 3, quoting producer Mert Kaplan's congressional testimony; see also "Making Money by Giving It Away," p. 27; *Twenty-One* 14 Nov. 1956, collection of the Museum of Broadcasting.

22. William M. Blair, "Pit Farmer against City Slicker, Ad Man Told TV Quiz Producer," *New York Times* 15 Nov. 1959:1; David Wise, "Secret Files Show Headaches with Rigged Quiz Gimmicks," *New York Herald Tribune* 15 Nov. 1959:1; "Making Money by Giving it Away," p. 27; "A Big Fake—Stempel," *New York Daily News* 4 Nov. 1959:42; House Fans TV Quiz Ashes to Life," p. 79; *Twenty-One* Oct. 1956, collection of the Museum of Broadcasting. Some quiz shows occasionally experimented with celebrity contestants, including a highly rated *$64,000 Challenge* which pitted Edward G. Robinson against Vincent Price on the subject of art, and one on which the uncoached son of Winston Churchill missed the opening, elementary question from the host. A memo from one advertising executive suggested re-

cruiting Bishop Fulton Sheen, SAC Commander Curtis Le May, Mickey Spillane, Ernest Hemingway, Boris Karloff (on the subject of children's literature), and J. Edgar Hoover; see David Wise, "Rigged TV Quiz Sought FBI Chief and Sheen," *New York Herald Tribune* 22 Nov. 1959:1, quoting a Revlon-BBD&O memo of December 27, 1956. Orson Welles appears to be the only invited celebrity contestant who refused on moral grounds, despite the offer of a guaranteed 7–12-week run and $170,000 from a producer looking for a "genius type"; see "Orson Welles Sez He Nixed Promise of TV Quiz Riches," *Variety* 28 Oct. 1959:1.

23. *The $64,000 Challenge* 7 Sept. 1958, collection of the Museum of Broadcasting, New York. A Hunter College political science professor who appeared on the rigged *Name That Tune* justified his cooperation and later silence about the fraud thus "As a lowly paid teacher I could use the prize money. . . . As a political scientist, I was anxious to see what makes a show like this tick." See "Why Prof Won on TV Quiz—And Why He Lost," *New York Post* 11 Nov. 1959:6; "Got Help, TV Prof Admits," *New York Daily News* 12 Nov. 1959:5; Stan Fischler, "On Fixed TV Quiz, Second Professor Reveals," *New York Journal-American* 11 Nov. 1959:5, quoted the professor's rationale for not reporting the rigging to the district attorney: "because no one asked me."

24. "Getting Rich on TV," *New York Times* 22 Jan. 1957:59; "The Wizard of Quiz," *Time* 11 Feb. 1957:44. In his speech, Barrow argued that the rigging of the quiz programs had indeed inflicted harm, not the least upon the general television audience: "It may also have lowered the moral tone of the community, for the young leaders of tomorrow may suspect that there is no difference between 'eggheads' and professional wrestlers," Roscoe L. Barrow, "The Rigged Quiz Shows and Payola Deceptions—Symptoms of a Lack of Responsibility in Broadcasting," speech before the Kiwanis Club, n.p., 1 Feb. 1960:1; collection of the Television Information Office. The full text of Van Doren's testimony was reprinted in the *New York Times* 3 Nov. 1959; "A Sad Ending to the Quiz Era," p. 40; Hans J. Morgenthau, *New York Times* 22 Nov. 1959:vi, 17; one letter to the editor of a New York newspaper complained: "I am truly disgusted by the TV quiz scandal. If the contestants had been just ordinary little people it would have been forgivable. But to have these big shots in the intellectual world bought and paid for, and so gutless that they couldn't face the music! How low can intellectuals fall? Is there no honor left in America?" Terry Smith, Manhattan, *New York World Telegram and Sun* 12 Nov. 1959:30.

25. John Tulloch, "Gradgrind's Heirs: The Quiz and the Presentation of 'Knowledge' by British Television," *Screen Education* 19 (Summer 1976):3–13; Wendell Brogan, "Television," *New Republic* 8 Aug. 1955:23; "The American Dream," *Commonweal* 22 Feb. 1957:525.

26. "Stempel in Rebuttal: Derides Producer's View That Quiz Show Had Merit," *New York Times* 10 Nov. 1959:42.

27. One article counted fifty-seven reporters plus camera crews at the hearings, and noted: "The female occupancy of the spectators section probably approximated the makeup of the televised quiz show audiences—about three women to each male." "Probe Seeks Way to Stop Quiz 'Fixing,' " *Editor and Publisher* 10 Oct. 1959:14; also see *Congressional Quarterly 1959 Almanac*, p. 744; for an account of the Mutual-Trujillo affair, see "Grand Jury Indicts Guterma Trio," *Broadcasting* 7 Sept. 1959:68–76, and "Guterma Bares Mutual Pact," *Broadcasting* 5 Oct. 1959:29–30. For an account of Doerfer's resignation from the FCC, see "Week of Shock, Sorrow," *Broadcasting* 14 Mar. 1960:31–38.

28. Joseph R. Dominick and Millard C. Pearce, "Trends in Network Prime-time Programming, 1953–74," *Journal of Communication* (Winter 1976):76; Frank Henry Jakes, "A Study of Standards Imposed by Four Leading Television Critics with Respect to Live Television Drama," diss., Ohio State University, 1960, p. 9.

29. Quoted in Erik Barnouw, *The Television Writer* (New York: Hill and Wang,

1962), p. 36; U.S. Federal Communications Commission, Office of Network Study, *Second Interim Report: Television Network Program Procurement Part Two* (Washington D.C.: Government Printing Office, 1965), p. 546.

30. *New York Journal-American* 1 Nov. 1959.

31. *Variety* 7 July 1960, quoted in Weinberg, p. 103. CBS reported its highest earnings in its 32-year history for 1959: see Columbia Broadcasting System, Inc., *Annual Meeting of Stockholders Report of the President* 2 Apr. 1960:1, collection of the Television Information Office; "Happy New Year," editorial, *Broadcasting* 28 Dec. 1959:74; "TV Future Bright," *Television Age* 11 Jan. 1960:21, 23.

32. Dr. Sidney J. Levy, "The Sponsor: More to Be Pitied Than Censured," *Sales Management* 6 Nov. 1959:46; "Hardly a Scratch in TV's Image," pp. 41, 48. Also see "Will the Hearings Hurt the Quiz Sponsors?" *Sales Management* 6 Nov. 1959; the magazine polled nine sponsors of quiz programs, all of whom reported being unhurt by the scandals.

33. "TIO's First Year: An Appraisal," *Broadcasting* 26 Sept. 1960:27–30; Philip N. Schugler, "TV Industry's PR Office Undertakes Rebuilding Task," *Editor and Publisher* 2 Jan. 1960:11, 47; "TV Goes after the Intellectuals—but Gently," *Printer's Ink* 16 Mar. 1962; *Business Week* 7 Nov. 1959:30.

34. Quoted in Fairfax M. Cone, *With All Its Faults: A Candid Account of Forty Years in Advertising* (Boston: Little, 1969), p. 267; NBC president Robert Kintner, testimony before the House Committee on Legislative Oversight, reprinted in an NBC press release, 5 Nov. 1959:3, collection of the Television Information Office.

35. *New York Times* 12 Oct. 1959, quoted in Weinberg, p. 79; FCC, 1965:553.

36. Charles A. Siepmann, "Moral Aspects of Television," *Public Opinion Quarterly* (Spring 1960):12–13.

37. Jack Gould, "Quiz for TV: How Much Fakery?" *New York Times Magazine* 25 Oct. 1959:74; Jack Gould, "TV Quiz Aftermath," *New York Times* 23 Oct. 1960, II:13; Van Horne is quoted in Harold Mehling, *The Great Time-Killer* (Cleveland: World, 1962), p. 53; for similar sentiments, see Mauringe Christopher, "Après le Déluge . . . TV Looks the Same Though Programs Alter," *Advertising Age* 14 Dec. 1959:87.

38. *Variety* 2 Nov. 1960, quoted in Weinberg, p. 153; *Variety* 7 June 1961, quoted in Weinberg, p. 278.

39. *Chicago Sun-Times* 21 Mar. 1960, quoted in Weinberg, p. 51; David Sarnoff is quoted in Richard Austin Smith, "TV: The Light That Failed," *Fortune* Sept. 1958:16.

40. Silverman is quoted in "Curtain Falls on FCC Hearing," p. 62; Wylie in Mehling, p. 27. Robert Sarnoff on the eggheads is quoted in Mehling, p. 17; and on cultural democracy in Solomon Simonson, *Crisis in Television* (New York: Living Books, 1966), p. 148.

41. "Curtain Falls on FCC Hearings," p. 60; "Haynes Blasts TV's 'Cultural Tyranny,'" *Variety* 14 Feb. 1962:34; see also Mary Ann Watson, "Commercial Television and the New Frontier: Resistance and Appeasement," diss., University of Michigan, 1983, p. 34, where Watson argues that by the fall of 1961, leaders of the three networks united in defense of industry practices around the ideas of "cultural democracy" versus government intervention.

42. *New York Times* 23 Oct. 1960, II:16.

43. "Moral Aspects of Television," p. 14–15.

44. FCC, 1965:751.

45. *Advertising Age* 14 Dec. 1959:88.

WHY WE DON'T COUNT

The Commodity Audience

Eileen R. Meehan

US intellectuals have little influence in shaping popular taste or in designing the cultural commodities that are mass-distributed to the US public. This is not simply a reflection of the esteem accorded to our intellectual minority by the general populace. Nor is it simply a reflection of differences in training, temperament, and taste that separate the professional intellectual from the average television viewer. Of the 86.3 million households owning television sets,[1] one can safely assume that only a narrow slice of those households shelter our intellectual minority, with a still narrower slice sheltering scholars of cinematic or televisual texts. Perhaps, as Dr. Frank Stanton of CBS argued,[2] our tiny numbers mitigate against a role for us in a democratic mass medium such as television. But where other nations have sought to ensure minority participation in mass media by creating structural openings in their media systems,[3] the commercial nature of the US system leaves few, if any, structural openings for minorities—intellectual or otherwise. In the US, then, intellectuals have no formal role in the multimillion-dollar industry that produces and distributes television to masses and intellectuals alike. In our television industry, intellectuals simply don't count.

But if we don't, who does? According to national networks, national advertisers, and national ratings firms, the answer is democratic in the extreme: the people count.[4] The preferences of millions of viewers, as scientifically measured in the ratings, determine what gets on and what stays on. Perhaps we may not like *Alf, Murder, She Wrote,* or *Wheel of Fortune,* but millions of people do, as demonstrated by the ratings. With raters measuring the people's choices in programming and programmers selecting shows that conform to these demonstrated preferences, then surely television reflects the public's taste.

All this rests on the claim that ratings are research—a claim that has been cultivated by raters in their promotional materials, in the trade press, before congressional committees, and in the mass circulation press.[5] If that claim is accurate, then the ratings firm's scientific sample is representative of television viewers. If that claim is accurate, then television programming reflects the forced choice behaviors of the mass of television viewers. That would mean that most people's preferences would count in the television industry, even if any particular individual was not in the sample. In short, we would all count, although only our forced choice behaviors would matter.

Most critics of television ratings and television taste have accepted the basic claim that ratings are research. Hence, their work has focused on the manipulation of network schedules to skew ratings, whether because of greed[6] or the desire to "prove" that a certain genre or particular show is not popular.[7] Others, equally accepting of the objectivity of ratings, have focused on the use of ratings to measure the naturally occurring viewership in order to package that viewership for sale to advertisers as the commodity audience.[8] But to accept the claim of scientificity without scrutinizing the historical development of ratings and the economic conditions that constrain ratings production is naive.

The purpose of this essay is to dissolve that naiveté. By examining the historical development of the market for ratings, I will demonstrate how ratings become fully commoditized through producers' manipulation of continuities and discontinuities in corporate demand for estimates of the commodity audience. I will show how economic self-interest restricts and reformulates measurement techniques, transforming these techniques from scientific measures into business practices, into corporate tactics in the struggle for market control, profitability, and low production costs. From this perspective, ratings do not count the viewers, but only the commodity audience which is saleable to national advertisers and networks. In fact, within the closed market where raters sell their commodities—the ratings—to national advertisers and networks, only the commodity audience counts. In this way, both intellectuals and masses have been defined out of this market and out of the audience. Neither intellectuals nor masses count.

Let me anticipate some objections: we all know that television is the massest of mass media. Millions of people watch television for eight to sixteen hours a day; programs are constructed to play to the lowest common denominator in taste and understanding. We all know that in millions of homes—maybe even our own—the set is not watched but remains on as constant soundtrack and moving wallpaper. We know all this as professional intellectuals, and we know it as everyday folks.

We know it, but does it make a difference? Do these behaviors, does this knowledge count? Consider another bit of common knowledge: television shows live and die by the numbers—that is, the ratings currently produced by the A. C. Nielsen Company and sold to national networks and national advertisers. These numbers are used by the networks to cancel shows, rearrange schedules, commission new shows, and set prices for advertising slots. The same ratings are used by advertisers to buy commercial time and target subgroups of consumers. The result is a cultural system run by magic numbers, numbers that shape content, creation, and availability. The question then becomes: Who counts in the ratings?

To answer that question, we need to develop a historical and analytic perspective on the macroeconomic structure of US commercial broadcasting. Constraints of space, however, preclude a full account, which would require a detailed examination of the internal struggles and national security connections of the Radio-Telephone Patent Pool, an essentially illegal cartel that dominated and defined US telecommunications from World War I into the 1930s.[9] Instead, I will look briefly at the Pool's radio operations directly after the Armistice. I will examine AT&T's innovation of "toll" broadcasting and the creation of corporate demand for audience measurements and program ratings in the late 1920s and early 1930s. I will analyze the structure of that demand and show how the measurement methods were selected by raters to both serve continuities in demand and manipulate discontinuities in demand.[10] I do this to demonstrate the artificial nature, the manufacturedness of the market for ratings, of the ratings themselves, and of the rating's object—the commodity audience. Finally, I will offer a brief observation on the people meter controversy.

The point of all this is to uncover the underlying macroeconomic structure that has set and continues to set the limits, parameters, and operating rules of national broadcasting as show *business*. In this corporate "game," players come and go. The balance of power between players shifts. But the basic structure of the game remains, and the longevity or success of any particular corporate player depends on its ability to adapt to and creatively manipulate the underlying structure.

TELEPHONY VS. RADIO: TAKING THE TOLL

So let me begin by noting that the Patent Poolers had divided the world into two territories: wired telephony controlled by AT&T and wireless or radio telephony controlled by General Electric (GE) and Westinghouse.[11] To manufacture equipment, AT&T had its wholly owned subsidiary, Western Electric; to distribute and sell radio equipment, GE and Westinghouse used RCA (co-owned by AT&T, GE, and Westinghouse). All three principals had research units, and all three dabbled in the experimental application of wireless telephony which we now call radio.[12]

Throughout World War I, the three had manufactured equipment for radio telephony for the armed forces, but the Armistice in 1918 meant a dramatic decrease in the military's demand for radio equipment. This left AT&T, GE, and Westinghouse geared up to produce radio equipment at levels that far exceeded civilian demand. At this time, radio was primarily a hobby that attracted college students, engineers, and tinkerers of all ages who built their own sets in order to communicate with other "ham" operators. GE and Westinghouse funneled their components through RCA into the home market where they competed with independent inventors but not with AT&T, since AT&T had agreed not to produce or sell radio sets in this market, just as its two partners had agreed to stay out of telephone manufacture. In 1922, GE and Westinghouse began selling fully assembled radios in the hope of expanding their equipment sales from do-it-yourselfers to the general consumers who lacked the ham's mechanical skills.

However, consumers had little incentive to buy radio sets in order to eavesdrop on conversations between hams or hear occasional experimental transmissions.[13] To persuade people to buy sets, manufacturers and retailers realized that they needed to provide something to hear on a regularly scheduled basis. Programs, then, were used to promote the sale of radio sets. Thus, radio broadcasting earned no direct revenues for itself; instead, it was an advertising device that earned indirect revenues by boosting set sales. The strategy was successful; sales rose from 100,000 sets in 1922 to 500,000 in 1923, and shot to 1.5 million only a year later.[14] Clearly, programming sold sets.

AT&T enjoyed none of the revenues from set sales. Despite this, the company remained active in broadcasting research and pioneered the use of long-distance telephone lines to link its station in New York (WEAF) to other AT&T stations. AT&T proposed to form a great chain of stations across the country that would serve as common carriers bringing to listeners the messages of any person or company that would pay the necessary "toll" for transmission. Rather than provide programs itself, AT&T would network the programs of any sponsor wishing to advertise its wares to a national listening audience. This proposal was the foundation of commercial broadcasting. It also signaled the start of a serious crisis for the cartel as AT&T sought to change the basic definitions upon which GE, Westinghouse, and AT&T had divided radio from telephony. AT&T essentially argued that toll broadcasting made radio a form of telephony and hence part of AT&T's territory.

The story of that crisis rivals the best spy fiction for intrigue, complexity, and drama. Unfortunately, that means I cannot delve into its web of detail;[15] suffice it to say that the outcome was a reaffirmation of the split between telephony and radio. AT&T would continue to monopolize telephony, but added to its activities the exclusive right to interconnect broadcast networks. GE and Westinghouse retained their hold on radio, especially in manufacturing. RCA secured a more independent role, taking over AT&T's network and coordinating those stations with GE's and Westinghouse's through RCA's new subsidiary, the National Broadcasting Company (NBC). The resulting NBC-Red and NBC-Blue networks would earn income by selling time to national manufacturers. These advertisers would produce programs to persuade consumers to buy their products, programs which listeners would receive free of charge.

This reorganization of the radio business was so promising that other networks were started on national and regional bases, with CBS emerging as NBC's strongest rival.[16] By 1927, then, through the struggles of private corporate interests, the basic structure of both radio and television broadcasting had largely emerged: three national networks, advertisers as the basic source of revenues, access to audiences as the basic commodity sold by networks. But if AT&T had solved the problem of direct revenue, the company had created a new problem by doing so—namely, how to figure out the cost of that access.

INFORMATION, PLEASE

The cost of such access hinged on advertisers' demand for listeners. However, because advertisers were being asked to pay per listener, not any listener would do. Clearly, the listeners worth paying for were those most likely to buy the product—in short, potential consumers. Since advertisers also bore the costs of programming, the number of potential consumers listening would have to be sufficiently large for advertisers to shoulder the combined costs of programming and access.

Advertisers, then, needed information about the radio audience in order to select a time slot that would reach their targeted subgroup, to assess the performance of their shows, and to evaluate the costs charged by networks for the time slot and its audience. Similarly, broadcasters needed information about the size and the value of the audience in order to both set and justify prices. Advertisers and broadcasters both needed information on the size and demographics of radio's audience in order to establish radio's ability to produce the right audience—an audience of consumers rather than of listeners.

This posed a problem: how to measure radio's productivity, that is, its ability to produce the invisible "commodity audience." The obvious solution was for CBS and NBC to measure their own productivity, reporting the aggregate numbers of listening consumers and describing the demographics of these consumers. The networks did this through their research departments which consistently found that radio drew vast audiences of eager consumers.[17] Such reports were used to justify the rates that networks charged advertisers.

For advertisers, however, these reports were simply promotional material. How could advertisers trust such glowing numbers when those numbers served the networks' economic self-interest? Since prices were tied to reaching the right audience in the right numbers, higher estimates of that audience's size meant higher prices. Although advertisers wanted fairly accurate demographics describing targeted listeners, their economic interests lay in methods of measurement that focused on the commodity audience yet underestimated the size of that audience, and thereby kept network prices down. This bifurcation of demand has persisted to the present. Advertisers and networks share an interest in ratings that measure audience *quality*; but their interests conflict over the accuracy of ratings that measure audience *quantity*.

In the face of the networks' self-reports, advertisers decided to do their own measuring. By 1928, the Association of National Advertisers (ANA) hired Archibald Crossley to devise a means to measure radio listening.[18] One year later, the ANA accepted Crossley's findings and officially institutionalized his suggestions in a new organization, the Cooperative Analysis of Broadcasting (CAB), which began operation in 1930. The CAB was directly under the control of the ANA, its members, and representatives of their advertising agencies. Using Crossley's method, CAB produced radio ratings that were circulated only to advertisers. Although the numbers usually leaked out to the networks and the trade press, CBS and NBC were barred by the ANA from buying the numbers and from using them in price negotiations or for self-promotion.

But if the circulation of CAB ratings was a problem for the networks, so too were the ratings themselves. Crossley's method favored the advertisers but offered no trade-offs to the networks. Let me briefly consider Crossley's methods and the socio-cultural setting in which he used them.

First, we need to remember that by 1929 radios had become a mass medium; more than 50% of the nation's homes were equipped with a radio, and sets were located in many public places (diners, bars, soup kitchens, etc.).[19] In all, 13 million sets had been sold, and sales had remained strong even during the recessions of 1924 and 1927 when other commodities had suffered sales decreases. Radio was well on its way to universality by 1929.

In contrast, telephony remained a rather somber medium. Still connected in the public mind with business and middle-class status, residential telephone subscription had nevertheless climbed to 41% of the nation's households.[20] While having a radio was taken for granted, having a telephone listing was still a mark of prestige. The acceptance of radio outstripped that of telephony so that radio homes were not necessarily also telephone homes. However, having a radio *and* a telephone was a mark of membership in the thoroughly modern, consumer-oriented middle class. Those were the homes that Crossley's methods targeted—not radio homes *per se,* but telephone homes with radios, the homes of the new consumer consciousness.

Crossley did this by using a telephone survey.[21] He randomly selected residential listings from directories and then called these households to inquire about their radio listening. Specifically, the interview followed a two-prong pattern: first, ask if anyone listened to the radio yesterday; then, ask for the titles of the shows and the names of the sponsors. Since many programs were only fifteen minutes long, Crossley was asking people to perform an incredible feat of memory. But it was not memory alone that served to bias Crossley's ratings in the advertisers' favor; social mores also skewed his results.

Crossley was dealing with a state of society whose code of conduct emphasized politeness, indirection, and avoidance of conflict in interpersonal relations.[22] When confronted by unpleasant situations, one tried to extract oneself gracefully, often by the use of polite lies. If one did not wish to speak with a particular telephone caller, one might be "indisposed" or "unable to come to the telephone" or forever "in a meeting." Often criticized as hypocritical, these conventions had important implications for Crossley's measurements. Should householders find onerous the task of detailing twenty-four hours' worth of listening for a perfect stranger on the telephone, they could politely escape the situation by suddenly remembering that they hadn't listened yesterday, that they had confused yesterday with the day before. Crossley could not tell real nonlistening from polite claims of nonlistening. Thus, reluctant respondents could systematically deflate the size of this middle-class audience. Indeed, ratings produced by these methods "found" that radio audiences were rather small.

Given Crossley's reliance on telephone households, his reports were systematically limited to those consumers that advertisers wanted. Given the interaction of socio-cultural codes and the difficulty of the task, his methodology deflated the number of listeners. In this way, Crossley and CAB produced ratings limited to the type of audience that advertisers wanted and delivered a quantity of audience that suited advertisers' interest in depressing network prices. No wonder the networks were quick to support an alternative, independent ratings service.

HOOPLA AND HOOPERATINGS

As early as 1930, C. E. Hooper contemplated a challenge to CAB.[23] The problem was to craft a measurement method that would rebalance the interests of both advertisers and networks in a way that would make the new ratings more attractive than CAB's numbers. Hooper's solution was based on changing economic conditions and on the bifurcation of demand. Where networks and advertisers shared an interest in better measures of the middle-class consumer at a time of downward socio-economic mobility, Hooper offered a sampling method that would further constrict the definition of the commodity audience. Where networks' interests conflicted with advertisers' interests over the accuracy of estimates of audience quantity, Hooper offered networks an interview that increased the number of listeners. To balance this, advertisers were offered a higher quality of listener at a lower price. Since Hooper sold his ratings to all comers—advertisers, agencies, networks, and local stations—he could decrease the cost for any single unit of information by spreading the production costs over more ratings consumers. (This is, of course, a central tenet of mass production.) Hooper gambled that advertisers would accept higher estimates of audience size (and thus higher network prices) if the sample was more carefully constricted to potential consumers and if unit costs were low. Essentially,

Hooper promised both higher quality and larger quantity in ratings production, but at lower prices.

He achieved these manufacturing goals by selecting a particular form of measurement. Like CAB, Hooper used telephone listings to restrict his sample to the middle class. With the Great Depression in full swing, residential telephone subscription had fallen 10% in only three years (1929–1931).[24] But Hooper further restricted that sample by using only urban directories. The big cities, although seriously hurt by the Great Depression, remained centers of consumption, especially when compared with small towns or rural areas.[25] The concentration of people in cities meant that the cities housed more potential consumers, more members of the middle class with sufficient disposable income who were willing and able to purchase name-brand goods. From an economic perspective, ratings that measured the preferences of the urban middle class were more cost-efficient than ratings that measured the entire middle class. Consumers in New York City, Chicago, and San Francisco were a more valuable audience than consumers in Bangor, Sheuyville, or Rio Osso. In this way, Hooper further restricted who counted, but did so in a manner consonant with advertisers' preferences.

Hooper also redesigned the interview.[26] Rather than ask people to recall yesterday's listening, he first inquired whether the radio was on when the telephone rang. If so, the respondent was asked to identify the program and sponsor. Respondents were also asked for simple demographic information about themselves and anybody else who might be listening with them. Finally, they were asked if they had been listening fifteen minutes earlier; if so, the same information was solicited for that program. These changes had an immediate effect on the results that Hooper gathered: suddenly people were listening to radio in droves. Clearly, this played into the networks' interests.

From 1932 to 1936, Hooper struggled to oust CAB from its monopoly over ratings. On the scientific front, he conducted a series of proprietorial studies to demonstrate the superiority of his interview, christened the "telephone coincidental," over Crossley's "recall interview." This culminated in Chappell and Hooper's *Radio Audience Measurement*[27] in 1942, the definitive attack on the recall interview, published long after that method had fallen from advertisers' favor. The book, however, does provide a systematic account of Hooper's criticisms.

Hooper argued that the CAB's method was flawed by its reliance on the human memory. In contrast, his coincidental method was cast as directly tapping the listening behaviors of respondents. To illustrate this, Hooper contrasted his ratings with CAB's, arguing that differences in ratings reflected the weaknesses of CAB's methodology. He claimed that the ability to remember a program varied with the age of the program, its previous status in the ratings, and the status of its network. Hooper reported that CAB's methods favored older shows on NBC that had long placed in CAB's top ten. People simply remembered them better having been exposed to more information about them and thus reported them as the shows heard the previous day. But memory was even more slippery than that; Hooper also found that people could not reliably recall when they were home. However, by substituting memory for direct report of behavior, he promised a scientific breakthrough to advertisers and networks alike.

The ANA responded to this challenge by reorganizing the CAB and changing its interview to more closely resemble Hooper's coincidental. This *de facto* admission of methodological inferiority may have improved its measurement of the commodity audience, but it did little to stem the tide of Hooper's criticism or his in-house studies.

On the promotional front, the self-effacing image dictated for the CAB by ANA was easily overwhelmed by the outgoing Mr. Hooper. Known as both "Mr. Ratings" and "Hoop" in the trades and the popular press, Hooper challenged CAB's ratings secrecy by holding weekly press conferences in which he would unveil the ratings winners. "Hoop" was often featured in the gossip columns, particularly in Walter Winchell's column after Winchell dubbed Hooper's product the "Hooperatings." While he constructed his public persona as the approachable, affable, and honest fellow in the ratings business, Hooper used these public occasions to assert the objectivity and scientificity of his product. Hooper established himself as a "show biz personality," but always as a personality whose work was in scientific audience measurement.

Overall, his blend of showmanship and scientificity complemented his careful balance of advertiser and network interests. And after four years of two raters producing different ratings for the same shows, public confidence in ratings generally may have been shaken. Certainly the business of buying and selling audiences had suffered from the wealth of contradictory ratings. Hooper's stance as the objective scientist provided a rationale for dumping CAB: it was not that ratings *per se* were faulty, only the particular methods used by the partisan CAB. By 1936, Hooper emerged as an objective third party, able to mediate between advertisers and networks through the scientific production of ratings. By 1936, then, Hooper effectively monopolized ratings production for national, networked radio. Hooperatings were *the* determinant of sponsors' programming decisions and *the* basis for network prices. This monopoly remained firmly entrenched until 1942.

THE HIDDEN ECONOMICS OF RATINGS

With Hooper's success, the macroeconomic structure of the market for ratings is set into place. First, there is a bifurcation of demand. Demand for ratings is unified in that advertisers and networks want measures only of potential consumers; this means that the audience to be measured is only a subgroup of the listening public. However, demand for ratings is disunified by the connections between price and size of the saleable audience; a big audience means a higher price. Thus, if ratings underestimate the size of the commodity audience, they work in the advertisers' economic interest; if ratings overestimate the size of the commodity audience, they work in the networks' economic interest. This discontinuity in demand opens up the possibility of independence for a ratings producer. And that possibility is strengthened by the fact that advertisers and networks need only *one* set of numbers as the basis for their transactions.

This crucial second element in the macroeconomic structure is made clear by the CAB-Hooper rivalry. Different methods will produce different ratings for the same program, partly as an artifact of the methods themselves. For Hooper, the selection of a particular method was a decision guiding both ratings production and the marketing of Hooper's particular brand of ratings. The selection of a method both positions a company in the ratings market *and* differentiates that company's numbers from those of its rival. Because ratings serve as the basis on which audiences are bought by advertisers and sold by networks in routinized transactions, having multiple, contradictory ratings for any single time slot complicates and disrupts the routine business of buying and selling the commodity audience. Only a single set of official numbers is required. This predisposes networks and advertisers to accept a monopoly in ratings production. If a ratings firm can take advantage of this predisposition and of bifurcation in demand in a way that satisfies continuities while balancing discontinuities in demand, that firm may gain control of national ratings production.

Such control also depends on the ability to discredit the methodology of any prior monopolist. Crucial to such an attempt is the selection and redesign of measurement methods to emphasize those groups of consumers that are targeted by advertisers. This brings up the worrisome problem that ratings may, in some sense, be tautological—that the design of the sample and measurements may determine the results. It should be clear from the analysis that the selection of the sampling method sets the definition for the commodity audience, which excludes some of the listening public in deference to continuities in demand. It should also be clear that methods can favor some networks over others, thus making the state of network rivalry another factor that must be weighed by ratings firms. However, for a ratings firm to remain independent and thereby retain its control over its own pricing policies, production costs, and profits, it must be able to sell its product to all comers interested in the commodity audience regardless of whether these purchasers are rivals in advertising, manufacturing, or broadcasting. Bitter rivals read the same reports, and for the ratings firm to succeed, such rivals must be willing to subscribe to those reports for years. This provides an economic reason for relative honesty in ratings within the limits set by economic considerations. The ratings may fairly be said to reflect the forced choice behavior of the commodity audience within limitations set by continuities in demand, market conditions, production costs, and changing conditions in the general economy.

The effect of this tripartite structure is important, but usually hidden behind a wall of clichés. We are constantly told by the networks, advertisers, and ratings monopolist that free programming is a reflection of what we want, that scientific measurements determine how people "vote" on content, that programming is just a mirror of public taste. If you don't like what's on, that means you're out of step with the people. While this may insult the populists among us, it is somewhat flattering for intellectuals to be out of step with those who find their cultural satisfaction in reruns of *Gilligan's Island* or repeats of *Entertainment Tonight*. However, whether insulting or flattering, the effect of such claims is to brand as elitist those who would change the programming policies of national, networked television and to trivialize serious criticism of televisual programming by making it a function of membership in the intellectual elite.

By analyzing the macroeconomic structures beneath the programming, it becomes obvious that the clichés have no basis in economic reality. Ratings are tools designed by firms to achieve economic success—control over ratings production. Forms of measurement are selected on the basis of economic goals, not according to the rules of social science. Not everybody is wanted by advertisers, so a ratings firm must try to exclude those persons who are not in demand. Programs, then, reflect the forced choices of the commodity audience when its constituents select between networked offerings. The differences between the commodity audience and the public viewership, between manufacturing the commodity audience through ratings and measuring the public taste through social research, cannot be overemphasized.

I have concentrated on the emergence of the market for ratings and the commodity audience. For most analysts of the televisual text, if the names Crossley and Hooper ring a bell, the chimes are very faint indeed. Yet Crossley and Hooper, in conjunction with the national advertisers and national networks in the 1920s and 1930s, effectively defined the market structure for the production of two commodities still crucial to broadcasting and cable—commodity ratings and the commodity audience.

THE TRANSITION TO TELEVISION AND METERS

Into this preexisting market structure came the best-known of the ratings firms, the A. C. Nielsen Company (ACN), which entered the market in 1942 and achieved its monopoly position in 1950. It is important to note that ACN did not invent the market for ratings. The company spent six years developing its measurement techniques and promotional strategy[28] in order to challenge Hooper's monopoly of that preexisting market. Like any firm entering a new market, ACN crafted its production techniques in terms of existing demand structures, established products, and current rivalries.

Three examples are particularly noteworthy in suggesting the care that ACN took in constructing its measurement practices as business strategies. Like Hooper, ACN promoted its method as the latest breakthrough in the scientific measurement of audiences and produced numerous in-house studies to show the superiority of the meter over any other method, including the telephone coincidental. But by grounding its ratings in a metered sample, ACN enjoyed a promotional advantage over Hooper in the technology-minded postwar era. ACN's Audimeters were promoted as impartial machines recording the facts about viewers, facts that viewers might be embarrassed to reveal to interviewers. The meters thus produced numbers untainted by human interaction. Furthermore, meters, unlike interviews, could be protected by patents and patent litigation. Thus, ACN could draw on the legal intricacies of the patent system and infringement litigation to forestall the entry of other firms into metered ratings production.[29] This gave ACN a new defense against rival ratings firms.

But ACN's strategies were also mindful of rivalries between clients, both within and across its client industries. For example, the metered sample went beyond the cities, where Hooper still found NBC preferred over CBS, to include the small towns and rural areas of the US, where CBS outdrew NBC. But where the particular sample might favor CBS, ACN's meters generally favored networks by treating tuning as if it were listening, thereby skewing audience estimates overall in the networks' favor. Finally, the metered sample offered advertisers a minute-by-minute account of audience tuning over a twenty-four-hour period. This capability would become more important to advertisers as they moved out of sponsorship and into spot advertising on television.

Importantly, ACN did not achieve industry dominance until after the networks took effective control over their schedules and after the nation entered the post–World War II economic boom. With economic imperialism abroad and real economic growth at home—plus the employment and inflationary effect of the limited war economies generated by various "police actions"—mass consumption in the US entered an expansionist phase. As more categories of people became bona fide consumers, advertisers sought media with greater coverage of the general population than ever before. The postwar boom shifted housing patterns so that more of these consumers became suburbanites, thus shifting advertisers' focus away from marketing strategies that emphasized urban living to those of suburban domesticity. Placing television at the center of the family room, the networks (NBC, CBS, and ABC rising out of NBC's divested second network) cast television in the role of the massest mass medium. With many advertisers reluctant to finance the expense of televising their radio shows but eager to advertise on television,[30] the networks took control over their schedules. Replacing sponsorship with the practice of selling sixty-second spots to advertisers, they manipulated their program schedules according to "flow," and created programs designed to appeal to the lowest common denominator.[31] With millions more people promoted to consumer status and suburban living and with network control over scheduling, ACN's particular methods of measurement suited the shifting relations between advertisers and broadcasters.

The upshot was simple and of great significance for television programming. In 1950, ACN achieved monopoly status when its two years of rivalry with Hooper culminated in its buying his national ratings operation and securing a promise from him that his company would never again produce national ratings for television or radio. With Hooper pushed out of national production, ACN's fixed sample of 1,200 designated households became *the* audience. And that sample was based on radio homes—not television households—some of which had participated in ACN's field tests as far back as 1938.[32] The company simply waited for its radio sample to buy television sets and then metered the televisions. This pool of radio households formed the backbone of the ACN sample until the mid-1960s. With investigations by the House Special Subcommittee on Investigations, Federal Trade Commission, and Federal Communications Commission plus pressures from advertisers and networks (especially ABC and NBC) for an updated sample, ACN announced plans for raising its quality controls on ratings production generally and for updating its sample specifically to reflect changes in housing patterns since the end of World War II.[33] ACN promised to begin turning over sample households and to turn over the entire sample by 1970, replacing the old radio homes with households that would be younger and more urban. The effect on programming was dramatic: ex-vaudevillians and radio stars who had moved from network radio to network television were replaced by a flood of youthful protagonists dealing with modern problems in urban settings—resulting in television's "Year of Relevance."[34] However, despite such turnover and regardless of increases from 1,200 to 1,700 households over the years, the definition of the commodity audience has remained synonymous with the people in the ACN metered sample. Only their forced choice preferences count.[35]

THE NEW SELECTIVITY: PEOPLE METERS

A downshift in economic conditions, changing relations between networks and advertisers vis-à-vis cable and satellite superstations, and emerging rivalry in ratings production, however, have had significant effects on the industrial definition of the commodity audience. The confluence of these forces has produced a redefinition that uses cable subscription as a barrier to inclusion much as CAB and Hooper once used telephone subscription, thereby narrowing the definition of the commodity audience and introducing a new selectivity into the ACN ratings operation. To see how this affects us and the definition of who counts, I will briefly review the current state of affairs.

With the advent of cable and superstations, the number of effective television networks has more than tripled for the 35,444,000 households subscribing to cable television.[36] The households paying for this expansion of channel choice constitute roughly 41% of the total 86.3 million television homes. Access to cable subscriptions, however, is neither randomly nor universally available to every television household. In some municipalities, city government and potential cable operators have disagreed on terms, typically leaving an area unwired as long as a franchise is not granted. In other areas, cable operators have bypassed opportunities when the potential for profit seemed surpassed by the high costs of capitalization involved in wiring a small town or rural area. While this has created a space in the cable industry for small companies similar to the "mom and pop" operations of 1950s CATV, the industry remains dominated by large companies that have secured franchises across the nation (called multiple system operators or MSOs in the trade press). Control over the cable industry has been concentrated in the hands of these MSOs, most of which are themselves divisions of even larger media conglomerates.[37] Thus, cable is generally available where cable operations are deemed profitable by MSOs and their parent corporations. And profitability is determined by the relations between cost of capitalization, density of potential subscribers within the population, and the changing balance between the ability of local government to require services and federal commitments to deregulation.

When MSOs do make cable available to a community, only about 50% of the households usually subscribe to the service. Cable subscribers, then, are households with sufficient discretionary income and sufficient interest in television programming that they pay for access to expanded television service. This separates them from ordinary viewers and marks them as active consumers. With 41% acceptance nationally, this pool of cable subscribers is now sufficiently large enough to merit special attention from advertisers. Yet the pool is also somewhat selective since subscribers must live within economically attractive areas and must pay monthly fees for service. Presumably, after subscribing to cable service, these households will organize a significant slice of their leisure around watching television. In this way, cable subscribers have come to be regarded by advertisers as an increasingly desirable part of the viewership.

But where advertisers have come to regard cable with interest, networks have not. With 40–50% acceptance, cable has attracted serious interest from advertisers and seems posed to expand the oligopoly that networks have long enjoyed in the distribution by expanding the number of available channels. Previously, advertisers had little interest in paying for ratings that included cable channels. Network demand for ratings did not include measures of rival cable channels, particularly during the period when regulation forbade network participation in cable. When neither advertisers nor networks wanted the numbers on cable, there was little in the marketplace to encourage ACN to measure cable viewers.

However, with cable's subscription rate reaching acceptable levels, advertisers' interest expanded to include cable consumers. Also, the proliferation of cable channels created a new clientele for ratings, ranging from the superstations (WTBS, WGN, WOR, KTVU) to satellite-distributed channels (ESPN, CBN, FNN, MTV, etc.), some of which were wholly or partially owned by the networks (CBS Cable Arts, A&E). Eventually, ACN was persuaded by Turner Broadcasting System's willingness to pay for extra measures to begin reporting cable as part of television's commodity audience. Thus began the official decline in network audiences.

We are now beginning to see the cumulative effect of these shifting relations between networks, broadcasters, cablecasters, and advertisers. At a time when classes are polarizing into yuppies and yuffies, when the middle class is increasingly pushed into the underclass, when wealth increasingly flows into the hands of the sparsely populated ruling class, cable subscription in the late 1980s provides the sort of barrier that telephone subscription provided in the late 1920s and early 1930s. Cable subscription can be used as a guarantee of consumer status; hence, cabled households are more in demand by advertisers even as cable channels seek to purchase more cable ratings.

With these pressures on ACN, compounded by the entrance of aggressive new competitors (AGB and Percy) pushing people meters, ACN has turned to a metering technology that deflates the numbers in a sample that emphasizes consumers, i.e., to people meters in a sample emphasizing cable. Here the task discourages long-term viewers from recording their viewing, as people are expected to press a button every fifteen minutes to record their presence, without any Skinnerian reinforcement. Further, ACN has adjusted its sample to the new balance in the marketplace by emphasizing cable households in the installation of its new people-metered sample.

The networks have fought this redefinition of the commodity audience and gained some concessions for the short run.[38] At this point, ABC agreed to pay ACN $500,000 to gain various considerations, including the right for its ratings to be based on households reporting useable data and not on the number of households with people meters or designated for the people meter sample. ACN has agreed to make the same service available to NBC and CBS. However, AGB's recent withdrawal from the US ratings market will probably weaken the networks' bargaining position.

The current trend suggests that ACN's people meters will in the long run eschew broadcast households to embrace cable households as the commodity audience. Network programming practices will thus necessarily shift as the networks and the satellite-distributed channels begin competing for the newly redefined commodity audience. This should produce another programming shift, à la the Year of Relevance, but whether that shift will mean an increase in the number of forced choices or a greater diversity in the content of those forced choices remains to be seen.[39] However, the driving force behind such a change will again be essentially economic, not cultural.

WHO COUNTS

The implications of this analysis are startling. Unless you have a meter, you don't count. Unless you live in a cable area and subscribe, you have almost no opportunity to count. In market terms, then, the Great American Public—washed or not, intellectual or mass, textual analyst or couch potato—is irrelevant. All that counts are the meters. The decision to install the meters is a function of demand in the closed market for ratings. There, advertisers, networks, and now cable channels buy ratings from a ratings firm whose success rests on the ability to serve continuities in demand, to manipulate discontinuities through measurement practices, and to design measurement practiced as strategies for market control. This means that ratings and the commodity audience are themselves manufactured in the strictest sense of the word. And it is only the manufactured commodity audience, measured by commodity ratings, that counts.

In social scientific terms, the metered group is not a scientific sample of the viewing public since it is not randomly selected from and not representative of that public. Hence, the forced choice behavior of the metered group cannot be generalized to the viewing public. Nor can the choices of that metered group be taken as representative of public taste. In short, the massest of mass media, television, is programmed for a narrow slice of the total viewership—for the commodity audience.

Thus it is macroeconomic structure—not taste, not training, not temperament—that determines who counts in television.

NOTES

1. United States Bureau of the Census, *Statistical Abstract of the United States* (Washington: GPO, 1978), p. 534.

2. Frank Stanton, "Parallel Paths," in *Culture for the Millions?* ed. Norman Jacobs (1959; Boston: Beacon, 1964), p. 90.

3. For examples, see Anthony Smith's discussion of Dutch broadcasting in *The Shadow in the Cave: The Broadcaster, His Audience, and the State* (Urbana: University of Illinois Press, 1973), pp. 264–78; Gertrude J. Robinson, *Tito's Maverick Media* (Urbana: University of Illinois Press, 1977); and Armand Mattelart and Seth Siegelaub, *Communication Liberation, Socialism*, vol. 2 of *Liberation and Class Struggle* (New York: International General, 1983).

4. Perhaps the strongest articulation of this view is by Arthur C. Nielsen, Jr., *If Not the People . . . Who?*, an address to the Oklahoma City Advertising Club, June 20, 1966. See also Stanton, "Parallel Paths." For a slightly cynical presentation of the same argument, see Paul Klein, "The Men Who Run TV Aren't That Stupid— They Know Us Better Than You Think," *New York Magazine* 25 Jan. 1971:20.

5. Cf. A. C. Nielsen Company, *Everything you've always wanted to know about TV ratings (but were maybe too skeptical to ask)* (Northbrook, Ill.: A. C. Nielsen Company, 1985); Arbitron, *Understanding and Using Radio Audience Estimates: Inside the Arbitron Television Report* (New York: Arbitron, 1985); testimony given by representatives from A. C. Nielsen Company, C. E. Hooper Company, Arbitron, Sindlinger & Co., Trendex, Plus, and Bideodex first to the US Congress, Senate, Committee on Interstate and Foreign Commerce, *Television Inquiry, Part 7: The Television Ratings Services*, 85th Congress, 2nd session, June 1958 (Washington: GPO, 1959), and later to the US Congress, House, Committee on Interstate and Foreign Commerce, *Broadcast Ratings*, Hearings before the Special Subcommittee on Investigations, 88th Congress, 1st and 2nd session, 1963–1964 (Washington: GPO, 1964 and 1965). See also US Congress, House, Committee on Interstate and Foreign Commerce, *Evaluation of Statistical Methods Used in Obtaining Broadcast Ratings*, House Report 193, 87th Congress, 1st session, 1961 (Washington: GPO, 1961), generally known as the Madow Report.

6. Erik Barnouw, *The Sponsor: Notes on a Modern Potentate* (Oxford: Oxford University Press, 1978); Harry J. Skornia, *Television and Society: An Inquest and Agenda for Improvement* (New York: McGraw-Hill, 1965), p. 120.

7. Erik Barnouw, *Tube of Plenty: The Evolution of Television* (Oxford: Oxford University Press, 1975), p. 160 on dramatic anthologies; Barnouw, *The Sponsor*, pp. 101–109 on the episodic series; Laurence Bergreen, *Look Now, Pay Later: The Rise of Network Broadcasting* (Garden City: Doubleday, 1980), p. 173 on anthologies and *Omnibus*; and Danae Clark, "The State vs. Asner in the Killing of Lou Grant," *Journal of Communication Inquiry* 11.2 (Summer 1987):87.

8. Dallas Smythe, "Communications: Blindspot of Western Marxism," *Canadian Journal of Political and Social Theory* 1(1977):1; Graham Murdock, "Blindspots about Western Marxism: A Reply to Dallas Smythe," *Canadian Journal of Political and Social Theory* 2(1978):109; Bill Livant, "The Audience Commodity: On the 'Blindspot' Debate," *Canadian Journal of Political and Social Theory* 3(1978):91.

9. The definitive account remains that of N. R. Danielian, *AT&T: The Story of Industrial Conquest* (New York: Vanguard, 1939).

10. Demand is often defined in one of three different ways: as the desire, willingness, and ability of a buyer to purchase a particular good (cf. Douglas Greenwald and Associates, *McGraw Hill Dictionary of Modern Economics* [New York: McGraw Hill, 3rd edition, 1983], p. 126); as the quantity of a good or service that a buyer or group of buyers desire at the prevailing price (David W. Pearce, *The MIT Dictionary of Modern Economics* [Cambridge: MIT Press, 1986], p. 100); or as the amount of a commodity or service that will be bought at a certain price (Alan Gilpin, *Dictionary of Economic Terms* [London: Butterworths, 3rd edition, 1973], p. 49). None of these dictionary definitions capture the sense of the term that emerges from Adam Smith, *The Wealth of Nations*, ed. Edwin Cannan (London: Methuen, 1961), where Smith clearly sees demand, supply, and market transactions as human processes—that is, as negotiated, argumentative, conspiratorial, and fractious (see vol. 1, pp. 144 and 278; vol. 2, p. 284). Recapturing Smith's notion of demand, then, allows one to thoroughly examine the demand for ratings, discovering in it a complex and sometimes contradictory expression of vested interests that both conflict and coincide. For ratings, this is particularly important since ratings form the basis for a second transaction between the buyers of ratings, national advertisers, and networks, in which the price demanded by networks rests squarely on the ratings. To capture some of the complexity in demand for ratings, I have selected the phrase "continuity in demand" to indicate those parts of demand where the interests of national advertisers and national networks coincide. By extension, to indicate where their interests diverge, I use the term "discontinuity in demand." This seems consonant with Smith, but it also draws on the spirit, if not the phrasing, of Paul A.

Baran and Paul M. Sweezy, *Monopoly Capital: An Essay on the American Economic and Social Order* (1966; New York: Monthly Review Press, 1968), pp. 79–217; John Eaton, *Political Economy* (New York: International Publishers, 1979, new revised edition), p. 29; Karl Marx, *A Contribution to the Critique of Political Economy*, ed. Maurice Dobb (New York: International Publishers, 1981), pp. 27–53 and 188–99, originally published in German in 1859; Karl Marx, *Capital*, vol. 3 *The Process of Capitalist Production as a Whole*, ed. Frederick Engels (New York: International Publishers, 1967), pp. 171–98, originally published in 1894; and Howard J. Sherman, *Elementary Aggregate Economics* (New York: Appleton, 1966), pp. 28–63.

11. The Patent Pool was originally composed of American Marconi, AT&T, its wholly owned subsidiary Western Electric, GE, Westinghouse, and United Fruit. American Marconi was forced to sell out to its fellow poolers when the Navy Department refused to return American Marconi's ship-to-shore stations after the Armistice on grounds of national security. United Fruit restricted its operations and its radio applications to its plantations in Central America. In the United States, the division of industrial territories was reflected in corporate policies on equipment: while AT&T offered its equipment for rental only, GE and Westinghouse sold both transceivers and receiving sets outright. Besides Danielian's *AT&T*, this account is drawn from the following texts: William Banning, *Commercial Broadcasting Pioneer: The WEAF Experiment* (Cambridge: Harvard University Press, 1946); Erik Barnouw, *A Tower in Babel: A History of Broadcasting in the United States to 1933* (Oxford: Oxford University Press, 1966); George Blake, *The History of Radio Telegraphy and Telephony* (1928; London: Arno, 1974); John Hammond, *Men and Volts: The Story of General Electric* (Philadelphia: Lippincott, 1941); Hiram L. Jome, *Economics of the Radio Industry* (Chicago: Shaw, 1925); W. Rupert Maclaurin, *Invention and Innovation in the Radio Industry* (New York: Macmillan, 1949); Paul Schubert, *The Electric Word: The Rise of Radio* (New York: Macmillan, 1928). The aggregate analysis, however, is entirely my own.

12. For an insider's account of AT&T's radio operations, see Banning.

13. Early broadcasts were generally organized around materials that were freely available (Barnouw, *Tube of Plenty*, pp. 27–31). Pioneering broadcaster Frank Conrad, a Westinghouse employee, became well known for his "evening phonograph concerts" (ibid., p.21), which occasionally included recitations by his sons. One Conrad concert was reported as a news story in an advertisement by the Joseph Horne Department Store for a $10 radio. Similar phonograph concerts were offered by electrical engineer Fred Christian in Hollywood, contractor Fred M. Laxton in Charlotte, North Carolina, and others. Some pioneers, such as Professor Earle M. Terry of Madison, Wisconsin, and William E. Scripps, publisher of the *Detroit News*, reported weather, news, and sports events as well as playing phonographs. Occasionally, public speakers visited these pioneers or were visited by them, resulting in transmissions of church services, sermons, uplifting talks, and political oratory.

14. United States Bureau of the Census, *The Statistical History of the United States from Colonial Times to the Present* (New York: Basic, 1976), p. 796.

15. See Danielian, *AT&T*, or an excellent account of the negotiations given by Dane Yorke, "The Radio Octopus," *American Mercury* 23(1931):385.

16. See Bergreen, *Look Now*, p. 50.

17. Some of CBS's internal studies on radio audiences included *Does Radio Sell Goods?* (1931), *Has Radio Sold Goods in 1932?* (1932), *Ears and Incomes* (1934), and *Listeners at Half Cost* (n.d.). NBC's offerings included *Little Books on Broadcasting*, series 1–12 and A–F (1927–1931), *Straight across the Board* (1932), *Improving the Smiles of a Nation: The Ipana Story* (1928), and *A New Measurement of the Size, Location, and Occupations of NBC Radio Audiences, Supplemented by Dealers' Opinions of Radio Advertising* (n.d.).

18. The discussion of Crossley and the CAB is drawn from Archibald Crossley,

Watch Your Selling Dollar (New York: B. C. Forbes, 1930); reports from Cooperative Analysis of Broadcasting: *The Invisible Audience: First Four Month Comprehensive Report* (New York: CAB, 1930); *Station Area Studies* (New York: CAB, 1933); *Ten Years of Network Program Analysis* (New York: CAB, 1939); Mark James Banks, "A History of Broadcast Audience Research in the United States, 1920–1980, with an Emphasis on the Rating Services," diss., University of Tennessee, Knoxville, 1981; A. B. Blankenship, *Professional Telephone Surveys* (New York: McGraw, 1977); Donald Lee Hurwitz, "Broadcast Ratings: The Rise and Development of Commercial Audience Research and Measurement in American Broadcasting," diss., University of Illinois, Urbana, 1983; Eileen Rose Meehan, "Neither Heroes nor Villains: Towards a Political Economy of the Ratings Industry," diss., University of Illinois, Urbana, 1983; and numerous articles in the serial trade publications *Variety, Broadcasting,* and *Advertising and Selling* for the years 1929–1930.

19. United States Bureau of Census, *Statistical History,* p. 796, and Frederick Lewis Allen, *Only Yesterday: An Informal History of the 1920s* (1931; New York: Harper, 1964), p. 137.

20. United States Bureau of the Census, *Statistical History,* pp. 783, 784.

21. See Crossley, etc., cited above.

22. Allen, p. 73; Boorstein, *The Americans: The Democratic Experience* (New York: Vintage, 1974), p. 525.

23. The discussion of Hooper and CEH is drawn from Matthew N. Chapell and C. E. Hooper, *Radio Audience Measurement* (New York: Stephen Daye, 1944); *Hooperatings Hi-lites* (CEH's newsletter); CEH's testimony to the Senate Committee and House Subcommittee investigating ratings; Banks, *History of Broadcast Audience Research*; Hurwitz, *Broadcast "Ratings"*; Meehan, "Neither Heroes nor Villains"; numerous articles in the serial trade publications *Variety, Broadcasting,* and *Advertising and Selling* for the years 1930–1946; and "Behind the Ratings System, Part V: Hooper Riding the Big Radio Room," *Sponsor* 18 Oct. 1945:42.

24. United States Bureau of the Census, *Statistical History,* pp. 783, 784.

25. See Boorstein, *The Americans,* p. 89; Malcolm P. McNair, "Trends in Large-Scale Retailing," *Harvard Business Review* 10 (1931):6; and Irwin M. Heine, "The Influence of Geographic Factors in the Development of the Mail Order Business," *American Marketing Journal* 3 (Apr. 1936):127–30.

26. See *Hooperatings Hi-lites*; Chapell and Hooper, *Radio Audience*; CEH's testimony before the Senate and House; and the Madow Report for details of the methodology.

27. Chapell and Hooper, *Radio Audience*; for an analysis and concise summary of their case, see Blankenship, pp. 11–14.

28. The discussion of Nielsen and ACN is drawn from A. C. Nielsen, Sr.'s, published writings: *Advances in Scientific Marketing Research* (Chicago: ACN, 1944), *New Facts about Radio Research* (Chicago: ACN, 1946), *A Researcher Replies* (Northbrook, Ill.: ACN, 1963), and *Greater Prosperity through Market Research: The First Forty Years of the A. C. Nielsen Company* (Northbrook, Ill.: ACN, 1963), originally given as an address to the Newcomen Society, Chicago, Apr. 30, 1964; testimony by ACN representatives before the House and Senate; the Madow Report; Banks, *History of Broadcast Audience Research*; Hurwitz, *Broadcast "Ratings"*; Meehan, "Neither Heroes nor Villains"; numerous articles in the serial trade publications *Variety, Broadcasting,* and *Advertising and Selling* from Jan. 1930–Aug. 1988.

29. See particularly testimony of Albert Sindlinger to the House Subcommittee and memoranda introduced into the record by Subcommittee counsel in the questioning of ACN's representatives, pp. 1592, 1596, 1587–603.

30. See Barnouw, *Tube,* pp. 190–95 on NBC's innovation of selling spots, and *Sponsor,* pp. 45–48 on the early move to network control; see Bergreen, *Look Now,* pp. 159–240 on network schedules.

31. See Klein, "The Men Who Run TV," p. 20, and Bergreen, p. 208; for an analysis of the cultural meaning of "flow," see Raymond Williams, *Television: Technology and Cultural Form* (1974; New York: Schocken, 1975).

32. See the questioning of ACN representatives by House Subcommittee 954–1618.

33. See ACN testimony, pp. 954–1019, House Subcommittee, pp. 1068–1618.

34. Barnouw, *Tube of Plenty*, p. 430; Morris Gelman, "A New Search for Relevance Next Season," *Variety* 17 Nov. 1969:52, 56; George Swisshelm, "CBS Inking of 3 New (Old) Stars Seen as Tipoff That Rube Image May Be Shucked in Next 2 Years," *Variety* 1 Oct. 1969:35.

35. The term "forced choice preferences" is widely used in research in psychology and marketing. It describes a situation in which respondents are required to select a single option (or good) from a limited number of options (or goods). The resulting selection is a choice, taken as reflecting a preference, but it is not a truly free choice since the range of possibilities is determined by the experimenter's interests. Skornia, *Television and Society*, p. 120, and Klein, "The Men Who Run TV," p. 20, extend the notion of "forced choice preference" to television viewing in the discussion of ratings and programming (120). The viewer picks one program from the roster that the networks have selected to offer. Instead of reflecting the desires and tastes of viewers, such forced choice selections are taken to reflect the least offensive program (Klein's LOP principle) or the program that resonates with the lowest common denominator of social experience. Most critical researchers would add to this an analysis of how the networks' economic agenda in selecting programming then feeds back to shape personal and cultural preferences in programming. For examples of such analysis see Philip Elliott, *The Making of a Television Series: A Case Study in the Sociology of Culture* (London: Constable, 1972, and Beverly Hills: Sage, 1979), or Herbert Schiller, *The Mind Managers* (Boston: Beacon, 1973), pp. 8–31 and 79–103.

36. United States Bureau of the Census, *Statistical Abstract*, p. 714.

37. The issues of corporate control, technologies of distribution, and diversity of programming/information have been taken up by critical researchers in a number of forums. For an analysis suggesting that economic concentration and new technologies will lead to more highly targeted and fractionalized commodity audiences, see Oscar H. Gandy, Jr., *Beyond Agenda Setting: Information Subsidies and Public Policy* (Norwood, N.J.: Ablex, 1980). For an analysis suggesting that the outcome will be a redesign of television as "more of the same" programming delivered to slightly fewer viewers, see Eileen R. Meehan, "Technical Capability vs. Corporate Imperatives: Toward a Political Economy of Cable Television and Information Diversity," in *The Political Economy of Information*, ed. Vincent Mosco and Janet Wasko (Madison: University of Wisconsin Press, 1988), and "Towards a Third Vision of the Information Society," *Media, Culture, and Society* 6 (1984):257.

38. At this point, directly prior to the 1988 fall season, ACN continues to install people meters with a projected sample of 4,000. The networks have received guarantees that houses will be turned over every two years rather than the three-to-five-year period originally envisioned by ACN, and that more households with children will be included in the people meter sample. ABC will receive rebates if the number of households in tabulation does not reflect the national population in terms of county size, men 18–49, women 18–49, and children 2–11. It is noteworthy that AGB has ceased operations in the US, claiming insufficient support from the networks, as the trade press indicates that the networks' ability to secure concessions from ACN rested on the threat of supporting AGB. For the trade discussions of the networks' attempts to secure concessions from ACN over the people meter sample, see Morrie Gelman, "Gloom Looms for TV Webs As Woes Grow," *Variety* 8 July 1987:55, 71; Morrie Gelman, "NBC First Up at Bat with Peoplemeter: No

Other Choice Available Now," *Variety* 29 July 1987:95, 118; Tom Bierbaum, "CBS' Poltrack Sez Meter Cooperation Key for Success," *Variety* 12 Aug. 1987:56, 84; Elizabeth Jensen, "Guarantees Yield Nielsen ABC-TV Pact—Will Have to Pony Up Extra $500,000," *Variety* 23 Sept. 1987:123, 154.

39. Compare Gandy and Meehan on programming. The possibility that cable channels will be programmed according to formats brings up serious issues of diversity and choice. The main question is clear: Will such formatting result in narrowcasting to consumers who fall in highly specified demographic groups, or will it result in slightly different content distributed to slightly fewer people? Where Gandy argues for the former, noting the ideological significance of such narrowcasting, Meehan suggests that media conglomeration, MSO control of cable systems, advertiser demand for generalized consumers, and the costs of narrowcasting militate against that practice. Perhaps some illumination on this question might be shed by the case of radio formats.

TECHNO-ETHICS AND TELE-ETHICS

Three Lives in the Day of Max Headroom

Andrew Ross

In November, 1987, four weeks after ABC canceled its primetime *Max Headroom* show, a video pirate in Chicago commandeered the signals of two local TV stations to make an unauthorized appearance in the guise of the video cult personality Max Headroom. The pirate broadcast skit, inaudible for the most part, ended with "Max" exposing his bare buttocks to be paddled by a fly swatter wielded by a woman off-screen. An extraordinary and expensive feat of video hacking was thus presented in the miscreant hacker spirit of adolescent delinquency. But the pirate Max's chastisement at the maternal hand was a trifling blow compared to the possible prison sentence facing the pirate himself. And as the *Chicago Tribune,* ever strong on law and order, pointed out, punishment by death was the penalty for such a crime in the futuristic TV world of *Max Headroom,* where justice is wholly bound over to laws protecting the proprietary flow of information, and where it is meted out in the Network Courts. In fact, not so long before on *Max Headroom,* a network prosecutor had actually argued the case against signal-zipping:

> [Zipping] is a threat to television, to our lives . . . we are talking about *interruption.* When decent, honest television-loving people cannot watch a *Shopping Spree* without these savage attacks on their viewing freedom, we have to ask this question. Are we being too lenient? When our wives and daughters cannot shop from their own homes in peace, we must ask—Is consumerism itself under attack?

Such a conceit, like many others in the show which were directly leveled at television's business interests, depends for its irony on a certain degree

of audience cynicism about commercial television's not-so-glorious historical mission of providing its sponsors with a human market. Week in, week
out, this primetime appeal to an audience's bad attitude toward TV did
little to boost ratings, however, and the show, which had established a cult,
if not a broadly popular audience, was canceled in mid-season.

TECHNO-ETHICS

But the concern, in primetime and at the FCC, about acts of video piracy
is no joke. In fact, it reflects the crisis in property law generated over the
last two decades by the newfound economic status of electronic information
systems. The urgency and uncertainty with which property laws have been
redefined to cover the ownership of "intangible" information in the form
of transmitted electronic blips have been matched only by the explosive
increase in techno-crime, running at a reported level of $10 billion a year,
while most of it goes unreported by corporations and government agencies
anxious to avoid exposing the vulnerability of their security systems.
Techno-crime is a glamorous and painless activity for career criminals and
saboteurs alike, and it has penetrated every sphere of traditional criminal
activity while creating many new variants for the postmodern security state
organized around the new economic principles of electronic funds transfer
and information trading. Exotic operations such as logic bombs, trojan
horses, trapdoors, salami techniques, and check kite simulations and modeling go hand in hand with such strategies as superzapping, scavenging,
piggybacking, impersonation, data diddling, interception, and other well-
known forms of information and credit fraud. At one end of this spectrum
are motivated political groups, including terrorist and foreign espionage
outfits, who steal, erase, or alter politically significant information, or else
sabotage the facilities of military or corporate command centers. At the
other end is the celebrated subculture of juvenile pranksters or trespassers,
whose tightly articulated hacker's ethic—which condones harm to corporations but not to individuals—is in danger of losing whatever juridical
immunity it once enjoyed, now that career criminals habitually cover their
tracks by posing as hackers. In the information sphere of a control society
that seems to be aimed, theoretically at least, at interlocking systems of
deep surveillance, local deterrence, and the global management of low-
intensity conflicts, the securing of logically safe data environments has become a political priority and a huge growth industry based upon data
encryption techniques.[1]

Accompanying the rise of this imaginary monolith of a security state has
been the organized concern of hi-tech intellectuals (manifest in groups such
as Computer Professionals for Social Responsibility) about the need for a
special ethics among technocrats working in the information industries and
research spheres. Beyond the shifting terrain of legality and illegality, they
say, we have to learn new standards of responsible conduct in our use of

information technology; we need to reformulate what's right and what's wrong, especially in a world in which human and social relations increasingly are endlessly reprogrammable, after the fashion of human/machine interfaces. Ethics is very much back on the agenda for intellectuals in a technocracy where efficiency and rationality are seen as presiding, without passion, over a regime of instrumental problem solving. In fact, ethics is the form taken by politics in a modern capitalist bureaucracy of the sort which seeks legitimation through scientific and technical expertise. In this paper, I will be concerned with how television represents its own place in our technocratic consciousness, and how it articulates techno-ethics in its own domestic form of *tele-ethics*.

Because ethics is associated with a process of maturational learning, its illegitimate forms are often cast as infantile or juvenile, as in the case of the hacker's naive commitment to free and egalitarian access to information; a libertarian ethic that condones, finally, those Robin Hood–like guerrilla acts of wealth redistribution, from the information-rich to the information-poor, that make such popular news copy. This is a naughty idea, for which the pirate "Max," for example, has his bottom spanked. It is an idea that is associated with a body as yet untutored and undisciplined in the pragmatic world of sexuality and power, a body that has not yet developed expertise which meshes with the system rules. In his primetime show, the sexual meanings of Max Headroom's lack of a real body are displaced elsewhere. He is the computer-generated memory image of a real person, the telejournalist Edison Carter, and so his access to memories of sexual activity is more or less complete but is unsupported by carnal knowledge. In this respect, his sexual incompetence mirrors and matches the adolescent curiosity of his creator, the sixteen-year-old tech nerd Bryce. Max, however, has had three lives, or three roles so far to play on US television: on network primetime, on a cable talk show, and in Coca-Cola time. In the autonomous space of his own cable talk show, then, Max's lack of sexual self-possession is given fuller expression and is often presented with camp imperiousness, as here in his confrontation with Dr. Ruth Westheimer:

> DR. RUTH: Max, I have a question for you. How can you masturbate without hands? Where's your answer?
> MAX: (abashed at first, then swelling with mock pride) I hire people to do it for me.

Here, at least, is one solution to the cybernetic version of the mind-body problem. But it also tells a story about how machines mediate sexuality and power. Max's inflated show of sovereignty is a parody of the old power of the autocrat industrialist in the new technocratic world, where machines, however smart or intelligent, are still serviceable, especially to those who own them, and who can afford to hire labor to service them. If Max's autoeroticism is just another fantasy of technical self-sufficiency, then it is a fantasy—a very technocratic fantasy—that nonetheless belongs to someone else, someone with the money and the power to use it to legitimize his or her own interests.[2] This is why part of the bad mythology of the information technocrat is the perennial adolescent and social pariah whose nerdy sexuality is arrested forever in "bachelor mode," and who thinks of sexual difference in terms of differences in hardware. His (this mythology is almost wholly masculine) monastic commitment to the defense of the tech faith is fully integrated, and is supposed to be immune to the realm of ethical judgments. Bryce, Max's primetime creator, is the representative of this bad mythology, who says, "I only invent the bomb, I don't drop it." For him, the human brain is an information processer, like any other, and so his sense of morality is confined to that which can "compute"; "right" and "wrong" are nonempirical concepts, although they can, at a stretch, be calculated according to laws of probability.

> EDISON: Life is more than just an interactive systems analysis.
> BRYCE: Not really, it's a matter of information. Once we collate our ideas, life will be much simpler. It's a matter of number-crunching.
> EDISON: Life is based on something more than logic. It's based on feelings. Switching off feelings makes you a byte less human. . . . What if you create an artificial intelligence that disagrees with your principles?

Bryce, however, is unregenerate. He is a graduate of the Academy of Computer Science, an elite school for teaching techchild prodigies mastery of and loyalty to the principles of cybernetic wisdom. Ethics for him is a gray area, lost somewhere in the abyss that separates logic from the swamp of subjective opinion. In addition to receiving lectures from Edison, Bryce is maternally chastised for treating people like machines by the show's representative of the good mythology of the technocrat, the career professional Theora, whose adult application of technology is socially well adjusted, and who brings a woman's sense of pragmatism to a boy's fantasy milieu of computer microworlds, cybernetic animals, and simulated war games.[3]

Bryce's bad attitude toward fellow humans is an adolescent stereotype of the positivist philosophy of AI which views smart (and now "brilliant") machines as the next step in evolution. The adult version of this technophilia is more often associated with covert fantasies of global domination/liberation. On the one hand, the prophetic bravado of the AI experts has been seen as a scary expression of instrumental rationality, the culmination of the reign of technological domination over a rationalized social world, freed from its servitude to Nature at the same time as it is delivered into the bondage of Science.[4] Behind the hubris of the AI pundits lies the Enlightenment's promise of a more rational regime of truth, justice, and power, wielded by intellectuals and experts and not by old-style despots and capitalists; in front of it lies the heady fantasy of the fully automated battlefield. Behind the promise of a postindustrial leisure utopia lies the likely result of the ultimate division of manual and mental labor—a vast deskilled population for whom knowledge and power are always located elsewhere, in the remote memory banks and integrated decision making of the new knowledge-processing technology. And for anyone with even the slightest knowledge of labor history and the long social agony, for working people, of industrialization and proletarianization, today's sub-culture of hi-tech AI wit that flourishes around the idea that "people are machines" retains a legacy of awfully bad taste.[5]

There is another story to tell, however, about the recent history of tech-nocratic autonomy in a knowledge society. It is one that cannot be so easily trivialized by the caricature of the adolescent control freak, whose relation to his body is invariably one of self-loathing. This caricature is a folkloric legacy from the Golden Age of hacking among MIT students in the late fifties and early sixties. Their philosophy of decentralization, free access to machines and information, and "computing for its own sake" as well as for social improvement was aesthetically fleshed out in the West Coast com-puter counterculture of the seventies.[6] There, the delinquent ethic of hack-ing was rearticulated in the adult language of computer liberation. Alternative communication networks, knowledge co-ops, and community memory facilities run on populist principles and united by the vision of a harmonious cybernetic eco-system sprang up in response to the demands of the time for a participatory politics. Electronic populism took on the contours of a New Age fantasy, fashioned out of medievalesque or Middle Earth mythologies of natural and industrial magic (in contrast to the mili-tary—Star Wars orientation of the MIT fantasy microworlds, financed from the beginning by the Department of Defense). The opposition of this com-munity-minded culture to the knowledge monopoly of the business ma-chine establishment, especially IBM, was to be most visibly and most ironically played out in the commercial struggle over the market for per-sonal computers, first secured by the countercultural crusaders behind Ap-ple. Apple's software was free, in accord with the hacker commitment to making available the technology of personal liberation. The ideology of IBM was not so user-friendly, and its domination of the information world was easily demonized as neo-totalitarian. To this day, Apple runs an ad-vertising campaign which identifies IBM as a Big Brother monolith, while IBM has long since responded by recuperating, with the kind of inscrutable logic that is often manifested by huge faceless corporations, the "little guy" image of Charlie Chaplin, complete with all of its potential anti-industry meanings generated by *Modern Times*.

The alternative, even oppositional, spirit of the hacker ethic lives on in bulletin boards and community information networks. But the cutting edge of its research avant-garde in the universities and institutes is still funded, as it always has been, by military-industrial interests, government and corporate alike. It is these interests which profit from the fractured code of professional responsibility to which scientists, as professional technicians, subscribe when they sell their skills to the highest bidder. Increasingly, the politics of scientific pressure groups and journals is based on a principled refusal of government funding for explicitly military-related research. But the call for a professional techno-ethics is usually more abstractly aimed at the protection of the privacy, sanctity, and human dignity of the individual in an age of massive public surveillance, where the information stored in corporate and government data banks far exceeds the limits deemed appropriate in a society that honors individual rights.[7]

Critiques of the decision-making regime of the technocrat which present themselves as ethically opposed to positivism or utilitarian instrumentality can often be as disembodied and remote from questions of power as the most stereotypical "laboratory mentality." The ideological claim of technocracy, after all, is to rule without passion or social bias, in other words, to be above political interests that are grounded in moral visions. In practice, that claim is everywhere compromised by the material and political interests of technocrats themselves, who, as citizens, consumers, parents, etc., occupy many more subject-positions than that of the professional technocrat alone. So, too, it is obscured by the fact that the social legitimacy of technocrats cannot be secured by expert competence alone; competence has to be applied "on behalf of the interests of those from whom legitimacy is sought," in other words, the nontechnical officials and owners.[8] Thus, the principled refusal of certain kinds of state funding on the grounds of professional integrity or autonomy is often the work of a left hand that doesn't want to know what the right hand and other parts of the body are doing. Technical competence and expertise is never simply applied, it is always exercised in the name of ideological interests—more consumer gratification, easier access, greater control—and in the service of those who can pay for it. It is in the gray area between the scientific humanist conscience and the myth of professional autonomy that ethics (the requisite binary code of an age of binary technology) comes to represent the professional's legitimacy in a hegemonic system where power is negotiated through contractual responsibilities and not exercised by bureaucratic fiat.

TELE-ETHICS

The primacy of ethics is nowhere more evident than in the case of representations of how television is produced in a corporate, technocratic world where the same ethical themes are pronounced again and again. Humans or Ratings. Truth or Profit. Edification or Entertainment. Public or Private. Service or Cost Efficiency. Giving the People What They Want, or Giving Them What's Good for Them, and so on. When liberal Hollywood takes the high ground, in such films as *Network* ("the story of Howard Beale, the first man to be killed for having bad ratings"), *Broadcast News*, and *The Running Man,* it usually depicts television at a distance, as an inevitably degenerate industry in which such ethical choices are always resolved for the worst. When television addresses these ethical themes, in many of the MTM shows, for example, it appeals to the everyday dialectic of anguish and satisfaction faced by culture professionals in a technocratic hierarchy whose scale of expertise is warped to conform to the rules of pricing and profits.

More generally, broadcast TV is permeated by a discourse of self-criticism, some of it stylized showbiz, like the convention whereby a performer will say "My producer will kill me for saying this, but . . . "; some of it slightly more risqué, as in the case of the recent critique of General Electric, owners of NBC, from within the confines of the David Letterman show; and some of it outrightly fractious, as in the widely publicized "struggle" of the CBS News Division to maintain its autonomy from the Entertainment Division. In this respect, television's self-criticism is more than just a self-sustaining ritual or spectacle of liberal guilt. It also constitutes the visible level at which labor conflicts between performer-professionals and manager-owners-capitalists are manifest to the public eye. This political conflict is represented by the code of tele-ethics, which allows professionals to believe that not everything they do must be determined by its exchange value, just as political conflicts are represented in the code of techno-ethics which encourages professionals to believe and act as if machines are not infallible. Tele-ethics denies the principle of the inevitability of profits; techno-ethics denies the principle of the inevitability of a posthuman future.

In *Max Headroom,* there is a more or less direct encounter between the humanistic conscience of tele-ethics and the scientific conscience of techno-ethics—or "the two cultures," as they used to be known. Naturally, the show, which features the activities of the beleaguered but prestigious news team of a leading TV network, works to resolve the resulting contradictions. On the one hand is the liberal consensus that the commercial television of the future, for the most part, will be awful but that responsible telejournalism will always be able to redeem some of its prestige. On the other hand is the liberal consensus that the rule of computational intelligence will be despotic but that our essential humanity will prove superior. Of course, these turn out to be quite compatible, but this can be achieved and demonstrated only by a "failure to compute" within the narrative, in this instance, by the character and function of Max himself, the wayward mutant "soft machine" offspring of these two ethical systems. Max is supposed to be a purely videoactive program which can also draw upon the store of Edison's memories in order to learn about human behavior. He turns out to be a program with a human glitch, whose circuits start randomizing the instant he utters his first sounds—"Mama . . . mama . . . mama . . . max" (it sounds maternal but turns out to be a self-reference, in keeping with his mercilessly narcissistic personality). Consequently, he circulates uncontrollably around the television and other telematic systems, making unpredictable appearances as a TV celebrity with such a popular following that his commentary has an instant effect on ratings.

Similarly, in real-time TV, Max won't go away; even when his network show was canceled, he cropped up in commercials, on his cable talk show, on other people's talk shows, in rock videos, in acts of video piracy, and in comic strips, including the Doonesbury series which featured the president as the recursively inane Ron Headrest. Incessantly hyped, he became an icon, with a human face, of an age of telematics—the conjuncture of information-processing and telecommunications systems. But his celebrity owed just as much to his popular reception as an electronic folk hero who somehow beats the system, or at least mobilizes a set of erratic, often critical, often nonsensical, meanings that cannot be readily contained; in other words, he is seen as beyond the control of his technocrat creators.

What is curious about this popular image is that a good deal of what Max represents is not at all heroic, alternative, or subversive; in fact, he presents himself as cowardly, shamelessly mainstream, and despicably narcissistic. His true ambition is to be a doyen of entertainment, and he delights in all of the schlockiest rituals of the world of TV showbiz. On his talk show, his guest list is often composed either of personalities whose celebrity rests upon their own excessive self-promotion—Robin Leach, Dr. Ruth, Don King, Ron Reagan, Paul Shaffer, Penn and Teller, Grace Jones, Jerry Hall; camp icons, like William Shatner and Mary Tyler Moore; musical freak shows such as Bobby McFerrin; or the most gimmicky of comedians, including Emo Phillips and Gilbert Gottfried.[9] His role models are Flipper, Lassie, and Dobie Gillis, and his favorite music is the theme from the Doris Day movie *The Glass-Bottom Boat*. He has an entertainment view of history, and since he is an electromorph and lives in a television, he responds only to form and not content, and he can't tell the difference between TV and real life. Max Headroom was Jean Baudrillard's best trip yet, and Todd Gitlin's worst nightmare.

In common with *Blade Runner, Alien,* and cyberpunk science fiction, *Max Headroom* shares many of the unsentimental, socially realistic features of a recognizable future; in particular, it focuses, understandably, upon the future of television. The messy, dystopian environment of the show itself is set "twenty minutes into the future" when TV is the only growth industry, and when TV ratings appear to be the determining measure of all social and cultural life. TV sets are a welfare handout to the needy, who live in "cardboard condos"; video narcosis is administered to the masses in the form of game shows containing subliminal endorphin-releasing digital messages; urban guerrillas are offered lucrative contracts to produce spectacular network-sponsored terrorism; sponsors are forever exploring the technology of direct neural stimulation in order to get their messages across without the mediation of broadcast TV; and the networks' own political candidates campaign through programs that are consumed while people are asleep. In this respect, it is clear that the show has absorbed and reissued as primetime material those critiques of the society of the spectacle and of mass media manipulation that were once presented as fresh and radical by the left. Here, all of the lessons about spectacle, commodification, surveillance, social control, disinformation, and McLuhanesque TV/brain stimulation are offered as palatable network fare (even though it is unclear to what extent ABC was ever very comfortable with this state of affairs). Recently, as the sixties have begun to come under retrospective media scrutiny, it has become rote to meditate on the grisly irony of such developments, when yesteryear's images of revolution are recirculated as models of today's revolution of images. *Max Headroom* presented an opportunity for many to consider how cogently the critical power of these earlier media critiques had come to be incorporated into mainstream network programming (while retaining some of their bite). But *Max Headroom* was also science fiction. More important than its lessons about co-opting the past was its capacity to suggest how TV, in a technocracy, defines our temporality with regard to the future.

Clearly, there is a difference between writing in 1948 about 1984, as Orwell did, and writing in 1984 about "twenty minutes into the future," as Max's creators did. Perhaps the difference here may be only one of speed rather than conceptions of temporality. For example, Annabel Jankel and Rocky Morton, the directors of the original *Max Headroom* telefilm, claim that they generally watch movies on fast-forward, especially French films.[10] But while the dystopias of 1984 and *Max Headroom* are founded on futuristic projections of political ideology and consumerist ideology respectively, they are both recognizable products of the technocratic imagination. As Alvin Gouldner points out:

> Technocratic consciousness promises that its project is already at hand and already exists. It is in this respect not future oriented, but is oriented to that which already is. . . . It tells us the future is already here, in essentials if not in its full maturity. The future comes, then, as incremental addition rather than as structural transformation.
>
> From another perspective, this says: things are not going to get better; there are no culminations to come; it is the present that counts. The technocratic consciousness, then, is the end of transcendental hope. It says we have much and will get more, but not all we have dreamed of and really wanted.[11]

In a technocracy proper, there is no future shock; the future arrives by increments, every twenty minutes or so. Or, as Max sardonically puts it, the TV system which he inhabits is "a network with a great future behind it." In this future, it is promised that the rule of reason and knowledge will be strengthened, and consumer gratification will be augmented. Gouldner adds, however, that the weakness of this technocratic promise is that it invites people to judge it on the basis of their present experience of the world, and if things are bad for them, then they can only be imagined as getting worse. In such a world—*Max Headroom*'s world—the rule of reason becomes a despotic rule of TV ratings, and the increase in consumer gratification is manifest in shows such as *Lifestyles of the Poor and Pitiful, Porky's Landing,* and *Lumpy's Proletariat,* or else the kind of shows, as Max puts it, that "go over nobody's head." In such a world, single corporations have access to more information than any single government, while a vast population of derelicts and noncitizens are fair game for the body banks which collect spare parts for biotechnology. Twenty minutes is a long time in a technocracy which only guarantees more of the same, but worse.

In such a world, the saviors are sentimental technocrats, or else they are like Edison Carter and his crusading telejournalist team, officially hired as the promoters, for twenty minutes a day, of a liberal tele-ethics and thus authorized to expose corporate corruption in the best interventionist tradition of the maverick TV cop. In this respect, the show fuses the heroic mythology of critical power claimed by TV's news divisions with the structural narrative of the cop show, TV's privileged representation of ethical debate about the rules of power: When does a cop step out of line? When are the rules simply a hindrance in the way of police expertise or humane conduct? When is self-restraint the price to pay for loyalty to bureaucratic superiors? These quandaries serve as dramatic representations of ethical dilemmas faced by ordinary people in responding to power in the workplace and in daily life. True to the *policier* tradition of serving the "honest commodity," Edison's reporting (the good cop on the metrocop beat is often an ally) often exposes top-level scandals at his own network, usually by implicating their corporate sponsors. In fact, this is the source of his high ratings appeal and his journalistic immunity. Because Edison is part of him, Max is often an accomplice to Edison's muckraking, but he is usually reluctant to play this game, especially when its results do not reflect upon the greater glory of the TV medium to which he would rather devote his loyalties. So, too, Max can often function as Edison's alter egotist, presenting the same critique for TV entertainment as Edison does for TV news coverage; "we just tell the truth differently," Max points out. One speaks the traditional rhetoric of liberal humanism in order to expose corruption "out there"; the other speaks in the assembly language of television itself, accessing fifty years of broadcast memory in order to inform his critical role as the TV spectacle's own conscience-in-residence.

The genius of this role becomes evident if we consider the contrast between the US pilot and the original British version of the show. In the British version, Max is appropriated by a pirate TV station with a punk profile, called Big-Time, which operates in the low-tech "500 watt ghetto" of broadcasters. Max's popularity helps Big-Time put a dent in the ratings dominance of Network XXIII, the industry monolith. In the US version, however, Max is contained within the system of Network XXIII itself, where his erratic appearances boost the network's ratings, especially when he savages network policy. The US pilot closes with a quip: "How can you tell when our network president is lying? His lips move." In the British version, Max is speaking on Big-Time, from the broadcasting periphery, when he offers the more abstract comment: "Parrots are only one rung above politicians though. You always know when *they're* lying—their lips move." No doubt conclusions could be drawn from this restructuring of the narrative about the respective roles of TV in British and US politics. In the ABC series, Max's often-biting anticorporate commentary reaches vast audiences and is tolerated because it is exploited for profit by Network XXIII. His popularity attracts the attention of even the biggest sponsors, who want him to front their ads, in the same way he fronts for Coca-Cola products in his other primetime life. In the British version, he is outside the system, speaking from a minority or marginal position which has little or no stake in attaching political significance to the media's routine and ritualistic exposures of politicians and their scandals.

Given the choice, of course, Max would probably take the media center over the media margin because of his addictive craving for respectability, popularity, fame, and glamor, those same qualities which originally satirized for British audiences the plastic-fantastic world of US entertainment values. He wants to play host to a global audience, and his entertainer's motto is "My world, my empire, my voice, *your* pleasure." *Playing host to the world* is the ambition of the transnational celebrity, but it is also the will to power of the transnational communications empires which have come close to monopolizing the global flow of information in our time. Their imperial power stems from the capacity to distribute media abundance to regions of material scarcity, and to administer "information colonies" by trading access to the hi-tech sublime. By way of his relentlessly parodic personality, Max comes to both represent and undercut this will to imperial power which is his inheritance, if you like, as an icon of techno-intensive America. His full name, Maximum Headroom, bespeaks the empty vanity of brainpower, as well as the arrogance of expansionism. So, too, in his cable talk show his campy worship of celebrity capital pushes the culture of spectacle toward its conventional limits. There, his overzealous devotion to the role of domineering showbiz diva generates discomfort in his guests, specifically chosen because their own celebrity is founded on dubious talents. Above all, his sexual affect is unstable and nonthreatening; the gaudy narcissism which he cultivates is a running joke on legitimate masculine authority.[12] How could it be otherwise for someone who models himself so fastidiously on Ted Baxter, the crassly egotistical news presenter on the *Mary Tyler Moore Show*?

In many respects, then, Max can be associated with the new pop sensibility that not only is comfortable with the politics of media analysis but also takes for granted the gratifications of media culture. Reconfigured today in the hi-tech environment of postpunk cynicism, his lineage is the sixties politics of pop and camp, cheerfully direct about its rejection of sincerity, and devoted to its ironic use of light entertainment and pop folklore.[13] Far from militantly anticonsumerist, it is a politics of artifice, self-conscious about the commercial limits of its construction, and critically set out on the plastic, or in Max's case silicon, surface of shared media memories. Its appeal today is primarily the basis of "youth TV," most evident on MTV's *Remote Control,* or in Lettermanism, and more generally in the appetite for junk shows, nostalgia reruns of fifties and sixties TV, the trivia craze, couch potatoism (a movement whose motto is "the recline of western civilization"), and the brittle consumerism of the "born-to-shop" sensibility. But Max's irony is also a cultural feature of an older baby boom audience, whose stylized pop quotationalism presents a way of reconciling its own dissident youthful past with its professional-managerial present. So, too, the ironic competence of this thirtysomething audience in the field of pop knowledge is also a correlative to its positivistic application of professional or technical knowledge in the realm of work. In this respect, Max's techno-scepticism represents an argument, even if it is the weakest possible argument, for cynicism-in-the-workforce (if not radicalism-in-the-professions): "we may work within the system, but we're not really serious about it." That's all very well, one might say, but in a command-and-control culture, this "bad attitude" is just as likely to be legitimized as a form of strategic intelligence, a "smart" way of getting the job done by bodies and minds that might otherwise be ideologically inert in the face of postmodern expertise and labor. Consequently, pop irony becomes the architectural norm of the new consumer credibility, constructing a framework for the successes of the future.

Take, for example, the TV ads for New Coke (dir. Ridley Scott) which featured Max on a vast video screen as the star attraction at a "cokeologists' convention" attended by thousands of cheering, video-happy teenagers. These ads were a direct riposte to the highly successful "Pepsi generation" ads featuring "live" appearances by such megastars as Michael Jackson, David Bowie, Lionel Richie, Tina Turner, and Don Johnson. Despite their "leading-edge" meanings, the Pepsi ads adopted the traditional manner of establishing a demographic community of consumers bound together by association with celebrities whom they themselves have helped to make famous. The Max Headroom ads, which fronted Coca-Cola's attempts to promote New Coke, could be read as an inside joke shared by the audience about the fake or artificial construction of celebrity, as well as the audience's collusive role in that process. In addition, the reference to technical expertise suggested by an academic convention of cokeologists was circulated even as this image was cast in the shape of a popular audience of nonaccredited experts. It was the people, after all, who had rejected the taste of New Coke, imposed on them by the technocrat experts who wanted to change the old cola recipe. Now the people, the true experts in cokeology, would make "America's choice" in the Cola Wars.[14]

Max's commercial appearances were the result of a restructuring of management after the New Coke crisis at Coca-Cola. With his inbuilt flair for debunking the technocrat style, Max was an effective marketing strategy for Coca-Cola to negotiate its embarrassment over the New Coke debacle. Max clearly suggested the new wave of a cybernetic future, but he is also an ironic version of it, always ready to revel in its fallibility at the same time as he accepts its inevitability. Under Max's tutelary genius, the future of New Coke, it was suggested, would surely be decided by the popular expertise of consumers who reject the falsity of merchandising and the arrogance of the experts, and who decide for themselves. This is the advanced management principle that underlies Max's brand of electronic populism, fleshed out in later New Coke ads (1988), which feature Max running for the presidency as the youth choice: New Voters! New Coke![15] Trading on a contradictory appeal to electoral populism, these spots were also in keeping with the kind of advertising which is aimed primarily at complimenting its target audience on their media sophistication and video literacy.[16] If the future is going to be smarter than the present, then consumers will need to have an image of their knowledge that stresses its self-consciousness, and not simply its functionalism. To "catch the wave," as Max exhorts us in the Coke ads, is to be tuned in, then, but it is also to be hip to the absurdity of a future constructed around spectacles. For the "new wave" is a liquid future with no guarantees, a future in which we are given the leeway to believe, if we are smart enough, that *trend is not destiny*. Classic Coca-Cola is there on the grocery shelf to remind us of the past mistakes of believing otherwise, while an eternity of electronic presidents like Ron "Headrest" Reagan wait off-camera to prove us wrong.

In this way is Max's hipness employed to strategically manage a consumer future that is both inevitable and indeterminate. So, too, his uncertain physical presence points to the question of our possible bodily future. What is it like to have a body and a memory in a "posthuman" world engineered by biotics systems which won't need to distinguish between machines and organisms, whether naturally born or artificially replicated, and what can techno-ethics do to prepare a critical awareness for this future? For the avant-garde imaginary, a politics that wants to be able to contest the new, impure space of cyborg subjectivity between nature and technology will need to critically apply the lessons of postmodernism about fantasy and fragmentation to the new conjuncture of knowledge/power which knowledge-processing technology will usher in; it will be a politics of the interface, not a politics of essences.[17] As for the realm of work and production, at least one, hardly metaphysical, response to the techno-ethical question can be found today in the new slave markets of Third World female labor that support the global microelectronics industry, and in the low-wage, deskilled, and nonunionized service-sector revolutions that are its byproduct in the "developed" world. The ethics that accompany these developments are an old, familiar ethics of survival. What used to be called "keeping body and soul together" is no less a material problem in the new cybernetic world than it was for earlier technological work forces, although its terrain, its strategies, and its symptoms (including techno-stress) have shifted, geographically, demographically, and physiologically. In this respect, the growth of these new forms of bodily exploitation, by gender and race as much as by class, is *ethically* linked to the spread of the knowledge industry and its technological production. The "feminization of poverty" and other effects of deindustrialization must be seen as the neglected underside of the professionals' debates about such techno-ethical questions as the erosion of privacy, or the tyranny, within human thought, of instrumental reason. Set against the backdrop of its new labor markets, the postindustrial dream of freedom and leisure in a telecommunications utopia looks like a zero-sum game to those who service the dream.

MEN IN BOXES

It's no surprise that the program which the Chicago "pirate Max" broadcast was timed to interrupt was *Doctor Who*. Like Max, the Doctor is a privileged expression of the conjuncture of vernacular science and tele-ethics, but he represents an older and largely outmoded system of beliefs and values about the role and conduct of technologues. Both, however, are men in boxes, trapped in the apparatus of old and familiar telecommunications technologies, the police phone box and the television set, which they use for their own relatively autonomous purposes. In this respect, they both demonstrate what Marshall McLuhan called rearview mirrorism, whereby the "message" of the new media tends to be articulated through old media environments.

The somewhat undependable Tardis is a shrunken expression of the faded British power to "police the galaxy" through its control of communication highways. British invention and technology, in the shape of the Doctor's eccentric, amateur genius, is now survivalist, not colonizing, and in fact is tied to a vaguely liberal, postcolonial conscience about the recent history of patronizing alien cultures. So, too, with each successive Doctor redefining his role, the strong ideology of BBC paternalism about popular education has become less of an embodied component of the show.[18] The schoolmasterism of the original concept has dropped some of its more avuncular features and embraced some of the younger technocrat style. But the Doctor is likely to remain an institutional expression of the erratic style of the free-floating intellectual who is a guardian and not a functionary of knowledge.

Like the Doctor, Max uses his box as an electronic passport to other telematic systems and locations in time and space, but he generally uses this privilege for information retrieval, the better to play his ambassadorial role as *a popular host to the world*. This sense of pragmatism, spliced with his goofy egotism, pays tribute to the gurgling optimism of US science and technology. So, too, his plastic good looks mirror the preppy blandness of Carl Sagan, America's technocratic equivalent in the field of vernacular science of the likes of Patrick Moore, Magnus Pyke, and other batty BBC paragons of absent-mindedness. Max may be the creation of a mischievous hacker, but functionally speaking, he is a product and a bureaucratic prisoner of feedback technologies, specifically the TV ratings system, which is a constant measure of his success or failure as a television host. His accountability to producers, sponsors, network executives, and audiences defines the limits of his mobility as a technocratic intellectual, whereas the Doctor's allegiance to the distant fraternity of the Time Lords allows him to be the traditional, universal defender of a much more disinterested faith.

Max articulates this limited mobility in various ways, but nowhere so succinctly as in the coda to the last episode of his ABC show, about to be cancelled because of its poor Friday evening performance against *Miami Vice* and *Dallas:*

> We will fight them on the beaches of Miami Vice. We will fight them on the sidewalks of Dallas. We will fight them on the Knots Landing stages. We will n-n-never . . . never . . . never surrender. And if the ratings system lasts for a thousand years, men will still say, this was Max Headroom's finest hour.

Here in Max's mock-heroic world of ratings warfare, his invocation of the fighting spirit reminds us of the military-industrial research environment of which he (and broadcast television itself) is a technological offspring. And so it is with a technocrat's indignation but with the besieged voice of military empire—the "rearview mirrorist" voice of Winston Churchill— that he announces his termination.[19] Max's TV world, then, is like a giant video game; the protagonist is constantly under military siege and struggles to survive in an environment where, no matter what level of expertise is applied, the zero-sum game rules are always made by others. Max is an actor in a microworld owned and programmed elsewhere, but if he doesn't know it, if *he can't tell the difference,* then he is dreaming for the ethicist the textualist nightmare of technocracy (best captured elsewhere in the film *War Games,* by its war computer's response—"What's the Difference?"—to the query about whether its "game" of Thermonuclear War is real or simulated). There is nothing immoral, of course, about technologies of representation that compromise our ability to tell the difference; that complaint is a recognizable anxiety, born of reaction, and as old as Plato. In a more democratic world, simulation technologies would be technologies of liberation. As it is, they are owned and developed in the interests of the powerful, and their modeling codes are the result of programming based on assumptions about reality that are highly contestable. Techno-ethics is not a radical challenge to that system of ownership, it is a code developed by professionals to guarantee their contract with the powerful, to signify that they have been dealt a hand in the game of power.

As I have suggested, the same can be said of tele-ethics, a code which signifies that television professionals—actors, writers, journalists, critics, producers, commentators—have been awarded certain bargaining powers in the business of determining the ideological shape of broadcast TV. Like other shows about work within the culture and media industries, *Max Headroom* represents how that bargaining power is intellectually negotiated by professionals; as a guide to life and labor in a technocracy, it shows what is possible and what is illegitimate under the hegemonic compromise that is monitored by the ethical codes of professionals. When that compromise breaks down, as happened in the case of the writers' strike of 1988, the material underpinning of the intellectual's cultural bargaining power is more exposed, despite the tendency to represent that power always in ethical terms of its defense of creative freedom and quality.

In the spring of 1988, ABC ran two previously unaired *Max Headroom* episodes to fill in a programming vacuum created by the writers' strike. The second episode dealt with the official suppression (ordered by a computer) of a printing press used to help educate children in "the fringes." A "good cop" helps Edison save the day by turning a blind eye to the existence of the press; when asked whether his principled action means that he is "turning revolutionary," he replies, invoking normative police ethics: "if you consider decency revolutionary then you can call me one." Edison signs off his broadcast report in the terms of his own ethical mode by observing that the "pen" may even be "mightier than the video camera." And finally, Max's sign-off, a paraphrase of Portia's plea for mercy in *The Merchant of Venice,* is an identificatory salute to the plight of the TV writers with whom he feels he shares the ethical code of creative or artistic integrity.

"The quality of TV is not strained, it droppeth as the gentle ratings droppeth, to a very tiny percentage share, and lo! 'tis none." Of course, Shakespeare would have loved your ratings system. *Twelfth Night* would have been lucky to have lasted one.

NOTES

1. See Donn B. Parker, *Fighting Computer Crime* (New York: Scribners, 1983); August Bequai, *Techno-Crimes: The Computerization of Crime and Terrorism* (Lexington, Mass.: D. C. Heath, 1987).

2. For those in a technocratic world who rule by knowledge and expertise, shows of impotency, whether technical or sexual, are supposed to be less of a problem than for the unskilled bureaucrats of the old order whose positions depended not on real skill and knowledge but rather on their loyalty to their superiors and to the system itself.

3. Sherry Turkle's book *The Second Self: Computers and the Human Spirit* (New York: Simon and Schuster, 1984) offers a perceptive commentary on many of the sexually differentiated features of the technocratic mentality.

4. The most well known and outspoken critique from within the AI establishment has come from Joseph Weizenbaum, *Computer Power and Human Reason* (San Francisco: W. H. Freeman and Co., 1976).

5. See Elizabeth and Stuart Ewen, "The Bribe of Frankenstein," in *Critical Com-*

munications Review, vol. 2: *Labor, the Working Class, and the Media,* ed. Vincent Mosco and Janet Wasko (Norwood, N.J.: Ablex, 1982), pp. 3–22.

6. Steven Levy has written the history of the "hacker ethic" from its origins at MIT through the period of the computer counterculture in *Hackers: Heroes of the Computer Revolution* (New York: Dell, 1984). For a brief polemical account of the computer counterculture, see chapter 7 of Theodore Roszak, *The Cult of Information: The Folklore of Computers and the True Art of Thinking* (New York: Pantheon, 1986).

7. Crucial books in the "privacy movement" of the last two decades have been Alan Westin, *Privacy and Freedom* (New York: Atheneum, 1967); James B. Rule, *Private Lives and Public Surveillance* (New York: Schocken, 1974); James Rule, Douglas McAdam, and David Uglow, *The Politics of Privacy* (New York: Elsevier, 1980); David Burnham, *The Rise of the Computer State* (New York: Random House, 1983).

8. Alvin Gouldner, *The Dialectic of Ideology and Technology* (New York: Seabury Press, 1976), p. 270.

9. Questioned about his own views of Utopia in an *Omni* symposium, Max concludes: "For centuries people have made personal pursuits for Utopia. Some thought they'd found it after being invited on the Johnny Carson show. But I know that the cruel reality of life is that there is no Utopia, unless you're a Tibetan monk or you've been invited back on Johnny Carson." *Omni* 10.7 (Apr. 1988):38.

10. Quoted in Peter Goddard, "Videos Push Movie-making Forward Fast," *Toronto Star* 19 Mar. 1988. The *Max Headroom* concept itself was the brainchild of British TV producer Peter Wagg, who enlisted the help of computer graphics experts Jankel and Morton. Legendary directors of computer-animated music videos and editors of *Creative Computer Graphics* (New York: Cambridge University Press, 1984), Jankel and Morton belong to the first wave of music video veterans who have moved into filmmaking (*D. O. A.* was their first major production). Of their films, they boast that "you won't be able to push the [FF] button, because we're already on fast-forward."

11. Gouldner, p. 261.

12. On the other hand, his genetic intimacy with the eroticized Edison Carter on the *Max Headroom* show often puts him in the position of homophilic protector of Edison's body when on assignment, and this puts him in direct competition with Theora, Edison's TV controller. As a woman, she is assumed to understand less about Edison than Max does.

13. In her article "Max Headroom: V-V-Very Bigtime TV," *Socialist Review* 17.6 (Nov.-Dec. 1987):31–43, Elayne Rapping asks the traditional question of *Max Headroom* for the left: "Is it after all possible to subvert commercial TV from within?" and concludes that the show comes very near to doing so by "ironically mocking the very 'hand that feeds it.'" For Rapping, Max uses his "cuteness" to "fight the good fight" by employing his charm "to undermine the network's own agenda." Writing in the summer of 1987, after the first spring run, she predicts that the show, for all of its promise to avoid "mushy" family viewing, is likely "to have its political lifeblood, and entertainment value, cloned out of it by the next season."

This kind of response from left media critics to new postmodernist shows is locked into the dialectic of "subversion" and "recuperation" which has governed cultural criticism ever since the first airings of the Frankfurt position. It assumes that articulate political positions or meanings, which are self-evidently oppositional, can be recognized and isolated and allowed to act in the world and that they are then contained and compromised by the monolithic mainstreaming tendencies of the culture industry. Aside from the fact that political meanings are never distorted or diluted—they are "made" in the process of making TV programs or in the process of viewing by individuals—the problems posed by this kind of approach to popular entertainment are myriad. By whom exactly are these sentiments seen as articulate and "subversive"? Are they articulate only for intellectuals who still dream of politically "educating" popular culture? If, as Rapping contends, "Max is pop culture at its most lovable, positive and progressive," is this not the leftist's dream of politically correct pleasure? Is the pleasure afforded by popular culture simply to be seen as part of a recruitment drive for political reeducation, a strategy that is used to win viewers over to the "subversive" messages of the show?

In the case of *Max Headroom,* it became clear that Max could no more be relied upon to consistently "undermine" the corporate values of the network than he could be trusted to play the functionary role required of him as a TV technocrat. His truancy, not his militancy, is more likely to be the source of our pleasure. Moreover, if we consider the meanings that Max generates as an intertextual celebrity—on his talk show, in the Coke ads, and elsewhere—then his presence is much less easy to recruit in the way Rapping would like. The popular "meaning" of Max is a cumulative one, incomplete, and likely to be redefined in his future "lives," if he is ever resurrected.

14. The "cokeology" reference was a witty retort to Pepsi's prize-winning ad featuring an archaeology professor who, along with his Pepsi-sucking students, unearths objects from the past, all of which he can identify—a split-level ranch house, an electric guitar, a baseball—except for an old green Coca-Cola bottle, which is assumed to be too prehistoric for its significance to have survived.

While the Max Headroom commercials were a success—Video Storyboard voted them the best-remembered commercials of 1986—they failed to stem the decline in sales of New Coke. As the Pepsi president put it, "this might sound funny from the guy who signed Michael Jackson twice, but Max Headroom seemed too strange for a mainstream product. The more Coke ran these commercials, we figured, the more they'd turn consumers off." Roger Enrico (and Jesse Kornbluth), *The Other Guy Blinked: And Other Dispatches from the Cola Wars* (New York: Bantam, 1988), p. 285.

15. MTV's presidential candidate is Randee of the Redwoods, a zonked-out hippie hangover whose campaign of enigmatic appeals to his narcissism rearticulates the erstwhile sixties values of "youth politics" as a merely inane commentary on the rhetoric of today's electoral process.

16. Diet Pepsi's TV ads in the spring of 1988 are a good example of the conflation of media literacy and product appeal. The claim that Pepsi is "generations ahead" refers in the ad to the generation of (video) images as well as to Pepsi's youthful generations of consumers.

17. Donna Haraway, "Manifesto for Cyborgs: Science, Technology, and Socialist Feminism in the Eighties," *Socialist Review* 80 (Mar.-Apr. 1985):65–107.

18. See John Tulloch and Manuel Alvarado, *Doctor Who: The Unfolding Text* (New York: St. Martin's Press, 1983).

19. This ending might be compared, however, with the ending of the *Mary Tyler Moore Show* ten years earlier in 1977. Faced with falling ratings, MTM decided to wind up the show with a story involving a takeover of the WJM station, in which all of the news teams were fired except for Ted Baxter, the inept, narcissistic presenter whose blunders had probably cost the station its ratings. To the new owners of the station, however, Baxter's showbiz "personality" was invaluable. Jane Feuer argues that his persona was partially revived in the 1983 summer comedy show *Buffalo Bill,* in which Bill Bittinger, like Max, was featured as a talk show host who delivered a barbed commentary on the image-making celebrity business. *MTM "Quality Television,"* ed. Jane Feuer, Paul Kerr, and Tise Vahimagi (London: British Film Institute, 1984), pp. 52–56. In its structure, and its particular configuration of characters working together on a TV news team, the ABC *Max Headroom* show resembled the *Mary Tyler Moore Show* in many ways other than Max's obsession with Ted Baxter, carefully studied by Matt Frewer, the Canadian comic who played both Max and Edison.

CRITICAL AND TEXTUAL HYPERMASCULINITY

Lynne Joyrich

I'd like to begin my discussion of TV, postmodernism, and the cultural connotations of femininity by referring to an image from David Cronenberg's film *Videodrome*. In this film, video signals are used to literally open their viewers to total control: exposure to these signals transforms the human body into a living VCR which can then be penetrated by videotapes, preventing the subject from differentiating reality from video simulation. Not only does this illustrate the worst fears of mass culture critics (fears concerning the power of the media to seduce and rape the viewer), but it clearly and violently marks the receptive TV body as feminine—the tapes are thrust into a gaping wound that pierces the hero's stomach. *Videodrome* thus brings together the image of the cyborg body—a postmodern hybrid of human, animal, and machine—and the image of the "feminine body"— a body yielding to manipulation, too close to the image to properly evaluate it.[1]

Such conceptual ties between TV, postmodernism, and femininity (or, more accurately, the meanings our culture assigns to "femininity") are symptomatic of shifting gender relations in our technologically mediated culture. Television, today's cyborgian "machine-subject,"[2] can be seen as playing out these relations in all their contradictions, revealing a terrain in which gender figures prominently in a network of differences we have only begun to explore. By "reading" several television texts against texts marking TV's critical reception, I will attempt to map out the connections forged between TV and postmodern culture, focusing on the veiled references to sexual difference and the figuration of gender constituted within this field.

Noting the ways in which TV has been portrayed as feminine in both film and mass culture criticism—a situation exacerbated by the fluctuating ground of postmodernism—I argue that while such tropes of analysis are seductive, they are also potentially dangerous, encouraging critics to ignore the complexities and contradictions of gender inscription as well as the other fields of difference (race, class, age, and so on) which traverse the TV text and audience alike.[3] In fact, attending to the complex dynamics of gender within both television and TV criticism might lead us to a very different conclusion from that implied by *Videodrome*'s sexual imagery. Despite the prevalence of such figures and images in accounts of TV, we cannot simply claim that television is itself either feminine or feminizing. Rather, this ontological premise recuperates the feminine and the critical insights of feminism within a new version of masculinity which inhabits television studies as well as television texts. In other words, the focus on TV as "feminine" masks a deeper cultural concern with masculinity—a concern which may express itself through the construction of a "hyper-masculinity" that renders the presence of women within TV representation and TV criticism unnecessary.

Several theorists have noted that consumer culture and the culpable masses blamed for its existence have often been figured as feminine. Tania Modleski examines this aspect of historical accounts and emphasizes the problems involved in either simply condemning or celebrating these feminine inscriptions.[4] Andreas Huyssen has also explored attacks on sentimental culture—slurs based on fears of the engulfing ooze of the masses which provoked the "reaction formation" of a virile and authorial modernism. Yet he concludes his analysis by claiming that such gendered rhetoric has diminished with the decline of modernism: "mass culture and the masses as feminine threat—such notions belong to another age, Jean Baudrillard's recent ascription of femininity to the masses notwithstanding. . . . "[5] Nonetheless, despite Huyssen's optimistic conclusion, such gendered imagery can still be seen in many analyses of television. While, as Huyssen argues, the "great divide" between art and mass culture may have narrowed (or even imploded) in the postmodern age, this rupture does not necessarily extend to a generalized dissolution of binary categories of analysis. Rather than an age in which bipolar thinking is no longer operative, we exist in a transitional space in which new dichotomies are erected as fast as the old ones break down. In fact, the very rupture of traditional modes of thought provokes a panicked attempt to create new divisions rather than working to dispel our society's felt need for oppositions. Thus, the kind of binary divisions used to discount mass art by the modernist critics Huyssen discusses continue to exert an influence over critics associated with the rise of postmodern theory in spite of their apparent reluctance to condemn all forms of mass and subcultural production. In other words, distinctions of value seem to hold sway within the realm of mass texts themselves even if the grand opposition between high and low art can no longer describe today's aesthetic theory or practice. Television theorists regularly define their object through such polarities; by constructing a duality in which television is placed in opposition to some other, more

"respected" medium, these theorists articulate cultural and textual difference in terms that are reminiscent of what is still posed as the dominant
binarism of our culture—sexual difference.

In *Understanding Media,* for example, Marshall McLuhan compares today's media to the previously dominant print, arguing that the new holistic
and participatory modes promote a "global embrace" and the implosion of
margin to center. Associating these media with the nonconformity of criminals, children, blacks, cripples, and women, McLuhan distinguishes the
heterogeneity of television from the regularity of book culture.[6] The "rational" form of print, allied with "literate man," is uniform, linear, and
isolated—it is, like film, a "hot" medium based on exclusion. It thus creates
the centralized, autonomous subject motivated toward impersonal domination, expansionism, and departmental organization. On the other hand,
the "irrational" media of the electric age, particularly television, return us
to the mythical form of the icon in which distance—the distance between
subjects as well as the distance between sign and referent—is abolished.
The mosaic of TV requires the involvement of all senses in a tactile, primitive intimacy that produces, according to McLuhan, retribalization, organic
interlacing, proximity, and empathy.

These qualities are clearly drawn from sterotypes of femininity, and while
McLuhan values them, he nonetheless believes that what he terms the
"threat from within the gates" (the new media) must be kept under control
by the masculine logic of print.[7] This phrase comes from Hegel who, in
theorizing the disruption provoked by Woman, writes that the community
"creates its enemy for itself within its own gates, creates it in what it sup-
presses, and what is at the same time essential to it—womankind in general.
Womankind—the everlasting irony in the life of the community—changes
by intrigue the universal purpose of government into a private end. . . . "[8]
McLuhan's metaphor for the disruptive media then clearly genders television as feminine—intrinsically feminine if "the medium is the message."
Any enthusiasm he expresses for the organic qualities of television thus
evades important historical questions. For example, McLuhan's claim that
TV is inherently decentralized allows him to ignore the fact that it is very
much economically centralized and that its femininity consists more in the
gender of its primary consumers than in its moral or aesthetic nature.
Ignoring the particular social construction of both TV and femininity,
McLuhan produces a celebratory reading of television in which sexual difference, once again polarized and essentialized, is made to uphold a historically specific mode of consumption.

Several other critics comparing television to earlier media similarly figure
opposition in gendered terms. John Fiske and John Hartley, for example,
use McLuhan to support their theory of television as our culture's bard,
also describing it as immediate and illogical, failing to support the individualism upheld by linear, abstract print. Arguing that TV is criticized
merely because it fails to conform to the standards of "Rational Man," they

too employ unacknowledged gender codes in their evaluation of television as a "separate but equal" medium. While Fiske and Hartley do not recognize their oppositions as gendered ones, their description of television as an intimate, personal, familiar medium, working to bond all viewers in an inclusive world, repeats common sexual stereotypes.[9] The cultural denigration of television is thus related to the marginality of an unnamed femininity—as Fiske and Hartley claim, TV is scorned merely for being TV: nonlinear, illogical, and unmasculine.[10]

Similarly, John Ellis compares television to the cinema, arguing that today, the culturally respectable is equated with the cinematic. According to Ellis, cinema's mode of narration constructs a scenario of voyeurism, granting the spectator power over the image and centering the look on the female body. TV, on the other hand, has little narration in the cinematic sense: it offers itself as an immediate presence, failing to produce a sufficiently voyeuristic position for its viewers. TV involves what Ellis calls "the glance"—a look without power—rather than cinema's gaze. The viewer then delegates his/her look to television itself, forging a sense of intimacy as events are shared rather than witnessed.[11] In other words, the glance of the TV viewer is a domestic, distracted, and powerless look that implies continuous co-presence—a "feminine" look that is too close to the object to maintain the gap essential to desire and full subjectivity.

As this brief survey shows, the use of feminine imagery to describe our "lowest" cultural form (in opposition to whatever is held up as more respectable and "masculine"—print or film) has not faded away with the passing of modernism.[12] In fact, such gender implications take on new meaning in the postmodern age as the threat of fluctuating signs, unstable distinctions, and fractured identities provokes a retreat toward nostalgia for firm stakes of meaning.[13] As the " 'natural' grounding principle" once seemingly offered by sexual difference erodes, new anxieties are created which are often projected onto television (a medium which stands as the ultimate in fluctuating signs even as it tries to remain a bastion of family values). Describing television in a world in which distance and contemplation are impossible, for example, Baudrillard writes, "the opposing poles of determination vanish according to a nuclear contraction . . . of the old polar schema which has always maintained a minimal distance between a cause and an effect, between the subject and an object. . . . "[14] In the circular logic of simulation, classical reason threatens to vanish, and separate positions merge. In Baudrillard's words, "positivity and negativity engender and overlap . . . there is no longer any active or passive . . . linear continuity and dialectical polarity no longer exist."[15] As dialectics collapse, the oppositions which maintain sexual difference and the stability of the sexed gaze seem to shift, if not fully disappear.

This collapse of the oppositions which have always upheld the primacy of the masculine subject is further suggested in Baudrillard's description of television as he discards what film theory has taken to be the terms of sexual difference: "TV is no longer the source of an absolute gaze . . . no longer . . . a system of scrutiny . . . playing on the opposition between seeing and being seen. . . ."[16] In rejecting the applicability of the categories subject/object, active/passive, and seeing/being seen, Baudrillard rejects the divisions that have been seen by many feminist film critics as constitutive of the male spectator.[17] In other words, for Baudrillard, postmodernism—and television in particular—seems to disallow the security and mastery of the masculine position, and as this stable site disappears, we are all left floating in a diffuse, irrational space—a space traditionally coded as feminine.

In the essay "In the Shadow of the Silent Majorities," Baudrillard describes the masses as soft and sticky, lacking attribute and reference. They are like a black hole that engulfs all meaning in an implosion of the social, an overpresence that collapses inward, producing a lack of distance or defining feature, and through this account, the masses are figured in clichés of femininity. But like women, the masses have access to a certain excess—they over-conform and over-consume, reduplicating the logic of the media. Referring, like McLuhan, to Hegel's analysis of "womankind," Baudrillard writes that this "destructive hyper-simulation" is "akin to the eternal irony of femininity of which Hegel speaks—the irony of false fidelity, of an excessive fidelity to the law, an ultimately impenetrable simulation of passivity and obedience . . . which annuls . . . the law governing them. . . ."[18] This theorization of subversive hyperconformity is very familiar. It mimics both Luce Irigaray's analysis of feminine mimicry—a playful repetition in which women resubmit themselves to a masculine discourse so as to show they remain "elsewhere"—and the notion of feminine masquerade elaborated, for example, by Mary Ann Doane in which women flaunt their femininity in order to hold it at a distance.[19]

Yet as many critics have noted, Baudrillard (unlike Irigaray and Doane) is not advocating acts of political resistance—he assumes the position of the feminine in order to stress the vacuum of the enveloping mass rather than the possible differences that may be constituted within it. He thus argues against those theorists who "would like to make a new source of revolutionary energy (in particular in its sexual and desire version). They would like to . . . reinstate it in its very banality, as historical negativity. Exaltations of micro-desires, small differences, unconscious practices, anonymous marginalities . . . and to transfer it back to political reason."[20] For Baudrillard, the goal of politicizing such fields is an impossible one. Substituting the fear of an all-consuming mass for the older notion of an all-controlling industry, he insists upon the anonymity of the feminized masses who are neither subject nor object.[21] In rejecting any theory of subjectivity which might valorize the deconstruction of identity (in a play of differences) as politically progressive, Baudrillard sentences the political (and political resistance) to annihilation. Nonetheless, as "a direct defiance of the political," the masses' feminine hyperconformity, their ironic excess, is still a show of strength, a mode of resistance escaping control.[22] In this way, Baudrillard employs the concept of the feminine, but deprives it of the progressive force suggested by some feminist critics—he simply recasts the division between mass culture and high culture in terms of a routine gender dichotomy.

Baudrillard is not the first male theorist to claim the position of the feminine as a way to signify ironic strength (whether deemed political or not). His analysis of hyperaffirmation recalls Jacques Derrida's discussion of the feminine in *Spurs* (part of which occurs, interestingly, in a section entitled "Simulations"). Considering Nietzsche's "affirmative woman," Derrida writes, "she plays at dissimulation, at ornamentation, deceit, artifice, at an artist's philosophy. Hers is an affirmative power. . . . " Woman is thus an indeterminable identity, "a non-figure, a simulacrum."[23] It is the very breakdown in logic that dismays readers of Baudrillard's *Simulations* that delights Derrida here, and the creation of a space between the self and the image through an exaggeration of this breakdown, the hypersimulation associated with feminine irony, is the only "hopeful" possibility that even Baudrillard seems to offer.

Yet feminists must approach a hope figured as feminine salvation with suspicion. As Modleski points out, figuring both the masses and their subversive mode as feminine does not necessarily give feminists concerned with the historical and cultural position of women any cause for celebration. Noting the (masculine) sexual indifference that arises when the position of feminine difference is claimed by everyone, Modleski insists that the ascription of femininity to the anonymous mass glosses over crucial distinctions.[24] Attending similarly to Nancy Miller's warning, we must not lose sight of the ways in which a theoretical position that deems the question "who speaks?" irrelevant can also maintain the institutional silencing of women. As Miller states, "Only those who have it can play with not having it."[25]

Not only must we be leery of male theorists playing with the demise of a social and political representation that we have never had, but we must not obscure the differences that do exist for men and women within the realm of mass culture. Returning to Huyssen's claim that images of a feminized mass culture no longer apply to the postmodern world, let me continue his point: "If anything, a kind of reverse statement would make more sense: certain forms of mass culture, with their obsession with gendered violence, are more of a threat to women than to men. After all, it has always been men rather than women who have had real control over the productions of mass culture."[26] In other words, while television spectatorship may be figured as generically feminine, two crucial differences are overlooked: the historical split between consumption and production (in which women are the primary consumers while men largely control television production) and TV's reaction against the feminine through the construction of a violent hypermasculinity.

Turning first to the issue of a gendered consumption, many television critics and historians have explored the material conditions of female consumption, women's viewing patterns, and advertisers' address to this audience.[27] Furthermore, several theorists suggest a relationship between constructions of femininity and the consumer subject. Elsewhere, I have argued that such theoretical accounts of femininity accord in many ways with popular images of women in relation to looking and buying.[28] In the popular imagination, the woman is too close to what she sees—she is so attached that she is driven to possess whatever meets her eye (or, as the pun suggests, her "I"). The labels commonly applied to film and television genres addressing a female audience—"weepies" and "tearjerkers"—convey the same assessment: there is an almost physical closeness assumed to exist between the overinvolved female spectator and the image which forces her tearful response. Such everyday appraisals of women as subjects who lack the distance required for "proper" reasoning and viewing are mirrored by theoretical and psychoanalytic accounts of femininity which similarly stress women's lack of subject/object separation.[29]

While feminist theorists may offer these tropes of female proximity, fluidity, and "nearness" as a subversive or hopeful alternative to the masculine model of identity, such overpresence cannot be divorced from consumer desires. As several critics have remarked, it is the emphasis on self-image that invites the consumer to attend to the images of advertised products, and the woman who must purchase in order to enhance her own status as valued commodity becomes the prototypical consumer—the same overpresence that ties her to the image allows her to be situated as both the subject and the object of consumerism at once.[30] It is thus no coincidence that (what has been seen as) the particular "feminine" textuality of television supports the psychology of the perfect consumer. One of TV's most devalued genres, the soap opera, clearly exposes this intersection of cultural notions of femininity and consumerism: within the form seen by many critics as emblematic of female subjectivity, there are almost twice as many commercials as occur on prime-time TV. Furthermore, television theorists have suggested a relationship between soap opera form—a continuously interrupted present which refuses closure—and the effectivity of its commercials which, rather than truly interrupting the soap opera, continue its narrative patterns while offering "oases of narrative closure."[31]

Yet the conditions that link consumerism and femininity (both related to an overidentification with the image and commodity object) affect all of postmodern culture—today men also attend to self-image and their value of exchange, similarly losing the distinction between subject and object that has characterized the female consumer. Not only, then, are women presumed to be the best of consumers, but all consumers are figured as feminized—a situation yielding tension in a culture desperately trying to shore up traditional distinctions even as its simulations destabilize such attempts. As the distance between subject and object diminishes in the weightless space of postmodern culture, the threat of feminization as well as an all-encompassing consumerism hangs over all subjects, and television (discussed, like femininity, through tropes of proximity, overpresence, and immediacy) is central to this process.

While TV's appeal then does not stop with women, its consumers have been belittled in such terms in the critical and popular imagination alike, provoking contemptuous assessments of genres in addition to those traditionally associated with female audiences. Music Television, for example—a form which also addresses a culturally devalued (but economically desirable) audience, youths in this case—further reveals the relations between a fractured Oedipal logic, postmodern form, and consumerism: these videos completely dissolve the distinction between program, product, and ad in texts which can only be described as commercials for themselves.[32] TV soap operas and music videos, the programs most disparaged, are thus in many ways the most telling, displaying the conventions of continuity and difference, presence and interruption, viewing and consuming invoked by the television apparatus. In other words, the forms that seem to best illustrate TV's specificity also reveal a consumerism associated with the address to an audience deemed infantile or feminine, a spectator "not fully a man."

Yet as the "feminine" connotations attached to television and consumer closeness are diffused onto a general audience, contradictions of gender and spectatorship emerge, and television is placed in a precarious position as it attempts to induce consumer overpresence even as it tries to achieve cultural status by mimicking the more respectable cinema. It is interesting in this context to look at texts which exaggerate or foreground the specific representational strategies and discursive configurations of contemporary television. For example, a program such as ABC's on-again, off-again series *Max Headroom* rejects the cinematic model as it self-consciously announces television's difference, and as it calls attention to the characteristics of television (which are, as we have seen, shot through with connotations of gender), it would also seem to be among the shows most vulnerable to charges of feminization.

Max Headroom does, in many ways, raise this fear as it both extends and defends itself against the vacuum of simulation and the threat of a feminized world. In the premiere episode, for example, we are introduced to Max, a computer-generated "video subject" who is born in an attempt to answer an enigma. The enigma at the root of this "birth" centers on a mysterious death and cover-up—an event investigated by ace news reporter Edison Carter, the man who furnished the mind given to Max. In the scene in which this enigma is made visible, we see a large and lazy man at home in his armchair, watching television as an ad comes on the air. The ad he sees makes use of a diegetically new representational form—instead of presenting a logical and linear argument, a miniature narrative, or a coherent series of associational images, it involves a rapid flow of sound and images, chaotically thrown together so that nothing can be clearly identified or isolated. In other words, this ad is simply an intensified microcosm of TV as we, the home viewers, know it. The effect of this commercial on the diegetic viewer, however, is that of a literal inflation—the man swells up as consumer s(t)imulation builds inside of him until he actually explodes (or, for Baudrillard, implodes). What we witness, then, can almost be described as a form of hysterical pregnancy—TV provokes a generation of sensations, meaning, and animated force until this energy short-circuits and bursts to the surface, destroying the human body but providing the narrative origin of the cyborg, Max. Because Edison Carter has seen this event (although on videotape), he is captured, and his brain is scanned by a computer in order to disclose the full extent of his knowledge. In the process, Max Headroom is created. Eventually, of course, Edison recovers, solves the case, and reports the crime through another simulation—he broadcasts the contents of Max's memory which contains the videotape of the viewer explosion.

Exploring the sexual and textual issues raised in this episode, it is first of all apparent that TV is caught up in a web of simulations—any access to "the real" is mediated through a series of video images (the original video ad, the videotape of the ad and explosion, the computer scan of Edison's memory of the tape, and finally, Edison's retaping of Max's computerized memory of the tape—a broadcast which is at that point at least four times removed). In the show's brief second run, such simulations are even further exaggerated. While Max gained Edison's mind in the opening season, in the "second premiere" Max returns the favor, allowing Edison to be programmed with the contents of his computerized memory in order to save Edison from "going out of his head" after being brainwashed by some junk food and its accompanying prize.[33] The question, then, of whose mind either Edison or Max can go out of (or into) raises the ultimate problem of simulation and its twisted yet seemingly all-encompassing order. Max Headroom, in other words, presents a completely technologically mediated world, the ultimate in postmodern hyperreality that, as the program's logo tells us, is only twenty minutes into our own future. Furthermore, in its form as well as content, this show draws on postmodern textual devices—the program is known for the ways in which it refuses to subordinate its visual effects to a clear narrative progression and multiplies the look through a dense layering of simulated images and a fractured diegesis. As this program plays with TV's multiplicity of signs, time flow and shifting space, editing techniques derived from advertising, and fluctuating levels of reality/reproduction/fabrication, it carries TV form to its limits, shifting the critique of television into a celebration of its specificity.

But like critical accounts of television, Max Headroom's depiction of TV simulation is not divorced from questions of gender: this scene figures both the receptive TV body and the threat of a simulated world in terms of denigrating images of femininity. The viewer-victim, while a man, is an emasculated one—flabby and passive, he sits in front of his TV set until his body blows up in the pregnancy that ultimately results in Max. As (literally) a "talking head," Max himself is likewise feminized—he lacks the body of a man and constantly tries to sort out a man's sexual memories that he can't really understand. While Max masquerades as male, his constantly shifting contours provide him with a fluctuation of being that refuses even the illusion of unity and stability. Unable to differentiate himself from the matrices that bear him, he does not master the order of hyperreality but can only flow within it, losing the distinction between self and other that is (however fictionally) required to attain the status of a man. This condition, however, is not confined to Max—even the experts of this simulation, the computer operators who help Edison solve his cases, lack powerful masculinity: Max is created by a pre-adolescent (and pre-sexual) whiz kid, while Edison's computer guide is female. Here, as in Baudrillard's vision, the dangers of hyperreality, as well as its perpetrators, are feminized.

Yet while it plays with textual figures and devices that have been theoretically linked not only to postmodernism but also to feminine subjectivity, various strategies with which to contain TV's "feminine" connotations are also employed. *Max Headroom* literally splits its hero in two, displacing postmodern consumer consciousness onto Max and leaving Edison Carter free to play the role of traditional hero. While Max is there for comic effect (much of the show's humor is based on his lack of a stable identity and his literal existence in the perpetual present of the TV mosaic—in the show's jargon, Max is "in the system," essentially bound to the flow of TV), it does, nonetheless, take a "real man" to free us from the adverse effects of this simulated world. Edison Carter, a typical melodramatic hero, battles crime and exposes wrongdoing in order to keep his world in line. This program thus exists in the tension between modern and postmodern forms, projecting the "feminine" cyborgian elements onto a dominated other (Max) while still allowing its male protagonist to control the diegetic space and the flow of the narrative.

In a similar way, television as a whole exists in an odd tension, balanced between the modern and the postmodern (its reliance on melodrama, for example, in the midst of its own self-referential texts) and between culturally constituted notions of the feminine and the masculine (both sustaining and rejecting the positions offered by critical, as well as commercial, discourses). This places television in a curious bind—a situation perhaps most evident in many prime-time programs which, in order to be "culturally respectable" and appeal to male viewers, attempt to elevate the infantile and deny the feminine conventionally associated with television (particularly with the texts I have noted). A common strategy of television is thus to construct a violent hypermasculinity—an excess of "maleness" that acts as a shield. In this way, TV's defense against the feminine may be seen to correspond with television theory's attempts to dispense with the same— by their either resisting the feminine position (as many television texts do) or else incorporating and so speaking for it (as occurs in many recuperative critical texts, as discussed above), the real presence of women within these particular TV representations and critical texts is deemed unnecessary.

Within the realm of TV itself, there are a number of possible methods of defense. By aiming for the status of "quality" television (producing texts that can function under the name of an author), creating "proper" spectator distance by mimicking cinematic conventions, or obsessively remarking the masculinity of their thematics, some programs attempt to evade TV's feminization. Yet attempts at denial and male masquerade can produce problems which emerge on the surface of "masculine" texts.[34] Faced with the contradictions created by the imperative to inscribe order in a medium that disallows resolution and the demand to be "manly" in the "feminized" world of TV, these texts yield a realm of masculine excess that demonstrates their fragile position within both TV's hyperreality and a "hypermasculinity" that is its defense.

In her article on televised sports, Margaret Morse notes that despite cultural inhibition, "the gaze at 'maleness' would seem necessary to the construction and . . . replenishment of a shared . . . ideal of masculinity"[35] —an ideal that, in the light of my earlier remarks on consumer culture, particularly needs replenishing. Morse examines the discourse on sport as "a place of 'autonomous masculinity,' freed even from dependence on woman-as-other to anchor identity."[36] Sport, however, is not the only area in which the male body is displayed. In her analysis of *Magnum, p.i.,* for example, Sandy Flitterman traces the mobilization of the male spectacle, revealing the ways in which an eroticized masculinity is foregrounded.[37] Furthermore, such displays do not necessarily establish a masculinity free from relation to the feminine, despite their location within the (generally) all-male preserves of sports and the cop/detective show. They can instead be seen as an attempt to save masculinity even in the "feminized" world of TV, even in the vacuum of a crisis-ridden postmodernism (which, not incidentally, also includes the crisis of Vietnam—a crisis in masculinity which has been dealt with explicitly in several cop/detective shows, including *Magnum, p.i.,* and which may also be partially responsible for the popularity of the genre in general).[38]

Even more than *Magnum, p.i., Miami Vice* is a show of male excess and display which can be analyzed as a response to a feminine "contagion." In his insightful analysis, Jeremy Butler reveals the ways in which *Miami Vice* aspires to the cultural position of the cinema through its use of *film noir* conventions.[39] Yet *Vice* differs from *film noir* in some important ways. In place of the duplicitous woman—the trouble that sets the cinematic plot in motion—the motivating forces in *Miami Vice* are all men. Women may be visible as background detail or decor, but in a world in which male criminals are the primary enigmas and objects of voyeurism, the woman is divested of all potency, including, and most importantly, her power of masquerade, her ability to manipulate her femininity. Here, the power of masquerade belongs to men, most frequently Crockett and Tubbs who display themselves as criminals in order to lure their prey into captivity. (This display can also be seen in the ways in which the images of Crockett and Tubbs have been taken up by advertising and fashion—again, it is the male image which is now the focus, the men who masquerade.) While *film noir* investigates female identity and masquerade, *Miami Vice*'s central dilemma revolves around the identity of "V/vice" and the possibility of differentiating between the cops and the crooks, the men and their roles.[40] Clearly at stake here is a question of masculinity in a world in which all stable distinctions have dissolved, in which the feminized object of the look and trouble of the text constitute a position shared by everyone. This is a crucial question for postmodern, post-Vietnam America as well as an issue for television—the "feminine" cultural form of our time.

An episode entitled "Duty and Honor" (one of the episodes confronting Vietnam) exemplifies the textual disturbances provoked by such displays of manliness. The narrative traces the paths of both an assassin—a black Vietnam veteran, called only "the Savage," who is responsible for a series of prostitute murders (all of the victims are marked by the words "VC Whore" despite the fact that most of them are not Vietnamese)—and a Vietnamese police officer, a former friend of Lieutenant Castillo who comes to Miami to solve the murders that have haunted the two since their meeting in Vietnam. From our first sight of the Savage, he is marked as an object of the gaze as he appears before a mirror, eyeing himself and rehearsing a pose. He is thus constituted as spectacle—the spectacle of a perfect machine, a cyborg weapon of war, and a feminized icon demanding to be looked at.

Discussing the spectacle of the cyborg body as well as the aesthetic of slow motion, Morse analyzes the athlete in terms of the cultural fantasy of the perfect machine body, a body moved by an "inner logic" beyond space and time, at one with nature and "unimpeded by acts of the ego." In the ritualized experience of this unified "flow," she writes, "man can overcome his separateness from nature, God, other men and his own body, and achieve grace, signified by slow motion."[41] In other words, as a cyborg body, an object displayed for the fascinated gaze, the male athlete can ritually experience a subjectivity usually coded as feminine. This analysis of slow motion applies to the visual style of *Miami Vice*, and specifically here to the cyborg, the Savage, who is positioned as both a (feminized) visual object and a perfect machine of death. His status as image is constantly emphasized as we see him primp in a black leather coat, repeating a gesture of smoothing his hair. In one scene, he even competes with a televised display of male bodybuilding as he yells at his landlady for watching too much TV and failing to look at him when she speaks.

As both spectacle and object of the investigatory gaze, the Savage is assigned the role traditionally aligned with femininity. In fact, as the narrative progresses, we learn that he is literally feminized; he has been castrated in Vietnam, the reason for his hatred of Vietnamese women and

their simulated stand-ins. Hypermasculinity as a response to such feminization, the underlying structure of texts of male spectacle, is then made
manifest in the episode's central murder scene.[42] The scene is marked by
a flattened pictorial space fully dominated by the Savage. Staring into the
camera, he is posed against a stark wall, apparently naked, with an enormous knife emerging from the bottom of the frame. Sharing the prostitute's
point of view, we see the Savage approach and almost leap into the camera,
returning the look of the spectator with a violent retribution that obscures
our vision and concretizes the excess of his status as spectacle as well as
the discord of such hypermasculinity, a reaction to castration.

In the logic of the episode, this castration is infectious—after the intro-
ductory flashback to the initial crime in Vietnam, the episode begins as
Sonny Crockett is interrupted at the height of a sexual encounter by the
news of the latest homicide. Sonny is also a Vietnam vet, and there is an
odd mirroring thus established between two "couples": Sonny and the Savage, and Castillo and Nguyen Van-Trang, Castillo's former partner. In both
couples, each "partner" has immediate knowledge of the other which goes
beyond language but is distorted by a masquerade. Furthermore, in these
"pairs," the conventional terms of sexual difference have been displaced
onto racial difference, a situation also key to *Miami Vice*'s primary part-
nership—that of Crockett and Tubbs. In this episode, however, the focus
shifts to the couples Sonny and Savage, Castillo and Trang—two familiar
heroes and their "others." Sonny mirrors the Savage in two scenes as shots
of his search for the killer are intercut with shots of the Savage looking
for prostitutes. Finally, Sonny exhibits the contagion of feminization by
smoothing his hair in the characteristic gesture of his prey moments before
the Savage arrives and is instantly recognized through the crowd (although
Sonny has never seen him before) while making the same gesture.

While the chase scene locates Sonny and the Savage as (literally) moving
down "parallel roads," the successful joining of Castillo and Trang is located
in the hope for an impossible future world. It is only after Trang has saved
Castillo from attack, tenderly examined his wound, and quickly disappeared that Castillo reads of his friend's masquerade—Trang is an alias,
assumed for undercover work in South Vietnam and Miami. While he
remains unnamed, his voice-over explains his real status as colonel in the
Army of the Republic of Vietnam, his new understanding of the Savage
as victim (of the true savages in both of their countries who nurture war),
and his appreciation of Castillo's care despite the masquerade. He ends his
letter asking for friendship: "I dream of a more perfect world in which we
could also be comrades." The dream of male bonding, occurring against
a backdrop in which it is impossible to distinguish opposing sides, assert
right or wrong, or secure masculinity apart from a violent defense, is here
played out in all its excess and contradiction.

While the politically progressive "message" of this episode is striking in
relation to the usual fare of TV cop shows, it exposes the problematic of

which I am speaking in chillingly clear terms, embodying the hypermasculine defense against a feminization associated with TV, postmodernism, and post-Vietnam America in the cyborg character of the Savage. As such, it reveals TV's masquerade of masculinity—a masquerade which may be seen as a violent response to the feminine connotations attached to television and its receptive viewers. In other words, while theoretical and popular discourses alike may figure television in terms of femininity, we should not accept such views uncritically, failing then to notice other crucial differences which run through television—differences related to class and racial positioning, for example—as well as the contradictions of gender that do exist within television's multiple address. While the gender inscriptions of U.S. broadcast television are complex, intertwined, and unstable, it is important to note that even the temporary securities offered in shows of male spectacle require the neutralization or absence of women (while still disavowing any overt homosexual eroticism). The family offered is a family of man, and the gender positions cast are significant for both the men and women watching. In a medium in which the familial is the dominant theme as well as mode of address, this is the final irony that cannot yet be explained by current theories of sexual and textual difference—the masculine threat that lurks "within the gates" of a medium deemed feminine.

NOTES

1. The concept of the cyborg body comes from Donna Haraway, "A Manifesto for Cyborgs: Science, Technology, and Socialist Feminism in the 1980s," *Socialist Review* 80 (Mar.-Apr. 1985):65–107. See also Tania Modleski's discussion of *Videodrome* in "The Terror of Pleasure: The Contemporary Horror Film and Postmodern Theory," in *Studies in Entertainment: Critical Approaches to Mass Culture*, ed. Tania Modleski (Bloomington: Indiana University Press, 1986), p. 159.

2. The term "machine-subject" comes from Margaret Morse who analyzes the ways in which TV seems to address its viewers from a position of subjectivity in "Talk, Talk, Talk—The Space of Discourse in Television," *Screen* 26.2 (Mar.-Apr. 1985):6.

3. For a related analysis, see Patrice Petro, "Mass Culture and the Feminine: The 'Place' of Television in Film Studies," *Cinema Journal* 25.3 (Spring 1986):5–21.

4. Tania Modleski, "Femininity as Mas(s)querade: A Feminist Approach to Mass Culture," in *High Theory/Low Culture*, ed. Colin MacCabe (New York: St. Martin's Press, 1986), pp. 37–52.

5. Andreas Huyssen, "Mass Culture as Woman: Modernism's Other," in *After the Great Divide: Modernism, Mass Culture, Postmodernism* (Bloomington: Indiana University Press, 1986), pp. 62 and 53–55.

6. Marshall McLuhan, *Understanding Media: The Extensions of Man* (New York: McGraw, 1964), pp. 16–17.

7. McLuhan, p. 17.

8. Georg W. F. Hegel, *Phenomenology of Mind*, trans. J. B. Baillie (New York: Harper, 1967), p. 496.

9. John Fiske and John Hartley, *Reading Television* (New York: Methuen, 1978). See, for example, pp. 15, 85–87, 112, and 116–26. The chart of oppositions between television and literate media that Fiske and Hartley offer in this book (pp. 124–25) mirrors the one that Fiske employs to differentiate feminine and masculine forms in *Television Culture* (New York: Methuen, 1987), p. 203.

10. According to Fiske and Hartley, it is in the space between TV's irrational mode and the masculine logic of print that the viewer can position him/herself so as to decode TV differently. Through the (unspoken) metaphors of sexual difference, then, these theorists construct a theory of television's difference—a view that echoes a common position in literary theory which has also aligned textual difference with figures of femininity.

11. John Ellis, *Visible Fictions* (London: Routledge, 1982). See, for example, pp. 57, 116, 137–39, 141–43, 146.

12. Perhaps the most obvious case of this tendency to associate television with the feminine is the Lacanian reading offered by Beverle Houston in the article "Viewing Television: The Metapsychology of Endless Consumption," *Quarterly Review of Film Studies* 9.3 (Summer 1984):183–95. I don't discuss this analysis in the text precisely because the thesis that TV is feminine is so clear in her work. The more interesting cases, in my opinion, are those in which gendered metaphors creep into discussions of television by critics not expressly making this claim.

13. See, for example, Huyssen's discussion of nostalgia as a response to postmodernism's "various forms of 'otherness'" (including feminism) on pp. 199 and 219–20. Janice Doane and Devon Hodges discuss the anxiety provoked by the erosion of traditional categories of gender in *Nostalgia and Sexual Difference: The Resistance to Contemporary Feminism* (New York: Methuen, 1987).

14. Jean Baudrillard, *Simulations* (New York: Semiotext[e], 1983), p. 56.

15. Ibid., pp. 30–31. See also pp. 52, 54.

16. Ibid., pp. 52, 54.

17. See, in particular, Laura Mulvey, "Visual Pleasure and Narrative Cinema," *Screen* 16.3 (Autumn 1975):6–18. Recently, many feminist film theorists have retheorized spectatorship so as to account for shifting and contradictory identifications and more powerful and pleasurable positions for the female viewer. See, for example, Elizabeth Cowie, "Fantasia," *m/f* 9 (1984):71–105; Teresa de Lauretis, *Alice Doesn't: Feminism, Semiotics, Cinema* (Bloomington: Indiana University Press, 1984); Tania Modleski, *The Women Who Knew Too Much: Hitchcock and Feminist Theory* (New York: Methuen, 1988); Kaja Silverman, *The Acoustic Mirror: The Female Voice in Psychoanalysis and Cinema* (Bloomington: Indiana University Press, 1988); and Linda Williams, "Something Else Besides a Mother: *Stella Dallas* and the Maternal Melodrama," *Cinema Journal* 24.1 (Fall 1984):2–27.

In discussing the female spectator in the latter part of this paper in terms of narcissism and tropes of proximity, I am not claiming that these are the only or essential positions available for an actual female viewer. Rather, I am focusing on the *representation* of women in both popular and critical accounts of cinematic spectatorship. In other words, the historically and culturally sanctioned positions for female viewers are quite limited even though other constructions of viewing pleasure are certainly possible, particularly for viewers who have been positioned "differently" by the discourses of feminism.

18. Jean Baudrillard, *In the Shadow of the Silent Majorities . . . or The End of the Social and Other Essays* (New York: Semiotext[e], 1983), p. 33.

19. Luce Irigaray, *This Sex Which Is Not One*, trans. Catherine Porter (Ithaca: Cornell University Press, 1985), pp. 76, 150–51; and Mary Ann Doane, "Film and the Masquerade: Theorizing the Female Spectator," *Screen* 23.3–4 (Sept.-Oct. 1982):74–88. Doane employs and expands the concept of masquerade developed by Joan Riviere in "Womanliness as Masquerade," in *Psychoanalysis and Female Sexu-*

ality, ed. Henrik Ruitenbeek (New Haven: College and University Press, 1966), pp. 209–220. Also see Mary Ann Doane, "Masquerade Reconsidered: Further Thoughts on the Female Spectator," *Discourse* 11.1 (Fall-Winter 1988–89):42–54.

20. Baudrillard, *In the Shadow*, pp. 40–41. See also p. 39.

21. Rey Chow, "Tofu: The Protein and Protean Dietetics," Cornell Graduate Student Conference on the Culture Industry, Cornell University, New York, April 1987.

22. See Baudrillard, *In the Shadow*, p. 39.

23. Jacques Derrida, *Spurs: Nietzsche's Styles*, trans. Barbara Harlow (Chicago: University of Chicago Press, 1978), pp. 67, 57, 49.

24. Modleski, pp. 50–51.

25. Nancy Miller, "The Text's Heroine: A Feminist Critic and Her Fictions," *Diacritics* 12.2 (Summer 1982):53. Also addressing this issue is Naomi Schor, "Dreaming Dissymmetry: Barthes, Foucault, and Sexual Difference," in *Men in Feminism*, ed. Alice Jardine and Paul Smith (New York: Methuen, 1987), pp. 98–110; and Patricia Mellencamp who examines sit-com simulations that are inflected differently by the female voice in "Situation Comedy, Feminism, and Freud: Discourses of Gracie and Lucy," in *Studies in Entertainment*, especially p. 87.

26. Huyssen, p. 205. The "threat to women" revealed by mass culture's gendered violence can also be seen in my example of *Videodrome*—a film that thus demonstrates how TV has been figured as feminine as well as how this figuration masks a violent hypermasculinity.

27. See, for example, the essays in *Camera Obscura*'s special issue on "Television and the Female Consumer," *Camera Obscura* 16 (Jan. 1988), and in the anthology *Boxed In: Women and Television*, ed. Helen Baehr and Gillian Dyer (New York: Pandora Press, 1987).

28. Lynne Joyrich, "All That Television Allows: TV Melodrama, Postmodernism, and Consumer Culture," *Camera Obscura* 16 (Jan. 1988):141–47.

29. See, for example, Nancy Chodorow, *The Reproduction of Mothering: Psychoanalysis and the Sociology of Gender* (Berkeley: University of California Press, 1978); Carol Gilligan, *In a Different Voice: Psychological Theory and Women's Development* (Cambridge: Harvard University Press, 1982); Irigaray, *This Sex Which Is Not One*; and Michèle Montrelay, "Inquiry into Femininity," *m/f* 1 (1978):83–102. For an illuminating discussion of such tropes of feminine proximity, see Mary Ann Doane, *The Desire to Desire: The Woman's Film of the 1940s* (Bloomington: Indiana University Press, 1987).

30. On advertising and self-image, see T. J. Jackson Lears, "From Salvation to Self-realization: Advertising and the Therapeutic Roots of Consumer Culture, 1880–1930," in *The Culture of Consumption: Critical Essays in American History, 1880–1980*, ed. Richard Wightman Fox and T. J. Jackson Lears (New York: Pantheon, 1983), pp. 3–38. Relating this to the specific position of women is Rosalind Coward, *Female Desires: How They Are Sold, Bought, and Packaged* (New York: Grove Press, 1985), and Doane, *The Desire to Desire*, especially pp. 13 and 22–33.

31. See Sandy Flitterman, "The *Real* Soap Operas: TV Commercials," in *Regarding Television: Critical Approaches—An Anthology*, ed. E. Ann Kaplan (Frederick, Md.: University Publications of America, 1983), pp. 84, 94. See also the essays on soaps by Tania Modleski, Charlotte Brunsdon, and Robert Allen in the same volume.

32. On MTV and postmodernism, see, for example, E. Ann Kaplan, *Rocking Around the Clock: Music Television, Postmodernism, and Consumer Culture* (New York: Methuen, 1987); Peter Wollen, "Ways of Thinking about Music Video (and Postmodernism)," *Critical Quarterly* 28. 1–2 (Spring-Summer 1986):167–70; and the essays on music video in *Journal of Communication Inquiry* 10.1 (1986).

33. After *Max Headroom*'s initial introduction in the US on March 31, 1987 (a remake of the original British text), its "second premiere" aired on ABC on April

28, 1988. Throughout this episode, we witness an argument between the two heroes which erupts when Max (who gets better ratings) steals Edison's airtime. When Max is later projected into Edison's brain in order to provide what is referred to as "a jumpstart" (a phrase which implies that Edison too is a technological being, another cyborg), they continue the argument. Edison exclaims, "You're always in my way—you're too close to me," and Max responds, "I can't help being that close and being a threat to you." Edison then asks, "Have you any idea what it's like having a part of me competing against me?" to which Max replies, "And have you any idea what it's like just being a part?" This exchange, coupled with the plot concerning the power of consumerism, is interesting for the ways in which it explicitly employs the tropes of "nearness" and overpresence that have been raised in both popular and critical portrayals of the cyborg, the female, and the "consuming" body. Furthermore, it reveals the threat to a (presumed) separate and unified male subject that is posed by such "feminized" objects as well as by the operations of postmodern culture which confuse the distinction between part and whole, self and "other."

34. The analysis of such shows as "hysterical" texts that yield contradictions emerging as textual fissures suggests a reading of these programs as "male melodramas." Noting that melodrama's search for clearly marked oppositions historically arises in periods of crisis, one can analyze television—the medium of hyperreality which is defined as *the* age of crisis—as the melodramatic forum of postmodernism. Because of both the specific suitability of melodrama for television and the demands of postmodernism, even genres not typically associated with the melodrama—such as the cop show—have turned toward the more personal issues associated with melodramatic form, thereby inheriting some of this genre's tensions as well as the tensions provoked by such generic hybrids. See Joyrich, "All That Television Allows," pp. 129–53.

35. Margaret Morse, "Sport on Television: Replay and Display," in *Regarding Television*, p. 45.

36. Ibid., p. 44.

37. Sandy Flitterman, "Thighs and Whiskers—the Fascination of *Magnum, p.i.*," *Screen* 26.2 (Mar.-Apr. 1985):42–58.

38. The crisis in masculinity provoked by Vietnam has also been discussed by Andrew Ross, "Masculinity and *Miami Vice*: Selling In," *Oxford Literary Review* 8.1–2 (1986):150. Comparing *Miami Vice* to *film noir*, Jeremy Butler reminds us of the historical connection between *noir* style and postwar disillusionment—a connection which suggests that the popularity of *Miami Vice* may be related to post-Vietnam despair. See *"Miami Vice:* The Legacy of Film Noir," *Journal of Popular Film and Television* 13.3 (Fall 1985):129.

39. For Butler's analysis of these issues of sexual difference, see pp. 129–30, 132–33.

40. On this core dilemma, see Butler, pp. 131–32. On the double meaning of "Vice" as it relates to masquerade and the "right stuff" of masculinity, see Ross, p. 152.

41. Morse, pp. 44, 56.

42. In other words, in "Duty and Honor" (which NBC first aired on February 6, 1987) hypermasculinity can be seen as a response to (or defense against) the literal embodiment of the Oedipal structure and the castrating woman.

SUPERMAN AND THE PROTECTIVE STRENGTH OF THE TRADEMARK

Jane Gaines

The television text's characteristic segmentation, its capacity to ingest everything, to repeat infinitely, to stamp its imagery on every conceivable object of everyday life are the dimensions of television described as aesthetic symptoms of postmodernism, which, as Stuart Hall has so aptly put it, is really about "how the world dreams itself to be American."[1] In the US, then, where late capitalism looms large and postmodern culture, *its* symptom, flows abundantly both within the country and across its borders into "the ones only dreaming," we would expect to find in operation certain codes or rules which govern this flow. Along with the formal conventions which regulate works of cultural production in general, there are other conventions organizing television texts. I will look to the field of entertainment law and examine the connection between the advent of television and the increased preference for trademark over copyright as a legal remedy since the late forties and early fifties.

If intellectual property and unfair competition laws can be said to rule cultural texts, is this regulation in any way comparable to the governance of literary, cinematic, and televisual conventions? We may think that the laws of the state are significantly different from other kinds of codes because of the sharp edge of enforcement, but we might also consider how law silently shapes even when not actually enforced. Legal commentators deal with this function of the law by referring to *norms* which they discuss in much the same way that cultural theorists talk about codes and conventions: users put codes into practice, and comprehension and order depend upon a loose agreement between users. One way in which the study of the law has differed significantly from the study of culture has been in the availability of the concept of ideology which did not find its way into legal studies until the late 1970s in Britain and the US.[2] The almost ten-year lag between legal studies and cultural studies presents an interesting problem for scholars: while it is crucial for legal theorists to begin work on the way law has functioned ideologically, those of us who study culture and society are currently looking for more elasticity in the concept of ideology; whereas legal scholars may now be refining their analysis of the structural function of ideology, scholars in cultural studies are looking at the points of opposition to ideology. The following represents an attempt to deal with the confluence of law, culture, and economics—the recurring dilemma is whether the law asserts itself as material base or disengaged superstructure.

Some Marxist legal theorists have noted the way the law *appears* to be both of the base and of the superstructure. Commenting on the way rights to the land and its agricultural uses seemed inseparable in seventeenth-century England, E. P. Thompson says that the law is "deeply imbricated" in the relations of production, so much so that it is often indistinguishable from the mode of production.[3] This neither-here-nor-there aspect of the law is its "mystery," say Paul Hirst and Elizabeth Kingdom. But its illusiveness is also its efficacy: "it stands to production in a mysterious form in that production is absent in it and yet by this 'absence' capitalism's conditions of operation are secured."[4] Do we have an inkling of the way the law silently "secures" capitalist "conditions of operation" in the way the very design on the face of the object of culture (for example, a scene from the television show *Star Trek* reproduced on sheets and pillowcases) has an economic function as a bona fide registered trademark? The case of the bed linens suggests that the mode of the law is also to represent economics as absent all the while it "secures" the requisite conditions for economic production. The trademark function disappears into the representational function of the scene from *Star Trek*.[5]

The success of Paramount Pictures in registering the *Star Trek* design as a trademark (which involved arguing to the US Trademark Trial and Appeal Board that it was not mere ornamentation) is part of a larger picture, in fact, part of a marked historical shift in the use of particular legal theories in entertainment law from 1940 to the present. I view the US Trademark Act of 1946, known as the Lanham Act, which took effect July 5, 1947, as a participant in rather than an absolute determinant of developments, an interpretation which allows me to look at the orchestration of the various levels. Thus I can ask if the increased use of trademark law to protect popular icons is not part of what some might see as television's eclipse of the theatrical film.

The transition of the character Superman from comic strip through radio and motion picture serials, television series, and motion picture features corresponded with the period in which trademark law overtook copyright law as the governing principle of character protection in popular formats. Since 1940, DC Comics, the corporate proprietors of Superman, have aggressively defended their entitlement to the character in the US courts.

The eight cases I have studied, spanning the years 1940 to 1983,[6] are a remarkable record of realignment around legal theories of character protection which would best strengthen the company's market position by reinforcing legal barriers around their image properties. The DC Comics cases testify to the basic conflict between copyright and trademark as legal theories and practical remedies, and in another realm they speak of conflict over cultural values.

The Superman text, then, is the cultural turf over which an important conflict between copyright and trademark has been waged. On the side of copyright, we have authorship: the older, bourgeois, cultural value which has protected the comic strips since 1938 and which was invoked to defend the cartoon hero Superman against the infringing comic book hero Wonderman in 1940. Historically, the spirit of Anglo-American copyright law has been protection of the author's expression, and in the name of this, copyright has justified the limited monopoly it allows over a creative work by linking exclusive use with an idea of the livelihood of the author-originator. Although Anglo-American law retains the Romantic notion of authorship in its emphasis on expression, uniqueness, and the self-contained work of art, in copyright law, *originality* really means point of origin rather than novelty or creativity.[7] The technical synonymity between origin and author here allows for theoretical consistency since copyright law recognizes the owner of rights over the real author. Thus any legal entity can stand in as author just as DC Comics has stood in for Jerry Siegel and Joe Shuster, Superman's creators, who tried for forty years to reclaim their work.[8]

If Anglo-American copyright law has evolved from an idea of protection for an author against marketplace pirates, trademark law, a branch of unfair competition law, has evolved from a general philosophy of protection *for the public* against merchants who might deceive them about the true source of the goods or services they were purchasing. In principle, the merchant's mark has been protected because it stood to the consumer for *goodwill*, the guarantee that the buyer could expect from the source behind the goods the same values and qualities received with the last purchase. Significant for us, however, is the inversion of this principle in US common law, so that the trademark comes to ensure that the merchant-owner of the mark is protected from infringers, *not* that the public is protected from merchant fraud.[9] With the weight of unfair competition law behind them, merchants are able to defend their trademarks against others who would use them, thus shielding what US, although not European, law has increasingly come to recognize as an asset or property. While copyright still upholds some remnant of the older cultural valuation of individual enterprise and creativity, the trademark unapologetically stands for market expansion and control. It is precisely this reversal in common law, the result of a shift in legal decisions after World War II, which makes it possible for DC Comics to defend the character Superman as their trademark, giving them a significant market advantage not realizable under copyright theory.

Copyright as the preferred theory of legal defense for popular characters fell out of fashion in the entertainment industry with the often-cited 1954 Sam Spade case. The question in *Warner Brothers* v. *Columbia Broadcasting* turned on whether Warner Brothers's motion picture rights to the novel *The Maltese Falcon* included the right to enjoin author Dashiell Hammett from using the character in sequels. It would appear that the sympathy of the court was with Hammett since the decision allowed him to continue to use his literary creation. But in the process of giving Spade back to the author, the court defined characters as mobile pieces in relation to the *work,* the wholeness and totality of which is crucial to copyright law. Characters, the "mere chessmen," devices or vehicles for telling the story, were substantially less than the work itself, and following this reasoning, the character had to constitute the work as a whole in order for it to be protected by copyright.[10] After the Sam Spade case, entertainment law literature associated copyright more and more with enigma and intellectual puzzle; in contrast with trademark law, copyright was as tenuous as the works of authorship it protected.[11] Sam Spade also demonstrated the consequences of the copyright preference for the single work-as-a-whole, since the work had previously protected the character as its component part. Especially in combination with the companion case *Nichols* v. *Universal Pictures, Warner Brothers* v. *Columbia Broadcasting* seemed to say that the literary character had to take on the complex proportions of the narrative undergirding in order to qualify for copyright protection.[12] Furthermore, the case reiterated the difference between the ephemeral literary character, often constructed with word portraits which were too abstract and vague to be visualized (and hence protected), and cartoon characters whose concrete existence as artistic renderings made uniqueness (or imitative proclivities) easier to verify in court.[13]

The Sam Spade decision, a relic of the Golden Era of Hollywood cinema when copyright law alone protected valuable literary properties from which so many films were derived, became a textbook case, and the field of entertainment law gravitated toward trademark doctrine as a remedy for securing the profitability of either popular titles or characters. Copyright law was found to be inadequate since it could not protect the title of a novel or a motion picture which the doctrine of intellectual property understood as descriptive of the work or like the proper name of something—in other words, not part of the work as a whole.[14] Trademark law, in contrast, with its emphasis on source, origin, and sponsorship as opposed to authorship, protected both title and character if they indicated programs or a series of stories emanating from the same source.[15]

It is interesting to note that the legal displacement of the author in the shift from copyright to trademark corresponds roughly in time with the phenomenon postmodern theory has diagnosed as the eclipse of the author by his or her own text. Legal theorist Bernard Edelman, in the context of commenting on the same feature in French trademark law that I have identified in US law, suggestively argues that the character which breaks away from its author is a feature of the very kind of writing which produced this character: "With the character, the writing circle closes—one could even claim that the author disappears. The author alienates himself within an infernal machine of his own making. The writing takes on a form beyond that of its own origin, a product that moves about freely on a stage, playing out its non-human role."[16] Perhaps because of my US vantage point, I would stress the facilitating role of trademark law in the tendency of popular characters to leave their textual origins and disclaim their authors. In US law based on copyright (as opposed to author's right as in France),[17] where real authors may be contractually canceled out forever, it seems more the case that trademark law has encouraged the detachment of the character from the work. This seems especially true considering the importance of trademark law to the merchandising of programs which grew out of early television programs.

From the first days of television, series titles, as indicators of origin (as opposed to motion picture titles which were considered to be like proper names), attained legal status as trademarks. From the point of view of merchandising, then, *Maverick, Howdy Doody, Annie Oakley*, and *Superman* were ideal vehicles because both the name of the main character and the series title could be protected by trademark law. To indicate the way trademark law works to reinforce a character name or series title, all of the US registered trademarks discussed hereafter will be designated by all caps in the text, following the graphic convention used in the legal literature on unfair competition.

One of the early tests of trademark law in relation to television suggests the potency of this legal remedy and hence its attractiveness to television producers who were interested in turning popular characters and program titles into further capital. In *Wyatt Earp Enterprises* v. *Sackman, Inc.* (1958), the court held that the owner of the program entitled *The Life and Legend of Wyatt Earp* could enjoin or stop a clothing manufacturer's use of the name "Wyatt Earp" on playsuits. Without prior knowledge of trademark law, it seems strange to us that any party could lay claim to the name of a legendary figure, since we would assume that history, of all the territories of shared culture, could not be monopolized. However, one of the basic concepts in trademark law, the doctrine of *secondary meaning*, sorts commercialized signs into a second (protected) order of meaning on the basis of their demonstrated popularity. Scholars have recently called attention to the way television programs exist to deliver viewers to advertisers who calculate the matches between commercial airing and hypothetical viewing as "impressions" made on consumers. Here, the titles of the programs, as well as the names, physical appearances, and costumes of the characters, are also impressed upon viewers whose later recognition then substantiates the trademark status of these high-circulation signs.[18] The very fact of having been broadcast to millions of homes then makes it possible for the producers of *The Life and Legend of Wyatt Earp* to first license Sackman, Inc., to use the name WYATT EARP on children's clothes and, after the company's continued production beyond the expiration date of the license, to restrain them from using the name of the legendary hero.

Product licensing, a parasitic industry which traces its parentage to the sound, motion picture, and radio industry, thrived in the post–Lanham Act early days of television, enjoying a heyday it had not known since the thirties when Herbert Kamen established the Walt Disney character licensing program, and Shirley Temple and the the Lone Ranger were licensed so successfully for dolls, games, and school supplies.[19] The 1978 STAR WARS merchandise boom, which reignited licensing after its lapse in popularity in the sixties and early seventies, was followed almost immediately by Warner Brothers's duplication of the phenomenon with SUPERMAN: THE MOVIE. The past ten years have seen further reduplication with four motion picture sequels and at least forty half-hours of syndicated television programming per week.[20]

Merchandise licensing depends entirely on the protectibility of the trademark; it is the legal shield around the name, logo, slogan, shape, or character image which makes it possible for the original proprietor to transfer this sign to second and third parties for a limited period of time, in exchange for royalties. In addition to the total reversal whereby injury to the owner takes precedence over injury to the consumer, the theories basic to trademark law also seem to have reversed themselves. While unfair competition law would be based on the prohibition against *palming off* one's goods as the goods of another, licensing itself is essentially a "passing off."[21] If, for instance, RJR Nabisco, Inc., through its merchandising agent, Columbia Pictures, licenses the image of Niagara Falls on the Shredded Wheat cereal box to a manufacturer of beach towels, does Nabisco stand directly behind the towel in the same way it stands behind the box of breakfast cereal? This unlimited transference is anticipated and aptly described by a 1938 provision in British law against "trafficking in trademark." The provision was invoked recently when American Greeting Cards tried to register their HOLLY HOBBY mark in the U.K. and were denied registration because, rather than preserving their reputation, licensing would help them to "dispose of [that] reputation as though it were a marketable commodity."[22]

SUPERMAN AND SERIES FORM

The point most often made about television series characters is that the narrative returns them to the same situation and frame of mind in which we left them in the previous week. They learn nothing new; they neither grow nor change significantly.[23] Superman, the ideal series character, created to fit the frames of the comic book, fights the same battles every week, and for all of his powers is unable to restore law and order or bring peace to the world. Each new story, says Umberto Eco in "The Myth of Super-man," is a "virtual new beginning," which means that the character exhausts the narrative material he is given and requires more, parceled out week after week, year after year. For Eco, this "iterative scheme" is written into the conditions of Superman's double (human/superhuman) existence, as though Superman and series form were eternally one.[24]

There are two other important ways of considering Superman and form suggested by recent developments in cultural studies. First, following Tony Bennett and Janet Woollacott's paradigm for studying James Bond, Super-man may be seen as one long intertext of all of the narratives, reviews, and biographies, laid end to end. In their scheme, the ancillary products I am describing become "textual meteorites" shooting off from the textual chain.[25] In this configuration, each story would not necessarily start from a virtual beginning, but would be written onto as well as over the earlier story, creating a paradigmatic build-up. The lethal powers of kryptonite, introduced in the radio series, are now firmly embedded in the accumulation of retellings. The second approach would be to look at the character as material which is significantly altered as it is cast in different media. Superman, then, does not necessarily carry his narrative scheme within him like a genetic map. He can always be rewritten for another medium, so that although Superman would seem to epitomize the television series character who must always return to the beginning, in his earlier incarnations, cast in different narrative schema, he followed somewhat different rules.

Three years after SUPERMAN's famed launching of DC's *Action Comics* in June, 1938, the stories took their first moving image form in the Max Fleischer/Paramount Pictures animated cartoons. Seventeen were cartoons produced between 1941 and 1943. Columbia Pictures then produced two fifteen-part series starring Kirk Alyn in 1948 and 1950. But the relative success of the 1948 series compared to the 1950 series suggests that the logic of the connection between television and series form had occurred to audiences as well as producers. A single transitional feature film, *Superman and the Moleman* (1951), introduced George Reeves as Superman; thereafter, Reeves embodied the part in the 104 television episodes produced and aired between 1951 and 1957.[26]

Pre-television—in his comic book, animated cartoon, and motion picture serial incarnations—the Superman character is ruled by the law of copyright, while in the fifties, in television, he comes more and more under the influence of the trademark. Since under copyright law the body of the text theoretically protects the character, and since the character alone, outside the work, can be protected *only* by trademark law, the expansion of the story as a continuing serial is simultaneously the legal survival of the popular character. The first of two Columbia serials retells Superman's early life history—from the disintegration of the planet Krypton, the arrival of the infant Superman on earth, and the death of his foster parents, to his arrival in Metropolis City. The feud with Lois Lane and the discovery of the powers of kryptonite are unfolded chronologically with each episode ending with cliff-hanging anticipation of the consequence of a former action. Using the novelistic time frame, the continuing serial asserts its status as a work and reveals its ambition to be a motion picture feature, an aspiration it has historically had since the mid-teens when it served as a compromise format in the transition from the short to the full-length feature.[27]

Significantly, in the period in which Superman is first represented by a mortal body (that of actor Kirk Alyn), the narrative takes the form of a continuing serial. One might also say that the 1948 serial tested the protectibility of the character against the powers of the real, for in the serial's combination of animation and live action, we are made aware of the continuity between DC Comics's thoroughly protected cartoon drawing and the new motion picture. Superman in cartoon form, the form with an already established record of toughness in court battles against pirates,[28] is imprinted on the film like the merchant's mark ensuring against infringement and defending against property claims made by the real-life actor playing the character. Although legal commentators have concurred that cartoon characters cannot lose their identities to actors, the Lone Ranger and Bela Lugosi–Dracula cases (in which the actors' rights to the roles they had played were asserted) are often cited in cautionary footnotes.[29] In other words, the actor playing the part introduces a potential challenge to the total monopoly DC Comics would have on Superman since the actor could conceivably argue that he had an ownership in a role with which he had become synonymous. The sign of the cartoon creator's hand which validates the iconic Superman as a protectible artistic rendering is invoked in the animated flying sequences in the 1948 serial which, in their unbounded defiance of physical laws, also show up the limitations of the live-action representation of flying "faster than a speeding bullet."

The difficulty that intellectual property (the branch of the law concerned with copyright protection) has had with the literary character within the work tells us something about the antithetical relation between the novelistic character and narrative form. Taken together, *Warner Brothers* v. *Columbia Broadcasting* (Sam Spade) and *Nichols* v. *Universal Pictures* display a high culture preference for the rounded character against the flat type. These cases suggest that the ordinary character is subservient to the narrative work in which it appears, and that in order for a character to be protected, it must rise to the condition of a uniquely created work of art in its own right. In other words, it must be the psychologically deepened, novelistic character whose development and change is charted along the chronology of classical narrative form (although of course we know that novelistic time is only borrowed to help create the illusion of the birth-to-death sequence of human life). But we begin to suspect that the novelistic character has structural limitations unknown to narrative which has, of course, a miraculous, tapeworm-like capacity to regenerate and ensure its own continuance. While narrative can assure its self-perpetuation into infinity, the novelistic character, who must change in the same direction, will make life choices which only bring him closer to his own obliteration—through aging and eventual death. As Eco has explained, the prohibition against action, change, and sexual encounter built into the Superman character has to do with the danger that with every humanlike act he would, in approaching death, "consume" himself.[30]

If we compare the time frames of the novelistic character and the continuing narrative, we find an impending contradiction between the two. While the narrative can permutate *ad infinitum*, the character modeled after the human individual will be exhumed because of the very action-oriented growth and development that classical narrative requires of him or her as its agent. The mortality of the character, of course, explains why the continuing serial—the first model of the cultural-industrial form with the potential to carry on forever—requires multiple characters who reproduce over several generations, thus adhering to codes of realism and still following its inclination to endure into infinity.[31] Consider, in contrast, the mythic hero, Eco's "inconsumable" character, whose actions will never extinguish him, but who, because he is doomed to repeat, seems most at home in the series form which reconstructs the key components of his type each week. That the immortal, semihuman character and the form which could expand infinitely to tell the history of the universe are ultimately incompatible says something about the inherent limitations of narrative realism and novelistic time. To get out of this bind, the Superman story resorts to fantasy time schemes and experimental temporalities. But finally, the profitability of the literary property requires this impossibility: a semihuman character who is immortal and a story which never really ends.

Capital and literary form appear as competing interests in Superman as with no other popular figure because of the peculiar conditions of his existence as both a consumable and an inconsumable character who obeys the temporal orders of earth and the universe, or as Eco has put it, "Superman is a myth on condition of being a creature immersed in everyday life."[32] Capital puts entirely different stipulations on the character who, from the point of view of profit, is under threat from two vantage points. First, the very human form which the character assumes in his live-action motion picture and television manifestations is a potential danger to profit. But a greater threat, whose effects are as dire and as certain as the effects of kryptonite on the body of this hero, is the fear of copyright expiration. During the period of copyright protection (in the US, the life of the author or the date of the first publication plus fifty years), the character may be somewhat shielded by the story. But inevitably, if the story stands absolutely alone as a work, it will fall into the public domain. That is, it will fall into the public domain and the character along with it *unless it is part of a series.*

This is where, in this story, television and trademark law come to the rescue of Superman. As I have already noted, the title of a television series is protected as a trademark because it indicates the source of the programs. A character becomes a trademark when and if it comes to identify a series of narratives produced by the same creator; by the same token, if the character indicates the same sponsored television program, it has a trademark function. And here, one can faintly see the philosophy of producer "goodwill" and the ostensible concern for television viewer-consumers who are protected by the promise that the trademarks MORK AND MINDY, THE DUKES OF HAZZARD, CHARLIE'S ANGELS, and STARSKY AND HUTCH mean that viewers can expect the same quality from the makers every time they choose one program over another.[33]

The status of SUPERMAN as a television series title is not the only source of the trademark's protective strength. By virtue of the character's popularity, "super" and "man" no longer are two descriptive words belonging to a common English language but have achieved a legal *secondary meaning* in the minds of the public. The physical appearance and costumes denoting SUPERMAN (but not the physical abilities or personal traits) are also protected as trademarks,[34] and as a trademark, the name and the physical likeness of SUPERMAN are protected in perpetuity. DC Comics, proprietors of the character, have an invincible monopoly on the character that is guaranteed into infinity. It would seem, then, that the character SUPERMAN, as a free-floating entity, could outlast even the stories that launched him. Yet there is one final danger facing SUPERMAN as private property, a danger which is always lurking in nonuse and its antithesis, overuse. I will explain these cliff-hanging possibilities in my conclusion, but first I want to return to the pending crisis in entertainment law between copyright and trademark, a crisis which is bound up as well with motion picture and television form.

With television, then, SUPERMAN has found the ideal medium for ensuring his immortality. Because it is potentially never-ending, television, for THE MAN OF STEEL, could be the narrative form that corresponds with the conditions of his immortality. Theoretically, this would resolve the contradiction between narrative progression and character by acknowledging that only the inconsumable, mythic character is temporally compatible with the never-ending proclivity of narrative. But for all of its apparent continuousness, television is also intermittent; its characteristic segmentation which, as John Ellis argues, means that it "tend[s] never to coalesce into an overall totalising account," would make it the perfect medium for the character who must never fulfill his mission in one episode.[35] And yet the weekly regularity of the 1950s series, now in syndication on US television, underscores the temporal and spatial impossibility of the Superman premise.[36]

Each week on television, the Superman story defies the logic of narrative progression, doubling back against the current of causality; in each program, the continuity construction defies the physical, spatial logic which asserts that since Clark Kent and Superman are never in the same place, they must be one and the same. Clark Kent's secret identity—a problem more insurmountable than the difficulty of finding more action for the character which would not slowly consume him—requires increasingly ingenious aesthetic solutions, pushing the series into an experimental and even self-reflexive mode at times. (As in the episode where Lois and Jimmy watch Clark Kent interview Superman on television, and he uses voiceover to speak to himself, eluding them once again.) The irresolvable time-and-space problems which place the stories in peril are compounded in the television series by George Reeves's portrayal of Clark Kent. Reeves makes us interested in the motives of a morally committed journalist which, in combination with the insistent tug of the black-and-white video image, take Superman in the direction of the hard-hitting crime show and closer to social realism than at any time in his career. (In the 1950s, on black-and-white television, SUPERMAN had its resemblances with DRAGNET and ELIOT NESS AND THE UNTOUCHABLES, but today, seen in the color in which it was originally shot, instead of hard edge we see soft nostalgia.) Although, as Eco reminds us, it is Superman who is "real," and Clark Kent who is the fiction, it is in the Kent role that the personality split erupts as the full-blown troubled psyche of the novelistic character.[37]

At this juncture in history, then, tensions between copyright and trademark are played out in the Clark Kent–Superman dichotomy. George Reeves as Clark Kent would dramatize the artist locked into the role; as the actor developed a penetrating mind and a conflicted psychology for the character, he would produce the very stuff of intellectual property—abilities and traits—which trademark law is not equipped to comprehend. Meanwhile, SUPERMAN the trademark, which subsumes and overrides the *Daily Planet* reporter, would with each episode (every one of which constituted another use) continue to stake out the DC Comics claim in culture and in consciousness.

It is the Super half of the character which we associate with the "immobility" and the historical short-sightedness that Eco and Thomas Andre diagnose as the political paralysis of the Superman format. This format binds us into a "continuum" and a "repetition" rather than an orientation toward a future we can create. These terms which reoccur in the political and aesthetic critique of Superman are, of course, the very same terms which are so often used to describe the conditions of US television as postmodern—its fragmentation, its infinitude, and its static quality.[38] However, describing the temporal immobility of television's episodic series (always a return to a position never outgrown), Ellis asks that we consider another possibility—that this stasis is "more a basic contradiction or power relation than a zero degree."[39] Or the Clark Kent–Superman tension figures the mythic, immortal character bound by conscience to outdated, mortal, time-linked notions of mankind and the values of humanism; locked as the two are into this antithesis, the episodes can only re-present a contradiction, at base one of the structural faults of bourgeois society.

This structural fault, or in Macherey's terms the "defect" at the core,[40] is more clearly written in the copyright-trademark dichotomy since it is here that capital announces its motives, and its clash with bourgeois humanism appears so striking. Recent trends in the interpretation of trademark law in the US, which have been such a boon to character merchandising, have also encouraged the growth of a new industrial practice.[41] Corporations recoup their advertising expenses and further diversify their interests by licensing corporate logos, so that, for instance, R. J. Reynolds and Philip Morris can license their CAMEL and MARLBORO trademarks for leisure wear.[42] In addition, with every successful defense against merchandise piracy and with every license issued for these ancillary products, and even, in a sense, with every pair of MARLBORO jogging shorts produced and with every purchaser's wearing of them, Philip Morris shores up its monopoly on the word MARLBORO, which enables the company to rent it again. Trademark law, as it has evolved in the entertainment industry over the last forty years, makes it possible for the owners of popular image properties to transfer them onto the surface of the culture like a decalomania is transferred onto a T-shirt.

To what extent, then, is SUPERMAN overlaid on the surface of contemporary culture? Imagine for a moment that you are growing up in the American suburbs in 1988. At home, you wear SUPERMAN house slippers, drink "kryptonite-free" DIET COKE, and eat pretzels in the shape of the SUPERMAN shield while you watch "Superman Week," an episode from the 1950s television series rebroadcast on your local cable channel. During school, you mark your place in the SUPERMAN novelization with an American Library Association SUPERMAN book mark, and take a test on the official *SUPERGIRL Seatbelt Safety* book. After school, you go to your Girl Scout meeting at the YWCA where you work on your WONDER WOMAN badge which requires you to cook a meal from recipes in the *DC Super Heroes Super Healthy Cookbook*. On the way home from the scout meeting, you and your friends decide to get off the bus at the mall to play the SUPERMAN pinball machine (manufactured by ATARI, another subsidiary of Warner Communications), and after you run out of quarters, you snack on the free samples of SUPERMAN Trail Mix handed out by a man dressed up in the official trademarked red-and-blue tights and cape.

My parody, I hope, will suggest that the experience of growing up in urban culture under advanced capitalism eludes the postmodernist notion of the contemporary image surround. But also that once these commodities are linked with use-practices, it begins to seem that such an image colonization may not be a surface phenomenon, but rather that consumer product tie-ups, once produced, are blended into daily life. Baudrillard might describe this as the "collusion of Image and life, of the screen and daily life," experienced at this time in history as "the most natural thing in the world, you feel it every day." However, neutralizing the apocalyptic pessimism in his diagnosis produces a more comprehensive analysis: SUPERMAN tie-ups are inextricably intertwined with everyday life and deeply rooted in the culture.[43]

Imagine, then, that you are growing up in an American small town in 1948. The usher punches your SUPERMAN Club Card as you enter the local motion picture theater to see Chapter Three, "The Reducer Ray," and as you enter the dark house you carefully slip the card back into your SUPERMAN billfold, anticipating the fifteenth week when a completely punched card entitles you to a free admission. As you leave the theater, still chewing the free SUPERMAN bubble gum, compliments of the exhibitor (who paid 52 cents for a box of 80 sticks), you pass the dry-goods store where you see a SUPERMAN movie viewer exhibited in the window. You dig in the pocket of your SUPERMAN jacket to see if you have seventy-eight cents, almost two months' allowance, and since you don't, you decide to enter the SUPERMAN contest advertised on the radio. With visions of SUPERMAN watches, school bags, and record albums in your head, you walk toward home thinking (in 25 words or less) "If I Were Superman, I Would. . . . "

DC COMICS IN COURT

There is a temptation, understandable in materialist analyses of culture (and film theory has been particularly prone to this), to represent the production of meaning as the production of commodities. The production metaphor itself encourages a homology which may not have been intended.[44] And yet, to say that the sign is the commodity is often an apt description of how the economy works under advanced capitalism. I am thinking here of the "use" stipulation in US trademark law which can be seen as encoding the transformation of sign-vehicles into commodities. US trademark law gives an emphasis to "use" that it doesn't have in other countries where, for instance, it is not necessary to demonstrate "use" and secondary meaning *before* registering a mark. Whereas in other countries first registration guarantees the monopoly (which is why you will find Donald Duck ice cream in Hong Kong not licensed by Walt Disney), in the US "use" stakes out the claim.[45] In other words, to industrially produce an aluminum cake pan in the shape of Superman is to reassert (by a kind of high-finance squatter's rights) ownership and economic control over the most commonplace signs of culture in everyday circulation.

Unwittingly, the consumer then participates in a kind of marking off of the territory of culture, which designates particular sign areas as out of bounds for users, some of whom are the very consumers whose use-practices have helped to establish the claim. Legally, if secondary meaning exists

"in the minds of the consuming public," then, even if a copyright or trademark has expired, the owner of this cultural capital can reestablish pro-
prietorship.[46] *DC Comics* v. *Jerry Powers* (1978) exemplifies this problem: in
a case in which neither party held a registered trademark in a name, the
party that could demonstrate consumer awareness was able to assert prior
claim to the name. This dispute over the name DAILY PLANET illustrates,
in addition, the struggle over language in more of an apparent confirmation
of the old ruling-class manipulation thesis of instrumentalism that Marxist
legal theory would currently want to see.[47] DC Comics is better able to
prove its entitlement to the name DAILY PLANET than an underground
newspaper which had a limited circulation in Miami, Florida, between 1969
and 1973, during which it published an article entitled "Superman Smokes
Dope." To claim a monopoly on the DAILY PLANET, DC Comics needed
only to show evidence that the newspaper title had figured in licensing
contracts for SUPERMAN, while the publishers of the underground
DAILY PLANET (public awareness of which never reached beyond the
audience of the 1969 Woodstock Music Festival) could not demonstrate the
"duration and consistency" necessary to hold onto their expired trademark
which they had held from 1970 to 1976.[48] While in copyright law, allowance
of parody and the doctrine of fair use (with its freedom-of-speech feature,
which the law needs in order to preserve the appearance of an open society)
might allow some oppositional elements to stand rather than find them
infringing; trademark law, the strong man for the expansion of capital,
however, can stamp out oppositional culture.

   Coincident with the release of SUPERMAN: THE MOVIE and its sequels
between 1978 and 1982, DC Comics successfully enjoined at least three
other uses of what the company calls the "family of SUPERMAN" properties. In 1979, they won judgments for copyright and trademark infringement as well as unfair competition against Crazy Eddie, Inc., an electronic
equipment company. DC successfully argued that the advertisement which
included the line "It's a bird, it's a plane, it's Crazy Eddie . . . " was not a
parody but more of a "detailed copying" of the trailer for the reruns of
the 1950s show in syndication in New York City on the same channels.[49]

   A year later, another New York court found in DC Comics's favor. It
ruled that the television cartoon characters Superstretch and Manta and
Moray had the same abilities as DC's PLASTICMAN and AQUAMAN.
Relying on copyright law, but also on Section 43a of the Lanham Act referring to the dilution of trademark, the court restrained Filmation Associates from producing their television series.[50] In Chicago, an Illinois
court concluded that the students of Richard J. Daley City College could
not name their college newspaper the *Daley Planet*. The state court found
that the students' use of the title violated the section of the Lanham Act
pertaining to the falsely designated source of origin, that the use was *likely
to cause confusion,* and finally that it was *likely to dilute* the *distinctiveness* of

the DAILY PLANET trademark.[51] Citing *DC Comics* v. *the Board of Trustees* (1981) along with the Marx Brothers and the John Philip Sousa cases from the same period,[52] David Lange has identified a wide move in copyright and trademark law which indicates to him an "unconscionable overreaching" that significantly reduces the area of the public domain. As he describes this realignment within case law, the "field of intellectual property can begin to resemble a game of conceptual Pac Man in which everything in sight is being gobbled up."[53]

There is confirmation of this in a *Harvard Business Review* article which recommends corporate logo licensing and trademark protection because of the limited number of brand names available. Some market researchers, the author says, find that nearly all of the desirable brand names have already been registered.[54] While this may indicate the failure of corporate imagination as much as US multinational dreams of "gobbling up" the domain of culture, Lange's suspicion that the public domain is being devoured provides a metaphor for and an insight into a relationship between popular culture and the state. The question which I will not pursue here is whether US law facilitates the penetration of capital into popular forms while discouraging its penetration into high cultural forms.

Just when it appeared that DC Comics had gone too far in their overreaching and that US law was clearly rigged in favor of concentrated power, the financial forces that protect SUPERMAN lost a landmark court case. In 1983, two years after the publication of Lange's article focusing on the Richard J. Daley City College case, Warner Brothers (along with DC Comics, a subsidiary of Warner Communications) unsuccessfully tried to restrain ABC from producing its SUPERMAN take-off, a television series entitled *The Greatest American Hero*. The US Second Circuit Court found, among other things, that the character, Ralph Hinkley, who crash-landed in his flights and cowered at bullets, was "sufficiently dissimilar" and that he exhibited "Superman-like abilities in a decidedly unSuperman-like way." In the decision in favor of ABC and its unhero, Hinkley, the court, describing Hinkley as part of a "genre of superheroes," concluded that "Superman has no monopoly among fictional heroes self-propelled in outer space."[55]

At issue here is a theory lurking in copyright and trademark law, a stipulation which comes to the rescue of the law in the nick of time, just when it is about to appear unfair. This stipulation is a loose translation of one of the basic dilemmas of capitalism: it fosters competition and at the same time remains deeply tied to a scale of economic expansion which wipes out all competition. In copyright law, this dilemma becomes the doctrine that a limited monopoly rewards creativity but that a complete monopoly on the materials available for expression doesn't foster creativity; creative breakthrough depends upon the circulation of materials. Even the legal distinction between underlying *ideas* which are not protectible and their *expression* which can be reserved has, specialists admit, awkwardly dealt with the problems that arise from the need to free up the languages that are the materials from which works are drawn.[56] The same general principle is at work in trademark law's prohibition against tying up language, and hence the Lanham Act's distinctions between what the law calls the *descriptive meaning* (defined as the literal or dictionary meaning) and the *secondary meaning* which a word (or figure) acquires through use. Thus, the primary meanings of the words "daily" and "planet" or "mickey" and "mouse" are not removed from the language pool. This suggests why US trademark law exhibits a preference for what are termed *fanciful* or *arbitrary* marks such as the coined words "clorox," "sanka," and "kodak" which have no initial utility in the culture other than their use in reference to companies and products.[57]

Warner Brothers v. *ABC* (1983) is a shift back to the other side as the law defends an idea of shared culture, speaking about the need to maintain a balance between "public interest in the free flow of ideas and the copyright holder's interest in exclusive use of his work."[58] In his argument that Superman is part of a genre of superheroes, Circuit Court Judge Newman affirmed the theory developed in the case law on characters since *Nichols* v. *Universal Pictures* (1954)—that the underlying "type" (much like an underlying "idea") must remain available to producers who need to use the basic features as building blocks.[59] The "superman" type must freely circulate in order for others to make use of the idea of a man with phenomenal powers who saves the human race, a concept made generic by the very success of the original SUPERMAN character. DC Comics's multiplication of the type into BATMAN, AQUAMAN, WONDER WOMAN, SUPERBOY, and SUPERGIRL, which, by their mere use, can deny existence to imitations such as Wonderman and Superstretch, is a vision of the monopoly on culture that trademark and copyright law in practice encourage but in theory stand against.

Thus, under the protection of trademark law, the only fear of extinction that SUPERMAN could conceivably have, a fear which is the opposite of nonuse and abandonment (which could hardly be the concern of such a popular character), is the threat of emasculation brought on by popularity itself as a direct result of fifty years of merchandising and licensing. Built into the Lanham Act of 1946 is a seldom-invoked provision which gives the US Federal Trade Commission the power to cancel a trademark in the name of competition if, through the success of its proprietors, it really does become the household term they set out to make it. Thus it was that Abercrombie and Fitch lost "safari" and Bayer lost its monopoly on "aspirin," which went the way of thermos, zipper, escalator, cellophane, ping-pong, yo-yo, brassiere, and shredded wheat: all from protected trademark to generic *descriptive* term available to competitors. The specter of a final peril for the protectors of SUPERMAN is raised by the concern in the plastic laminate business; because the trademark may become generic through universal recognition, SUPERMAN might face the fate of "formica."[60]

NOTES

1. Stuart Hall, "On Postmodernism and Articulation: An Interview," *Journal of Communication Inquiry* 10.2 (Summer 1986):46.

2. For an overview of these developments, see Hugh Collins, *Marxism and Law* (New York: Oxford University Press, 1984); David Kairys, ed., *The Politics of Law: A Progressive Critique* (New York: Pantheon, 1982); Peter Fitzpatrick and Alan Hunt, eds., *Critical Legal Studies* (Oxford: Basil Blackwell, 1987).

3. E. P. Thompson, *Whigs and Hunters: The Origin of the Black Act* (New York: Pantheon, 1975), p. 261.

4. Paul Hirst and Elizabeth Kingdom, "On Edelman's 'Ownership of the Image,'" *Screen* 20.3–4 (Winter 1979/80):139.

5. Paramount Pictures Corp, *US Patent Quarterly* 217 (1983):292–94.

6. Detective Comics, Inc. v. Bruns Pub. (1940); Detective Comics, Inc. v. Fox Pub., Inc. (1942); Detective Comics, Inc. v. Powers (1978); Detective Comics, Inc. v. Crazy Eddie, Inc. (1979); Detective Comics, Inc. v. Filmation Associates (1980); Detective Comics, Inc. v. Board of Trustees (1981); Detective Comics v. Reel Fantasy, Inc. (1982); Warner Brothers, Inc. v. American Broadcasting Co., Inc. (1983).

7. See Bleistein v. Donaldson Lithographing Co. (1903) for a definition of originality as it has been employed in US law.

8. Otto Friedrich, "Up, Up and Away!!!" *Time* 14 Mar. 1988:69, says that Warner Communications, now the owners of D. C. Comics, finally paid each author $20,000 per year for life at the time the company produced SUPERMAN: THE MOVIE.

9. Frank Schechter, *Historical Foundations of Trademark Law* (New York: Columbia University Press, 1925), p. 5; Frank S. Moore, *Legal Protection of Goodwill* (New York: The Ronald Press, 1936), p. 40; David Lange, "Recognizing the Public Domain," *Law and Contemporary Problems* 44.4 (Autumn 1981):168.

10. Warner Brothers Pictures, Inc. v. Columbia Broadcasting Co. (1954).

11. Paul E. Adams, "Superman, Mickey Mouse, and Gerontology," *Trademark Recorder* 64 (1974):191.

12. Nichols v. Universal Pictures Corp. (1930); Thomas E. Harrison, "The Protection of Titles and Characters," *The Merchandising Reporter* 4.7 (Aug. 1985):9–10.

13. E. Fulton Brylawski, "Protection of Characters—Sam Spade Revisited," *Bulletin of the Copyright Society of America* 22 (1974):83–84.

14. Gregory Battersby and Charles Grimes, *The Law of Merchandise and Character Licensing* (New York: Clark Boardman, 1985), Sec. 8.10.

15. Bernard Edelman, "The Character and His Double," in *Post-modernism and the Question of Identity: ICA Documents 6*, ed. Homi Bhabha (London: Institute of Contemporary Arts, 1987), p. 36.

16. Edelman, p. 36; Franklin Waldheim, "Characters—May They Be Kidnapped," *Trademark Reporter* 55 (1965):1030.

17. See R. F. Whale and Jeremy J. Phillips, *Whale on Copyright* (Oxford: ESC Pub., 1983), chapter 2, "Theory of the Author's Right."

18. Wyatt Earp Enterprises, Inc. v. Sackman, Inc. (1958), p. 622, at 2 and 3, uses as evidence for the establishment of *secondary meaning* the fact that between 1955 and 1957, 107 programs were produced and aired for 52 weeks each year, "viewed weekly on millions of television receivers by additional millions of persons."

19. Weston Anson, "A Licensing Retrospective and Glimpse into the Future," *The Merchandising Reporter* 3.5 (June-July 1984):4–5, cites Theodore Roosevelt's 1913 royalties earned from the sale of "'Teddy' bears (which supported the National Parks system) as the earliest American use of licensing, followed by the radio, television, and film licensing campaigns for Buck Rogers (1929), the Lone Ranger and Shirley Temple (1930s), Hopalong Cassidy and Tom Mix (1940s), and Zorro

and Davy Crockett (1950s); Battersby and Grimes, Sec. 1.6, say that in the 1950s over 17 ANNIE OAKLEY trademark registrations were approved for more than 70 products.

20. Kenneth Turan, "Superman! Supersell!" *American Film* 4.3 (Dec.-Jan. 1979): 49–52; "An Interview with Maggie Young—The 'Force' at Lucasfilm," *The Merchandising Reporter* 3.5 (June-July 1984):15–16.

21. Melville Nimmer, *Cases and Materials on Copyright and Other Aspects of Entertainment Litigation* (St. Paul: West, 1985), p. 837, says: "the essence of unfair competition consists in the palming off of the goods or business of one person as that of another."

22. Charles Grimes and Gregory Battersby, "English Legal Decision Jars Licensing Commission," *The Licensing Book* 1.5 (Apr. 1984):10, 12; Walter J. Derenberg and Paul B. Morofsky, eds., *European Trademark Law and Practice* (New York: Practising Law Institute, 1971), p. 452.

23. John Ellis, *Visible Fictions* (London: Routledge, 1982), p. 125; see Jane Feuer, "Narrative Form in American Network Television," in *High Theory/Low Culture*, ed. Colin MacCabe (New York: St. Martin's, 1986), pp. 108, 112, for an important challenge to the notion that series characters do not develop which is at the same time aware of the political significance of the concept of character development.

24. Umberto Eco, *The Role of the Reader* (Bloomington: Indiana University Press, 1979), pp. 117, 120.

25. Tony Bennett and Janet Woollacott, *Bond and Beyond: The Political Career of a Popular Hero* (New York: Methuen, 1987), p. 44.

26. Gary Grossman, *Superman: Serial to Cereal* (New York: Popular Library, 1976), pp. 318–20.

27. Raymond Stedman, *The Serials* (Norman: University of Oklahoma, 1971), p. 10.

28. Warner Brothers, Inc. v. American Broadcasting Co. (1983), p. 240, cites King Features Syndicate v. Fleischer (1924) [Barney Google's horse, Spark Plug], Hill v. Whalen & Martell, Inc. (1914) [Mutt and Jeff], and Empire City Amusement Co. v. Wilton (1903) [Alphonse and Gaston].

29. The Lone Ranger, Inc. v. Cox (1941); The Lone Ranger, Inc. v. Currey (1948); Lugosi v. Universal Pictures (1979).

30. Eco, p. 111.

31. Robert C. Allen, "*The Guiding Light:* Soap Opera as Economic and Cultural Document," in *American History/American Television*, ed. John E. O'Connor (New York: Ungar, 1983), p. 311, describes the character Bert Bauer who was played by the same actress for thirty years in this soap opera which, if we count its origin in radio in 1937, had been broadcast continually for over forty years. My point is merely polemical. Broadcast television *could* produce a narrative that continued into infinity, but even the serial which runs over several years is the exception.

32. Eco, p. 111.

33. Paramount Pictures Corp., *US Patent Quarterly*, p. 213 (1983) [MORK AND MINDY decalomanias]; Warner Brothers v. Gay Tops, Inc. (1981) [DUKES OF HAZARD—the General Lee car]; Spelling-Goldberg v. Levi (1978) [STARSKY AND HUTCH, CHARLIE'S ANGELS iron-on heat transfers].

34. Thomas J. McCarthy, *Trademarks and Unfair Competition*, vol. I (Rochester, N.Y.: The Lawyers Co-operative Pub. Co., 1984), chap. 7.

35. Ellis, p. 120.

36. Eco, p. 115, says the "confused notion of time is the only condition which makes the story credible."

37. In a strange foregrounding of the mortal time to which Superman is bound, and which is signaled in the human fallibility of Clark Kent, Reeves would commit suicide in 1959, two years after the series ended.

38. Thomas Andre, "From Menace to Messiah: The History and Historicity of Superman," in *American Media and Mass Culture: Left Perspectives,* ed. Donald Lazere (Berkeley: University of California Press, 1987), pp. 124–38; Umberto Eco, "Innovation and Repetition: Between Modern and Postmodern Aesthetics," *Daedalus* 114 (Fall 1985):179–80.

39. Ellis, p. 125.

40. Pierre Macherey, *A Theory of Literary Production,* trans. Geoffrey Wall (London: Routledge, 1978), p. 197.

41. Kaz Kuzui, "Japanese Licensing: An Ever-Changing Market," *The Merchandising Reporter* 3.5 (June/July 1984):30–31, describes how in 1962, "shohinka-ken," a new word meaning "product-making rights," had to be added to the Japanese language as the number of animated television series with licensing programs increased.

42. John A. Quelch, "How to Build a Product Licensing Program," *Harvard Business Review* (May-June 1985):187.

43. Jean Baudrillard, "Beyond Right and Wrong or The Mischievous Genius of Image," in *Resolution: A Critique of Video Art,* trans. Laurent Charreyron and Amy Gerstler, ed. Patti Podesta (Los Angeles: Contemporary Exhibitions, 1986), p. 10; I am indebted to Angela McRobbie, "Postmodernism and Popular Culture," *Journal of Communication Inquiry* 10.2 (Summer 1986):108–116, for this way of reading Baudrillard as well as an idea of how we might see realities and fictions as intermingling at this time in history.

44. See Fredric Jameson, *The Political Unconscious* (Ithaca, N.Y.: Cornell University Press, 1981), p. 45.

45. Battersby and Grimes, *The Law of Merchandise and Character Licensing,* Sec. 5–35.

46. Ibid., Sec. 4–18.

47. See Collins, p. 41, for further information on the instrumentalist theory which saw the law as carrying out the interests of the ruling class.

48. D. C. Comics, Inc. v. Powers (1978), p. 847.

49. D. C. Comics, Inc. v. Crazy Eddie, Inc. (1979), *US Patent Quarterly* 205 (1979):1178.

50. D. C. Comics, Inc. v. Filmation Associates (1980).

51. D. C. Comics, Inc. v. Board of Trustees (1981), as quoted in Lange, p. 166.

52. In Groucho Marx Productions, Inc. v. Day and Night Co., Inc. (1981), the heirs of the Marx brothers successfully enjoined the off-Broadway comic spoof *A Day in Hollywood, A Night in the Ukraine* which, they argued, used Groucho, Chico, and Harpo in violation of their right of publicity; in Instrumentalist Co. v. Marine Corps League (1981), an Illinois court awarded the exclusive use of the name and likeness of John Philip Sousa to a relatively unknown magazine, in effect prohibiting its use by the Marine Corps League. Lange (p. 170) argues that trademark and unfair competition law in this case could not take account of the cultural or historical significance of Sousa's relationship to the Marine Corps Band, which Sousa directed at the time he wrote "Semper Fidelis," and which took its name from the Marine Corps motto.

53. Lange, p. 156.

54. Quelch, p. 186.

55. Warner Brothers, Inc. v. American Broadcasting Co., Inc. (1983), p. 233.

56. Nimmer, p. 89; See J. Frow, "Repetition and Limitation—Computer Software and Copyright Law," *Screen* 29.1 (Winter 1988):7, for an analysis of the problems posed by this distinction from the point of view of linguistics.

57. McCarthy, pp. 656–79; British trademark law often cites Lord Justice Farwell on the need for vigilance in registering only those marks which genuinely "distinguish" lest "the large and wealthy firms with whom the smaller folk are unwilling

to litigate, could by a system of log-rolling, divide amongst themselves all the ordinary words of description and laudation in the English language"—as quoted in Derenberg and Morofsky, pp. 81–82.

58. Warner Brothers, Inc. v. American Broadcasting Co., Inc. (1983), p. 242.

59. Note "Protection for Literary and Cartoon Characters," *Harvard Law Review* 68 (1954):359.

60. Walter P. Marqulies, "FTC v. Formica, Inc.: Trademarks Face Challenge of their Lives," *Advertising Age* 13 (Aug. 1979):13.

AN ONTOLOGY OF EVERYDAY DISTRACTION

The Freeway, the Mall, and Television

Margaret Morse

> Thus television turns out to be
> related to the motor car and the
> aeroplane as a means of transport for
> the mind
> —Rudolf Arnheim

The following essay articulates an intuition which has been expressed from time to time in critical literature—that television is similar or related to other, particular modes of transportation and exchange in everyday life. This investigation of the subjective and formal bases of this intuition is limited here to the built environment of freeways and malls.[1] Television and its analogs, the freeway and the mall, are conceptualized as a nexus of interdependent two- and three-dimensional cultural forms which don't so much *look* alike as observe similar principles of construction and operation. These shadows or inverse aspects of the work world are forms of communication which also function interdependently.

Freeways, malls, and television are the locus of an attenuated *fiction effect*, that is, a partial loss of touch with the here and now, dubbed here as *distraction*. This semifiction effect is akin to but not identical with split belief—knowing a representation is not real, but nevertheless momentarily closing off the here and now and sinking into another world—promoted within the apparatuses of the theater, the cinema, and the novel. Its difference lies primarily in that it involves two or more objects and levels of attention and the copresence of two or more different, even contradictory, metapsychological effects. Ultimately, distraction is related to the expression of two planes of language represented simultaneously or alternately, the plane of the subject in a here and now, or *discourse,* and the plane of an absent or nonperson in another time, elsewhere, or *story.*

However, beyond the invocation of an *elsewhere* and a "spacing out" or partial absence of mind described here, many aspects of "distraction" are left to the imagination or to later treatment: a review of the rich field of the iconography of automobiles, freeways, malls, and television,[2] an account for the shifting relations between mastery and bondage and the feelings of pleasure and boredom involved in their use, and the ambiguous value the analogs of television enjoy in our culture—each in its own way being considered a "vast wasteland" and a waste of time as well as a devotion allied with the American dream.

The preconditions of distraction are postulated in the phenomenon of "mobile privatization," and the general features which promote this divided state of mind are described as "the phantasmagoria of the interior." Furthermore, freeways, malls, and television are posed as interrelated and mutually reinforcing systems organized in a way which allows for "liquidity," the exchange of values between different ontological levels and otherwise incommensurable facets of life, for example, between two and three dimensions, between language, images, and the built environment, and between the economic, societal, and symbolic realms of our culture.

Television is a key element of these exchanges and transformations, not only because it invests images with exchange value but also because it models exchange itself, both as an apparatus which includes the viewer virtually in discourse and via representations of constant shifts through various ontological levels, subjective relations, and fields of reference. The dualism of *passage* and *segmentation* which is part of the freeway, mall, and televisual realms is discussed more theoretically in relation to *discourse* and *story.*

There is nothing discrete about television, for its very nature is to annex pretelevisual culture and leisure time to itself. This essay seeks, in broad strokes, to situate television as a cultural form in a larger socio-cultural context of everyday life. This speculative project draws explicitly and tacitly on previous works of synthesis to support its premises, for example, Raymond Williams's relation of broadcasting to the changing social context of mobile privatization in which it developed; Walter Benjamin's *Passagenwerk* or arcade project of research on the genealogy of commodity fetishism in the nineteenth century in glass-and-ironwork-enclosed shopping arcades, dioramas, and exhibition halls such as the Crystal Palace; and, Mikhail Bakhtin's notion of the *chronotope* or unit of space/time which oscillates between literary representation and the spatio-temporal experience of everyday life. The archetypal chronotope, the *road,* for instance, invites comparison with the *freeway,* as does Benjamin's conception of the *arcade* with the *mall.*

Michel de Certeau's *The Practice of Everyday Life* is an inspiration to the basic premise of interchangeability between signs and objects described here. Noting that "in modern Athens, the vehicles of mass transportation are called *metaphorai*" (115),[3] de Certeau articulates concepts of language and narrative with such forms of everyday life as architecture, transportation, and food. His vision of liberation from formal determination, surveillance, and control is based on the distinction between language and society as formal systems versus language as it is enunciated or as a social form enacted in practice at any one time. This distinction is expressed spatially, for example, as the difference between *place*, a proper, stable, and distinct location, and *space*, composed of intersections of mobile elements, taking into consideration vectors of direction, velocities, and time variables. He concludes that "*space is a practiced place*," a geometry of the street redefined and made habitable by walkers (117).

De Certeau's vision of liberation via enunciative practices bears the marks of its conception in another time and place, that is, in a premall, prefreeway, and largely print-literate, pretelevisual world. In the meantime, in the United States at least, the very nature of the street and pedestrian activity as well as the predominant modes and media for linguistic communication has changed. However, the notion of praxis as enunciation, be it linguistic, pedestrian, or other, which evades predetermined paths and escapes from literal reality into an *elsewhere* and to other levels of consciousness is, as we shall see, one fully congruent with the operation of malls, or, for that matter, freeways and television. Indeed, *distraction* is based upon the representation of *space* within *place* (in which, as we shall see, space becomes displaced, a *nonspace*) and the inclusion of (for de Certeau, liberating) *elsewheres* and *elsewhens* in the here and now.

Thus, de Certeau's very means of escape are now designed into the geometries of everyday life, and his figurative practices of enunciation ("making do," "walking in the city," or "reading as poaching") are modeled in representation itself. Could de Certeau have imagined, as he wrote on walking as an evasive strategy of self-empowerment, that there would one day be video cassettes that demonstrate how to "power" walk? This investigation takes stock of this new cultural environment.

To contour this new terrain is less to map postmodernity than to explain why a map per se is virtually impossible to construct. For the level of iconicity shared by television and its analogs is one of common preconditions and principles of articulation rather than one of resemblance in shape or the boundedness of contiguous or even specifiable locations in space. Rather, these analogs share the *nonspace* and the simultaneous temporalities of *distraction*.

1. DEREALIZED SPACE

The late twentieth century has witnessed the growing dominance of a differently constituted kind of space, a *nonspace* of both experience and representation, an *elsewhere* which inhabits the everyday. Nonspace is not mysterious or strange to us, but rather the very haunt for creatures of habit. Practices and skills that can be performed semiautomatically in a distracted state—such as driving, shopping, or television watching—are the barely acknowledged ground of everyday experience. This ground is without locus, a partially derealized realm from which a new quotidian fiction emanates.

Nonspace is ground within which communication as a flow of values among and between two and three dimensions and between virtuality and actuality—indeed, an uncanny oscillation between life and death—can "take place." One finds the quintessential descriptions of nonspace in the postwar generation which was first to explore suburbia. Tony Smith's description of a car ride along a newly constructed section of the New Jersey Turnpike at night[4] expressed a formative experience of *elsewhere* out of which grew (in the 1960s) the conception of environmental art by artists like Robert Smithson. With earthworks such as *Spiral Jetty,* Smithson undermined the objecthood and the locus in space of his sculpture, lost somewhere between documentation in a gallery or museum and an inaccessible referent somewhere else. Robert Hobbs explains Smithson's nonsite and nonspace sculptures as a profound assessment of mid-twentieth-century experience:

> In an era of rootlessness, massive reordering of the landscape, large-scale temporary buildings, and media implosion, he viewed people's essential apprehension of the world as a rejection of it. Vicariousness, projection to some other place by rejecting where one actually is, has become a dominant mid-twentieth-century means of dealing with the world. Making the Nonsite (which brings together nonseeing and nonspace under one rubric) a primary determinant of his aesthetic forms, Smithson emphasized ways people nonperceive.[5]

Later descriptions of nonspace (for example, Baudrillard's notion of simulation) also emphasize it as a focus of derealization. Baudrillard conceives of simulation as a loss of referential anchorage to the world or the insecurity of denotation as it applies primarily to objects, whereas his own spatial allusions to *networks,* inert *masses,* and *black holes* lay claim to a kind of poetic scientificity. But this mixed metaphor in "The Ecstasy of Communication" is the vehicle which conveys the full complexity of his conceptualization of spatiality in postmodernity: "The vehicle now becomes a kind of capsule, its dashboard the brain, the surrounding landscape unfolding like a televised screen (instead of a live-in projectile as it was before)."[6] The interiors of the home television viewing space, the automobile, the space capsule, and the computer are ultimately associated with the interiority of the human mind. The image of the exterior world from these interiors is no longer a "Western window" onto reality but, for Baudrillard, the dubious vision of television.

In his popular and playful ontology of the shopping mall, *The Malling of America,* William Severini Kowinski goes even further, calling the mall a "TV you walk around in." Here the mode of locomotion is different, but the interiority (not just exterior vision) of the viewer is equated with television itself: "The mall is television, [in terms of] people's perceptions of space and reality, the elements that persuade people to suspend their disbelief."[7] These spatial comparisons depend on a common experience of some degree of fictitiousness within their (un)realities. The implication is that television epitomizes a new ontology of the everyday: vast realms of the somewhat-less-than-real to which significant amounts of free time (unpaid leisure, the shadow of work) are devoted on a routine, cyclical basis. The features of this derealized or *nonspace* are shared by freeway, mall, and television alike.

The first distinguishing feature of nonspace is its dreamlike *displacement* or separation from its surroundings:

Freeways are displaced in that they do not lie earthbound and contiguous to their surroundings so much as float above or below the horizon. The freeway disengaged from its immediate context is "a bridge over the barriers of both social and natural geography," offering as well "a continued shelter from engagement with ghetto areas."[8] In Kevin Lynch's famous study of cognitive maps of the city, from the point of view of the streets, the freeway is almost invisible, "not felt to be 'in' the rest of the city" (31). Similarly, from the subjective point of view of a driver or passenger experiencing motion blur, the city isn't visible either, except at times as a distant miniature seen from a freeway which is usually also physically depressed, elevated from its surroundings, or shielded by its own greenbelt. To paraphrase Charles Kuralt, the freeway is what makes it possible to drive coast to coast and never see anything. In fact, the freeway divides the world in two, into what David Brodsly calls "local" and "metropolitan" (24) orientations. These also denote two realities: the one, heterogeneous and static; the other, homogeneous and mobile. The passage between them can be accompanied by a shock, a moment of "severe disorientation" (24).

Furthermore, the process of displacement is a prelude to condensation. The freeway not only represents transportation from the city in the suburbs, but it is also a greenbelt and an escape "from the world of stucco into an urban preserve of open space and greenery" (49). Suburbia is itself an attempt via serial production to give everyman and everywife the advantages of a city at the edge of the natural world. Thus, the suburbs are "a living polemic against both the large industrial metropolis and the provincial small town," which nonetheless manage to "maintain the facade of a garden patch of urban villages, a metropolitan small town, without ever compromising the anonymity that is a hallmark of city life" (33; 45).[9] Freeways and the suburbs they serve are thus examples of the "garden in the machine," which provides mass society with a pastoral aesthetic and rhetoric.

Malls are similarly "completely separated from the rest of the world."

Kowinski calls this separation "the first and most essential secret of the shopping mall":

> It was its own world, pulled out of time and space, but not only by windowless walls and a roof, or by the neutral zone of the parking lot between it and the highway, the asphalt moat around the magic castle. It was *enclosed* in an even more profound sense—and certainly more than other mere buildings—because all these elements, and others, psychologically separated it from the outside and created the special domain within its embrace. It's *meant* to be its own special world with its own rules and reality. (60)

The mall is a spatial condensation near a node where freeways intersect, serving a certain temporal radius; it is "a city, indeed a world in miniature."[10] Shops that are four-fifths of normal size[11] are linked together within a vast and usually enclosed multileveled atrium or hall devoted solely to the pedestrian consumer (albeit served by autos and trucks).[12] A regional center saturated by chain stores which turns its back on local shops,[13] the mall is the paradoxical promise of adventure on the road within an idyll[14] of Main Street in a small town before the age of the automobile.

The mall is not only enclosed, Kowinski adds, but it is protected from exposure to the natural and public world through unobtrusive but central control. This private surveillance escapes the kind of sharp vigilance in the light of democratic values to which it would be subject in the public world: we do not expect the consumer to possess the same kinds of rights or responsibilities as the citizen. Shopping malls are essentially governed by market planners (i.e., by a fairly limited pool of mall entrepreneurs, builders, owners, and managers) and market forces. Each mall is carefully situated and designed in terms of its architecture; the "retail drama" of its syntax of shops and types of commodities, promotions, and advertising conveys a unified image which attracts some parts of the surrounding population and discourages others.

Consumers of all ages (but probably not all social conditions) come together to re-create the lost community of the street and the agora now under the private management of the arcade. The courts of foot traffic allow consumers and "mall rats" (nonconsuming loiterers) to intermingle in an attenuated and controlled version of a crowded street. Thus, the mall retains elements of the milling crowd, but as a private space in which anonymous individuals, preferably ones with particular demographic characteristics, gather *en masse*. So the paroxysms of release from individuality via bodily contact described by Elias Canetti in *Crowds and Power* are unlikely; the street celebrated by Bakhtin as a place of festival which erases boundaries between self and other is scarcely imaginable.[15]

Rather than a site of "contamination," the mall is a place to shore up the boundaries of the self via commodities which beckon with the promise of perfection from beyond the glass or gleam from beyond the threshold in brightly lit shops. These commodities with roles in retail drama have a somewhat dreamlike quality even in terms of their use value, for they are less often connected with labor or the small necessities of life (e.g., needles and thread, nails and hammers, seed and fertilizer, et cetera) than with leisure and a designer lifestyle (note the category shift of pots and pans, now that cooking is linked to luxury living). Rather, the preferred commodities of retail drama are "lost objects," the very things a subject desires to complete or perfect his or her self-image. And, rather than being unique, these objects are mass-produced, the very ones to be seen advertised on television, in print, and on display beyond the glass.

Television is likewise premised upon private reception in an environment isolated from events "out there," which determine the conditions of life outside the home. John Ellis has described this practice as the "double distance" of television's complicity with the viewer against an "outside world" represented as "hostile or bizarre," and the viewer's delegation of "his or her look to the TV itself."[16] Both means of distancing constitute "the opposition 'inside/outside,' which insulates the viewer from events seen by TV" (169).[17]

But this division of the world is complicated by the reconstruction of an idealized version of the older forms of transport, social and media communication within the very enclosures from which they are excluded. The past inscribed within the present is constructed *as past* through this very act of separation; a local and heterogeneous world beyond continues to exist but with fading resources, a phantom from an anterior world. This interior duality has symbolic dimensions as well: oppositions between country and city, nature and culture, sovereign individual and social subject are neutralized only to be reconstituted within nonspace in a multilayered compromise formation, a Utopian realm of *both/and*, in the midst of *neither/nor*.

This process of displacement from context is also one of *dislocation*. In a quite literal, physical sense, freeways, malls, and television are not truly "places." That is, they cannot be localized within the geometrical grids that orient the American city and countryside:

As Brodsly explains in his essay on the *L. A. Freeway*, a freeway is not a place but a *vector* (25f.);[18] even its name or number is a direction rather than a location. Channels of motion dedicated solely to one-way, high-velocity travel, freeways are largely experienced as "in-betweens," rather than enjoying the full reality of a point of departure or a destination. And magnitude on the freeway is popularly measured in minutes rather than miles. Yet, within that waste of time spent in between, usually alone and isolated within an iron bubble, a miniature idyll with its own controlled climate and selected sound is created. In this intensely private space, lifted out of the social world, the driver is subject, more real and present to him- or herself than the miniatures or the patterns of lights beyond the glass, or farther yet, beyond the freeway.

Television is also dislocated, insofar as it consists of two-dimensional images dispersed onto screens in nearly every home in the United States, displaying messages transmitted everywhere and nowhere in particular. Television is also a vast relay-and-retrieval system for audio-visual material of uncertain origin and date which can be served up instantaneously by satellite and cable as well as broadcast transmission and video cassette. Other two-dimensional media including newspapers and periodicals (the prime example being the hybrid satellite/print production of *USA Today*, now appearing as a television magazine program as well) are increasingly identified less with the specific location(s) from which they emanate (insofar as that can be ascertained) and more with a *range* or area of distribution they "cover"—indeed, mass-circulation media have constituted the "nation" as a symbolic system of common associations as well as a legal and political creation. The freeway and the mall provide the greatest evidence and manifestation of a homogeneous, material culture, just as television is the main source of shared images (visual and acoustic). There is even a "national" weather within these enclosed spaces of mall and home and auto—the even temperature of the comfort zone.[19]

Nonspace is not only a literal "nonplace," it is also *disengaged* from the paramount orientation to reality—the here and now of face-to-face contact. Such encounter with the other is prevented by walls of steel, concrete, and stucco in a life fragmented into enclosed, miniature worlds. As Brodsly explains: "Metropolitan life suggests the disintegration in space and time of individual's various dwelling places. Often living in 'communities without propinquity,' the individual metropolitan must somehow confront the task of reintegrating his or her environment. . . . One does not dwell in the metropolis; one passes through it between dwelling places" (2). This task of reintegrating a social world of separated, dislocated realms is accomplished by means of an internal dualism, of *passage* amid the *segmentation* of glass, screens, and thresholds. Thus, each form of communication becomes a *mise-en-abyme*, a recursive structure in which a nested or embedded representation reproduces or duplicates important aspects of the primary world within which it is enclosed.[20]

The freeway, for instance, is divided into a realm of passage, both over the outside world and from inside an idyllic, intensely private, steel-enclosed world of relative safety. At the same time, the sociality with the outside world that has become physically impossible inside the automobile is re-created via radio, disc, and tape.

Television is similarly derealized as communication, i.e., the primacy of discourse in television representation is not anchored as enunciation in a paramount reality of community, propinquity, and discursive exchange. While every act of enunciation disengages an utterance from the subject, space, and time of the act of enunciation,[21] television—with its temporal and spatial separation of interlocutors into a one-way, largely recorded transmission—is *doubly disengaged*. Hence televisual utterances waver uncertainly in reality status. However, the primary levels of "interface" with the viewing audience of television are those televisual utterances which represent direct engagement or address oriented proxemically on face-to-face discourse, that is, the discursive level of presenters, hosts, and spokespersons. The discursive plane of television includes all sorts of unrelated, nonprogram material, from ads, logos, and I. D.'s, public-service announcements, to promotions and lead-ins, as well as the discursive segments within programs themselves, from openers and titles to presentational segments. This primary plane of discourse seems to be an overarching presumption of television representation even when it isn't directly on-screen, and it builds the framework of television flow as a whole.[22]

Further acts of internal disengagement install second- and third-level segments as units of narrative (disengaged) or dialogue (engaged) within the primary discursive plane of the television utterance. However, the nesting order of disengagement does matter, for Greimas notes that the effect is different when dialogue is included in narration rather than when narrative is included in dialogue. In the former situation, predominant in the novel, for example, dialogue is referentialized, that is, given a spatio-temporal locus (however fictive) by the narration; in the latter situation, predominant in US televisual representation, narration is dereferentialized, that is, lifted out of a spatio-temporal context (however real) into a symbolic or affective realm. That is to say that even in nonfiction genres such as the news, the dominant reference point of the utterance will be a simulacrum of an ultimately fictitious situation of enunciation rather than a world outside.

2. METAPSYCHOLOGICAL EFFECTS OF PRIVATIZATION

In "Paris, Capital of the Nineteenth Century," Walter Benjamin anticipated the everyday world to come and discovered the roots of nonspace in the phenomenon of *privacy* and enclosure. Indeed, the nineteenth-century arcades of Milan served as direct model for the contemporary American mall.[23] While *privatization* has largely been conceived as an economic and political term,[24] it appears to have metapsychological effects associated with its derealized surroundings—the postmodern development of what Benjamin called the *"phantasmagoria of the interior,"* a mixture of levels of consciousness and objects of attention. The process of distancing the worker from the workplace and the enclosure of domestic life in the home, separated from its social surroundings, allowed a compensatory realm of fantasy to flourish, a conglomeration of exotic remnants in which new and old are intermingled. This *phantasmagoria of the interior* broke with the immediate present in favor of a primal past and the dream of the epoch to come. However, the twentieth-century phantasmagoria idealizes not the primal but the immediate past, and is an agent responsible for its decay. And the u- or dystopia which these forms anticipate seems less a vision of a future earth transformed for good or ill than a hermetic way of life liberated from earth itself.

The temporal world is also lifted out of history in favor of cyclic repetitions less determined by than modeled secondarily on daily and seasonal cycles of the sun, the stages of life, and the passage of generations. As labor is more and more liberated from solar and circadian rhythms, cycles of commuting, shopping, and viewing become shiftable as well. Television program schedules are "intricately woven into the fabric of our routine daily activities,"[25] because they are organized by the same division of labor outside and inside the family which recruits the daily commuter and the recreational shopper. And it is the demands of labor itself which may produce a state of mind and body which is best compensated within the comfort zone.

Time is largely experienced as duration on the freeway, a "drive time" guided by graphics in Helvetica (connoting a clean, homogeneous, or unmarked publicness and a vague temporality "from the 1960s on"). Continuity with the past is represented largely in terms of automobile model and year. Similarly, within the mall (as in Disneyland, McDonald's, and other realms of privately owned mass culture), decay or the fact of time itself has been banished from cycles of destruction and regeneration via a scrupulous cleanliness and constant renewal of worn parts.

On television, duration of viewing time is also the prime experience of temporality. The work of time itself as decay is seldom represented in images of the human body or everyday life. Nor is the past so much remembered via narrative as it is rerun or embedded as archival images within contemporary, discursive presentation. Even the image quality of the past—records of grainy black and white—is gradually undergoing electronic revision to meet today's expectations. The phantasmagoria of television and its analogs is thus to be imagined less as escape to flickering shadows in the cave than as a productive force which shapes spatio-temporal and psychic relations to the realities it constitutes. The state of mind promoted within the realms of nonspace can be described as *distraction*.

Distraction as a dual state of mind depends on an incomplete process of spatial and temporal separation and interiorization. The automobile, for instance, is connected to the world outside via the very glass and steel which enclose the driver. However, the dualism of outside/inside within these separate realms means that a connection with "outside" drifts between a "real" outside and an idealized representation.

A sheet of glass alone is enough to provide a degree of disengagement from the world beyond the pane. Add to this the play of light which appears to be part of the *mise-en-scène* of the mall, the freeway, and television—the world beyond the glass glows more brightly than the darker passages and seats we occupy. Beyond its glow, even the "real" world seen through a clear glass windshield, shop window, or screen has a way of being psychically colored and fetishized by the very glass which reveals it; the green glasses of the inhabitants of the Emerald City of Oz are a mythic expression of this vitreous transformation.[26]

However, green visions promote a state of mind which remains somewhere between Oz and Kansas, or between regression to the primal scene and a commercial transaction: because mental life on the freeway, in the marketplace, and at home is linked to very real consequences for life, limb, and pocketbook, it requires vigilance while it also allows for and even promotes automatisms and "spacing out." "Being carried away" to a full-blown world of fantasy is not in order—but the "vegging out" of the couch potato is a well-publicized phenomenon. Malls and freeways also can induce a state of distraction: For example, the very design and intentions of the mall taken to extreme can induce what the "cosmallogist" Kowinski diagnoses as the "zombie effect" (floating for hours, a loss of a sense of time and place) which he diagnoses as a copresence of contradictory states of excitement enhanced to the point of overstimulation mixed with relaxation descending into confusion and torpor (339). In discussing the habit of driving, Brodsly calls "detached involvement" (47) an awareness of the outside environment mixed with that of an intensely private world within the interior of the automobile. Noting that the automobile is one of the few controlled environments for meditation in our culture, he describes how even the temporal link with the outside world may fade: "Perhaps no aspect of the freeway experience is more characteristic than the sudden realization that you have no memory of the past ten minutes of your trip" (41).[27]

In his mythological investigations of everyday life, Roland Barthes made the subjective experience of driving a metaphor for the operation of mythology itself. In "Myth Today," he turned from analysis of objects and scenes such as the "cathedral-like" "New Citroën" to the practice of driving as an alternation between two objects of attention:

> If I am in a car and I look at the scenery through the window, I can at will focus on the scenery or on the window-pane. At one moment I grasp the presence of the glass and the distance of the landscape; at another, on the contrary, the transparency of the glass and the depth of the landscape; but the result of this alternation is constant: the glass is at once present and empty to me, and the landscape unreal and full.[28]

For Barthes, this constant alternation constitutes a spatial category of a continuous *elsewhere* which is his model for the alibi of myth. If we were to expand Barthes's metaphor of semiotics and driving with concepts of discourse, the alternation of which he wrote would also be one which shifts between planes of language and subjectivity. That is, the awareness of a subject would shift between a here/now in the interior of the automobile and awareness of a world elsewhere beyond the glass (in which the interior is also lightly reflected) through which the subject speeds. But because the interior of the auto is disconnected and set in the midst of a new kind of theater of derealized space, the experience of what is normally the paramount reality—the experience of self-awareness in a here and now—becomes one of unanchored mobility. This mobile subject in the midst of *elsewhere* is a cultural novum and the model for a new kind of fiction effect, unbound and uncircumscribed by the fourth wall, without a 180-degree line to separate the world of the imaginary and the subjunctive from the commonplace.

The freeway provides the most obvious examples of *mobile subjectivity:*

> Each [freeway] exit ramp offers a different visual as well as kinesthetic sensation. The interchange is like a mobile in a situation where the observer is the moving object. It is the experience of an effortlessly choreographed dance, with each car both performing and observing the total movement and the freeway architecture providing the carefully integrated setting.[29]

Yet from the observer/moving object's point of view, this mobility is a paradoxical feeling of stasis and motion. In *nonspace*, the body in motion is no longer a kinesthetic key to reality, for at the wheel of the automobile (or at the remote control of the television), engaged in small motor movements which have become highly skilled and automatic, it explores space as an inert mass, technically or electronically empowered with virtual or actual speed. Indeed, what we experience is not an erasure, circumvention, or fragmentation of the body but its investment with a second and more powerful skin within which a core remains secure, intact, and at rest in a vortex of speed.

Of course, mobility is a multifaceted and paradoxical concept per se, with many fields of reference: from displacement from one location to another, to the freedom of movement which is symbolically equated with social mobility, to the feelings of pleasure in effortless flight which has roots in infancy, to the fundamental psychic link of motion with causality and subjecthood first described by Aristotle. But mobility also suggests the opposite of subjecthood, the freely displaceable and substitutable part, machine or human, which enables mass production and a consequent standardization brought to the social as well as economic realm. *Nonspace* engages all of these possibilities.[30]

Motion is not only paradoxical, but it is also relative. Safe within the halls of consumption, the body may stroll with half a mind in leisurely indirection. But the shops passed in review are themselves a kind of high-speed transport, the displacement of goods produced in mass quantities in unknown elsewheres into temporal simultaneity and spatial condensation. And on the freeway as well as the airplane, a new and paradoxical experience of motion has evolved: on one hand, the relative motion of an enclosed space beyond which the world passes in high-speed review; or inversely, the dynamic sensation of movement itself experienced by a relatively inert body traversing the world at high speed.[31] At least before the advent of the simultaneous and multiple perspectives of Cubism, motion in Western representation was usually confined to the world of the story beyond the glass, stationary or moving images presented for the eyes of a stationary (and one-eyed) subject. A "bubble" of subjective here and now strolling or speeding about in the midst of elsewhere is one of the features that constitute new, semifictitious realms of the everyday.

Of course, any mobility experienced by the television viewer is virtual, a "range" or displaced realm constituted by vectors, a transportation of the mind in two dimensions. Our *idyll*, or self-sufficient and bounded place, is the space in front of the TV set, what Baudrillard calls "an archaic envelope."[32] Yet Baudrillard thinks bodies left on the couch are "simply superfluous, basically useless," "deserted and condemned," like the immense countryside deserted by urbanization. But these couch bodies are also travelers, responding in a checked, kinetic way to the virtual experiences of motion we are offered as subjects or view in objects passing our screens.[33] Television also offers the road in the midst of the idyll, reconstituting a virtual world of face-to-face relationships shared between viewer and television personalities displaced or teleported from elsewhere in the process, a fiction of the paramount reality of discourse. Thus *discourse* or represented acts of enunciation can be understood as a container for both the viewer and the personalities of television which provides protection from a world thereby constituted as beyond and elsewhere.

Discursive segments also constitute a plane of passage between the shows, items, and stories embedded within the plane. Sometimes *passages* are even marked as such via the motion of subjects who can speak as if directly to us, the viewers within the televisual representation. For instance, the syndicated yet local program *Evening Magazine* often shows its local hosts in motion, walking as they introduce unrelated, packaged stories (produced at many different stations) to the viewer.[34] While this practice seems strange and gratuitous, it is quite simply a visual realization of the virtual power of language as a means of transport. The use of movement as passage marker is echoed, for instance, in the work of visual anthropologists Worth and Adair,[35] who, in trying to understand the films they had incited members of the Navajo tribe to make, concluded that almost all of them "portray what to members of our culture seems to be an inordinate amount of walking" (144). Worth and Adair concluded that for the Navajo, walking itself was an event and "a kind of punctuation to separate activities" (148). On television, such marking may also be represented in far more minimal than spectacular ways, for example, spatially via shifts of an on-screen subject in body orientation and eyeline or verbally via the use of discursive shifters. Thus, the overall discursive framework of televisual representation, including the use of hosts and presenters of all kinds, provides a means of passing between object-worlds, be they stories provided for entertainment or fantasies that surround commodities, in a way which virtually includes the viewer.

In *Visible Fictions,* John Ellis determined that the *segment* is the basic unit of television (in opposition to or modification of Raymond Williams's notion of flow).[36] The basic dualism of televisual representation opts for neither concept alone but helps to explain why, despite its segmentation into un-related items, television is *not* commonly perceived as fragmented, but rather is experienced as unified and contained. Nor is that coherence achieved simply by virtue of "flow" or the juxtaposition of items on the same plane of discourse. The duality of *passage* and *segmentation* in physical as well as represented space is related in turn to the dual planes of language, the engaged discourse of a subject in passage and the disengagement of stories from the here and now of the subject.

The separate segments which disengage from discursive passages are recursive or embedded "hypodiegetic worlds"[37] at one level removed from the frame of passage. Segments with widely disparate topics in contrasting expressive moods from the tragic or the comic to the trivial or traumatic can be united via discourse into flow. Other sub- or "hypo" levels of nar-ration can appear within any one discursive or narrative segment—three, for instance, are typical of news reports (115).[38] Thus, television discourse typically consists of "stacks" of recursive levels which are usually quite dif-ferent in look and "flavor." These stacks are also signified at different spatial and temporal removes from the viewer and have different kinds of con-tents. Thus a shift of discursive level is also a shift of ontological levels, that is, to a different status in relation to reality. Television formats then amount to particular ways of conceptualizing and organizing "stacks" of worlds as a hierarchy of realities and relationships to the viewer.

Formally, shifting from one televisual segment to another may be a shift in the hierarchy of discourse—but shifts and passages between levels can also occur within segments. For instance, there is a category of television segment, including advertisements, logos, and rock videos,[39] the *raison d'être* of which is to engage the viewer with a sign, image, or commodity by means of a represented passage through a whole range of discursive and onto-logical levels. Such segments are *condensations* of what are ordinarily dis-persed in syntactic alternations of discursive segments with embedded stories or fantasies.

Furthermore, televisual representations may include several layers in the same visual field, *simultaneously*. An obvious example is the image of the narrating news anchor against "world" wallpaper and over-the-shoulder news windows. Like television, freeways and malls provide similar examples of multiple worlds condensed into one visual field: for example, the au-tomobile windshield is not merely glass and image of the world into which one speeds, but also a mirror reflection of the driver and passengers; the rear-view mirror displays the window of where one has been; the side-view mirror shows what to anticipate next. Meanwhile, the landscape unfolds right and left, distorted by speed.

The representation of the copresence of multiple worlds in different modes[40] on the television screen is achieved via division of the visual field into areas or via the representation of stacked places which can be tumbled or squeezed and which, in virtual terms, advance toward and retreat from the visual field of the viewer. Discursive planes are differentiated from embedded object-worlds via *axes:* the vector of eyelines and movements, and changes of scale along the z-axis of spatial depth indicate a proxemic logic of the shared space of conversation with the viewer. In contrast, embedded stories are oriented around x- and y-axes, actually or virtually by means of the field/reverse field of filmic, continuity editing. The primary logic of alternation in television segments is then not that of suture, as in filmic fictions,[41] but rather that of communication with a spectator in various degrees of "nearness." The constant reframings in and out along the z-axis of depth which David Antin saw as part of the television form[42] apparently do have a function as links with a spectator rather than as inexplicable or gratuitous reframings of a spatially continuous, diegetic world. Even in fictional worlds beyond the plane of discourse, a relation to the z-axis of discursive relations with the viewer can be discerned. For example, in her discussion of soap operas on television, Sandy Flitterman noted the lack of continuity editing and the practice of alternating framing of characters in a two-shot as nearer to and farther from the viewer.[43] This practice can be explained historically by the television studio situation of live editing by means of switching between two or more cameras. But it can also be explained as part of a proxemic logic of relations with the spectator which pervades even fictional worlds.

What is ultimately at stake in this insistent relation to the viewer is a site of exchange. For the representation of mixed and simultaneous worlds is deeply allied with the cultural function of television in symbolically linking incommensurabilities of all sorts—the system of goods or commodities and the economic relations it orders, the sexual-matrimonial system which orders sociality and the symbolic order of language, including images, symbols, and the spoken and written word. If television itself is a great storehouse for tokens of all these cultural systems, exchange values are created by their juxtaposition, but even more by means of passages through them, in which television programming offers many different itineraries from which to choose.

The viewer as mobile subject has remote control over trajectories and channels plus power to take the off ramp and leave the zone of televisual space. However, the television viewer who enters a car to go shopping, or even to work, hasn't left *nonspace* behind—these realms are variations thereof. (For this reason "home shopping" channels represent less the interaction of television with the world than a "short circuit" of communication and growing withdrawal into enclosed systems.)

Thus the realm of *nonspace* is divided again via the play of motion and stillness organized by passages and thresholds to the worlds behind the glass, by a *mise-en-scène* of light and darkness, and by proxemic indicators of nearness and distance within an unanchored situation. This very mobility allows what could be a profoundly disorienting and fragmented experience of life to act as a powerful means of reunifying the flow of time and space into a virtual here and now of a communal world. Voices and images offer community to a disengaged and enclosed world of the home, the automobile, and the mall. A banished, paramount reality is recreated as a phantom within elsewhere. The result may be the "secular communion"[44] of the freeway, the shared passages of the mall, or parasociality in relation to television personalities. Thus the institutions of mobile privatization restore a vision of the world from which they are disengaged and which they have largely displaced.

3. A NEXUS OF EXCHANGE BETWEEN ECONOMIC, SOCIAL, AND SYMBOLIC SYSTEMS

Realms of everyday experience—the freeway, the shopping mall, and television—are part of a socio-historical nexus of institutions which grew together into their present-day structure and national scope after World War II. Transportation, broadcasting, and retailing displaced the earlier socio-cultural forms of modernity such as the railroad, the movies, and the shop windows along a brightly lit boulevard.[45] These earlier forms of modernity were in themselves means of surveillance and control. Like the cinema, the railroad is an odd experience of immobile motility, virtual and actual, in which spatiality retains a semipublic nature.

Institutions of communication after World War II intensified processes of privatization and massification which had begun far earlier. Private life in the postwar era presumed a significant amount of leisure or discretionary time and "an apparently self-sufficient family home" which "carried, as a consequence, an imperative need for new kinds of contact" (27). Raymond Williams pointed out the paradox which the notion of "mass" communications hides—the increasing functional isolation and spatial segmentation of individuals and families into private worlds which are then mediated into larger and larger entities by new forms of communication.

In the United States, the paradox of mass culture and social isolation is even more acute, for to a far greater extent, the public airwaves, rights of way, and places of assemblage have been given over to private ownership or use and to market forces. Perhaps because the principles of mobile privatization are congruent with widely and deeply held American values of the good life along with dreams of social mobility which hold that ideal attainable for all, the choice of the private automobile over public conveyances, for instance, "seems to reflect an overwhelmingly popular consensus rarely matched by social movements, and it flourishes because it continues to serve that general will."[46] The principles of mobile privatization guided the creation of systems of transport and social communication which promise liberty in the midst of sociality, privacy amongst community, and an autonomy of protected selfhood nourished by its environment.

What the institutions of mobile privatization then represent is a means of social integration and control which can dispense with the need for any "central" or panoptical position of surveillance, visible display of force, or school of discipline, because they are fully congruent with the values of individualism and hedonistic pleasure, as well as desires for social recognition and dreams of community. Furthermore, the practices of driving, shopping, and television viewing are dreams become habit.

Take, for instance, the perception of freedom and self-determination experienced by the driver of the automobile in comparison with that public mode of transport, the train. An automobile driver, Otto Julius Bierbaum, exclaimed in 1902:

> The railway just transports you—and that's the immediate contrary to travelling. Travelling means utmost free activity, the train however condemns you to passivity. Travelling is getting rid of the rules. But the railway squeezes you into a time-table, makes you a prison of all kinds of rules, and locks you into a cage that you are not supposed to leave and not even to unlock whenever you want. . . . Who considers that travelling may as well call a march in review a stroll.[47]

The automobile represents an apparent freedom from the lock step of a public time schedule as well as "the complete subversion of the traditional sanctuary of the public realm—the street," so that merely driving a private automobile can be understood as a ritual expression of national faith: "Every time we merge with traffic we join our community in a wordless creed: belief in individual freedom, in a technological liberation from place and circumstance, in a democracy of personal mobility. When we are stuck in rush-hour traffic the freeway's greatest frustration is that it belies its promise."[48] This faith in mobility sustains cultural homogeneity rather than diversity; and, paradoxically, the feelings associated with vast improvements in the freedom of motion are in lock step with submission to demands for greater conformity.

A common faith in freedom of movement and of choice among commodities, destinations, and channels sustains the institutions of mobile privatization. They are the realms of answered prayers, embodiments of dearly held beliefs, and phantoms of desire become commonplace, a field of action constituted by the automatisms and chains of associations which make up vast networks in the symbolic system of our culture. Constraints built on these chains of associated ideas are owned, not imposed, and require very little surveillance. As an early theorist of representational punishment cited by Foucault in *Discipline and Punish* explained:

> this link [between ideas] is all the stronger in that we do not know of what it is made and we believe it to be our own work; despair and time eat away the bonds of iron and steel, but they are powerless against the habitual union of

ideas, they can only tighten it still more; and on the soft fibres of the brain is founded the unshakable base of the soundest of Empires.[49]

The Empire of the habitual is the matrix of mental and social life, made of mundane opportunities and choices and composed of practices conducted half-aware, which assemble one's very personhood. What is new in contemporary life are not these institutions of mobile privatization per se but the interpenetration of layer upon layer of built environment and representation, the formative and derivative, the imaginary and mundane. Embodying values as neither here nor there, both present and absent, they are ideal expressions of the *zones* of ontological uncertainty, expressions of both Kansas and Oz.[50]

Although we may perceive no alternative, no one forces people to watch television or to drive, particularly on the freeway, or to go to the mall or to buy anything on display there or on television. But few indeed resist. One prescription for an aesthetic mode of resistance to consumer culture requires the passerby to remain bewitched on this side of the window, glass, or mirror, poised at the moment between perfection and lack, never cashing in desire for the disappointments of fulfillment.[51] But aesthetic resistance depends on an older disposition of the subject in relation to the spectacle of an imaginary world framed and discrete behind the glass. The cycle of consumption in a "Highway Comfort" culture is designed for maximum mobility and circulation of a consumer inside the imaginary world of images and objects. One of the successes of this system of interrelations is on one hand the liquidity of images, objects, and commodities, and on the other the ease with which the subject passes from one role to another—driver, passerby, and consumer—each requiring a different mode of attention and psychic investment in objects.

Such *convertibility* between these various systems of communication and exchange is necessary; freeways, malls, and television are not merely similar in form, they are systems constructed to interact in mutually reinforcing ways.[52] Each institution is a kind of socio-cultural distribution and feedback system for the others: Television (most obviously as mass-audience network broadcasts) serves as the nationwide distribution system for symbols in anticipation and reinforcement of a national culture presented not only as desirable but as already realized somewhere else. The mall is a displacement and the enclosure of the walkable street and a collective site in which to cash in the promises of the commodities seen on television. The freeway is the manifestation of personal mobility at its most literal, its radius a lifeline that makes the consumption style of suburban living and shopping economically feasible as well as logistically possible. The auto on the freeway is a juncture between television and mall, a "home" and commodity fetish on wheels. Convertibility between systems means that values can be exchanged whether they are expressed as commodity objects or images, in two or three dimensions, or in gigantic or miniature scale.

Just as the mall is a miniature suburbia, a figure of desire become literal and three-dimensional, the television box is a quintessential miniature, both as copy *and* prototype; even in its gigantic form, the large-screen projection, it is no bigger than a picture window or an alternative to wallpaper. Bachelard explained how miniaturization is an attempt to master and control the world, which one can then enter in one's imagination by making oneself very small.[53] This *miniaturization* is responsible for the feelings of safety linked with malls, freeways, and television, what Susan Stewart in *On Longing*[54] termed "feminization," as opposed to a "masculine" metaphor of the gigantic, as abstract authority of the state in collective and public life. Miniaturization is a process of interiorization, enclosure, and perfection, one in which the temporal dimensions of narrative or history are transformed into spatial ones, a plenitude of description of seemingly endless details. This contraction of the world which expands the personal serves a process of commodification as well, the transformation of action into exchange, nature into marketplace, history into collection and property. The realm of the gigantic and exaggerated in public life, a collective body in pieces, has been shrunk into a perfect whole. Kowinski describes the technique of miniaturizing the shops and concessions in theme parks and malls as designed to evoke the nostalgic feelings the adult has when visiting the world of childhood, the once vast seen as tiny. The incomprehensible then comes near, no longer too far away or too foreboding: the distant and the exotic are sought in order to collapse them into proximity and approximation with the self.

However, once within the miniature, the universe looms endless, just as the stars shine through Benjamin's glass-topped arcades of nineteenth-century Paris. How are malls, freeways, and television as miniatures compatible with representation of the universal and the social? In *Learning from Las Vegas*[55] Robert Venturi et al. described a new kind of monumentality which began with the Las Vegas strip cut off from the surrounding desert and concluded within the darkened and low-ceilinged casinos, spotted with islands of activity, from glowing tables to garden oases. Rather than tall and imposing, like the skyscraper as upended panopticon and symbol of coercive or (via reflective glass) impenetrable power, the new monumentality is long and low, without discernible edges or ends or secure locus in place, rather like mirages lifted above the grids of homes, shops, and offices. Indeed, the very lack of panoptical positions afforded within the wings and cubbyholes of the typical mall is responsible for its sense of endlessness and a sense of disorientation within it. The freeway is "long and lowness" incarnate, but it also offers "kinks in the road" beyond which one can anticipate the unknown, in which accident and death can lurk, as a prime source of the monumental within a highly controlled, otherwise predictable system. "Kinks in the road" on television are temporal in order, possibilities of irruption of the unexpected in a plot or a schedule within an endlessness of parallel worlds which go on whether switched on or not, whether we watch or not, a world which is a primary reference in daily conversation, which we may be equipped to enter or not.

In principle, miniatures such as the mall are conceptual units which are invertible: that is, a mall can be lifted off the page, a scale model can be shrunk or expanded and plunked down in a nowhere that is anywhere suitable freeway access and (usually upscale) demographics prevail. This liquidity is certainly one of the secrets of commodity culture, allowing signs and images to become realized as objects of desire and also to circulate freely between different levels of reality. One still "unnatural" and hence disconcerting feature of postmodernity is the presence of glowing signifiers of desire realized in the midst of everyday life—images magnified into monuments (e.g., Michel de Certeau speaks of New York skyscrapers as "letters") or the big world shrunk down to the miniature size of a theme park or a mall. This invertibility between language and reality, i.e., world-to-image-to-world fit, is inherent in the performative aspect of language, or the capacity to declare worlds into existence within designated and proper boundaries. But those boundaries now extend to cover much of everyday existence: perhaps never before has it been so opportune or so feasible to realize a symbol or idea dramatically in 3-D. This expansion of the performative, making the actual virtual and the virtual actual, is behind the most recognizable features of postmodernity as theorized in Boorstein's culture of the image and "pseudo-events," in Callois's description of an indecidable state between the animate and inanimate,[56] and in Baudrillard's "simulations." Beyond liquid worlds that readily convert into one another, we are now undergoing a process of gradual convergence of the analogs of television with television itself. In the mall, not only can television screens be found in department stores and passages, but the mall as an architectural form has begun to sprout "video walls." On the freeway, we can soon anticipate the appearance of the virtual video screen or "head up display" which will float in a driver's field of vision like a freeway sign.[57] It seems that soon one will have to speak of one great machine.

4. CONCLUSION

The nonspace of privatized mobility is not neutral ground. It is rather the result of the dominance of one set of values over other values held a little less dear. Those other values, loosely allied with the "public sphere," are represented—but not included in a way that gives them substance. The dominance of the values linked with mobile privatization is also the result of a misunderstanding: ideas in the marketplace, that is, words and images as markers of economic and social exchange, are not the same thing as the free marketplace of ideas; and, correlatively, consumers are not the same thing as subjects of discourse. Broadcast and narrowcast ratings and cassette sales figures, for instance, are the measure of the first kind of marketplace, the pure exchange value of language and images. To the measure that the stock of ideas is determined by pure exchange value, the marketplace of ideas is diminished. (Deregulation and dismantling of obligation to a "public," however defined, are perhaps better understood as a "depublication" of transport, social and media communication, the legal and regulatory surface of the general phenomenon of privatization discussed here.) To strengthen the second kind of values—those related to discursive exchange among subjects, community, and a shared commitment to the just as well as the good life—requires foundation work. First, a widely held sense of the difference between the market value and the discursive value of ideas must be established. Then, recognizing the extent and scope of an attenuated fiction effect in everyday life—an effect now largely unappreciated or considered trivial and hence subject to little vigilance—might already be a step toward bringing distraction within a controlled psychic economy of disavowal. For distraction both motivates and promotes the "liquidity" of words and images in economic exchange by undermining a sense of different levels of reality and of incommensurable difference between them.

However, the analysis of the situation advanced in this essay suggests how difficult such a project has become. First, the means of advancing such notions are largely restricted to those very venues of privatization and distraction which work against them. Furthermore, older concepts of liberation in everyday life based on "escape attempts"[58] and figurative practices are no longer viable in a built environment that is already evidence of dream-work in the service of particular kinds of commerce, communication, and exchange. Indeed, older notions of the public realm and of paramount reality have been largely undermined, and a return to a pretelevisual world of politics, the street, or the marketplace is unlikely.

Not that there is nothing outside the built environment of freeways, malls, and television: there is indeed a heterogeneous world of local values; the decaying world of the city and town left beyond the enclosures is also becoming a gentrified and lively realm of privilege and experimentation. Because the realms of privatization present a facade of self-sufficiency and self-determination, means of change are easier to imagine as coming from those realms outside than from within. Thus, a prime strategy which has been devised for changing television is one of penetration of these enclosed worlds with other public and private voices.[59] What is ultimately at stake in puncturing everyday enclosures for low-intensity dreams are the rights and responsibilities of subjects in the public realm, a once gigantic, now shrunken terrain to be reclaimed from everyday life.

However, when included within television, the public and private worlds outside are distanced ontologically under several other layers of representation. That is why inclusion in representation per se is not enough to open the television apparatus out into the public world—for the privileged sites of subjectivity on television are those allotted first to the enunciation of televisual utterances and the interests those utterances serve; and second to those subjects in passage represented in the utterance, shifting between a relation to the viewer and relations to embedded object-worlds. That is, the very formats and conventions which have evolved in US televisual representation work against dialogue with the "other," the excluded outsiders. Or the past and otherness are included by proxy in a way that blunts the sense of an outside and of other possible worlds.

Furthermore, even the embedded narrative or dramatic segments under the plane of discourse are not conducive to the representation of change, either formally or at the level of social content. Narrative that embraces change, heterogeneity, and historical reach is undermined at a global level by the underlying serial organization of televisual representation per se: the notion of a linear sequence with a beginning, a middle, and an end, in which "something happens," is limited to the micro-level of the segment. The temporal-spatial organization of narrative on television can be compared with Bakhtin's analysis of the "road" chronotope in Greek romance. That is, the *road* was not a place where a change from one state or condition to another could occur—it was rather an obstacle course which merely delayed the eventual reunion of two characters who were destined to be lovers. These characters do not change, develop, or age in a journey governed solely by fortuitous incident. Like the romance, television narrative often manages to combine a sense of passage with an ultimately static situation. Like itineraries in the mall or the freeway, these stories are highly segmented enchainments which have largely given up any pretense of development. The itineraries of viewing will always pass by representations of cultural goods of various kinds, over and over, but the system of combination seems impervious to change.

So, when the dominant principles of alternation on television work against both the narrative process of change in characters and a rhetorical process of argumentation, how can they then challenge or encourage change in the mind of the viewer? Differentiation by means of lifestyle and disposable income which must be distinguished from the differences between subjects in "local" and "heterogeneous" outside realms. That is why the proliferating venues for ever more demographically segmented audiences for audio-visual representation bode well only if they also bring about formats which allow for the entry of new subjects from the outer world at the primary level of discourse. However, considering that this primary level of discourse is itself a fictional representation of discourse and part of a process which transforms outsiders automatically into insiders, the problem of representing discourse is one of degree. At best one can present a somewhat more intersubjective fiction of discourse and an only somewhat different kind of celebrity and momentary fame.

Yet, models of "penetration" and discursive exchange are necessary and useful precisely because the power relations of mobile privatization are the conventional expression of a kind of legal and social fiction based on widely held values. Changes in shared fictions, values, and beliefs occur over the long term, slowly and incrementally, not merely because once shared values are discredited or may be no longer viable, but because alternative values and their constituencies have labored to mark themselves in discourse. I believe the criticism of television can serve cultural change where it keeps such long-term goals in mind.

NOTES

1. Rudolf Arnheim's mention of the "aeroplane" along with the "motor car" suggests another analog of television in the airport, the experience of flying, and in the air transportation network. (Arnheim's remarks appear in *Rundfunk als Hörkunst* [1933; Munich: Hanser, 1979], p. 164, trans. Phillip Drummond, cited by Claus-Dieter Rath, "The Invisible Network: Television as an Institution in Everyday Life," in *Television in Transition: Papers from the First International Television Studies Conference,* ed. Phillip Drummond and Richard Paterson [London: British Film Institute, 1985], p. 199.) This investigation is primarily concerned with consumption and everyday experience. Because flying is not as everyday an experience as driving and shopping and because it is imbricated directly in corporate as well as military and surveillance uses of images (for example, Paul Virilio's *War and Cinema: The Logistics of Perception* [London, New York: Verso, 1989]), the aeroplane as analog of television is left to exploration elsewhere.

The mass-circulation periodical which preceded television, the magazine in print, is another obvious and important analog of television. The magazine format and the "magazine concept" were discussed in the paper on which this essay is based, given at the Conference on Television at the Center for Twentieth Century Studies in 1988, but they are omitted here for reasons of space and because the terms of comparison differ considerably from those between the built environment and television.

2. Todd Gitlin's discussion of the iconographic function of the automobile in the program *Miami Vice* and its juxtaposed ads exemplifies this kind of analysis. See "Car Commercials and *Miami Vice:* 'We Build Excitement,' " in *Watching Television* (New York: Pantheon, 1986), pp. 136–61. For a general description of the iconography of automobiles, the title essay of Marshall McLuhan's *The Mechanical Bride: Folklore of Industrial Man* ([Boston: Beacon, 1967], pp. 98–101) remains among the most insightful in making the link between technology and sexuality, the automobile and the female body as a love machine with replaceable parts. Stephen Bayley's *Sex, Drink, and Fast Cars: The Creation and Consumption of Images* (London, Boston: Faber, 1986) is a more recent monograph on the subject which notes pleasures of all kinds connected with the automobile, from kinesthetic/visceral and aesthetic to the sado-masochistic and death-driven. Bayley emphasizes the masculinity of that iconography. The difference between the two conceptions of automotive gender may be negotiated via the distinction between an interior womblike comfort zone versus the exterior, between driver and driven, the auto-woman as object of mastery and status display. Malls, on the other hand, are a predominantly female domain as recent papers by Ann Friedberg and Meaghan Morris demonstrate and develop, while the gender of the television even in terms of the machine itself is divided in ways related to division of labor in the home and work force.

3. Michel de Certeau, *The Practice of Everyday Life*, trans. Steven F. Rendall (Berkeley: University of California Press, 1984). The projects of synthesis drawn on here also have in common their work against the terror imposed by theory or intellectual discourse as well as the terror of the State. By returning to an earlier rich and highly validated cultural period at the cusp of the development of commodity culture, Benjamin's long-term view circumvents some of the immediate intellectual prejudices of his age which might foreclose the capacity to analyze cultural forms in the broadest sense. Bakhtin's appreciation of heterogeneity and the mixture of different voices in culture is designed to validate difference and make heard suppressed and otherwise voiceless parts of the social world. He developed the concept of the *chronotope* (in "Forms of Time and of the Chronotope in the Novel" [1937–38, 1973], from *The Dialogic Imagination: Four Essays* [Austin: University of Texas Press, 1981], in an age in which intellectuals sought tools for circumventing a closed discourse with concepts which reached into the manifestations of daily life in representation for reminders of what is not included in it. Compare other work which turns to the common, the everyday, and the "real" in the 1930s and 40s in the context of economic failure and the exposure of discourses of the "word" as tools of institutional power. The relations of class to culture which Williams studied were also the intellectual framework against and within which he articulated his ideas. Michel de Certeau's project of evasion and transformation of dominant and predetermined forms of everyday life can also be seen as an attempt to poke holes in a hermetic, structuralist notion of language as well as to find possibilities for liberation in the everyday.

4. Recalled in a conversation with Samuel Wagstaff, Jr., in *Artforum* Dec. 1966, and cited by Robert Hobbs, "Introduction," *Robert Smithson: Sculpture* (Ithaca: Cornell University Press, 1981), p. 14.

5. Hobbs, pp. 15f.

6. Baudrillard, "The Ecstasy of Communication," in *The Anti-aesthetic: Essays on Postmodern Culture*, ed. Hal Foster (Port Townsend, Wash.: Bay, 1983), pp. 126–34. E. Ann Kaplan cites Baudrillard's automobile metaphor in relation to a McLuhanian comparison of hot and cold media in *Rocking around the Clock: Music, Television, Postmodernism, and Consumer Culture* (New York: Methuen, 1987), pp. 50ff.

7. William Severini Kowinski, *The Malling of America: An Inside Look at the Great Consumer Paradise* (New York: William Morrow and Co., 1985), p. 71.

8. Kevin Lynch, quoted in David Brodsly, *L. A. Freeway: An Appreciative Essay* (Berkeley: University of California Press, 1981), pp. 39f.

9. Brodsly is here writing of Los Angeles. The same dream is in force today, despite smog and congestion. "The sustaining dream of most Southern Californians is to not live in, or even near, a city. Just as when millions of young families flocked to the small farming town on the fringes of a burgeoning Los Angeles after World War II, today people are seeking economically and socially homogeneous suburban neighborhoods. In short, they're looking for a comfortable small-town atmosphere within commuting distance of a big city, an almost idyllic place to watch the kids, the grass, the real estate values and the equity grow while they pursue the American dream." Sam Hall Kaplan, "The New Suburbia," *Los Angeles Times Magazine*, September 16, 1988, p. 28. The author explains that today people who look at computer screens all day do not want tract housing, but rather accept higher density in order to attain a "village atmosphere." Despite what is sometimes considered an infrastructure nearing the point of defeat and random outbreaks of freeway frustration into violence, surveys of Los Angeles commuters suggest surprising equanimity and even satisfaction with their lot.

10. "On both sides of these passages, which obtain their light from above, there are arrayed the most elegant shops, so that such an arcade is a city, indeed a world,

in miniature"—*Illustrated Paris Guide,* cited by Walter Benjamin in "Paris: Capital of the Nineteenth Century," p. 165.

11. Modeled directly on buildings in theme parks such as Disneyland, which was itself modeled on Disney's home town of Marceline, Missouri. Kowinski (reviewing the work of Richard Francaviglia), p. 67.

12. The typical layout of a mall includes two fully enclosed levels, a central court, and side courts, with one or more department stores or "anchors" at either end, and about 100 shops, services, and eating places. The interior typically mixes elements associated with exterior and interior design. The Urban Land Institute defines a mall as "a group of architecturally unified commercial establishments built on a site which is planned, developed, owned and managed as an operating unit. . . . " Design, temperature, lighting, merchandise, and events are all planned according to unifying principles. Cf. Kowinski, p. 60.

13. The difference between the two is not merely size and ownership but every facet of public relations, marketing, and retailing. Cf. Anthony DePalma, "The Malling of Main Street," *New York Times* 19 April 1987, Business, p. 1.

14. Dan Graham and Robin Hurst, "Corporate Arcadias," *Art Forum* Dec. 1987: 68–74. Note that corporate atriums are "parallel forms to the suburban shopping malls" which evidence the same tensions: "The urban corporate atrium is an attempt to smooth over contradictions between environmental decay and technological progress. As a miniutopian retreat from the stresses of city life, it reevokes the notion of a 'garden' as an idealized landscape (the return to a preurban Eden), attempting to reconnect it to the idea of technology as an aid to man." The authors conclude that because these atriums are largely separate from the fabric of the city, they represent exclusive enclaves which do not serve democratic values or the maintenance of community (71).

15. A recent application of the *chronotope* to film noir by Vivian Sobchack in " 'Lounge Time': Post-war Crises and the Chronotopes of Film Noir" (unpublished paper) suggests the importance of the semipublic *loungetime* as an idyllic contrast to the road for rootless postwar sexual-social relationships. Today's homeless and displaced people find public lounge space with difficulty, for it has been rededicated to driving and paying customers and linked to commercial sightlines.

16. John Ellis, *Visible Fictions: Cinema, Television, Video* (London: Routledge, 1982), p. 112. For an interpretation of pleasure and the home reception of the news related to this very distancing from the world, see Robert Stam, "Television News and Its Spectator," in *Regarding Television* (Frederick, Md.: University Publications of America, 1983), pp. 23–43.

17. Joshua Meyrowitz discusses displacement in the figurative sense of a loss of the sense of place in the social hierarchy in *No Sense of Place: The Impact of Electronic Media on Social Behavior* (New York: Oxford University Press, 1985). He argues that because televisual representation has provided a view of the "backstage" of adulthood and masculinity, as well as political power, the dominant positions in the social hierarchy have been essentially demystified for children, women, and the citizen. His observations about the "public-public" nature of events such as the press conference "that are carried beyond the time-space frame by electronic media, and therefore are accessible to almost anyone" (287), are plausible as applied to representation before it is mediated by the television apparatus. Here it is argued that the realm of controlled production and privatized reception as a framework within which such "public-publicness" is embedded has significant consequences not only for the representation itself but also for the metapsychology of its reception. Notions such as "nonspace" allow the imaginary aspects of Meyrowitz's unifying and leveling process to be conceptualized.

18. In many cities, the freeway once acted as a kind of container or beltway

around the city, eventually to become surrounded by suburbia. However, wherever the freeway may be drawn on the map, it is not really "located" in the grid of streets over or under which it extends, nor is it accessible without specially designed transitions, which are, as Lynch pointed out, not always easy to locate from the street.

19. The effects of an imaginary unity are not restricted to "nationhood," but can extend to smaller and greater units. See, for instance, Rath on the counternational effect of the broadcast transmission area in German-speaking countries.

Andrew Ross, in "The Work of Nature in the Age of Electronic Emission," *Social Text* 18 (Winter 1987–88):116–28, describes how the weather acts as an ideology, a means of naturalizing the social, and a way of explaining "an otherwise apparently contingent world of events" (123). Note that Ross is discussing the weather outside the venues discussed here—the world without comfort control beyond the window or glass. The "ideology" of the national weather inside is a more truly "lived relation" to the relations of production for most Americans. Meanwhile, the vagaries of traffic and the speed of travel to work, the beach, or the mall as impeded by accidents and contingencies, are most often considered and treated as if they were a force of nature like the weather "outside" of which Ross speaks.

20. Brian McHale, *Postmodernist Fiction* (New York: Methuen, 1987), pp. 124–28, provides an explanation of the *mise-en-abyme* and its importance for postmodernist literary fiction in expressions of ontological uncertainty.

21. A. J. Greimas and J. Courtes, *Semiotics and Language: An Analytical Dictionary,* trans. Larry Christ et al. (Bloomington: Indiana University Press, 1982). The engaged utterance is a simulacrum of the situation of enunciation, i.e., *discourse*. The disengaged utterance is story. Note that subject, space, and time can be engaged or disengaged separately rather than *en masse*.

22. "Flow" here is not the pure juxtaposition of unrelated segments that Raymond Williams found so fascinating in television. It is rather the result of conceiving a model hierarchy among segments, in a way related to Nick Browne's notion of the "supertext," in "The Political Economy of the Television (Super) Text," *Quarterly Review of Film Studies* 9 (Summer 1984):174–82, but conceived in terms of discourse and including other discursive material on a par with commercials. At some primary level, though, Williams's pure and unreconstructed flow undeniably plays a role in television reception.

23. Kowinski, in "The Mall as City Suburban," describes the motivation for building the first mall as providing needed opportunities for face-to-face contact among the isolated environments of cars, housing, and office. Victor Gruen modeled the first covered mall in the United States, Southdale Center in Edina, Minnesota, on covered pedestrian arcades, especially the Galleria Vittorio Emanuel in Milan in 1956 (119). The large department stores of Europe were in turn modeled on the garden city in such ideal realizations as the Crystal Palace.

24. Public and private are complex and historically shifting notions. While Jürgen Habermas is the best-known contemporary philosopher of the disappearance of the public realm, this concern has a long tradition in the United States, in the struggle between market forces and democratic values for dominance of areas of life. Hannah Arendt's *The Human Condition* traces the changing practices and concepts regarding *privacy* from the Greeks through the romantic period and is the most generally helpful on the concept.

25. Shaun Moores, " 'The Box on the Dresser': Memories of Early Radio and Everyday Life," *Media Culture and Society* 10 (1988):23.

26. See Stuart Culver, "What Manikins Want: *The Wonder World of Oz* and *The Art of Decorating Dry Goods Windows,*" *Representations* 21 (Winter 1988):97–116. Culver's enlightening link between Frank Baum's *Emerald City of Oz* and the growth of commodity display in shop windows is tied to a model of discrete fiction and identification rather than the utterly different disposition of the spectator "inside" the

glass which characterizes the most sophisticated development of consumer culture. Culver's main question can guide any investigation of the institutions of consumption: Why is it that Americans so willingly and apparently knowingly seek out and accept bogus substitutes, paper symbols, and commodity objects they know are inadequate to fulfill their needs, not to mention their desires? Culver presumes this occurs as an act of will—rather than in a state of distraction.

27. Spaulding Gray's "L. A., the Other" features a "real" story told by a woman who suddenly finds herself traveling in the opposite direction on the freeway miles from where she was last aware of her relative position. She interprets this lapsus as an intervention in her life by beings from outer space. Such experiences of "spacing out" are viewed here as endemic rather than otherworldy.

28. Roland Barthes, *Mythologies*, trans. Annette Lavers (New York: Hill and Wang, 1972), p. 123.

29. Brodsly, p. 50.

30. I might add that this experience of motility and subjectivity is divided differently by gender, much as David Morley has described the power relations around the dial and the remote control around the family television—the wife and mother decides what to watch only when no one else is there. Just so, the experience of driving is gendered. As his future bride said to Sonny Crockett in an episode of the 1987–88 season's *Miami Vice*, "I'll bet no woman has driven your Testosterone."

31. Cf. the chapter "Speed" in Stephen Kern's *The Culture of Time and Space, 1880–1918*, p. 120, for a discussion of this distinction between relative and absolute (subjectively intuited) motion. Note also that *nonspace* is not at all Kern's "empty space" or the void. Paul Virilio's meditations on the relation between speed and power of a coercive or military nature are only peripherally related to the "private" speed developed here.

32. "Ecstasy," p. 129.

33. Cf. Freud on jokes and body responses to "too much" and "too little" in *Jokes and Their Relation to the Unconscious*.

34. The two local hosts of the show address the home viewer directly across the heads of nameless other people, as if they were in a bubble of space which could exchange talk and looks with our home-viewing space, while an objectively closer realm in front of them remains an otherwise distant and unrelated diegetic world. This bubble of subjectivity can also be found in other televisual genres such as logos and rock videos. What seems to be at stake are two things: the end of a "line" or fourth wall which divides representational realms, and the notion of a mobile rather than stationary or positioned spectator and/or presenter, able to roam and cross the barriers between multiple worlds at will. The constant alternation of static settings with "driving" segments in *Miami Vice* is an inverse example of the process embedded within story, marking the interiorized subjectivity or "true" self "under cover," also reflected in music and conversation.

35. "For the Navajo, walking was an important event in and of itself and not just a way of getting somewhere. We expected the filmmakers to cut out most of the walking footage—but they didn't. It was the least discarded footage." Sol Worth and John Adair, *Through Navajo Eyes: An Exploration in Film Communication and Anthropology* (Bloomington: Indiana University Press, 1975), p. 146. "In reading the Navajo myths and stories later we were struck by how, in most Navajo myths, the narrator spends much of his time describing the walking, the landscape, and the places he passes, telling only briefly what to 'us' are plot lines" (147).

36. Ellis, *Visible Fictions*, pp. 120ff. and 140ff. and generally in his discussion of television. Ellis does not relate "segmentalization" to the development of spot advertising, whereas it could be argued that the struggle for control of the enunciation which led to spot advertising is served by segmentation, i.e., an argument of consequences not from particular events but from techniques of power.

37. McHale, p. 113.

38. Ibid., p. 115; cf. Morse, "Talk, Talk, Talk: The Space of Discourse in Television News, Sportcasts, Talk Shows, and Advertising," *Screen* 26.2 (Mar.-Apr. 1985):1–15, and "The Television News Personality and Credibility: Reflections on the News in Transition," in *Studies in Entertainment: Critical Approaches to Mass Culture*, ed. Tania Modleski (Bloomington: Indiana University Press, 1986), pp. 55–79, for more detailed reflection on these levels and on the notion of virtuality in direct address.

39. Cf. Margaret Morse, "Postsynchronising Rock Music and Television," *Journal of Communication Inquiry* 10.1 (Winter 1986):15–26.

40. These include mixtures of pictorial systems, two- and three-dimensional images, symbols, and the written word in a single image as well as different planes of language. Worth and Adair considered it odd that the Navajos made photos with layouts of painted words to "try out ideas" and that they linked clips of symbolic events without concern for spatio-temporal continuity. However, layouts of painted words would be quite compatible with contemporary televisual representation.

41. Especially in regard to fiction films on television, such alternation of story and discourse is perceived as interruption by all sorts of extraneous material and an incessant disruption of the psychological mechanism of disavowal that Beverly Houston explained in "Viewing Television: The Metapsychology of Endless Consumption," *Quarterly Review of Film Studies* 9.3 (1984):183–95.

Segmentation imposed on continuity editing is a mismatch of principles of coherence and dramatic unity of character, plot and setting, and editing, as well as conditions of viewing which promote fairly concentrated attention, and identification can only suffer thereby. What is interruption from the point of embedded fictions is more likely to be perceived as passage among segments and engagement with the viewer in discursive genres. Nonetheless, ads retain the sense of being foreign bodies in flow at least since the advent of spot advertising in the mid-1950s, whereas when sponsors controlled programming, the shift of subjects of discourse was smoother.

42. David Antin, "Video: The Distinctive Features of the Medium," in *Video Culture: A Critical Investigation*, ed. John Hanhardt (Rochester, N.Y.: Visual Studies Workshop, 1986), pp. 147–66.

43. Sandy Flitterman, "Psychoanalysis, Film, and Television," in *Channels of Discourse*, ed. Robert C. Allen (Chapel Hill: University of North Carolina Press, 1987), p. 200.

44. "It is hardly an exaggeration to call the freeway experience," as Joan Didion does, "the only secular communion Los Angeles has." Joan Didion, "The Diamond Lane Slowdown," *Esquire* 86 (August 1977), cited in Brodsly, pp. 36f.

45. Raymond Williams, *Television: Technology and Cultural Form* (New York: Schocken, 1975), p. 26; the boulevard is discussed at length in Marshall Berman's *All That Is Solid Melts into Air: The Experience of Modernity* (New York: Simon, 1982); street lighting in Wolfgang Schivelbusch, "The Policing of Street Lighting," *Yale French Studies: Everyday Life* 73 (1987):61–74.

46. Brodsly, p. 36.

47. Cited in Wolfgang Sachs, "Are Energy-Intensive Life-Images Fading? The Cultural Meaning of the Automobile in Transition" (unpublished paper 1982), pp. 3f. Sachs goes on to explain how the symbolic value of the auto is undermined as soon as it becomes generally accessible and how it actually generates social inequalities.

48. Brodsly, p. 5.

49. Michel Foucault, *Discipline and Punish: The Birth of the Prison* (New York: Random, 1979), p. 103.

50. McHale, especially chap. 3, "In the Zone" (43–58). McHale proposes that

the shift in dominance from epistemological to ontological questions is the primary distinguishing feature of postmodernism. The *zone* is a concept with a prior history in nineteenth-century Paris suburbs.

51. Culver, pp. 112f.: "In short, Dorothy loves the mechanism which turns display into a narrative of desire and enables her to experience the pastoral idyll vicariously. [. . .]She desires the figure that represents desire, recognizing in that image her own capacity for infinite desire."

52. Kowinski stresses the chain of relationships: "The shopping mall completed the link between the highway and television; once the department stores and the national chains and franchises were inside, just about anything advertised on the tube could be found at the mall. The mall provided the perfect and complementary organization for the national replicated and uniform outlets of the Highway Comfort Culture. The mall, too, was national, and it was also replicated and uniform in management as well as appearance—the chains knew what to expect just about everywhere. They could slip easily into any mall; one size fits all" (51).

53. Gaston Bachelard, "Miniature," in *The Poetics of Space* (Boston: Beacon, 1964), pp. 148–82.

54. Susan Stewart, *On Longing: Narratives of the Miniature, the Gigantic, the Souvenir, the Collection* (Baltimore and London: Johns Hopkins, 1984).

55. Robert Venturi, Denise Scott Brown, and Steven Izenour, *Learning from Las Vegas: The Forgotten Symbolism of Architectural Form* (Cambridge, Mass.: MIT Press, 1977).

56. Denis Hollier calls Callois's essay on the praying mantis in *Le myth et l'homme* (Paris: Gallimard, 1938) the first to deal with the issue of simulation (in "The Word of God: 'I Am Dead,' " *October* 44 [Spring 1988]:76f.).

57. Edward E. Duensing, "Television on the Move: In-Car Video Screen Small but Critics Question Safety," *Los Angeles Times* September 11, 1989, part II, p. 3. The article described the new technology recently patented by Jay Schiffman of Auto Vision Associates in Ferndale, Michigan. The virtual television is resisted for safety reasons, but its gradual acceptance is anticipated as a process comparable with the pioneering of the car radio by Bill Lear in 1929. What kind of programming the virtual television will display is discussed largely in terms of safety and attention. The process of looking at the virtual screen while driving is described in terms of "time sharing."

58. Stanley Cohen and Laurie Taylor, *Escape Attempts: The Theory and Practice of Resistance to Everyday Life* (London: Penguin, 1978).

59. Avenues for images and voices which might represent subjects other than network representatives, advertisers, and celebrities, that is, members of a general public, or for that matter other private voices, remain few: independent productions, the lowly public service announcement, cable community access programming, private networks for exchanging video cassettes, and computer networks. The growing segmentation of what was once broadcasting into cable channels and superstations supported by satellite as well as the video cassette is an opportunity for heterogeneous voices to enter into representation—but only if the discursive practices developed in network television are themselves changed. Venues of "publicness" that range from PBS and C-Span to Paper Tiger and Captain Midnight merit separate discussion as to how each contributed as a model of entry into the realms of distraction.

INFORMATION, CRISIS, CATASTROPHE

Mary Ann Doane

The major category of television is time. Time is television's basis, its principle of structuration, as well as its persistent reference. The insistence of the temporal attribute may indeed be a characteristic of all systems of imaging enabled by mechanical or electronic reproduction. For Roland Barthes, the *noeme* of photography is the tense it inevitably signifies—the *"That-has-been"* which ensures both the reality and the "pastness" of the object photographed.[1] The principal gesture of photography would be that of embalming (hence Barthes's reference to André Bazin). In fixing or immobilizing its object, transforming the subject of its portraiture into dead matter, photography is always haunted by death and historicity. The temporal dimension of television, on the other hand, would seem to be that of an insistent "present-ness"—a *"This-is-going-on"* rather than a *"That-has-been,"* a celebration of the instantaneous. In its own way, however, television maintains an intimate relation with the ideas of death and referentiality Barthes finds so inescapable in his analysis of the photograph. Yet, television deals not with the weight of the dead past but with the potential trauma and explosiveness of the present. And the ultimate drama of the instantaneous—catastrophe—constitutes the very limit of its discourse.

According to Ernst Bloch, "Time *is* only because something happens, and where something happens, there time is."[2] Television fills time by ensuring that something happens—it organizes itself around the event. There is often a certain slippage between the notion that television covers important events in order to validate itself as a medium and the idea that because an event is covered by television—because it is, in effect, deemed televisual—it is important. This is the significance of the media event, where the referent becomes indissociable from the medium. The penetration of everyday life by the media is a widely recognized phenomenon. But it is perhaps less widely understood that television's conceptualization of the event is heavily dependent upon a particular organization (or penetration) or temporality which produces three different modes of apprehending the event—information, crisis, and catastrophe. Information would specify the steady stream of daily "newsworthy" events characterized by their regularity if not predictability. Although news programs would constitute its most common source, it is also dispersed among a number of other types of programs. Its occasion may be politics, science, or "human interest." Information is noteworthy but is not shocking or gripping—its events are only mildly eventful, although they may be dramatized. The content of information is ever-changing, but information, as genre, is always *there*, a constant and steady presence, keeping you *in touch*. It is, above all, that which fills time on television—using it up. Here time is flow: steady and continuous.

The crisis, on the other hand, involves a condensation of temporality. It names an event of some duration which is startling and momentous precisely because it demands resolution within a limited period of time. Etymologically, crisis stems from the Greek *krisis*, or decision, and hence always seems to suggest the necessity of human agency. For that reason, crises are most frequently political—a hijacking, an assassination, the take-over of an embassy, a political coup, or the taking of hostages. There is a sense in which information and catastrophe are both subject-less, simply there, they *happen*—while crisis can be attributed to a subject, however generalized (a terrorist group, a class, a political party, etc.). The crisis compresses time and makes its limitations acutely felt. Finally, the catastrophe would from this perspective be the most critical of crises for its timing is that of the instantaneous, the moment, the punctual. It has no extended duration (except, perhaps, that of its televisual coverage) but, instead, happens "all at once."[3]

Ultimately, the categories of information, crisis, and catastrophe are only tenuously separable in practice. There are certainly phenomena which seem to annihilate the distinctions between them—a flood, for instance, which has elements of both the crisis (duration) and the catastrophe (it takes many lives), or an assassination which, although it may be experienced as a catastrophe, is a political action which must be attributed to a subject. But what is more striking in relation to this inevitable taxonomic failure is that television tends to blur the differences between what seem to be absolutely incompatible temporal modes, between the flow and continuity of information and the punctual discontinuity of catastrophe. Urgency, enslavement to the instant and hence forgettability, would then be attributes of both information and catastrophe. Indeed, the obscuring of these temporal distinctions may constitute the specificity of television's operation. The purpose of this essay is to investigate the implications and effects of this ambivalent structuration of time, particularly in relation to the categories of information and catastrophe.

Television overall seems to resist analysis. This resistance is linked to its sheer extensiveness (the problem of determining the limits or boundaries of the television text has been a pressing one), its continual barrage of information, sensation, event together with its uncanny ability to assimilate, appropriate, or recuperate all criticisms of the media. A story on the March 7, 1988, CBS Evening News detailed how the presidential candidates of both parties produced increasingly provocative or scandalous commercials in order to generate additional television coverage. The commercials would be shown several times in the regular manner and then, depending upon the level of their shock quotient, would be repeated once or more on local or national news, giving the candidates, in effect, free publicity. CBS News, in airing the metastory of this tendency, demonstrates how television news reports on, and hence contains through representation, its own exploitation. Its recuperative power is immense, and television often seems to reduce and deflate, through its pervasiveness and overpresence, all shock value.

Televisual information would seem to be particularly resistant to analysis given its protean nature. Not only does television news provide a seemingly endless stream of information, each bit (as it were) self-destructing in order to make room for the next, but information is dispersed on television among a number of genres and forms, including talk shows, educational/documentary type programs such as *Nova*, *National Geographic* specials, and *Wide, Wide World of Animals*, "how-to" programs such as *The Frugal Gourmet*, *This Old House*, and *Victory Garden*, news "magazines" such as *60 Minutes* and *Chronicle*, children's shows (*Sesame Street*), sports, etc. Furthermore, even the two generic forms which are most consistently associated with the concept of information—news and the educational/documentary program—exhibit diametrically opposed formal characteristics. Documentary programs such as *Nova* tend to activate the disembodied male voice-over whose authority has long ago lapsed in the realm of the cinema (it is a voice which, as Pascal Bonitzer points out, has irrevocably "aged").[4] News programs, on the other hand, involve the persistent, direct, embodied, and personalized address of the newscaster. Information, unlike narrative, is not chained to a particular organization of the signifier or a specific style of address. Antithetical modes reside side by side. Hence, information would seem to have no formal restrictions—indeed, it is characterized by its very ubiquity. If information is everywhere, then the true scandal of *disinformation* in the age of television is its quite precise attempt to *place* or to *channel* information—to direct its effects. Even if it is activated through television, it uses broadcasting in a narrowly conceived way. Disinformation loses credibility, then, not only through its status as a lie but through its very directedness, its limitation, its lack of universal availability. The scandal is that its effects are targeted. Disinformation abuses the system of broadcasting by invoking and exploiting the automatic truth value associated with this mode of dissemination—a truth value not unconnected to the sheer difficulty of verification and the very entropy of information.

Yet, in using the concept of information, I am accepting television's own terms. For the concept carries with it quite specific epistemological and sociological implications associated with the rise of information theory. As Katherine Hayles points out, the decisive move of information theory was to make information quantifiable by removing it from the context which endowed it with meaning and, instead, defining it through its own internal relations. According to Hayles, this results in what is, in effect, a massive decontextualization: "Never before in human history had the cultural context itself been constituted through a technology that makes it possible to fragment, manipulate, and reconstitute informational texts at will. For postmodern culture, the manipulation of text and its consequently arbitrary relation to context *is our* context."[5]

From this point of view, television could be seen as *the* textual technology of information theory. Insofar as a commercial precedes news coverage of a disaster which in its own turn is interrupted by a preview of tonight's made-for-TV movie, television is the preeminent machine of decontextualization. The only context for television is itself—its own rigorous scheduling. Its strictest limitation that of time, information becomes measurable, quantifiable, through its relation to temporality. While the realism of film is defined largely in terms of space, that of television is conceptualized in terms of time (owing to its characteristics of "liveness," presence, and immediacy). As Margaret Morse notes, television news is distinguished by the very absence of the rationalized Renaissance space we have come to associate with film—a perspectival technique which purports to *represent* the truth of objects in space.[6] Instead, the simultaneous activation of different, incongruous spaces (the studio, graphics, footage from the scene, interviews on monitor) is suggestive of a writing surface and the consequent annihilation of depth. Television does not so much *represent* as it *informs*. Theories of representation painstakingly elaborated in relation to film are clearly inadequate.

Conceptualizing information in terms of flow and ubiquity, however, would seem to imply that it lacks any dependence whatsoever upon punctuation or differentiation. Yet even television must have a way of compensating for its own tendency toward the leveling of signification, toward banalization and nondifferentiation—a way of saying, in effect, "Look, this is important," of indexically signaling that its information is worthy of attention. It does so through processes that dramatize information—the high seriousness of music which introduces the news, the rhetoric of the newscaster, the activation of special effects and spectacle in the documentary format. Most effective, perhaps, is the crisis of temporality which signifies *urgency* and which is attached to the information itself as its single most compelling attribute. Information becomes most visibly information, becomes a televisual commodity, on the brink of its extinction or loss. A recent segment of *Nova*, "The Hidden Power of Plants," chronicles the attempt to document the expertise of old medicine men who, when they die, take their knowledge with them (it is "worse than when a library burns down," the anonymous voice-over tells us). Similarly, the numerous geographic specials demonstrate that the life of a particular animal or plant becomes most *televisual* when the species is threatened with extinction. The rhetoric of impending environmental doom is today applicable to almost any species of plant or animal life given the constant expansion and encroachment of civilization on territory still designated as "natural." In this way, television incessantly takes as its subject matter the documentation and revalidation of its own discursive problematic. For information is shown to be punctual; it inhabits a moment of time and is then lost to memory. Television thrives on its own forgettability. While the concept of information itself implies the possibilities of storage and retrieval (as in computer technology), the notion of such storage is, for television, largely an alien idea. Some television news stories are accompanied by images labeled "file footage," but the appellation itself reduces the credibility of the story. Reused images, unless carefully orchestrated in the construction of nostalgia, undermine the appeal to the "live" and the instantaneous which buttresses the news.

The short-lived but spectacular aspect of information is revealed in the use of special-effects sequences where the drama of information is most closely allied with visual pleasure. In a *National Geographic* special entitled "The Mind," an artist's conception of the brain curiously resembles the *mise-en-scène* of information theory. The brain is depicted as an extensive network of neurons, synapses, and neurotransmitters regulating the flow of information. In one cubic inch of the brain there are 100 million nerve cells connected by 10,000 miles of fibers (laid end to end, the voice-over tells us, they would reach to the moon and back). The amount of information is so enormous that cells must make instantaneous decisions about what is to be transmitted. The sequence is organized so that music announces the significance of these data, and an almost constantly moving camera suggests the depths of the representation. The camera treats what is clearly a highly artificial, technologically produced space as the experienced real, while the voice-over provides verbal analogues to real space (the fibers which reach to the moon and back, the pinch of salt in a swimming pool which helps one to grasp what it would be like to look for a neurotransmitter in the brain). Yet, there is no pretense that an optical representation of the brain is adequate—it is simply *necessary* to the televisual discourse. The voice-over announces, "If it could be seen, brain cell action might look like random flickering of countless stars in an endless universe. Seemingly an infinite amount of information and variety of behaviors in an unlikely looking package," while the visuals mimic such a sight with multicolored flickering lights. Television knowledge strains to make visible the invisible. While it acknowledges the limits of empiricism, the limitations of the eye in relation to knowledge, information is nevertheless conveyable only in terms of a *simulated visibility*—"If it could be seen, this is what it might look like." Television deals in potentially visible entities. The epistemological endeavor is to bring to the surface, to expose, but only at a second remove—depicting what is not available to sight. Televisibility is a construct, even when it makes use of the credibility attached to location shooting—embedding that image within a larger, overriding discourse.

The urgency associated with information together with the refusal to fully align the visible with the dictates of an indexical realism suggests that the alleged value of information, like that of television, is ineluctably linked with time rather than space. And, indeed, both information and television have consistently been defined in relation to the temporal dimension. According to Walter Benjamin, the new form of communication called information brought about a crisis in the novel and in storytelling: "The value of information does not survive the moment in which it was new. It lives only at that moment; it has to surrender to it completely and explain itself to it without losing any time. A story is different. It does not expend itself. It preserves and concentrates its strength and is capable of releasing it even after a long time."[7] Information must be immediately understandable, graspable—it is "shot through with explanation." Meaning in storytelling has time to linger, to be subject to unraveling. It has "an amplitude that information lacks."[8] This tendency to polarize types of discourses with respect to their relation to temporality is evident also in Jonathan Culler's activation of Michael Thompson's categories of transience and durability: "we are accustomed to think—and tradition urges us to think—of two sorts of verbal, visual compositions: those which transmit information in a world of practical affairs—utilitarian and transient—and those which, not tied to the time or use value of information, are part of the world of leisure, our cultural patrimony, and belong in principle to the system of durables."[9] Benjamin might say that the loss of aura associated with electronic reproduction is a function of its inability to *endure*. In other words, there are things which last and things which don't. Information does not. It is expended, exhausted, in the moment of its utterance. If it were of a material order, it would be necessary to throw it away. As it is, one can simply forget it.

Television, too, has been conceptualized as the annihilation of memory, and consequently of history, in its continual stress upon the "nowness" of its own discourse. As Stephen Heath and Gillian Skirrow point out, "where film sides towards instantaneous memory ('everything is absent, everything is *recorded*—as a memory trace which is so at once, without having been something else before'), television operates much more as an absence of memory, the recorded material it uses—including the material recorded on film—instituted as actual in the production of the television image."[10] This transformation of record into actuality or immediacy is a function of a generalized fantasy of "live broadcasting." Jane Feuer pursues this question by demonstrating that a certain ontology of television, defined in terms of a technological base which allows for instantaneous recording, transmission, and reception, becomes the ground for a pervasive ideology of "liveness."[11] Although, as she is careful to point out, television rarely exploits this technical capability, minimalizing not only "live" transmission but preservation of "real time" as well, the ideology of "liveness" works to overcome the excessive fragmentation within television's flow. If television is indeed thought to be inherently "live," the impression of a unity of "real time" is preserved, covering over the extreme discontinuity which is in fact typical of television in the US at this historical moment.

From these descriptions it would appear that information is peculiarly compatible with the television apparatus. Both are fully aligned with the notion of urgency; both thrive on the exhaustion, moment by moment, of their own material; both are hence linked with transience and the undermining of memory. But surely there are moments which can be isolated from the fragmented flow of information, moments with an impact which disrupts the ordinary routine—moments when information bristles, when its greatest value is its shock value (in a medium which might be described as a modulated, and hence restrained, series of shocks). These are moments when one stops simply *watching* television in order to *stare*, transfixed—moments of catastrophe. But what constitutes catastrophe on television? And what is the basis of the widespread intuition that television exploits, or perhaps even produces, catastrophe? To what extent and in what ways is the social imagination of catastrophe linked to television?

Etymologically, the word "catastrophe" is traceable to the Greek *kata* (over) plus *strephein* (turn)—to overturn. The first definition given by *Webster's* is "the final event of the dramatic action esp. of a tragedy" (in this respect it is interesting to note that the etymology of the term "trope" also links it to "turn"). Hence, although the second and third definitions ("2. a momentous tragic event ranging from extreme misfortune to utter overthrow or ruin 3. a violent and sudden change in a feature of the earth") attempt to bind catastrophe to the real, the initial definition contaminates it with fictionality. Catastrophe is on the cusp of the dramatic and the referential, and this is, indeed, part of its fascination. The etymological specification of catastrophe as the overturning of a given situation anticipates its more formal delineation by catastrophe theory. Here, catastrophe is defined as unexpected discontinuity in an otherwise continuous system. The theory is most appropriate, then, for the study of sudden and unexpected effects in a gradually changing situation. The emphasis upon suddenness suggests that catastrophe is of a temporal order.

The formal definition offered by catastrophe theory, however, points to a striking paradox associated with the attempt to conceptualize televisual catastrophe. For while catastrophe is designated as discontinuity within an otherwise continuous system, television is most frequently theorized as a system of discontinuities, emphasizing heterogeneity. Furthermore, the tendency of television to banalize all events through a kind of leveling process would seem to preclude the possibility of specifying *any* event as catastrophic. As Benjamin pointed out in a statement which seems to capture something of the effect of television, "The concept of progress is to be grounded in the idea of catastrophe. That things 'just go on' *is* the catastrophe."[12] The news, in particular, is vulnerable to the charge that it dwells on the catastrophic, obsessed with the aberrant, the deviant. According to Margaret Morse, "The news in the West is about the *a*normal. It is almost always the 'bad' news. It is about challenges to the symbolic system and its legitimacy."[13] Furthermore, in its structural emphasis upon discontinuity and rupture, it often seems that television itself is formed on the model of catastrophe.

Given these difficulties, is it possible to produce a coherent account of events which television designates as catastrophe? What do these moments and events have in common? One distinctive feature of the catastrophe is that of the *scale* of the disaster in question—a scale often measured through a body count. By this criterion, Bhopal, the Detroit Northwest Airlines crash of August 1987, and the Mexican earthquake could all be labeled catastrophes. However, other events which are clearly presented as catastrophic—Chernobyl, the explosion of the *Challenger*—do not involve a high number of deaths, while wartime body counts (Vietnam, the Iran-Iraq war), often numerically impressive, do not qualify as catastrophic (undoubtedly because war makes death habitual, continual). Evidently, the scale which is crucial to catastrophe is not that of the quantification of death (or at least not that alone).

Catastrophe does, however, always seem to have something to do with technology and its potential collapse. And it is also always tainted by a fascination with death—so that catastrophe might finally be defined as the conjuncture of the failure of technology and the resulting confrontation with death. The fragility of technology's control over the forces it strives to contain is manifested most visibly in the accident—the plane crash today being the most prominent example. Dan Rather introduced the CBS story about the August 1987 Detroit Northwest Airlines crash with the rhetoric of catastrophe—the phrase "aftershocks of a nightmare" accompanying aerial images of wreckage strewn over a large area. The inability of television to capture the precise moment of the crash activates a compensatory discourse of eyewitness accounts and animated reenactments of the disaster—a simulated vision. Eyewitnesses who comment upon the incredible aspects of the sight or who claim that there were "bodies strewn everywhere" borrow their authority from the sheer fact of being there at the disastrous moment, their reported presence balancing the absence of the camera. What becomes crucial for the act of reportage, the announcement of the catastrophe, is the simple gesture of being on the scene, *where* it happened, so that presence in space compensates for the inevitable temporal lag. Hence, while the voice-over of the anchor ultimately organizes the event for us, the status of the image as indexical truth is not inconsequential—through it the "story" touches the ground of the real. Nevertheless, the catastrophe must be immediately subjected to analysis, speculation, and explanation. In the case of the airplane crash, speculation about causes is almost inevitably a speculation about the limits and breaking points of technology (with respect to Northwest flight 255, the history of the performance of the engine was immediately a subject of interrogation).

As modes of transportation dependent upon advanced and intricate technologies become familiar, everyday, routine, the potential for catastrophe increases. The breakdown of these technologies radically defamiliarizes them by signaling their distance from a secure and comforting nature. As Wolfgang Schivelbusch points out, this was the case for the railroad in the nineteenth century, its gradual acceptance and normalization subjected to the intermittent shock of the accident:

> One might also say that the more civilized the schedule and the more efficient the technology, the more catastrophic its destruction when it collapses. There is an exact ratio between the level of the technology with which nature is controlled, and the degree of severity of its accidents. The preindustrial era does not know any technological accidents in that sense. In Diderot's *Encyclopédie*, "Accident" is dealt with as a grammatical and philosophical concept, more or less synonymous with coincidence. The preindustrial catastrophes are natural events, natural accidents. They attack the objects they destroy from the outside, as storms, floods, thunderbolts, hailstones, etc. After the industrial revolution, destruction by technological accident comes from the inside. The technical apparatuses destroy themselves by means of their own power. The energies tamed by the steam engine and delivered by it as regulated mechanical performance will destroy that engine itself in the case of an accident.[14]

In the late twentieth century, the potential for technological collapse is more pervasive, characterizing catastrophes as diverse as Bhopal, Chernobyl, the *Challenger* explosion, earthquakes which science and technology fail to predict, as well as railway and plane crashes. But this massive expansion is perhaps not the decisive difference. After the Detroit crash, airport authorities spray-painted the burned-out grass green in order to conceal all traces of the accident and enable other travelers to avoid the traumatic evidence. Yet, this action was then reported on radio news, indicating that what is now at stake in the catastrophe, for us, is *coverage*. While the vision of catastrophe is blocked at one level, it is multiplied and intensified at another. The media urge us now to obsessively confront catastrophe, over and over again. And while the railway accident of the nineteenth century was certainly the focus of journalistic inquiry, its effects were primarily local. Television's ubiquity, its extensiveness, allows for a global experience of catastrophe which is always reminiscent of the potential of nuclear disaster, of mass rather than individual annihilation.

Catastrophe is thus, through its association with industrialization and the advance of technology, ineluctably linked with the idea of Progress. The time of technological progress is always felt as linear and fundamentally irreversible—technological change is almost by definition an "advance," and it is extremely difficult to conceive of any movement backward, any regression. Hence, technological evolution is perceived as unflinching progress toward a total state of control over nature. If some notion of pure Progress is the utopian element in this theory of technological development, catastrophe is its dystopia, the always unexpected interruption of this forward movement. Catastrophic time stands still. Catastrophe signals the failure of the escalating technological desire to conquer nature. From the point of view of Progress, nature can no longer be seen as anything but an affront or challenge to technology. And so, just as the media penetrate events (in the media event), technology penetrates nature. This is why the purview of catastrophe keeps expanding to encompass even phenomena which had previously been situated wholly on the side of nature—earthquakes, floods, hurricanes, tornadoes. Such catastrophes no longer signify only the sudden eruption of natural forces but the inadequacy or failure of technology and its predictive powers as well.

On the ABC Evening News of September 15, 1988, Peter Jennings stood in front of a map tracking the movements of Hurricane Gilbert for the first fifteen minutes of the broadcast. A supporting report detailed the findings of a highly equipped plane flying into the eye of the hurricane. The fascination here was not only that of the literal penetration of the catastrophic storm by high technology but also that of the sophisticated instruments and tracking equipment visible inside the plane—a fetishism of controls. Our understanding of natural catastrophe is now a fully technological apprehension. Such incidents demonstrate that the distinction made by Schivelbusch between preindustrial accidents (natural accidents where the destructive energy comes from without) and postindustrial accidents (in which the destructive energy comes from within the technological apparatus) is beginning to blur. This is particularly the case with respect to nuclear technology which aspires to harness the most basic energy of nature itself—that of the atom. And in doing so, it also confronts us with the potential transformation of that energy into that which is most lethal to human life.

While nuclear disaster signals the limits of the failure of technology, the trauma attached to the explosion of the *Challenger* is associated with the sheer height of the technological aspirations represented by space exploration. The *Challenger* coverage also demonstrates just how nationalistic the apprehension of catastrophe is—our own catastrophes are always more important, more eligible for extended reporting than those of other nations. But perhaps even more crucial here was the fact that television itself was on the scene—witness to the catastrophe. And the played and replayed image of the *Challenger* exploding, of diverging lines of billowing white smoke against a deep blue Florida sky—constant evidence of television's compulsion to repeat—acts as a reminder not only of the catastrophic nature of the event but also of the capacity of television to record instantaneously, a reminder of the fact that television was *there*. The temporality of catastrophe is that of the instant—it is momentary, punctual, while its televisual coverage is characterized by its very duration, seemingly compensating for the suddenness, the unexpected nature of the event.

A segment of Tom Brokaw's virtually nonstop coverage on NBC contained a video replay of the explosion itself, a live broadcast of the president's message to the nation, Brokaw's reference to an earlier interview with a child psychiatrist who dealt with the potential trauma of the event for children, Chris Wallace's report of Don Regan's announcement and the press's reception of the news during a press briefing, a mention of Mrs. Reagan's reaction to the explosion as she watched it live on television, Brokaw's speculation about potential attacks on Reagan's support of SDI ("Star Wars"), and Brokaw's 1981 interview with one of the astronauts, Judy Resnick. The glue in this collection of disparate forms is Brokaw's performance, his ability to *cover* the event with words, with a commentary which exhausts its every aspect and through the orchestration of secondary reports and old footage.[15] Brokaw is the pivot, he mediates our relation to the catastrophe. Furthermore, as with television news, it is a direct address/appeal to the viewer, but with an even greater emphasis upon the presence and immediacy of the act of communication, with constant recourse to shifters which draw attention to the shared space and time of reporter and viewer: terms such as "today," "here," "you," "we," "I." Immediately after a rerun of the images documenting the *Challenger* explosion, Brokaw says, clearly improvising, "As I say, we have shown that to you repeatedly again and again today. It is not that we have a ghoulish curiosity. We just think that it's important that all members of the audience who are coming to their sets at different times of the day have an opportunity to see it. And of course everyone is led to their own speculation based on what happened here today as well." The "liveness," the "real time" of the catastrophe is that of the television anchor's discourse—its nonstop quality a part of a fascination which is linked to the spectator's knowledge that Brokaw faces him/her without a complete script, underlining the alleged authenticity of his discourse. For the possibility is always open that Brokaw might stumble, that his discourse might lapse—and this would be tantamount to touching the real, simply displacing the lure of referentiality attached to the catastrophe to another level (that of the "personal" relationship between anchor and viewer).

There is a very striking sense in which televisual catastrophe conforms to the definition offered by catastrophe theory whereby catastrophe represents discontinuity in an otherwise continuous system. From this point of view, the measure of catastrophe would be the extent to which it interrupts television's regular daily programming, disrupting normal expectations about what can be seen and heard at a particular time. If Nick Browne is correct in suggesting that, through its alignment of its own schedule with the work day and the work week, television "helps produce and render 'natural' the logic and rhythm of the social order,"[16] then catastrophe would represent that which cannot be contained within such an ordering of temporality. It would signal the return of the repressed. The traumatic nature of such a disruption is underlined by the absence of commercials in the reporting of catastrophe—commercials usually constituting not only the normal punctuation of television's flow but, for some, the very text of television.

That which, above all, cannot be contained within the daily social rhythms of everyday life is death. Catastrophe is at some level always about the body, about the encounter with death. For all its ideology of "liveness," it may be death which forms the point of televisual intrigue. Contemporary society works to conceal death to such an extent that its experience is generally a vicarious one through representation. The removal of death from direct perception, a process which, as Benjamin points out, was initiated in the nineteenth century, continues today:

> In the course of the nineteenth century bourgeois society has, by means of hygienic and social, private and public institutions, realized a secondary effect which may have been its subconscious main purpose: to make it possible for people to avoid the sight of dying. Dying was once a public process in the life of the individual and a most exemplary one. . . . There used to be no house, hardly a room, in which someone had not once died. . . . Today people live in rooms that have never been touched by death. . . . [17]

Furthermore, the mechanization of warfare—the use of technologically advanced weapons which kill at a greater and greater distance—further reduces the direct confrontation with death. Consistent with its wartime goal of allaying the effects of death and increasing the efficiency with which it is produced, technology also strives to hold death at bay, to contain it. Hence, death emerges as the absolute limit of technology's power, that which marks its vulnerability. Catastrophe, conjoining death with the failure of technology, presents us with a scenario of limits—the limits of technology, the limits of signification. In the novel, according to Benjamin, death makes the character's life *meaningful* to the reader, allows him/her the "hope of warming his shivering life with a death he reads about."[18] What is at stake in televisual catastrophe is not meaning but reference. The viewer's consuming desire, unlike that of the novel reader, is a desire no longer for meaning but for referentiality, which seems to have been all but lost in the enormous expanse of a television which always promises a contact forever deferred. Death is no longer the culminating experience of a life rich in continuity and meaning but, instead, pure discontinuity, disruption—pure chance or accident, the result of being in the wrong place at the wrong time.

And it is not by coincidence that catastrophe theory, on an entirely different level, seeks to provide a means of mapping the discontinuous instance, the chance occurrence, without reducing its arbitrariness or indeterminacy. Catastrophe theory is based on a theorem in topology discovered by the French mathematician René Thom in 1968. Its aim is to provide a formal language for the description of sudden discontinuities within a gradually changing system. The points of occurrence of these discontinuities are mapped on a three-dimensional graph. In 1972, E. D. Zeeman developed an educational toy called the "catastrophe machine" to facilitate the understanding of Thom's theory. (The appeal of this toy is that you can make it yourself with only two rubberbands, a cardboard disk, two drawing pins, and a wooden board). The point of the catastrophe machine is the construction of an apparatus which is guaranteed to *not* work, to predictably produce unpredictable irregularities. For catastrophe theory is, as one of its proponents explains, "a theory about singularities. When applied to scientific problems, therefore, it deals with the properties of discontinuities directly, without reference to any specific underlying mechanism."[19] It is, therefore, no longer a question of explanation. Catastrophe theory confronts the indeterminable without attempting to reduce it to a set of determinations. Thom refers to "islands of determinism separated by zones of instability or indeterminacy."[20] Catastrophe theory is one aspect of a new type of scientific endeavor which Lyotard labels "postmodern"—a science which "by concerning itself with such things as undecidables, the limits of precise control, conflicts characterized by incomplete information, 'fracta,' catastrophes, and pragmatic paradoxes—is theorizing its own evolution as discontinuous, catastrophic, nonrectifiable, and paradoxical. It is changing the meaning of the word *knowledge*, while expressing how such a change can take place."[21]

Television is not, however, the technology of catastrophe theory, or if it is, it is so only in a highly limited sense. The televisual construction of catastrophe seeks both to preserve and to annihilate indeterminacy, discontinuity. On the one hand, by surrounding catastrophe with commentary, with an explanatory apparatus, television works to contain its more disturbing and uncontainable aspects. On the other hand, catastrophe's discontinuity is embraced as the mirror of television's own functioning, and that discontinuity and indeterminacy ensure the activation of the lure of referentiality. In this sense, television is a kind of catastrophe machine, continually corroborating its own signifying problematic—a problematic of discontinuity and indeterminacy which strives to mimic the experience of the real, a real which in its turn is guaranteed by the contact with death. Catastrophe thrives on the momentary, the instantaneous, that which seems destined to be forgotten, and hence seems to confirm Heath's and Skirrow's notion that television operates as the "absence of memory." But because catastrophe is necessary to television, as the corroboration of its own signifying problematic, there is also a clear advantage in the somewhat laborious construction and maintenance of a memory of catastrophe. The spectator must be led to remember, with even a bit of nostalgia, those moments which are preeminently televisual—the explosion of the *Challenger,* the assassination of John F. Kennedy (the footage of which was replayed again and again during the time of the recent twenty-fifth anniversary of the event). What is remembered in these nostalgic returns is not only the catastrophe or crisis itself but the fact that television was there, allowing us access to moments which always seem more real than all the others.

Catastrophe coverage clearly generates and plays on the generation of anxiety. The indeterminacy and unexpectedness of catastrophe seem to aptly describe the potential trauma of the world we occupy. But such coverage also allows for a persistent disavowal—in viewing the bodies on the screen, one can always breathe a sigh of relief in the realization that "that's not me." Indeed, the celebrity status of the anchorperson and of those who usually appear on television can seem to justify the belief that the character on the screen—dead or alive—is always definitively *other,* that the screen is not a mirror. Such persistent anxiety is manageable, although it may require that one periodically check the screen to make sure. But this is perhaps not the only, or even the most important, affect associated with catastrophe coverage.

Something of another type of affective value of catastrophe can be glimpsed in Slavoj Zizek's analysis of the sinking of the *Titanic* and its cultural and psychical significance. At the end of the nineteenth century, "civilized" Europe perceived itself as on the brink of extinction, its values threatened by revolutionary workers' movements, the rise of nationalism and anti-Semitism, and diverse signs indicating the decay of morals. The grand luxury transatlantic voyage incarnated a generalized nostalgia for a disappearing Europe insofar as it signified technological progress, victory over nature, and also a condensed image of a social world based on class divisions elsewhere threatened with dissolution. The shipwreck of the *Titanic* hence represented for the social imagination the collapse of European civilization, the destruction of an entire social edifice—"Europe at the beginning of the century found itself confronted with its own death."[22] The contradictory readings by the right and the left of the behavior of first-class "gentlemen" with respect to third-class women and children corroborate this reading of a social imagination seized by the shipwreck and treating it as an index to the maintenance or collapse of former class differences.

But Zizek goes on to claim that there must be something in excess of this symbolic reading. For it is difficult to explain satisfactorily the contemporary fascination with images of the wreck at the bottom of the sea: "The mute presence of wrecks—are they not like the congealed residue of an impossible *jouissance?* . . . One understands why, notwithstanding technical problems, we hesitate to raise the wreckage of the Titanic to the surface: its sublime beauty, once exposed to daylight, would turn to waste, to the depressing banality of a rusted mass of iron." It would be problematic to bring the *Titanic* too close—it is there to be watched in its "proper" grave, to be regarded as a monument to catastrophe in general, a catastrophe which, in its distance, makes you feel real. According to Zizek, the two aspects of the *Titanic*—the "metaphorical one of its symbolic overdetermination and the real one of the inertia of the thing, incarnation of a mute *jouissance*"—represent the two sides of the Freudian symptom. For although the symptom can be interpreted as a knot of significations, it is also always more than that. There is a remainder, an excess not reducible to the symbolic network (in the words of Jacques-Alain Miller, one "loves one's symptom like oneself"). This is why, according to Zizek, "one remains hooked on the real of one's symptom even after the interpretation has accomplished its work."[23]

It is this remainder, this residue, which televisual catastrophe exploits. The social fascination of catastrophe rests on the desire to confront the remainder, or to be confronted with that which is in excess of signification. Catastrophe seems to testify to the inertia of the real and television's privileged relation to it. In the production and reproduction of the metonymic chain—the body-catastrophe-death-referentiality—television legitimates its own discourse. This is why it is often difficult to isolate and define catastrophe, to establish the boundary which marks it off from ordinary television. Information and catastrophe coexist in a curious balance. According to Susan Sontag, "we live under continual threat of two equally fearful, but seemingly opposed, destinies: unremitting banality and inconceivable terror."[24] Television produces both as the two poles structuring the contemporary imagination.

This relation to catastrophe is by no means an inherent or essential characteristic of television technology. Rather, it is a feature which distinguishes television and its operations in the late capitalist society of the United States where crisis is produced and assimilated as a part of the ongoing spectacle— a spectacle financed by commercials and hence linked directly to the circulation of commodities. What underlies/haunts catastrophe but is constantly overshadowed by it is the potential of another type of catastrophe altogether—that of the economic crisis. According to Schivelbusch, "If the nineteenth century perceives the cause of technological accidents to be the sudden disturbance of the uncertain equilibrium of a machine (i.e., the relationship between curbed energy and the means of curbing it), Marx defines the economic crisis as the disruption of the uncertain balance between buying and selling in the circulation of goods. As long as buying and selling work as a balanced and unified process, the cycle goes on functioning, but as soon as the two become separated and autonomous, we arrive at a crisis."[25] Of course, economic crisis does not appear to meet any of the criteria of the true catastrophe. It is not punctual but of some duration, it does not kill (at least not immediately), and it can assuredly be linked to a notion of agency or system (that of commodity capitalism) if not to a subject. Yet, for a television dependent upon the healthy circulation of commodities, the economic crisis can be more catastrophic than any natural or technological catastrophe. Ironically, for this very reason, and to deflect any potentially harmful consequences, it must be disguised as catastrophe and hence naturalized, contained, desystematized. The economic crisis as catastrophe is sudden, discontinuous, and unpredictable—an accident which cannot reflect back upon any system.

In comparison with the lure of referentiality associated with catastrophe "proper," the economic crisis confronts us as an abstraction. Yet, the abstraction of catastrophe is difficult since catastrophe seems to lend itself more readily to an account of bodies. Hence, the reporting of the Wall Street crash of October 1987 strives to restore the elements of catastrophe which are lacking—the iconography of panic becomes the high-angle shot down at the milling crowd of the stock exchange, bodies in disarray. An interviewee claims, "It's fascinating, like a bloodbath." Furthermore, a catastrophe which seems furthest removed from the concept of a failure of technology is rebound to that concept through the oft-repeated claim that a major cause of the crash was computer trading gone awry. Economic crisis is also tamed by naturalizing it as a cyclical occurrence, like the change of seasons. This is a containment of a catastrophe which, unlike the others, potentially threatens television's own economic base, its own mechanism for the production of commodity-linked spectacle. And perhaps this is why catastrophe has become such a familiar, almost everyday, televisual occurrence. According to Ernst Bloch, "the crisis of the accident (of the uncontrolled things) will remain with us longer to the degree that they remain deeper than the crises of economy (of the uncontrolled commodities)."[26] The depth which television accords to the catastrophes of things is linked to the lure of referentiality which they hold out to us. Catastrophe makes concrete and immediate, and therefore deflects attention from, the more abstract horror of potential economic crisis. For the catastrophe, insofar as it is perceived as the *accidental* failure of technology (and one which can be rectified with a little tinkering—O-rings can be fixed, engines redesigned), is singular, asystematic—it does not touch the system of commodity capitalism.

The concept of crisis is linked to temporal process, to a duration of a (one can hope) limited period. This is why the time of crisis can coincide with that of politics, of political strategy. Crisis, *krisis*, is a decisive period insofar as it is a time when decisions have to be made, decisions with very real effects. The televisual representation of catastrophe, on the other hand, hopes to hold onto the apolitical and attach it to the momentary, the punctual. Here time is free in its indeterminacy, reducible to no system—precisely the opposite of televisual time which is programmed and scheduled as precisely as possible, down to the last second. Television's time is a time which is, in effect, wholly determined. And this systematization of time is ultimately based on its commodification (time in television is, above all, not "free"). As both Stephen Heath and Eileen Meehan point out, what networks sell to advertisers is the viewing time of their audiences.[27] Here the commodification of time is most apparent (and perhaps this is why, in the reporting of catastrophes, there are no commercials).

The catastrophe is crucial to television precisely because it functions as a denial of this process and corroborates television's access to the momentary, the discontinuous, the real. Catastrophe produces the illusion that the spectator is in direct contact with the anchorperson, who interrupts regular programming to demonstrate that it can indeed be done when the referent is at stake. Television's greatest technological prowess is its ability to be there—both on the scene and in your living room (hence the most catastrophic of technological catastrophes is the loss of the signal). The death associated with catastrophe ensures that television is felt as an immediate collision with the real in all its intractability—bodies in crisis, technology gone awry. Televisual catastrophe is thus characterized by everything which it is said not to be—it is expected, predictable, its presence crucial to television's operation. In fact, catastrophe could be said to be at one level a condensation of all the attributes and aspirations of "normal" television (immediacy, urgency, presence, discontinuity, the instantaneous, and hence forgettable). If information becomes a commodity on the brink of its extinction or loss, televisual catastrophe magnifies that death many times over. Hence, catastrophe functions as both the exception and the norm of a television practice which continually holds out to its spectator the lure of a referentiality perpetually deferred.

NOTES

1. Roland Barthes, *Camera Lucida: Reflections on Photography*, trans. Richard Howard (New York: Farrar, 1981), p. 77.

2. Ernst Bloch, *A Philosophy of the Future*, trans. John Cumming (New York: Herder, 1970), p. 124.

3. The time proper to catastrophe might be thought of as compatible with that of the digital watch where time is cut off from any sense of analogical continuity, and the connection between moments is severed. One is faced only with the time of the instant—isolated and alone.

4. Pascal Bonitzer, "The Silences of the Voice," in *Narrative, Apparatus, Ideology*, trans. Philip Rosen and Marcia Butzel, ed. Philip Rosen (New York: Columbia University Press, 1986), p. 328.

5. N. Katherine Hayles, "Text out of Context: Situating Postmodernism within an Information Society," *Discourse* 9 (Spring/Summer 1987):26.

6. Margaret Morse, "The Television News Personality and Credibility: Reflections on the News in Transition," in *Studies in Entertainment*, ed. Tania Modleski (Bloomington: Indiana University Press, 1986), p. 70.

7. Walter Benjamin, "The Storyteller," in *Illuminations*, ed. Hannah Arendt, trans. Harry Zohn (New York: Schocken, 1969), p. 90.

8. Benjamin, "The Storyteller," p. 89.

9. Jonathan Culler, "Junk and Rubbish," *Diacritics* 15.3 (Fall 1985):10.

10. Stephen Heath and Gillian Skirrow, "Television, a World in Action," *Screen* 18.2 (Summer 1977):55–56.

11. Jane Feuer, "The Concept of Live Television: Ontology as Ideology," in *Regarding Television: Critical Approaches—An Anthology*, ed. E. Ann Kaplan (Frederick, Md.: University Publications of America, and the American Film Institute), pp. 13–14.

12. Walter Benjamin, "Central Park," trans. Lloyd Spencer, *New German Critique* 34 (Winter 1985):50.

13. Morse, p. 74.

14. Wolfgang Schivelbusch, *The Railway Journey: Trains and Travel in the 19th Century*, trans. Anselm Hollo (New York: Urizen, 1979), p. 133.

15. This performance could also be seen as a masculinist discourse which attempts to reestablish control over a failed masculinized technology. In this sense, catastrophe is feminized insofar as it designates the reemergence of the nature technology attempts to repress and control. Brokaw's performance is thus a discursive management of catastrophe. Such a reading is problematic insofar as it equates nature and the feminine, technology and the masculine, but gains a certain amount of historical force from an influential mythology. It was, after all, a woman (Pandora) who unleashed catastrophe upon the world.

16. Nick Browne, "The Political Economy of the Television (Super) Text," in *Television: The Critical View*, ed. Horace Newcomb, 4th ed. (New York: 1987), p. 588.

17. Benjamin, "The Storyteller," pp. 94–95.

18. Ibid., p. 101.

19. P. T. Saunders, *An Introduction to Catastrophe Theory* (Cambridge: Cambridge University Press, 1980), p. 1.

20. René Thom, "Topological Models in Biology," *Topology* 8 (1969), quoted in Michael Thompson, *Rubbish Theory: The Creation and Destruction of Value* (Oxford: Oxford University Press, 1979), p. 142.

21. Jean-François Lyotard, *The Postmodern Condition: A Report on Knowledge*, trans. Geoff Bennington and Brian Massumi (Minneapolis: University of Minnesota Press, 1984), p. 60.

22. Slavoj Zizek, "Titanic-le-symptôme," *L'Ane* 30 (Apr.-June 1987):45.

23. Ibid.

24. Susan Sontag, "The Imagination of Disaster," in *Against Interpretation* (New York: Dell, 1969), p. 227.

25. Schivelbusch, p. 134.

26. Quoted in ibid., p. 131.

27. See their essays in this volume.

TV TIME AND CATASTROPHE, OR *BEYOND THE PLEASURE PRINCIPLE* OF TELEVISION

Patricia Mellencamp

US network television is a disciplinary time machine, a metronome rigorously apportioning the present, rerunning TV history, and anxiously awaiting the future. The hours, days, and television seasons are seriated, scheduled, and traded in ten-second increments modeled on the modern work week—day time, prime time, late night, or weekend. Time itself is a gendered, hierarchized commodity capitalizing on leisure. Along with selling public time and service for private homes (paradoxically over an electromagnetic spectrum which "belongs to the people"), TV quantifies the body, collectively imagined by the networks as "the audience"—measured by statistics, demographics, and people meters, correlated with supermarket purchases, and bartered according to calculations of time spent/money made. (Subcultural, in-person studies of specific local audiences depict other, idiosyncratic versions of the TV homebody, rephrasing the network obsession with "shares.") The expenditure of time, in contrast to cinema's tallies of box office attendance receipts (and spatial aesthetics), is what counts. Our time is money. Television is a machine capitalizing on the fear of the passage of time—as aging and death; like sponsors for whom time is money, we can also buy or stop time.

TV's "flow" of entertainment is an economics, including libidinal, which resembles Newtonian time—an old-fashioned view of history as relatively static, slowing changing, a notion emblematized by Darwin. Along with its origin in tourism—reportedly Raymond Williams came up with "flow" in a San Francisco hotel room—the structural model has another US lineage, a pragmatist dimension, from William James and others who argued around 1890 that time was a flux rather than a sum of discrete units, that human consciousness was a stream rather than a configuration of separate faculties; James wrote in 1894: "Consciousness does not appear to itself chopped up into bits . . . it is nothing jointed; it flows. . . . A 'river' or a 'stream' are the metaphors . . . let us call it the stream of thought, of consciousness."[1]

(A recent two-part commercial for Excedrin demonstrates the confident hold of flow, of continuity rather than rupture. In part one, a man with a headache takes an aspirin, seemingly a conclusion; but after two ads and station promos, the commercial returns like a program, incorporating the time lapse into the sell and brief narrative: two minutes later, the man's headache is gone. The interruption itself has been fragmented, mimicking conventions of program and flow. This tactic is practiced in a different way by the Ragu spaghetti sauce commercials which are miniature sit-coms, replete with laugh tracks and applause, planned as a long-running series. Television or publicity is one step ahead of its theorists; theory is humbled, taken from the realm of academia into popular culture, made accessible and parodic; our cultural objects are, like physics' unpredictable atoms or terrorists, moving, unstable targets.)

Turn-of-the-century Joycean figurations of time split public time, the time of crowds—the newly instituted world standard time which crossed national boundaries like the wireless, regulating war, railroads, and masses alike—from private time which, like memory, was capricious; both added simultaneity to successive time. Freud's theory of childhood and memory elucidates this temporal model, perfectly applicable to television programming; TV reruns and remakes Freud's "repetition compulsion": "Theoretically, every earlier state of content could thus be restored to memory again even if its elements have long ago exchanged all their original connections for more recent ones."[2] For Freud, as for Newton, Darwin, and reruns of "*I Love Lucy*," time is embedded in our embryonic beings . . . in which every experience leaves a trace.

However, the memories TV recalls via constant reruns, remakes, and parody, the past it recreates, rarely summon or echo personal experience, what Benjamin in "On Some Motifs in Baudelaire," referring to Bergson's "theory of experience" and Proust, called involuntary memory; rather, TV schedules memories of television, perhaps, as Benjamin argues, resulting in an "atrophy" of experience. TV's peculiarly democratic past is infrequently idiosyncratic; as exemplified by *Leave It to Beaver* and the return of June Cleaver in name to *Roseanne*'s promo and in body to *Baby Boom*, and by the appearance of TV game show history on the second episode of *Tattinger's* embodied as the legit, New Yorkers Kitty Carlisle (*I've Got a Secret*) and Arlene Francis (*What's My Line?*) looking exactly as they did in the fifties and making bad puns, TV's history personally, parodically belongs to everyone. "Therefore Proust, summing up, says that the past is 'somewhere beyond the reach of the intellect, and unmistakably present in some material object (or in the sensation which such an object arouses in us). . . . As for that object, it depends entirely on chance whether we come upon it before we die or whether we never encounter it.' "[3] Roland Barthes, in *Camera Lucida,* came upon the material object, the old photograph of his mother as a child, before he died.

TV is rarely the material object setting off involuntary (personal) memory, causing us to assimilate "the information it supplies as part of [our] own experience." "Where there is experience in the strict sense of the word, certain contents of the individual past combine with material of the collective past."[4] Rather than this amalgam of involuntary/voluntary memory, shifting from conscious to unconscious, from collective to individual past, in the realm of experience—as Marguerite Duras did in *The Lover,* or as occurred during the twenty-fifth-year commemoration of Kennedy's assassination—television's "intention is just the opposite, and it is achieved: to isolate what happens from the realm in which it could affect the experience of the reader."[5]

TV triggers memories of TV in an endless chain of TV referentiality. The newspaper techniques Benjamin cites are applicable to TV: "brevity, comprehensibility, and above all, lack of connection between the individual news items."[6] Instead of experience and memory, television's past, whether funny or not, evokes laughter and distance; it is a dissociated, dated history, out of synch with the present, with nothing, now, to do with us—it is over and thus, paradoxically, ahistorical or nostalgic—at least for most critics. With its raw appeals to and inscriptions of affect, television is a medium of remembrance more than memory: " 'The function of remembrance,' Reik writes, 'is the protection of impressions; memory aims at their disintegration. Remembrance is essentially conservative, memory is destructive.' "[7] TV enacts the contradiction of destructive conservation.

However, Benjamin's model of history as revolutionary or catastrophic exists as an inside premise of television's rhetoric. Like Proust who "immediately confronts this involuntary memory with a voluntary memory, one that is in the service of the intellect," or Benjamin in his encounters with the everyday or artifacts of popular culture which set off memories of, for example, the Berlin of his childhood, and in his formulations of time in "Theses on the Philosophy of History," we can analyze the present of television through our personal, generational, and intellectual histories—a "dialectical" or materialistic analysis which might "blast a specific era out of the homogeneous course of history—blasting a specific life out of the era or a specific work out of the lifework [which] is preserved . . . and at the same time cancelled,"[8] what I call, following Freud's cue, television's overriding process of creation/cancellation. (For "specific work," we might substitute "program"; for "lifework," "series.") Like Benjamin's famous formulation, TV partially gives us "a conception of the present as the 'time of the now' which is shot through with chips of Messianic time."[9]

This conception of the eruption of the past into the present as a simultaneity is inflected by Freud's model of shock which, along with the Soviet revolution, influenced Benjamin:

> To articulate the past historically . . . means to seize hold of a memory as it flashes up at a moment of danger . . . fashion is a tiger's leap into the past. . . . The same leap in the open air of history is the dialectical one. . . . Where thinking suddenly stops in a configuration pregnant with tensions, it gives that configuration a shock . . . a revolutionary chance in the fight for the oppressed past.[10]

While TV is usually a tiger's leap into fashion, a medium of remembrance rather than memory, it operates, particularly during catastrophe coverage—"the configuration of shock"—"as if" there might be a revolutionary chance. Catastrophe coverage, "the time of the now," is represented as a moment when thinking stops, a moment of danger that might portend change, which paradoxically is both thrill and preclusion. To suggest mechanisms of this containment is the goal of this analysis which, perhaps parroting Freud's tedious style of rephrasing or like the depleted TV coverage of parades and elections, unstylishly resorts to a determined repetition. (Could anything be more tedious than watching parades on television?)

Paralleling TV's temporal effects, anxiety is television's affect. If this is so, then we might consider shifting our analysis from theories of pleasure to include theories of unpleasure (and paradoxically, from constructs of work to models of leisure *as* work), moving *Beyond the Pleasure Principle* to *Inhibitions, Symptoms, and Anxiety*, away from desire, lack, castration, Oedipus, the unconscious and toward anxiety (and Colonus), loss, separation, the conscious (and, for Freud, women).

Successive, simultaneous time, measured by regular, on-the-half-hour programming (a historical expansion of the 15-minute radio and early TV base program unit), indefinitely multiplied by cable and satellite transmission, hypostatized by familiar formats and aging stars in reruns and remakes, trivialized by scandal and gossip, is disrupted by the discontinuity of castastrophe coverage. So-called heterogeneity or diversity ceases as do commercials and TV continuity time as we focus on a single event. My temporal model of television incorporates the imperfect and aging body addressed by TV (including plastic surgery, masquerade, and sexual difference) and speaks about gossip/scandal (including talk show "pluralism" and differentiation as difference) which are figured elsewhere.[11]

Newton's project of charting an unchanging universe—the equivalent of plastic surgery—was doomed, as are our sagging, wrinkled bodies, by his own laws of gravity: the natural state of matter (at least for now) is chaos, disorder. Einstein and relativity sketched an artistic universe where space is curved, the path of light is bent, and time is slowed. TV time of regularity and repetition, continuity and "normalcy," contains the potential of interruption, the thrill of live coverage of death events. It is here, in the potential and promise of disruption—a shift between the safe assurance of successive time and story and the break-in of the discontinuity of the real in which the future hangs in the balance, the intrusion of shock, trauma, disaster, crisis—that TV's spectatorial mechanism of disavowal, which is retroactive, operates most palpably. If a program begins off the half-hour, or we hear the alarm "We interrupt this regularly scheduled program," a catastrophe or political event has occurred;[12] that it is still not on the air reassures us that it was not a nuclear catastrophe, at least in the US. Our disasters require "continual coverage," nation over narrative; those of other countries are not worth a missed soap opera. Most critically, the US network trade of time for money is suspended during catastrophe coverage, formatted events too portentous for commercials; the news division's takeover of entertainment is also the daytime replacement of women by men. The break-in or disruption of continuity flow or narrative normalcy has rigid rules: in addition to the rare, unscheduled presidential address, or news conference, it must be economic (commercials, station IDs, or promos) or deathly. Imagine a mid-program break to the zoo, the classroom, or an art event.

Theories of catastrophe—mathematical (René Thom), psychoanalytic (Sigmund Freud), socio/geo/logical (the journal *Disasters*), historical materialist or dialectical (Benjamin), artistic (Andy Warhol in painting, Bruce Conner in film and sculpture, and Ant Farm in video), biblical (the catastrophists and TV evangelists), figural/aesthetic (Baudrillard and Derrida's "nuclear criticism"), and literal (US nuclear actions, testing, and policy)—are predicated on models of time and fear of death (functioning as denial, disavowal, and loss, of power/mastery). I have briefly referred to Benjamin and here have space for only the first three constructs, although the comparisons are intriguing.[13] In fact, catastrophe discourses echo each other across history, context, and discipline in quite remarkable ways, with a political distinction which breaks down into two opposing categories: those that embrace and detail the paradox of contradiction (and discontinuity), and those premised on apocalyptic, evolutionary, but invisible answers or originary causes—Derrida, Baudrillard, Jimmy Swaggart and cohorts, the biblical catastrophists, and the US government. (Sociology tries to treadle both ways via empiricism.)

I.

René Thom's mathematical system of topology (presented in academic papers in the late 50s, with his book appearing in 1972) is a qualitative rather than quantitative way of analyzing change that is not smooth but rather discontinuous. Rather than a scientific theory, Thom's is an "art of models."[14] While this resonates of simulation, suggesting Baudrillard, who, like Thom, has the will to totalizing answers, Thom is undone by observation, along with the magnitude of his "text" which includes the everyday. "Catastrophe theory" is concerned with "sudden and discrete changes . . . the stability of forms, and the creation of forms."[15] "Form" and "model" are crucial terms for his analysis of catastrophe—"jump behavior"[16] resulting from a state of conflict. Catastrophe is a problem of "the succession of form," and relies on "local models" applicable to common, everyday experience. "Our everyday . . . may be a tissue of ordinary catastrophes, but our death is a generalized catastrophe."[17] "Many phenomena of common experience [are] in themselves trivial . . . but is it not possible that a mathematical theory launched for such homely phenomena might, in the end, be more profitable for science?"[18] His homely examples are cracks in a wall and the shape of a cloud which suggest a "structural stability" of recurrent, identifiable elements. I would add television to the list of the homely.

As this theory is dependent on form, so is my model of TV catastrophe—real events and also form historically turned into learned convention. For Thom, catastrophe occurs for "formal reasons,"[19] is a process involving the creation or destruction of forms, their disappearance and replacement. As Woodcock and Davis point out, the models must depict both continuous and discontinuous change, summarizing the appearance and disappearance of stability: "To change discontinuously is to pass through non-equilibrium states." "The abrupt bursting of a bubble, the transition from ice at its melting point to water at its freezing point, the shift in the unconscious in the process of getting a joke or pun"[20] are examples of shifting moments of discontinuity—transformations which resemble linguistic shifters. Thom argues that these transitions are discontinuous because the intervening states of passage from one state to another are not stable. However, they are brief eruptions, as they are rare on television, in comparison to the time spent in stable states. "Jump behavior" is a state of unstable passage, signaled by the network news announcer's vocal break-in with a visual logo and the abrupt cut-away, *off the half-hour,* to the news studio and the anchor, a discontinuous shift from the taped and rehearsed into the live, irregular, and unpredictable which disrupts TV's "structural stability"—a catastrophe of TV "normalcy," continuity, and narrative. The pleasure of familiar repetition of the same as difference turns into the dangerous unpleasure of repetition, moving "beyond the pleasure principle." Many viewers of afternoon soap operas express their displeasure via the mail, angry that Chernobyl replaced thirty minutes of *One Life to Live.*

II.

As Thom's allusions to the double dealing of the joke work suggest, and as Benjamin argued, Freud rather snugly adheres to a catastrophe model.

Two texts, *Inhibitions, Symptoms, and Anxiety* (1925–26) and *Beyond the Pleasure Principle,* are central to my argument. Revising his position in 1926, Freud wrote: "I can no longer maintain this view . . . of the transformation of libido into anxiety."[21] Rather, "anxiety is a reaction to a situation of danger" (128) predicated on a fear of "being abandoned by the protecting super ego" (130). Anxiety both is an "affect" ("every affect . . . is only a reminiscence of an event" [133]) and is "freshly created out of the economic conditions of the situation" (130)—conventions of catastrophe coverage, the event being covered, and audience response. We respond to TV interruptions announcing earthquakes, airline crashes, and nuclear accidents with an affect of anxiety, which TV can decide to exacerbate by "staying on the air," eradicating the regularly scheduled entertainment, a narrative catastrophe. Anxiety is "something that is felt, . . . a very marked character of unpleasure," (132) unlike tension, pain, or mourning—although these are later stages of catastrophe coverage. Anxiety is a "physiological, motor manifestation" based on "an increase of excitation which produces . . . unpleasure and . . . finds relief through acts of discharge" (133).

The historical and *crucial* difference between Benjamin, Freud, and television is that television is shock *and* therapy; it both produces *and* discharges anxiety. Whereas for Benjamin shock came from the public "crowd" of modernity (and historical events), and for Freud the experience or affect was, with the critical exception of the war neuroses, individuated, TV administers shock and ameliorates the collective affects, imagined as shared, perhaps uniform. Via repetition, information, and constant coverage, TV is both source and solution.

The origin of anxiety is traced back to birth and then fear of castration, both of which are dismissed as explanations (to be honest, castration, Freud's favorite answer on *Jeopardy,* is abandoned rather sadly, or at least nostalgically); Freud finally settles on "missing someone who is loved and longed for" (136) as his favored analysis—not an answer/cause he savors as he does the former. "Longing turns into anxiety" for the child (the subject of psychoanalysis). "The situation, then, which it regards as a 'danger' and against which it wants to be safeguarded is that of non-satisfaction, of a *growing tension due to need,* against which it is helpless." In relation to the imperfect body addressed by commercials and explanations of the causes and even "facts" of catastrophe, TV preys on/creates nonsatisfaction, all the while staying on the air, waiting, repeating. In this "situation of non-satisfaction the amounts of stimulation rise to an unpleasurable height without its being possible for them to be mastered . . . or discharged" (137). Zapruder's film footage of Kennedy's assassination was endlessly repeated; the thirty-second *Challenger* explosion was rerun hundreds of times—attempts at mastery and discharge.

Like the rest of Freud, sexual difference circulates; however, in this text, there is a fascinating, albeit awkwardly reluctant if not begrudging, reversal—an almost whispered inscription of female subjectivity: "It is precisely in women that the danger-situation of loss of object seems to have remained the most effective." And, sounding like an ad copy man on Madison Avenue, aware of feminism: "All we need to do is to make a slight modification in *our* description of *their* [my emphasis] determinant of anxiety" which, he asserts, is the loss not merely of an object but of "the object's love" (143). Given the "determinant" of "their" or female anxiety (unstated though it is, from the mother's subjective position), Freud cautions us to "put ourselves on guard against over-estimating that factor [castration] since it could not be a decisive one for the female sex, who are undoubtedly more subject to neuroses than men."[22] While I doubt the neurotic claim, castration is not decisive—for women and this theory of anxiety.

Along with backhandedly privileging women, albeit neurotic females, there is another crucial distinction from pleasure, his theory of desire and the unconscious. In unpleasure and anxiety, "the ego is the actual seat of anxiety" (140). In current grey-tone ads for telephone and computer systems, middle-management/aged men and a few discriminately placed women with furtive brows and worried glances haltingly, quizzically fret anxiously in piercing, abrupt closeups about their wrongly chosen business system while, *vérité* style, hand-held camera shots literally signify "high anxiety." (TV coopts yet another tactic of the counterculture, *cinéma vérité*, direct cinema, or hand-held video, for commodity culture as "art"—a double whammy recuperation.)

Thus, while one dominant model of psychoanalysis developed for cinema is based on the unconscious, the male subject, desire/castration/lack, and Oedipus, this construct shifts to include the ego, the female subject, love/loss, with a subjective, hesitant place reserved for mother (no small gain)—critical distinctions which, for me, go a long way toward theorizing the mechanisms of both the TV text and its audience—with, however, historical differences, including the permutation and rearrangement of everyday US life, politics, and culture by television.

If the "danger situation" changes, "the impulse [anxiety] will run its course under an automatic influence . . . the influence of the compulsion to repeat . . . as though the danger-situation that had been overcome still existed" (153). That everyday and catastrophic television rely on repetition (an economic "compulsion to repeat") like no other activity (or medium) except assembly-line production is not without consequence. The sheer repetition of coverage serves a hypothetical purpose of "as if"—operating on the pretense "that the danger-situation still existed." Even Freud's description of anxiety resembles television. For example, as Freud often does, he tacks on an intriguing addendum which relates "angst" to expectation— "anxiety *about* something. It has a quality of *indefiniteness* and *lack of object*." As with television itself, a central trait of catastrophe coverage is indefiniteness; coverage involves a search for the answer, the explanation—in short, the object. On a metaphorical level, indefiniteness and lack of object define television—electronic, erasable circuitry with no visible, material base until transmitted. Freud differentiates "realist anxiety"—"about a known danger"—from "neurotic anxiety"—"a danger that has still to be discovered" (165). TV vacillates between realistic and neurotic coverage. The live, videotaped murder of Lee Harvey Oswald by Jack Ruby, rerun like the Zapruder film, triggered neurotic anxiety; Black Monday anchors awaited, like network vultures, a crash after the fall, prophesying back to 1929, the realist harbinger of the neurotic future.

To doggedly restate my earlier argument: Freud argues that "there are two reactions to real danger. One is an affective reaction, an outbreak of anxiety. The other is a protective action" (165). With its strategy of creation/contradiction/cancellation, TV is both the outbreak and the protective action, the latter accomplished by repetition, finding answers, and the rare result of assigning guilt. Like a doctor detailing medical procedures to a patient before and after surgery, information here provides a therapeutic service, a ritual akin to prayer or chanting. Cloaked as an epistemé, a desire to know, it soothes our anxiety, protecting us from fear. Thus, information, the raison d'être of coverage, becomes story, therapy, and collective ritual. Later it will be known as myth.

I can find no better description of catastrophe coverage than "anxiety is . . . an expectation of a trauma, and . . . a repetition of it in a mitigated form . . . expectation belongs to the danger-situation, whereas its *indefiniteness* and *lack of object* belong to the traumatic situation of helplessness—the situation which is anticipated in the danger-situation" (166). Although TV situations are mainly comedy, the TV spectator anticipates, fears, then relishes the danger-situation: "a recognized, remembered, expected situation of helplessness. Anxiety is the original reaction to helplessness. . . . The ego . . . repeats it actively in a weakened version . . . what is of decisive importance is the first displacement of the anxiety-reaction from its origin in the situation of helplessness" (166–67). Expectation is displaced anxiety. We await catastrophe as the ultimate promise and noble dream of television—when time is open-ended, commercial-free, and we are helpless. However, the audience is not passive but expectant; agitated by TV, it partakes of masochism, is soothed by mundane ritual, and is contained by contradiction.

The place of "mother" and the resolute determinance for Freud of sexual difference suggest that the response will necessarily be different for men and women. Deleuze's work on masochism is helpful in this regard because he argues that the scenario or contract revolves around "mother." As Sonja Rein has so lucidly argued: "what is important in masochism is the desire to return to the mother . . . thus, the masochist demands that he be beaten in order that the image of his father in him . . . is diminished." However, as Rein points out, "What is important for Deleuze is the nature of the agreement made between the masochist and his torturer . . . the contract functions . . . to invest the mother image with the symbolic power of the law."[23] The image of the mother in catastrophe events does not function as law—rather as loss; the image circulates within an economy of anxiety, not one of desire. Yet, like masochism, mother is at least subjectively there, albeit left over. However, the audience does make a contract with TV during catastrophe coverage, a painful ritual which mirrors masochistic (un)pleasure.

BABY JESSICA AND BLACK MONDAY

US TV was on disorder alert, in a frenzy of disequilibrium, anticipating a danger situation in October, 1987. Daytime entertainment was interrupted, punctuated by crises that failed to escalate, at least for the time being, into catastrophe. Issues were conflated and strangely gendered. Milwaukee was in a virtual frenzy of local news as a result of fires in the racially segregated core district—black children were dying by the dozens. The image of conflagration was lifted off by satellite and picked up in Sydney. Eventually, this local spectacle was analyzed in the newspapers as an issue of poverty, migration from the South, families living together in crowded, flimsy homes, without heat and using space heaters to keep warm, families headed by young women, without jobs or husbands. The families were black, the landlords were white.

After the hideous deaths of so many local black children (and the single solution of installing fire alarms!) the local, revved-up audience saw the blonde Baby Jessica emerge as a national star on Friday, October 16, in a TV nightmare of entrapment. TV kept breaking in; Connie Chung was not at the scene but more prestigiously at the catastrophe helm in New York, the throne of power, prestige, and stability usually occupied by anchormen—in this NBC case, Tom Brokaw, who was off for the weekend. While diagrams delineated Baby Jessica's (and our) Freudian nightmare, the camera focused on the rigging, a cable surrounded by men and media— in a Texas town, Midland, depleted by the US oil crisis, an image right out of *Radio Days* and the Depression, this time with a happy ending. There was little to see except the same cable and the passage of time; little to tell except the local story of the uncanny accident, teenage parentage, and community heroism. Drilling miscalculations were delays prolonging the suspense and time of coverage. Once the classic story of dead or alive had begun, the networks couldn't quit; it was only a matter of time, which would tell. She was rescued alive, looking like a little mummy, on NBC just before *Miami Vice*.

The next day, the story of Baby Jessica shifted to surgical details—her damaged foot and face. The drama of the separation of mother and child continued, but added Nancy Reagan's breast, cancer, and gender to the surgical agenda. Enter the symbolic mother. The two dramas were positioned together in the newspapers; the female body became headlines, a front-page event. Baby Jessica and Nancy were stories of loss for women. Although the coverage was mediated by men, particularly the medical news briefings, Connie Chung was one initial narrator; the female reporter covering Nancy wore a remarkably similar red dress. On Saturday, Jessica was "serious but stable." By Sunday's headlines, Nancy was fine, and Jessica's foot would be saved. (The Jessica story continued: the Oprah Winfrey show visited Midland with a program dedicated to Jessica, capitalizing on the bizarre *vis-à-vis* personal compassion. Later, participants in the rescue wrangled over monies for selling the rights to the story—organizing into unions for profits.)

The coverage and the events were the made-for-TV reenactment of *Inhibitions, Symptoms, and Anxiety,* including birth, loss, and several mothers—Jessica's teenage mother, Nancy Reagan, and Connie Chung. Along with helplessness, there was no visible object, only waiting, indefiniteness, and the expectation of either alive or dead. The weekend bodily drama of anxiety seemed suspiciously anachronistic (like the emergence of high-style Bakhtin), a symptom of something else. Black Monday and the stock market plunge interrupted *Days of Our Lives,* the soap in the twelve noon slot, with another version of the fall and loss—this time of money, not mother/child. Tom Brokaw was back as NBC anchorman, trying to explain this crisis of capitalism via talking heads, shots of the New York Stock Exchange, Wall Street, and later, international exchanges.

While it was argued that the problem was electronic, set off by computer trading via satellite transmission across standardized international time zones, it was difficult for the US audience to believe that the world and business carried on while it slept. The stammering reports, interspersed irregularly throughout the day, revealed a dual dilemma—significant for cultural studies scholars as well as the sad yuppies who were interviewed en masse on PBS financial programs, stricken with grief at the loss of million-dollar condos, BMWs, and Porsches: (1) the inability to analyze electronic, computerized conditions of production and (2) the difficulty of imagining international, rather than nationally determined, boundaries, economic structures, times, and points of view. The ultimate catastrophe for television would be a crisis of capitalism, resulting in change, which might unravel or alter TV's economic/commercial base above which catastrophe coverage is a superstructural raison d'être. (For example, one reason for TV's rigid temporality is to notify advertisers of the seconds their ads will air; different times have different costs.)

It is not surprising that these four days revealed a very old-fashioned sexual hierarchy of power: with women on the side of babies and the body—the visible referent, and men aligned with money and technology—the invisible symbolic. Yet, perhaps this move of the surgical body from scandal magazines to the nightly news might portend a challenge to the propriety or decorum called power. Granted that Reagan's (Ronald's) colon and nose had been spotlighted previously, Nancy's breast took over the headlines. And hers was not the only newsworthy surgical breast in 1987 (as Jessica Hahn revealed).

While it has been theorized in philosophy and art since the early 1900s that simultaneity has replaced succession, that electronics has annihilated space and time and extended the present, we are still caught in our thinking about television around the turn of the century (which, given capitalism and the snug fit of a Freudian model, might be apt). The stock market coverage frantically tried to locate a place or context, and an object—like the sinking of the *Titanic*. If, as for Stephen Kern, the *Titanic* is a historical border between the present as a series of local events (local news coverage and horizon-to-horizon transmitting towers) and a simultaneity of multiple, distant events (network, nightly news, and satellite transmission), then we have entered another historical phase. If in the *Titanic* "we recognize with a sense near to awe that we have been almost witness of a great ship in her death agonies," our history might be determined by what we cannot see.[24] In the 1987 crisis, electronic technology was no longer only the means of transmission and salvation but was also, like the *Titanic*, part of the problem—and an invisible, international, simultaneous crisis at that. As with time and money, the stock and trade of television, there was no stable, tangible object, only effects and victims (who made personal appearances on TV or committed suicide—an exaggerated re-creation of 1929). Our history might be determined by aftereffects.

III.

The field of disaster studies is a collaboration between academic sociology and behavioral psychology, sponsored by federal and local governmental agencies, with textbook titles such as *Organized Behavior in Disaster, The Disaster Handbook,* and *System Responses to Disaster* and professional journals such as *Disasters.* The field also provides a model for TV catastrophe, addressing a problem of contemporary theory as well—the conflation of natural with technological. "The problem of taxonomy is the most pressing issue confronting the field at this time."[25] *Behavior and Attitudes under Crisis Conditions* defines disasters as "forces of nature" and catastrophe as "manmade hazard actualizations"—the latter a good definition of TV coverage. This text divides disasters accordingly: Natural (eighteen), Technology (nuclear, building collapses, energy shortfall), Discrete Accidents (with beginnings and endings, such as toxic fumes, industrial/transportation accidents), Socio-political (war, assassinations, hostage taking, terrorism), Epidemics and Disease.[26]

The conflation of natural/technological by the Federal Emergency Management Agency in Washington is predicated on response—a "response to a crisis is phenomenological evidence of a crisis, which is dependent on perception which abruptly changes normalcy to crisis."[27] Also, as with the stock market coverage, "there are cumulative implications of trends of threat." No matter what the event, the response—termed "crisis expectant" and "crisis surge"—is uncannily similar and predictable. The public will (1) seek information, (2) confirm warnings, (3) tend to evacuate, and (4) unite in groups, particularly families, to ease tension. However, rather than evacuate, TV urges us to stay home, to continue watching. Meaghan Morris argues that the ultimate catastrophe for the audience is silence on TV (which might occur if Los Angeles earthquakes into the Pacific Ocean during entertainment programming; we feared this had happened in San Francisco when transmission of the 1989 World Series was interrupted by a major quake); however, the ultimate catastrophe for TV networks would be coverage without an audience—either a ratings dilemma or a sign that disaster had eradicated viewers; for TV, both are economic issues.

Like Thom and Freud, disaster studies position "normalcy" against crisis, arguing that "daily life is dependent on continuities, on repetition . . . a disruption of normalcy produces stress," "either by the event or the perception of a threat."[28] Along with Thom's emphasis on form and structural stability, disaster studies add perception, as does Freud, a response not dependent on the type of event. For me, the conventions of catastrophe coverage, mapped over the event, trigger and sustain audience response, and hence are determining. These conventions can transform a personal accident such as Baby Jessica's into a national catastrophe watched by millions. Disaster studies emphasize temporality: the timing of crisis events "cannot be encompassed."[29] Catastrophe coverage is open-ended; it ceases only when it has an answer or becomes exhausted from repetition. Once on the air, Connie had to keep going, although there was little new to tell.

A contradiction emerges in these manuals: disaster analyses, like the stock market coverage, are predicated on the belief that people will panic. (TV participated in the stock market panic, creating a "crisis surge.")[30] Yet, studies repeatedly demonstrate that this is resolutely not usually the case; instead of panicking, people confirm, reconfirm, and often deny the message. TV, believing that it is in control and we are not, is a source of reconfirmation; rarely does it deny—if it did, we would not need to watch. Disaster subcultures are people with experience in "repetitive situations,"[31] like the TV viewer familiar with conventions. That a subculture of catastrophe operates via TV is demonstrated by tele-evangelism and the creation of midday "newsbreaks" which combine the style of catastrophe break-ins (by a news announcer at a studio desk in New York or Washington) with the temporality of commercials and announcements. When a "newsbreak" comes on, Cher might have been married or England destroyed. Via metonymy and remembrance, catastrophe style, like avant-garde techniques on MTV, has become regular yet unsettling flow.

In the famous 1920 Halifax case study which poetically and rigorously analyzed the harbor explosion and fire that decimated that city, Prince points to the difference between catastrophe and crisis—"an instant when change one way or another is impending. Crises are those critical moments which . . . are big with destiny . . . the term . . . [precedes] change."[32] Prince criticizes the failure to distinguish between that which occasions the crisis and the crisis itself—a dilemma for television, and my argument, which conflates the two. For him, "crises . . . precede catastrophes . . . and catastrophes . . . generate the crisis-situation . . . the disintegration of the normal by shock and calamity" (21). After noting that change is only a premium in science, his crucial argument is that "catastrophe always means social change. There is not always progress" (32). TV mitigates against change by equating crisis and catastrophe and defusing both via repetition. Unlike the Halifax disaster which "smashed through social division, traditions,"[33] TV upholds institutions via containment. Catastrophe threatens "conventionality, custom, and law"—which TV, as exemplar, defends. In an argument remarkably similar to Freud's, Prince argues that victims repeat the initial shock, "reproducing the tragic or terrible scenes," deny them, or commit suicide.[34]

Prince accords import to communication agencies which set a good example that can be imitated. Heroes, what he calls a "disaster protocracy" (53), emerge—"often men were surprised at their own power for prolonged effort under the excitement of catastrophe."[35] These heroes are the anchors or the chance reporters on the scene—established stars or emerging stars. Prince cites the "stimulus" of the lookers-on: "citizens of Halifax knew they were not unobserved. . . . Halifax simply had to make good. She was bonded to the world" (78–79). However, one notion is anathema to television: "A disaster event happens in a particular social context . . . our primary focus is on the community as the locus of the event and as the social system that copes with the physical impact." What media events do to "disaster events" is erase "the particular social context"—like "the society of the spectacle."

KENNEDY AND *CHALLENGER*

The assassination of John F. Kennedy set the pattern for catastrophe coverage. Zapruder's amateur/tourist movie footage was endlessly rerun on television and scrutinized for clues. Because it had been recorded, the image, aligned with reality and tragic drama, would yield an answer, a truth, if, as with the riddle of the Sphinx, we could only get closer, deconstruct it. A shift from cinema to television was dramatized by the murder of Lee Harvey Oswald by Jack Ruby, live on television and rerun.

It could be argued that the assassination, not initially covered by the networks, was the first and last time for a united television audience: everyone compulsively remembered and minutely described, again and again, like reruns, where *they were* in real life, and where they were in relation to television, representation, a cultural moment when television and our daily lives were still separate but merging. While our emotional experience of the event came from television, our bodies remained distinct from television; "meaning" occurred to us in specific places. This is comparable to Benjamin's use of Freud and "shock": "Perhaps the special achievement of shock defense may be seen in its function of assigning to an incident a precise point in time in consciousness at the cost of the integrity of its contents."

Along with a precise time as a shock defense, viewers remembered where they were when they heard the news—a place contiguous to a television set. We took our grief into public places and watched TV together. The assigning of a time at the cost of content for Benjamin "would be a peak achievement of the intellect; it would turn the incident into a moment that has been lived" (163). The assassination—"a moment that has been lived" between individual memory and collective ritual, a moment that tended toward destruction rather than remembrance—and its coverage marked the passage from experience to information (the physical to simulation), from the *public crowd* as the source of shock ("collisions . . . nervous impulses . . . in rapid succession, like . . . electric energy" [175], an "experience" of the "passerby" which corresponds to "what the worker experiences at his machine") (176) to the *private audience* of television; in the 60s, we were still on the threshold. (Benjamin's argument, from Sergei Eisenstein [and Pavlov's reflex psychology along with William James], that "perception in the form of shocks was established as a formal principle" [175] in film marks a cultural shift from public to private, from work to leisure, from film to television.) We told stories about our personal experience of the event, set off by a film of the real; after this, we would speak of television and representation. (*Eternal Frame*, a performance/videotape by Ant Farm, restages the *film* of the assassination [and its reception] as simulation.)[36]

The constant coverage of the assassination was cited as realizing television's potential for collective identification—television's democratic dream that by informing us and setting a good, calm, and rational example via the protocratic anchors, the populace will be united, soothed, and finally ennobled by repetition of and patient waiting for information. As I argued earlier, TV administers and cushions shocks, is both the traumatic shock and Freud's protective "shield" which "both protects against excess excitation . . . and also transmits excitation from the outside to the inside of the organism."[37] This double function of "transmission and protection" is temporal, and is accomplished by narration—"temporizing the traumatic effects of an excess of energy . . . the death drive as another name for a story," according to Samuel Weber (145). Like the joke technique (described by Freud as an envelope or container), TV envelops the shock, delivering *and* cushioning us from stimuli which it regulates in acceptable levels—like the dosage of microwave ovens—turning news or shocks into story and tragic drama. Rather than an excess of stimuli which set off for Benjamin private recollection and memory, such as the assassination coverage initially provided, TV administers then defuses stimuli in containing doses.

Television promises shock and trauma containment over time via narration of the real. As Weber states, Freud's analysis of abstract time was connected to the psychic real as an *aftereffect* of events. This aftereffect is separate yet necessarily dependent on the event; examples are the "dream, in the narration that disfigures it, the joke, in the laughter that displaces it," citations which resemble Thom. Like "The Return to Space," as the October, 1988, *Discovery* flight was titled by CBS, "aftereffects repeat the event they follow, but they also alter it and it is precisely this process of repetitive alteration that renders the event psychically 'real'" (147). The stories do not repeat merely an event but each other, in a sequence that is both successive and simultaneous. Catastrophe coverage, rendering events psychically real, is "repetitive alteration" or disfigural representation resulting in aftereffects which read back, creating further disfiguration, in Weber's view. This process is stoppable for Freud, in the end, by myth and eros—a conclusion to which I will return.

Freud's analysis of consciousness as precisely "not consciousness *of* anything, and even less . . . self-consciousness," might describe the role of the anchor—along with repetition and narration, another means of cushioning excess. Covering catastrophes is the ultimate test of the top anchorman's mettle, his stamina measured by words, information, and calm demeanor. (The Los Angeles news announcer who panicked during the 1987 earthquake and ducked under his desk miserably failed anchorman protocol, becoming a joke for late-night comics.) Television fancies that if we have enough news, if it stays on the air with us, a vigil like sitting up with a sick or dying friend, we will behave like adults. Or, the stock market coverage of "Black Monday" demonstrates that television can also, like computer trading, panic us, creating a need *for* television. What was innovative then has become protocol which we have come to expect and which plays into and creates those expectations.

The *Challenger* catastrophe (January 28, 1986) exploded the modernist myth of technology (and also the Western frontier myth of the necessity of humans for space exploration) as unifying a dispersed audience. In this case the national audience was symbolically fragmented by images such as the unseeable and horrific imaginary nightmare of the human astronaut bodies, knowing and alive, for seconds plunging at unfathomable speed into oblivion. The technological catastrophe, our telescopic, distanced view from outside of an abstract speck, collided with the chance, personal drama of a mother and father at the liftoff watching—and then, in an instance and a glance, *knowing,* turning away, their teacher/daughter/mother blown up in space, unnecessarily. We were truly in the position of voyeurs, catching a glimpse of something private we shouldn't have seen and, in contrast to the Kennedy assassination, unable to really see what happened. We saw only the beautiful "aftereffect," the clouds of white, billowing smoke against a deep blue sky, reminiscent of the spectacular clouds after a nuclear explosion. This image of Christa MacAuliffe's mother and father staged Freud's trauma of separation, as the images of Jacqueline Kennedy in the motorcade car and beside the coffin restaged mother-child and loss. Mourning, with affects different from anxiety, was a later stage of coverage/response.

In keeping with the myth of the frontier which has dominated the US space program, MacAuliffe was the adventurous schoolmarm of the Western genre, an Easterner who had won a contest to bring civilization to space via the one-room satellite schoolhouse, conquering space and winning audiences with knowledge. Represented as mother/daughter/teacher/amateur, she dominated coverage before and after the explosion, an unusual situation of a woman being the focus of news and then catastrophe. That she was more like us increased (1) our identification and (2) our shock: because a mother of young children was aboard, we believed that the shuttle missions were sure-fire, foolproof occurrences. However determined by being "the first," the press became fascinated with a woman's work and home life which was news before her death became an event. (Notice how few obituaries are of women—like their lives, women's deaths are not as newsworthy as men's.)

While verbal facts and accounts detailing the horror of error and technological failure were piled onto that distant fragmentation to explain it scientifically, we imagined from the audio tapes the personal nightmare and terror inside the shuttle. Did they know? For how long? Afterward, the ocean floor was combed in mourning, the fragments of bodies and machine were brought back to create a funeral pyre—to retrieve, and later reconstruct, the real.

Standing by in Concord to record MacAuliffe's students celebrating her lift-off and subsequent space lecture, TV reran her death back in time, showing the initial register of the students' shock, disbelief, grief; twenty-five TV news crews descended on the town afterward and recorded weeping schoolchildren and trauma management—a pedagogical model for audiences of TV catastrophe, taking us from anxiety to grief and vicarious mourning, with psychological advice. The shift into mourning and pedagogy, for example, the historical details of a presidential funeral in Kennedy's case, is a significant part of the reassurance stage of catastrophe coverage, fear turning to grief, acceptance of loss, and a return to normalcy.

NASA was investigated as a trial of errors rather than murder, with videotaped evidence endlessly repeated. Seeing was not believing in this instance. While disavowal could not function in either tragedy as reassurance for onlookers or spectators, the difference between these two events is profound, and historical: the horror of Kennedy's assassination was in what we saw; the terror of *Challenger* was what we could not see—the bodies, the premises of the entire space program, the loss of technological superiority. The concern after the assassination was who shot Kennedy; the worry after *Challenger* was about communication satellites and space insurance—corporate purveys—and US space potency. The irony was that we saw so little of a communication mission for corporate profits which included product tie-ins. Spiegel's 1986 catalogue advertised an indoor/ outdoor *Challenger* tent where children could watch MacAuliffe's lecture.

CBS's "Return to Space" in October, 1988, reenacted the scenario of *Challenger,* remembering that primal scene of which this was the successful and professional remake. Countdown was scheduled for a lowly weekday morning (rather than a cynical prime-time slot), with a huge live audience of Florida tourists. Sitting behind a sleek desk in the modern studio mise-en-scène with Dan Rather was a former astronaut; rather than the usual tech talk, he described his *feelings* of anxiety when walking to the launch pad and sitting in the cockpit during lift-off. A teacher and a finalist in the contest that MacAuliffe had won was interviewed along with his students, remembering and rewriting the horror of that earlier scene; these students were older, fewer. The explosion footage was rerun as the danger situation—this horrific image had served as a trailer, rerun for two years to prepare us for the anxiety of this event. While the digital clock in the lower corner of the screen counted down, calm Dan reminded us of his and our anxious states. I was completely nervous—exactly as I was supposed to be. As in the second 1988 presidential debate, anxiety was a precondition or lure (or publicity) rather than a result of viewing. Without a catastrophe, the affects of coverage had been simulated by reruns, reminiscences. The return, both sequel and remake, resulted in mastery by NASA and the networks, who truly dazzled us with technique.

A telescopic, wide-angle zoom of the launch pad, clearly shot from a heavenly angle, opened the enclosed, framed, titled broadcast which *included commercials*—blatant clues that they expected no problems. A concluding zoom of the launch from this same godly view was poetically repeated at the end. The critical seventy-three seconds were clearly and multiply visible this time; the editing, camera placement, and clarity were technically remarkable, efficiently scripted. The visual and verbal style was rehearsed, not catastrophic—we should have relaxed. Blue-screened or keyed in as backdrop, the rumbling, fiery rocket, shuttle, and launchpad appeared to be right behind Dan's desk, with coverage dominating or equated with its subject, visible through a "picture window." There were no glitches by NASA or CBS; the smooth professionalism, resembling an error-free simulation rather than live coverage, and a performed public emotionalism akin to the nightly news, as much as the successful mission, reassured us that the US had not lost its standing in technocracy or in space. The two-year run of the explosion ended its long engagement (only to return, further contained, as a made-for-TV movie).

One protagonist of the initial drama was resolutely absent but determinantly figured as memory—Christa MacAuliffe (the aftereffect that was contained, erased as women are in TV [and newspaper] news). There were no women on board this flight. While one critic has argued that the sick jokes, mainly focused on MacAuliffe, which circulated after the *Challenger* tragedy testified to regard for and identification with her, I suggest the opposite, more in line with Freud. ("Where did MacAuliffe spend her summer vacation? All over Florida.")[38] Like the objects of Freud's jokes which are women, she is strangely at fault, guilty. While NASA took the rap, an unprofessional, a space amateur, is also to blame. When women assume subjectivity in masculine enclaves, claiming an equal if not superior status (as Joan Rivers did on Carson), disloyalty (not a better job) or disaster is the result. Thus, it is logical to banish women from that endeavor, at least momentarily. Women, as leftovers or aftereffects, become the objects of jokes or malicious gossip, their asserted subjectivity the real target, analyzed, as with Lucy, as lack of ability.

Baudrillard's prognoses of cultural elided with nuclear catastrophe are, like postmodernism, linked to or derived from television, particularly its instantaneous capacity to present "live" coverage of death events, both shocking and mollifying the audience, mediating and exacerbating the effects of the real—rerun and transformed into representation. We can await "live" catastrophe on TV, signaled by ruptures in the flow of programs, a disruption of time, TV's constancy. Catastrophe argues for the importance, the urgent value, the truth of television and its watching which will be good for us—providing catharsis or, better, mastery via repetition of the same which is fascinating, mesmerizing.

Catastrophe coverage thus functions *Beyond the Pleasure Principle* as an essentially verbal rendering of "fort/da" hinged on a "compulsively repeated" visual detail (Baby Jessica's cable, the thirty-second explosion, rifle shots) to acknowledge then alleviate fear and pain—the audience and the anchor, like the child, achieving mastery over loss, the departure, return, and, perhaps in the end, control of the mother, depending on who is throwing the ball. Perhaps masochistically, pleasure, aligned with death rather than life, a ritual determined by the mother rather than the father, comes from that game of repetition, with catastrophe as potent TV, coded as exception, yet one that doesn't come from TV techniques which are usually of extremely poor quality—shaky, minimal, indecipherable images, awkward editing glitches, missed cues and connections, filler speech and delimited language, endless repetition of the same facts and simple arguments—like muzak, yet overwhelming narrative, regular programming as we wait, with the anchor, either for further events and analysis or a conclusion before TV normalcy can return.

In the attempt to theorize, I have ignored specificity in two areas: textual analysis of crisis coverage and the variations among the three major networks. Different disfigurements create different aftereffects. In *Nightly Horrors: Crisis Coverage by Television Network News,* Dan Nimno and James E. Combs operate on the now axiomatic premise that US TV news is story or narrative in which the hero-motif is central as is melodrama. Their detailed content analysis of recent crises covered by NBC, CBS, and ABC, ranging from Jonestown to Three Mile Island, revealed variant patterns—what might be termed symptoms of ideology. NBC was more educational and contextual, acceptant of "the human condition"; CBS emphasized technology, which was sometimes represented as a monster, and searched for the high-tech causes of failures. ABC had the greatest appeal to anxiety, running interviews with survivors and heroes and citations of victim tolls rather than emphasizing the facts of the stories, whereas CBS appealed to experts and factual detail. While NBC had more and variant sources and location shots, ABC tended to remain in the studio. NBC's pluralist approach was more assuring than alarming, with more "straight" news placed in context. ABC, in contrast, depicted helplessness, chaos; Ted Koppel's ABC reports often contributed to a narrative of chaos and frustration in which no one was in control. (That Koppel is now the very powerful and famous host of *Nightline* is not insignificant; the program grew, like Topsy, from temporary coverage of the hostage crisis, the permanent, regular institutionalization of catastrophe *as* news format and content rather than the reportage of catastrophe *on* the news or as a special event; it is still a crisis program.) CBS had narratives of diplomacy, with technology a recurring star and issue; NBC used colloquialisms in a low-key, conversational style.[39]

Although Mary Ann Doane has recently defined TV catastrophe as technological catastrophe, a conclusion in line with CBS and a definition determined by the disaster event, I argue, as does Thom, that form, including temporality, inextricable from audience response (in line with Freud, Benjamin, and disaster studies), is the central determinant. No matter what the content, the form of the three networks tended toward similarity. That our crises are frequently technological is a historical argument. That the technological might serve as a symptom or cover-up of economics is also historical.

IV.

While Freud's is an apt theory for television, there are historical flaws: television addresses an older audience, a generational audience, not easily recapitulated, as is cinema, by childhood and Oedipus, Freud's focus. The Cold War was television's context, a history predicated on a defensive nuclear imaginary—an image of death that turned many of us into neurotics. The Cold War qualifies the interpretation of Freud as analyzed by Weber: "the very impulse that drove Freud beyond the pleasure principle to repetition, and beyond repetition to the death drive, also impels him to move beyond the death drive . . . toward a very different 'place' . . . in which the repetition of the same becomes the repetition of difference" (130). Although Weber's fatal conclusion of sexual difference, or death in the form of "the passive female" (134),[40] is not new or unimportant, as the dead MacAuliffe and pink-suited Jackie illustrate, Weber finds at the end of Freud's thought "a myth which counterbalances the death drive"—love stories, eros, myth.[41]

I want to partially disagree with Weber, and update Freud's historical assertion that "the unconscious seems to contain nothing that could give any content to our concept of the annihilation of life."[42] The second half of the twentieth century has an image of doomsday and annihilation which Freud could not have imagined. This image haunts the unconscious, politics, art, and now criticism; it is not a love story and, like "The Return to Space," excludes the female. With the abrupt 1988 end to the Cold War as yet uncelebrated, hanging in a virtual suspension of disbelief, its image has shifted from testing in 1946 and Operation Crossroads to simulation and Troop Test Smokey in the 50s, from avid discussion to silence, from civil defense to its futility, and from visual representation in government experiments and art to theory. The logic of governmental, nuclear argument was one of contradiction: a process of creation—showing us the visual spectacle of the bomb's capacity in elaborately staged films—and cancellation—the verbal denial that nuclear power would be offensively used. If precautions were taken, radiation's harmful bodily effects were also denied disingenuously. The nuclear image with its logic of conscious disavowal, including our reception, is historical. Like a few of us, this imaginary real has aged, its terror contained by forty years of disavowal. We grew up with it, terrified; my very Catholic grandmother convinced me that every airplane sound signaled imminent death from Russian planes; duck and cover in school encouraged fear of Soviet attack—the contradictory premise of US *defensive* policy—the ultimate exemplar of a logic of creation/cancellation. This is the repressed of catastrophe coverage, haunting its form and our reception; this could be its content, and we are almost relieved when it is not. (That the imaginary hold of this apocalyptic fear of the Soviet Union is over is demonstrated by the recent governmental acknowledgment that nuclear plants do have real and destructive effects on the human body.)

Along with television comedy, which distracted us by the "liberation" of laughter, these two institutions of Cold War foreign and domestic containment determined the 50s and audience memories. The US imaginary appears to be arrested at that adolescent moment which refuses passage into the symbolic and resists aging (with the necrophiliac resuscitation and sightings of the real Elvis and the photographed nude Marilyn as rituals of this arrested process); the Cold War generations of parents and children addressed by television are now well into middle and verging on old age. The historical point marked a move away from the real which could destroy us, into the imaginary, into simulation as positive, with offense figured by the government as defense, the rhetorical disavowal (and lie) of safe nuclear policy, with television rather than cinema as culture's dominant "theoretical object"—only recently recognized, albeit usually unstated, in the boom in postmodernism. In fact, early stages of postmodernism can be glimpsed in the 50s selling of television, coincident with and party to the rapid expansion of consumer markets, nuclear experiments, and the development of nuclear rhetoric. Shopping in the new centers was sold to the populace as one patriotic way of easing fear of "the bomb."

Unlike the claims of disaster studies, of Thom, and of Benjamin for catastrophe, television is rarely a model of change but rather one of incremental stasis, continuity, repetition; rather than wild heterogeneity, the return of the same, often *as* the same, albeit on two hundred channels; along with desire and pleasure, unpleasure, anxiety. Repeats and remakes, like the instant playback of sports, are games of mastery via a compulsive yet voracious repetition. This is not without consequence and need not result in condemnation. However, critical models predicated on change, radical reception, or democratic pluralism (and theories which rely on referents/realism, cause-effect/either-or dualisms, along with detectable authors and tangible objects) are limited in relation to television.

Television contains (and pleasures) us by contradictions, positing us in a halfway house, a netherland between subject/object—half-subject, half-object: rather than an "either/or" logic, one of "both/and" (the oxymorons of "working mother" or "single parent," "the middle-class poor")—an inclusive logic of creation/cancellation in which mimicry and simulation are stolid cornerstones rather than lofty embellishments. The cultural logic of television imitates the "diphasic" quality of obsessional neuroses, what Freud calls "the power of ambivalence": "one action is cancelled out by a second, so that it is as though neither action had taken place, whereas, in reality, both have" (113; 119). Every week for seven years, in reality, Lucy, the chorus girl/clown, complained that Ricky was preventing her from becoming a star. For twenty-four minutes, she valiantly tried to escape domesticity by getting a job in show business; after a tour-de-force performance of physical comedy, in the inevitable reversal and failure of the end, she resigned to stay happily at home serving big and little Ricky. The ultimate "creation/cancellation"—the series' premise which was portrayed in brilliant performances then denied weekly—was that Lucy was not star material. For keeping her home and out of show business, Lucy throws a pie in Ricky's face during his solo performance at the Tropicana; in the twenty-second end, she says, "You were right all along, Ricky. Forgive me?" Laughter. Applause.

To rephrase Freud: "an action which carries out a certain injunction is immediately succeeded by another action which stops or undoes the first one" (113). (Gracie Allen, to the contrary, takes Freud's "diphasic ambivalence" literally, as she does the shaggy dog story; illogical cancellation and reversal are the very stuff of story and comedy. However, after winning the story, she loses, too, in the end, to other systems.) Paralleling the structure of the Janus-faced enunciation of jokes (but unlike Freud's jokes, which are for men only, about women), TV addresses gendered subjects, often both sexes at the same time; the effect, however, is "as if neither action had taken place." Thus, it is complexly easy, after arduous labor, to produce

contradictions about TV, often shamelessly blatant about its equivoca-
tions—particularly regarding gender. Speaking overtly with a forked
tongue to males and females in the audience, TV is just not as seamless as
cinema. Yet, TV is trickier—"it is as though neither action had taken place,
whereas in reality, both have."

TV pinpoints our loneliness by providing companionship, advice, consolation, prayer, and therapy, assuring us we are not alone by assembling
audiences who have fun together. It materializes reality by simulation; ob-
sesses with time while eradicating it; and repeats catastrophes which tell us
that we are safe. TV catastrophes construct us as victims and onlookers or
audience, a division replicated by interviews with emotional eyewitnesses
or actual victims, intercut with the anchor's direct address to us; thus, we
are held between shifting identifications with the emotive participants and
the unemotive or "rational" anchor—linked to the safety of him—not
them—on an investigative search for truth or an outpouring of human
compassion, as is TV. In relation to victims, our response is an anti-iden-
tification, the relief of "not me" resulting in gratitude. It might be argued
that catastrophe coverage functions to ensure our feelings of well-being
and good fortune. This would hold true for anonymous victims and by-
standers. Celebrities or public figures elicit *very* different responses, however. The assurance for the viewer of catastrophe is that it is happening,
but elsewhere; or it already happened and is now historical, over. The
tantalizing threat, the true danger of catastrophe, is the here and now; if
it were happening to us, we wouldn't be watching television. We exist as
vicarious participants whose presence is critical, acknowledged, and flat-
tered, yet we are never in danger of being touched, seen, or heard; neither
do we need to act (the only action TV requests is dialing the telephone).
Television's participatory nonparticipation of direct looks and address,
structures of the joke and parody which incorporate us, the presence of
on-screen audiences, laugh tracks, viewer mail, telephone polls, pleas for
money, measuring us and charging accordingly, is the ultimate reassurance
of our status as safe outsider, yet holding an opinion as involved, concerned,
informed citizens. We are safe, at home, perhaps in bed, away from the
crowd.

However, television is a medium of containment with a significant difference from nuclear discourse—TV invokes the palpable body, often female, which nuclear policy and criticism have disavowed, eradicated.
Although the network "news" division is still a strong masculine preserve,
TV's address within "entertainment" incorporates women as half-subject,
half-object in need of physical improvement and domestication, but also
critically as subjects. This enunciation, and its specific textual practices
amidst the changing conditions of production which increasingly but spar-
ingly include women as producers, writers, and directors as well as performers, bears careful scrutiny. Instead of merely being satisfied that
television acknowledges that women do indeed exist, we must analyze the

terms of the enunciation. After all, contradiction and simulation are not new(s) to women.

NOTES

My gratitude to Mary Yelanjian for her splendid research efforts.

1. William James, *Principles of Psychology* (New York: 1890), p. 239. The earlier reference is to Raymond Williams, *Television: Technology and Cultural Form* (New York: Schocken, 1975).

2. Sigmund Freud, *The Complete Psychological Works of Sigmund Freud,* vol. 4 (London: Hogarth, 1959), p. 274.

3. Walter Benjamin, "On Some Motifs in Baudelaire," in *Illuminations* (New York: Schocken, 1969), p. 158.

4. Ibid., p. 159.

5. Ibid., p. 158.

6. Ibid.

7. Ibid., p. 160.

8. Walter Benjamin, "Theses on the Philosophy of History," in *Illuminations,* p. 263. Obviously, this formulation is Hegelian.

9. Ibid., p. 263.

10. Ibid., pp. 255, 261, 262 (collapsed together, in this order).

11. The "elsewhere" is in a book I am completing on television, the body, and anxiety.

12. Sports also cause network delays off the half-hour; this is an almost regular occurrence on CBS on Sunday evenings, pushing back *60 Minutes,* ironically, and hence the entire night schedule, to a frequently irregular scheduling. Along with sports, presidential addresses also cause off-hour temporalities. Because everything is so rigidly preprogrammed, there is no means of condensation to "catch up" other than eliminating ID's, promos, or commercials—now coded and hence necessary ellipses for program sense and continuity; TV can only run late, or over; it is never early.

13. The snug fit of Baudrillard, and to a different degree Derrida, with the early catastrophists (and their right-wing revival via tele-evangelism and US fundamentalism) and US nuclear tests and films of the late 40s and early 50s suggests a very distinct intellectual politics.

14. René Thom, *Structural Stability and Morphogenesis: An Outline of a General Theory of Models* (Reading, Mass.: W. A. Benjamin, 1975), p. 323. In *Catastrophe Theory* (New York: E. P. Dutton, 1978) Alexander Woodcock and Monte Davis trace the date of the appearance of Thom's seven archetypal structures, from "ideas contained in his paper published in the 50s . . . the book draft was finished in 1966, with a six year delay in publishing" (16).

15. A. G. Wilson, *Catastrophe Theory and Bifurcation* (Los Angeles: University of Calif. Press, 1975), p. 1. After Thom's book was published, there were hundreds of studies in countless areas using his models, including the work on urban retail structures by Wilson in *Aspects of Catastrophe Theory and Bifurcation* (Leeds: University of Leeds, 1979); in another *Catastrophe Theory,* a Soviet mathematician, a professor at the University of Moscow, V. I. Arnold, scathingly critiques its mass media circulation (it appeared as a "pocket book," something which had not happened in math since cybernetics, from which "catastrophe theory derived many of its advertising techniques" [2]) along with Thom's mystical bent and his stylistic incomprehensibility: "Neither in 1965 nor later was I ever able to understand a word of

Thom's own talks on catastrophes" (ix). Arnold links Thom with the catastrophists and God, in contrast to my model, arguing so on p. 89 by quoting Thom: "It is a fundamentally polytheistic outlook to which it leads us: in all things one must learn to recognize the hand of the Gods." For Thom, this is a Heraclitian battle between archetypes. After declaring that this theory has already been eulogized, Arnold presents his model of singularities, bifurcation, and catastrophes (Berlin, Heidelberg, New York, Tokyo: Springer Verlag, 1981, 1986).

16. Wilson, p. 5.

17. Thom, pp. 6, 251.

18. Ibid., p. 9.

19. Ibid., p. 290.

20. Woodcock and Davis, pp. 40, 4.

21. Freud, vol. 20, p. 109.

22. On the same page (143) Freud contradicts himself. After aligning women with neuroses, farther down the page he links hysteria with women and "obsessional neurosis . . . with masculinity." However, by mentioning castration so often as an explanation for almost everything, he inscribes his arduous difficulty relinquishing it. Also, when he refers to mother, he does so as an afterthought, for example, "such as its mother" when referring to children's fear of the dark (136).

23. Sonja Rein, "Whose Whip Is It?" unpublished graduate seminar paper, 1986/87.

24. Stephen Kern, *The Culture of Time and Space, 1880–1918* (Cambridge, Mass.: Harvard University Press, 1983), p. 67.

25. Thomas Drabek, *System Responses to Disaster* (New York: Springer Verlag, 1986), p. 6. He goes on to assert that "certain natural disasters can be compared to effects of man-made and technological disasters," presumably operating on the premise that technology has little to do with human intervention—a critical dilemma of *Challenger* which was explained by or blamed on human error or technological failure, which also were frequently conflated.

26. Federal Emergency Management Agency, *Behavior and Attitudes under Crisis Conditions: Selected Issues and Findings* (Washington D.C.). The problem of taxonomy reappears in *Natural Disasters: Acts of God or Acts of Man,* published by the International Institute for Environment and Development, which argues that when the ecology and the balance of nature are destroyed, no longer can natural and man-made events be differentiated.

27. *Behavior and Attitudes*, p. 17.

28. *Ibid.,* a notion repeated throughout this federal publication. Their model is derived from "stress" studies, not specifically influenced by Freud; rather, they are derived from US psychology, tested by sociologists. Reading the lists of catastrophes, mentioned almost as asides in flat language, becomes parody, comparable to the nightly news which casually refers to horrendous events without emotion and poetry of thought or word. One means of containing shock appears to be the deathly use of dull and boring language; or, in order to be either academic or official, the writer, the scholar, like the TV anchorman, must be "objective," in control, unemotional, bland, and expressionless. Thus, most writers' models of disaster, like the weather on TV, level difference, dulling the landscape, turning tragedy into routine. The reason Prince's book is effective is that it is also affective—his language recreates the scene rather than turning it into a list, a statistic, a distanced, impersonal event; equally, his analysis encompasses many disciplines with the unusual commitment, not Marxist but close, that disaster can lead to change and that it cuts through class divisions.

29. *Behavior and Attitudes*, p. 17 (I think).

30. *A Brief History of Panics* (New York: Knickerbocker Press, Putnam, 1893, copyright by De Courcy W. Thom, who "Englished and Edited" this French book)

is uncannily applicable to journalists' assessments of Black Monday: for example, the symptoms of a panic (based on the silver standard!) are wonderful prosperity, rising prices of commodities, lowering of interest rates along with a rise in salaries, large number of discounts, loans, banknotes, and decreasing deposits and reduced reserves, plus, critically, "growing luxurity leading to excessive expenditures." What he grandly but perhaps accurately observes is: "What must be noted is the reiteration and sequence of the same points under varying circumstances at all times, in all countries, and under all governments" (argued well before the Soviet revolution). After analyzing panics in thirteen countries, he asserts that the only common cause is overtrading, so credit and money become scarce. The difference is the focus on banks rather than the new brokerage institutions, which are replacing banks as gold did silver.

31. Samuel Henry Prince, *Catastrophe and Social Change* (New York: AMS Press, published in 1968 from the Columbia University Press, 1920), pp. 16–17. In Chapter I: "About midway in the last two years of war—to be exact December, 1917—a French munitioner heavily laden with trinitrotoluol, the most powerful of known explosives, reached Halifax from New York. . . . Suddenly an empty Belgian relief ship swept through the Narrows directly in her pathway. There was a confusion of signals; a few agonized maneuvers. The vessels collided; and the shock of their colliding shook the world!

"War came to America that morning. Two thousand slain, six thousand injured, ten thousand homeless, three hundred acres left a smoking waste . . . such was the appalling havoc of the greatest single explosion in the history of the world. It was an episode which baffles description. . . . It was all of a sudden—a single devastating blast; then the sound as of the crashing of a thousand chandeliers. Men and women cowered under the shower of debris and glass. . . . To some death was quick and merciful in its coming. Others were blinded, and staggered to and fro before they dropped. Still others with shattered limbs dragged themselves forth into the light— naked, blackened, unrecognizable shapes. They lay prone upon the streetside, un- der the shadow of the great death-cloud which still dropped soot and oil and water. It was truly a sight to make the angels weep. . . . It was an earthquake so violent that . . . the city shook as with palsy. The citadel trembled, the whole horizon seemed to move . . . the mute record tells not of the falling roofs and collapsing walls which to many a victim brought death and burial at one and the same time. . . . It was a flood. . . . It was a fire or rather a riot of fires. . . . It was like the flight from Vesuvius of which Pliny the Younger writes. . . . And when the hegira was over . . . a succes- sion of winter storms."

32. Ibid., p. 18.

33. Ibid., p. 46. The psychologists Prince uses for his behavioral model of shock and the ensuing emotions are William McDougall (*An Introduction to Social Psychology,* 1917), William James, M. Dide, a French psychologist who analyzed the hypnosis produced by shock, and several others writing between 1917 and 1920.

34. Prince, p. 60. After the initial shock and calamity, the community begins to reorganize. This protocracy arises initially from "the part of society which is most closely organized and disciplined in normality." Prince cites the militia as his ex- ample, mentioning not only the army's speed, its power, but "the attending psy- chological effects of orderly bearing and coolness in time of general chaos, bespeaking a care that is at once paternal and sympathetic." This is a good descrip- tion of the institution of TV and its stable, paternal anchors. Prince also describes and distinguishes the pattern of disaster events which have stages, over time.

35. Ibid., pp. 78–79. In *Disaster and the Millennium* by Michael Barkun (New Haven: Yale University Press, 1974), studies illustrate that the effects of Kennedy's assassination were "unique": that there was little difference between the Dallas spectators and TV spectators around the country, that the death of Kennedy was

comparable to the loss of a parent or close relative. Eighty-two percent in Dallas, versus 68% nationally, experienced "extreme nervousness and tension." TV viewers had the following symptoms, which disappeared after the funeral: "loss of appetite, crying, difficulty sleeping, unusual fatigue." "Television temporarily created disaster victims." This is an intriguing assertion in a rather strange book; Barkun goes on to discuss the effects of induced and constant catastrophe, for example, the Chinese Cultural Revolution, suggesting that the secret of permanent revolution is permanent disaster—which, from another political position, accords with Benjamin and Prince who argue that disaster is one critical means of instigating revolution and change. Thus, there is a politics to catastrophe. Prince, quoting Professor Shailer Matthews, who distinguishes between a crisis and a revolution: "The difference between a revolution and a crisis is the difference between the fire and the moment when someone with a lighted match in hand pauses to decide whether a fire should be lighted." When I was a child, and older, we used to wonder what we would do if the bomb were dropped. Rather than running to church or falling to our knees in prayer, we most likely would turn on television.

36. I have analyzed this videotape and its context, the counterculture and Ant Farm, in "Video Politics: Guerilla TV, Ant Farm, *Eternal Frame*," *Discourse* 10.2 (Spring-Summer 1988):78–100.

37. Samuel Weber, *The Legend of Freud* (Minneapolis: University of Minnesota Press, 1982), p. 143.

38. Patrick D. Morrow, "Those Sick Challenger Jokes," *Journal of Popular Culture*, 20.4:179; other examples of these jokes are "Did you hear that Christa MacAuliffe has been nominated for the 1986 Mother of the Year Award?" "Of course, she only blew up once in front of her kids this year." "What does Christa MacAuliffe teach?" "English, but she's history now."

39. Dan Nimno and James E. Combs, *Nightly Horrors: Crisis Coverage by Television Network News* (Knoxville: University of Tennessee Press, 1985). See also W. Lance Bennett, *News: The Politics of Illusion* (New York: Hangman, 1983); Barbara Matusow, *The Evening Stars: The Making of the Network News Anchor* (Boston: Houghton, 1983).

40. "Thus, if Freud's initial stories deal with men, betrayal, and ingratitude, death enters the scene with—as?—the passive female . . . a recurrent fatality linked to the female: she either eliminates the male or is eliminated by him. But nothing is more difficult to do away with than this persistent female." This, in Weber's interpretation of *Beyond the Pleasure Principle*, p. 134.

41. Samuel Weber concludes with the Greeks: the myth, as it were, of our cultural origins or consciousness, back, along with Freud, to the *Symposium*.

42. Sigmund Freud, *Inhibitions, Symptoms, Anxiety*, p. 129.

NOTE: This essay was written before the 1989 California quake; however, the model developed here was a snug fit.

REPRESENTING TELEVISION

Stephen Heath

Discussion of television is extensive today; more than extensive, indeed, if we do not immediately limit discussion according to some criterion of seriousness (of what counts as "serious discussion") but allow it to embrace the range of discourses in which television is now talked through: from the government report or the sociological study to the feature in this week's *TV Guide* or the commuter-train conversation, to this or that program commenting on itself and all the others (television has television as an abiding concern). This more-than-extensiveness corresponds, of course, to the sheer size of television, its seamless equivalence with social life; or rather, it is part of that size, a reflection of it but also a material element in it, in the general substance and reality of television which cannot be merely envisaged as a totality of transmitted programs. Hence television is a somewhat difficult object, unstable, all over the place, tending derisively to escape anything we can say about it: given the speed of its changes (in technology, economics, programming), its interminable flow (of images and sounds, their endlessly disappearing present), its quantitative everydayness (the very quality of this medium each and every day), how can we *represent* television?

Partly here there is a problem simply with the use of the term "television" which covers not just the extensive social fact but a number of things which are not at all homogeneous despite that fact. Think only of the historical volatility of the technology and of the realities of broadcasting: the television of the 1980s is not the television of the 1950s or 1960s, is not merely more of the same in some straightforward continuity of technological, economic, and social relations. Or think of the differences from television to television across the world, the differences we elide as we too readily extrapolate from and collapse into US television as television *tout court,* the essential realization and the certain destiny. Or think again, recognizing another dimension of the problem, of the uneasy relation of "television" to video: many artists work with television (television technologies), but the involvement of video art, video practice with television (broadcast television, TV) is problematic (aesthetically, culturally, ideologically): important in the history of video art is an initial—and continuing—practice against television, the mass broadcast form, leading in one direction into a typical modernist concern with the "essentials" of the medium in opposition to the whole idea of transmission, the dominant idea of the "medium," while in another (but the two can overlap) to a critical interventionist concern with the politics of television, with its critique and transformation. Such examples are a necessary counter to the usual assumption of "television"; assuming, the latter excludes; excluding, it homogenizes; homogenizing, it accepts a specific domination. This assumption, moreover, is a condition of the slide which compels so many of the public discussions and reactions toward the projection of some anthropomorphized originating force: television as the autonomous subject-cause of this or that. Nowhere do technological determinism and cultural pessimism meet with so much assent as in attitudes to television (the assumption of "television") which must, on the contrary, always be understood to involve in a given context the particular institution of a set of technical knowledges and procedures as an applied technology in a specific social formation.[1] It thus needs to be said that in most of what follows, "television" is used to refer to broadcast television as instituted in the US and—allowing nevertheless for characteristic differences—in the countries of Western Europe.

Yet to specify usage in that way is indicative. While homogenization is misleading, while the equation of US television with television is wrong, there is also an evident rightness, a necessary emphasis in it: to go no further, economic determinations have rendered such homogenization and equation powerfully real. Herbert Schiller, most vividly, has been analyzing for a number of years now the capitalist permeation of the informational realm, with information/communication services accounting for more than half of the economic activity in the US, and the emergence of a television based increasingly on world markets and multinational corporate over public ownership, with US television having the large monopoly of this television, being its very achievement. Imperialism translates into these terms of the media, economic and cultural appropriation, the world deluged by what Schiller calls "homogenized North Atlantic cultural slop."[2] To say which is to point to the tensions of television as medium and as (economic) culture, possible diversity and effective domination, forms and form. We must acknowledge not technological determinism but the historical reality of a particular institution as determining domination—where domination does not, by definition, exhaust differences but at the same time is, again by definition, exactly domination.

One of the main difficulties in approaching television is the increasing inadequacy of existing terms and standards of analysis, themselves precisely bound up with a specific régime of representation, a certain coherence of object and understanding in a complex of political-social-individual meaning. Representation in the régime we largely know ("we" in the democracies of Western industrial societies) involves together a depiction (something imaged for us), an argument (as we talk of representations being made regarding this or that), and a deputation (we are represented, taken up in the representativeness), an economy of message, communication, and subject-identity. That television is about messages, that it communicates, that it identifies in order to engage us, there is no need to doubt; clearly it is and does. At the lowest level, we can switch on and quickly find messages being delivered to us—political, religious, whatever, messages are constantly being proposed, time bought to make this or that offer of sense, some particular representation. Clearly there is nothing "pure" about these messages: they are enrolled in all the spectacle and ritual and procedure of television, televisuality, but they are nonetheless given as such, labeled thus, so many "this is a message" moments. Clearly again, messages are not to be limited to these declared moments; they are also everywhere else, television as a multiplication of messages through the whole range of programs and genres and slots with their various topics, narratives, dramas, constructions, strategies, all their diverse modes of presentation.

At this point, however, the idea of the "message" has begun to slip, has begun to lose its usefulness: extended across television, it both forgoes any specific analytic meaning and constrains understanding of television within a traditional framework that misses its reality, is too univocal, and this notwithstanding the added stress on "multiplicity." By "univocal" is meant that such an idea can suggest a single coherent functioning of television, a single coherent effectivity (the transmission of messages); that it can suggest a single relation between institution and audience (the reception of messages); that it is liable to conflate the problem of meaning in television, of the production of social meanings, with, precisely, "messages" in a way which holds back from the necessary new terms we will need for thinking about television and ideology, about its conditions and reality of representation (and the validity and sense of the latter term will then be in question); that it accepts an essentialization of television as "communication," which is—or was—after all a dominant respectable version of television (this having its other, complementary, lighter side: "entertainment"), the ideology of the noble social role with its accompanying rhetoric: criticize television and you criticize communication, democracy, the free flow of ideas and information (there was a time indeed in strong European "public service" televisions when every set was to all intents and purposes inscribed "this is communication—be grateful").

Messages, communication, that is, may be part of our perception of television but must also be part of the analysis, part of its critique; at once inasmuch as that perception has been a given of television itself and is far from adequately registering the nature of its institution, and inasmuch as, politically, the point in the end cannot be only to communicate alternatives—although this is now certainly crucial—but equally to produce al-

ternatives to this specific social version of "communication," where the latter
is both these particular orders of meaning and the terms of an ideological
miscognition: communicating alternatives, that is, involves moving beyond
"communication" in order to grasp the reality of the television institution
(and so of its modes of establishment and use of communication) as a
prerequisite for effective transformation, the condition finally of any alternative (significantly enough here, Godard entitled his initial set of television interventions "on and under communication," *Sur et sous la
communication*).

Thus we need, for example, to understand the institution in respect of
its fundamental universalizing function, universalizing not in the sense of
the creation of some one coherent subject, some representative reason for
its orders, but in that, more basically, of the universalization of the function
of reception. Television exists first and foremost as availability, as saying
everything to everyone, all of us receivers, assembled and serialized in that
unity ("the public," "the audience," "the viewer," what we have to be, exactly
the everyone, and not someone; the religious television stations—and the
prelapsarian Swaggart, for instance, was reaching a claimed 145 nations—
are forcefully brute expressions of this: the *Assembly* of God/TV). Along
with social security numbers we should also receive television recipient numbers (we have them now in one form or another, as most obviously in
countries with television license systems), certification of our being there
(no doubt it is not quite by chance that that last phrase finds the title of
the Hal Ashby film in which Peter Sellers played a character—himself in
fact just Chance—whose existence was entirely as viewer, not watching but
receiving television, always immediately switching channels, even when he
himself—but there is no such identity outside of reception—appeared on
screen). The hierarchy of message and medium on which notions of communication habitually depend here shifts: what is transmitted is important,
but it is the realization and maintenance of the function of reception that
is *all*-important, everything else then to be seen as simply something like
the minimum required to allow that realization and maintenance, to guarantee the fulfillment of the function.

This is to have come from the question of representing television as
how to represent it to the question of representing television as how it
represents, its relation to and of representation. The two go together,
since how it represents will have to be a decisive focus of attention for any
representation of television; to talk about the first is necessarily to raise
the issues of the latter, of the concepts and procedures for a validly critical analysis. In what follows, the aim is to provide some initial discussion
of how television represents, of thinking about it and representation; and
then, too, implicitly and later on rather more explicitly, to give some consideration to studying it, to terms of analysis. Needless to say, no doubt,
the determining perspective will be political: the questions of representing television are directly, from the start, a matter of a politics of representation.

Television is the displacement of representation from political into economic terms.

Representation, of course, is a basic reference for television itself which runs it into socio-economic constructions: "the audience," "the target group," and all the other expressions of such constructions. "The problem," a Nielsen ratings official once candidly said, "is picking the sample that is representative, that is representing what you want it to represent."[3] Which holds above all for the networks and advertisers who commission and use the ratings. The criteria of the representative are not political but economic; representation works that way. The problem is representatively packaging the market grouping that represents what commodity value needs it to represent. Sitting in front of the television screen, we have always to remember that, whatever else, programs are so much wrapping paper and that what is being wrapped up for delivery is us, an audience. The mention of packaging can also remind us that, like packaging in other areas of capitalist production, programs themselves have not usually been subject to price competition amongst the networks: the competition is for ratings (through "quality," scheduling, etc.), for audience representation as market asset. This representation, moreover, *is* the prime economic relation: consumers—the viewers—express their preferences precisely through ratings, not through any direct buying of a product (programs are like and unlike other products).[4]

The ratings institutes work with the idea of the "representative sample," but this is simply an economic majority, a commodity standard which the programs—the means to the realization of the commodity audience—are anyway set to fit from the very beginning (the Preview Theater on Sunset Boulevard where proposed new series are sent to be tested for audience response is well known; and, of course, the audience itself each time must be tested for standardness, its reactions measured to a Mr. Magoo cartoon, making sure it laughs in the right places, gives good "Magoos"). Arthur C. Nielsen himself in the 1960s once described how he dealt with objections to his small number of homes recorded by using—what else?—a television analogy.[5] Suppose for the sake of objection that someone in the sample is unrepresentative, which is to say "idiosyncratic" according to the Nielsen view of things; his example is a woman in Arkansas who, having once taken exception to some remark made by Jack Paar, turned off the set every time the latter appeared. The result would be equivalent to losing one out of the 525 lines scanned on your television screen: you would still have a good picture, "any one line by itself is meaningless"; the standard image is maintained and the standard representation too, "representing what you want it to represent." The contortions are evident: "while this woman statistically did stand for many viewers, she did not specifically represent them," "separately she represented no one. . . . " What they express, however, assertively defensive still (remember that this was some time ago), is the relocation of representation as the economic construction of a majority at the expense of any social or political reality outside of its assembly through television, any other reality then being so much interference that distorts the true—representative—picture. The point is the mean, the right audience, the whole lot of Magoos; and the ever-increasing precision in targeting specific groups, the interest in particular minorities, is a continuation and an intensification of this relocation: the social identity is again economic, minorities defined by spending power (in a nice loop, television then defines spending power, is itself economic identification: witness the way that subscription to cable has now become a key indicator of disposable income). Of course, that representation and its realization and discussion are in the province of the biggest marketing research firm on earth (television work is responsible for only 11% of the Nielsen Company's earnings but 99% of its fame) is indicative enough from the start, shows immediately the relocation. Representation is the economic relation of an audience, and it is no surprise that disputes about the accuracy of the ratings are about just that, economic representation; as in the compensation payment demands by advertisers after more sophisticated measurement techniques developed by the Percy Company challenged accepted figures, giving a 70% audience share to the networks at the time as opposed to a previously believed 76%: the disputed 6% equals some 7 million television households equals a sizeable difference in marketable audience equals a considerable variation in the price at which time can be sold to advertisers—representation is now caught up in that equation.

The displacement of representation from political to economic terms is a relation of culture to the economic in new forms that challenge a political culture of the individual subject.

Obviously, the relation of representation to the economic is part of its history from the beginning: suffrage is a political demand from economic power by the middle classes in Britain, for example, in the early nineteenth century (as later in the century one strand within suffragism was pressure for the enfranchisement of propertied women, women with social responsibility). At the same time, the history—that of *universal* suffrage—is one of political independence from the economic, representation as condition of full subjecthood, as social recognition of the individual and his or her freedom (thus, alongside the middle classes, the working classes struggled for parliamentary reform, the more so after the 1832 Act limited the franchise to £10 rated householders; thus the historical project of suffragism was the enfranchisement of all women). This individual version of representation brings with it a new elaboration of and attention to culture, at once in the sense that culture is produced as an area of value and achievement in an argument against democracy and, *a fortiori*, socialism from which indeed it would need to be protected (culture *or* anarchy) and in the sense that culture becomes the expression of a social concern with the individual who, given the movement toward the extension of the suffrage, must now be educated, socialized, cultured, indeed *acculturated* (to adapt a term that appears at our end of the history: the individual is as an alien to be brought into culture).

Historically, therefore, the idea of culture is a site of contradiction, both term of individual value (growth, development, self-realization through the attainment of a *true* perfection, Arnold's "the best which has been thought and said in the world") and term of social production (the realization of the individual in the social, its mesh of beliefs and customs and representations, *its* "reality"). In the history it then mediates the resolution of the two or rather the flattening out of any contradiction; and this finally by the holding together of the social as culture as value, value thus collapsing into an *indifference* of culture: culture is potentially everywhere and everything. "Culture," writes Fredric Jameson, "seems to me the very element of consumer society itself; no society has ever been saturated with signs and messages like this one . . . everything is mediated by culture to the point when even the political and the ideological 'levels' have initially to be disentangled from their primary mode of representation which is cultural."[6] This, in fact, was the historical necessity of structuralism, treating everything—and indifferently—as communication, message, sign ("the interpretation of society as a whole in function of a theory of communication," as Lévi-Strauss so influentially put it);[7] as it was and is then of poststructuralism, drawing its inevitable conclusion from the primacy of signs, namely, that of their disorigination from anything other than the nonorigin of their production, Derrida's *différance:* representation is taken no longer as record or expression of some existing reality but as production of reality, with a consequent suspicion of the term itself insofar as it cannot but involve the idea of a distinction between representation and represented with the latter "outside" of the former, its origin or cause or corresponding truth, this as against the generalized textuality within which representation works, which is its sole ground ("representations as signs that refer to other signs, which refer to still other signs," in Jonathan Culler's words).[8]

The interrelation of television with this development of culture and then also with that of poststructuralism is powerful. Television marks a qualitative change in the history in which it is included of the central cultural modes of representation in industrial societies. From the novel to cinema to television, these succeeding and overlapping one another in that history, there has been a prime concern with making individual-social sense, providing exactly the terms of *representation,* sense of the social in individual terms for the individual thus identified as a representative and represented subject, socially existent to him- or herself. Which brings us back to the logic of culture and its history and to the growth of mass culture. Representation, from the nineteenth century on, is a political fact and struggle *and* a market reality, the heavy investment in socially extensive representing modes that offer fictions, images, reports: so many repeatedly available

versions of how it is for me to be living in the new and changing society
(note the importance of realism in these modes), versions of the culture
that constitute the culture, that are the individual's social identity.

Mass culture may be understood as dependent on the following at least:
the imposition of market relations as the condition of production and reception; processes of industrialization; the incorporation of the vast majority of people into the dominant industrial production of culture.[9] Novel
and television can thus be seen equally as classic instances of mass cultural
production, as single history. Television, however, at the same time that it
continues also changes that history, quite decisively alters our experience
of mass culture (we need to think, too, of the position of radio, its inception
of broadcasting and subsequent accompaniment of television). What is at
stake here is the dominance of television as medium and culture—as mode
of cultural production—in the societies of its institution in a way that gives
new content to dominance, that is characterized by a quantitative-qualitative
shift in respect of: *extension* (television's massive penetration—the industry's
own word—of homes: 98% of US households with one or more sets);
sociality (owning and watching television has become an obligatory requirement for full membership of the modern capitalist state); *occupation* (a
French person born after 1970, for example, will spend on average 63,000
hours of his or her life in front of the television as opposed to 55,000 hours
working); and so on. This is precisely the realization of the saturation of
signs and messages, of representations, mediating everything, everyone in
a general spread of culture that operates the displacement of representation from political to economic terms and is the result of a determining
cultural-economic organization of the social (the increasing importance of
information/communication services can be noted again in this context).
Debates in the recent history of television in Western Europe with their
arguments over "public service" or "private, commercial" television are
indicative: political-representational versions of State and individual subject
are juxtaposed with economic-representational versions of media, network,
circulation (of sounds-images-capital), with the future—and the present—
on the side of the latter (inflation and reduced public spending have facilitated the shift from public to private and prompted new accommodations between State and market around communications). Culture is a
matter no longer of political calculation for the individual but of economic
calculation for the consumer as audience; and representation is now the
form of that calculation.

The displacement of representation to economic terms is the archaicization of all address to the individual as citizen, as individual subject.

In its most archaic systems ("archaic" from the perspective of its institution in advanced capitalist societies), television is exactly broadcasting,
the transmission of state speech to viewers as first and foremost citizens;
television as "a mirror of the principles of the State," as the director of the

USSR State Committee for Television and Radio put it in 1984, describing the reality in his country.[10] Such a television will be news-centralized, highly educational, and parsimonious; thus in China, where the average daily watching time is one-seventh of that in the US, some 70% of programs are informational, artistic, or pedagogic, with broadcasting a state monopoly and television under direct government control. The "public service" traditions of some European televisions mediated individual and state through culture (both as value and as general socialization) in a varied appeal to and identification of free subject plus state citizen plus socio-cultural being plus, more and more, consumer, with these instances "catered for" to a considerable extent by different programs and channels.

The current situation is one of that cultural saturation already mentioned, with television as main agency of the explosion of messages, signs, endless traces of meaning, a whole performance of the society as culture. This can be seen too as the recasting of the social into "the everyday," the culturalization of everyday life by and as television. Socio-political representation is turned into the commodification of a public that is television's economic representation of itself (its market existence); identities are leveled to that standard, the "other people" of the public (for the individual this is the serial consciousness that television gives: viewers are not me but all the others, and this is the same for everybody), and redeemed in the valuation of the everyday, constructed and presented as the truly real (television accounts for daily life: prime activity, taking up my time, and prime mode of its being, taking over reality in a constant domestic recycling in which the terms of my world are made and approved). The new intellectual interest in everyday life is critically important, grasping the need for an understanding of a material sphere usually left aside, if not contemptuously dismissed, by previous theoretical approaches—Habermas talks of "the no-man's land of everyday life" which for the Frankfurt School, for instance, "was a mere epiphenomenon either of the totalizing force of the administrative world or of suffering nature."[11] But it is also, like structuralism and poststructuralism indeed, caught up in a history in which television is crucial and in which the production of the sphere of "the everyday," the realization and proposal of that, is an erasure of the possibility of political meaning: the political as transcending the everyday as analysis and critique, project of transformation and action toward it. One initial mode of interest in the everyday, that of the Situationists in the 1950s and 1960s, was concerned precisely with critique and interruption of "*la société du spectacle*"; another, however, the more recent, is often given at best to retrenchment in a low-level pragmatism (the great projects have failed us, stick to the ordinary and its little adjustments), at worst to jubilation in "the screen stage" (forget politics, moral sense, truth, and all other such anachronisms: "Happily . . . the social will not take place").[12] Which, again, is not to suggest that there is not a necessary renegotiation of the political from and in respect of the everyday—think only of the way in which feminism has cut across the old political exclusions of the lives and oppressions of women by its attention to daily life, forging an everyday politics; it is simply to acknowledge an appeal to "the everyday," following television, that is just the reverse.

In *L'Entretien infini* Maurice Blanchot describes the everyday as "without subject, without object," as the dissolution of the one and the other, of the one with the other: the objective realm cedes to a series of compartment-alized actions, day-to-day indifference, "the medium in which alienations, fetishisms, reifications produce their effects"; the subjective cedes to an empty third-person, an anyone:

> The everyday escapes. Why does it escape? Because it is without a subject. When I live the everyday, it is anyone, anyone whatsoever, who does so, and this any-one is, properly speaking, neither me nor, properly speaking, the other; he is neither the one nor the other, and he is the one and the other in their inter-changeable presence, their annulled irreciprocity—yet without there being an "I" and an "alter ego" to give rise to a *dialectical recognition*.[13]

"Dialectical recognition" is another term for socio-political representation, dependent on the realization of specific identities, a historical process of subject and object; as "everyday speech," the title of the section in which Blanchot's description occurs, is a term for its neutralization, an omnipre-sent lateral movement of language, from moment to moment, "the leveling of a steady slack time," "this present without particularity."[14] Such speech is now the province of television, and we can note the sheer extent to which the latter has been developed for and as talk: talk shows, game shows, news shows, soap operas, situation comedies, and so on and on. Not surprisingly, the true stars and symbols of television are talkers, instigators of ever more talk: Johnny Carson or Oprah Winfrey or Phil Donahue or Barbara Walters or. . . . Television is meeting people over and over again (with programs inevitably about people meeting people—*The Dating Game*—and then too about whether people really met who they meet—*The Newlywed Game*) and talking over and over again (day in, day out, from *Good Morning America* through to Ted Koppel or David Letterman).[15] Before all else we are treated to a permanent serial of the public for the public in a circle of proximation: if I watch for long enough, I will get meeting and talking with everyone; and, in fact, the long enough is of no matter since at any moment, for any stretch of viewing, the ritual will be being gone through for everyone, anyone, me and the others and whoever it is in television's proximity, which we all are: near, next, before, after, round and round. This proximity, grounded in the huge production of everyday speech, is then the new representational reality, the new democratic condition: not *suffrage*, archaic historical expression of identity, but *reception*, today's social availability to, of, and for all—welcome in, reception's good, whoever-wherever; and who-where can you be but here-now on television's everyday life, serial days?

In representative elections in the US, less than half of those eligible to vote do so; 98% of homes in the US have television, and the networks still share between 60% and 70% of the audience, and anyway everyone watches network TV. Democratization is through the medium, not the state, parliamentary majority gives way to televisual—and commercial—majority, the viewing public at any and every moment. For as long as the networks are broadcasting, there is always a guaranteed majority: electronic assembly gives an instantaneous mass, creates a majority discourse. This is not to say that the program of the moment represents (in anything of the old sense) the discourse of the majority (it might, but that is not what is first and foremost at stake); rather, it *is* the majority discourse at this point by virtue of television: its representation is exhausted in its audience which is what makes it representative and which exists only as a function of television, its aim, standard, and product, its rating.

Classically, representation is bound up with some assumption of a stability of the subject, the imaginable and imagined individual in the social identity of his or her project (the subject *means*); television's imagination is a continuation of itself, the achieved distribution of a *network*. This imagination, moreover, is strong even in programs that are deliberately cast as appealing to the viewer as citizen, that assume the responsibility of the social-individual subject. Thus the producer and presenter of the West German *Aktenzeichen XY . . . Ungelöst* (from which *America's Most Wanted* now derives) calls his book on the program *Das Unsichtbare Netz*—the invisible net or network—and offers a powerful corollary definition of its audience-method:

> The method used is reminiscent of the operation of an electronic data-bank from which extraordinarily precise information can be called up in an extremely short time. . . . And the receptive capacity of millions of human minds, which can be checked at one and the same time with the help of the television screen, could be considerably greater than that of an equally powerful electronic robot.[16]

Which is a definition that can be applied throughout television: viewers as audience as *receptive capacity*. Note too that the network can operate only in television's electrification of it, switching it on: the presenters of *Crimewatch UK* (the equivalent British program) record that "for some extraordinary reason [but then not so extraordinary] . . . people only believe their experiences when they see something on *Crimewatch* [only, that is, when they—the experiences *and the people*—are *networked*]"[17] And, of course, what you see on *Crimewatch* is primarily television: a quarter of a million crimes are reported per month in Britain, but "it is remarkably difficult to find three crimes worthy of reconstruction."[18]

The archaicization of address to the individual is concomitant with a transformation of relations of time at the expense of the temporality of history.

The distinction is sometimes made in sociological studies between *pledged*

time (spent at work), *compulsive time* (spent fulfilling various necessary requirements, such as traveling to and from work, completing official forms),
and then *free time* (spent "as one chooses"). Television is the second proposed
as the third and running into the first: free time as compulsive time and
as economic relation. The point is the appropriation of free time as commodity, the watching time produced by the seller (the networks and cable
stations) for the buyer (the advertisers); the viewer has to watch—has to
be a viewer—not just as a social requirement but as an economic one too,
so as to produce the marketable commodity, time as that. Godard once
remarked how strange it was that people were not paid for watching television given the productive labor involved, the economic service performed.[19] Obviously, "free time" is always a concept and a reality within a
specific system of the organization of time, is always given socially and
caught up economically (as in capitalist societies for consumption, and it is
in just such societies that "free time" becomes important, along with the
elaboration of "public" and "private" life). What is new with television,
however, is the directness of the relation to and of this free time, the nature
and extent of its appropriation, both commodification and occupation—
time at home is time for television, the latter occupies the former, and more
and more.

This appropriation then finds expression in how and what we see on
television, in television's prodigious work on time. Time is monitored, the
day organized into time slots; there is a homogenization—every moment
contained within this organization—and a certain hierarchization of time—
the ordering of a time for learning, a time for news, a time for entertainment, and so on (although the multiplication of channels with cable is
shifting this somewhat to an anything anytime situation, news twenty-four
hours a day, for instance); with this ordering determining the form and
content of programs so that they can be read as signifying "six o'clock,"
"eight o'clock," as in every sense *meaning* time (Earl Hamner, producer of
Falcon Crest: "it was designed to be an eight o'clock show . . . CBS felt that
with some modifications it could become a ten o'clock show . . . one of them
was to shift the emphasis away—not totally away—from the attempt to
build a strong family . . . the kind of thing you do at ten o'clock. . . . ")[20]
Typically, time needs to be filled and accelerated, as much time *made* as
possible—the Lexicon time-compression process for speeding up movies
on TV, for gaining time on them, is symbolic enough of the general urge.
Days, hours, minutes, seconds, television is time and motion study in practice, assembly-line quantification for maximum efficiency. Hence the potential panic around time, the endlessly repeated dramatization of doing
things in the quickest time; as in game shows, that staple of television—
who can do this the quickest, answer the fastest, time always in jeopardy.
The liveness of television—whether real or fictive (liveness is a prime imaginary of television)—also has its significance here, that of a constant
immediacy, TV today, now, this minute.

Exhausting time into moments, its "now-thisness," television produces forgetfulness, not memory, flow, not history. If there is history, it is congealed, already past and distant and forgotten other than as television archive material, images that can be repeated to be forgotten again (Jameson: "Think only of the media exhaustion of the news: of how Nixon and, even more so, Kennedy are figures from a now distant past. One is tempted to say that the very function of the news media is to relegate such recent historical experiences as rapidly as possible into the past. The informational function of the media would thus be to help us forget, to serve as the very agents and mechanisms for our historical amnesia").[21] There is no place for anything other than actuality, the moments as they come; television actualizes rather than intelligibilizes time, this latter being the condition of time's achievement as history. Representation and the subject are terms of that achievement; television and the rated viewer are those of an ahistoricization of time—no distance, position, intelligible construction. Such a global description is not to ignore the possibility of historical terms and constructions in television; it is to suggest that these too are archaicized by the overall institution of TV time, the quantitative-qualitative appropriation.

All of this is to indicate the excess that television is. It has gone out of any simply graspable and comprehensible régime of representation and so over the edge of habitual terms, habitual approaches. The problem, then, is that of finding new approaches that are neither the mimicking of that excess nor the refusal of its implications and effects. Which, of course, is a political problem: television is a central site of politics today and any account of television is directly political discourse; indeed with the politics often derived from the reflection on, the description of the experience of television—witness Baudrillard, as we shall see.

Representation, classically, comes with a two-faced idea of representativeness, of likeness. What is the representative *like*? One answer invokes a general subjectivity, the individual as agent of a universal reason; he (the masculine is appropriate for this account), once elected, is then there not to represent any particular group or interest but to realize that reason, chosen to express it as best he can. The second answer, of course, is that he represents precisely an interest, a group, that he is chosen in that likeness; which is our actual political history, so many struggles for representation by the middle classes, the working classes, women. The struggle for women's suffrage is significant here in that it posed acutely the problems of the assumptions in representation and its versions of likeness. In what sense were women a group and what were they like? The arguments in Britain, for example (and they were duplicated elsewhere), from both those in favor of and those against this suffrage, went the two ways: women were like men, the same identity of human reason (thus they are as able as men to vote and be representatives, *or* thus there is no need for them to vote and be representatives since men can perfectly stand for them); women were unlike men, a different identity, like themselves (thus they need to vote and be representatives since men cannot perfectly stand for them, *or* thus they should not have the vote and be representatives since they cannot be really representative, can represent only their particularity).[22]

If a representative is like what he or she represents, then identity and interest determine representation, a consequence that preoccupied political thinkers during the nineteenth-century movement toward democracy. John Stuart Mill, for instance, author indeed of an essay "On Representative Government," argued strongly for a general extension of the suffrage (and to include women) but was also deeply apprehensive of the majority rule it would bring ("the natural tendency of representative government, as of modern civilization, is towards collective mediocrity"),[23] which is seen as exactly the removal of decision from reason, from the capacity developed by instruction to transcend local and immediate desires and inclinations (the effect of extensions of the franchise "being to place the principal power in the hands of classes more and more below the highest level of instruction in the community").[24] Such representation is thus, in fact, from this standpoint, no representation—what is the identity of a majority of the lowest common denominator created in this way, and what of the essential values that then find no expression? Mill turned to systems of proportional representation to ensure a voice to "the minority of educated minds," proposing multiple votes for those of "mental superiority" in order that disinterestedness—reason—should prevail over "class legislation."[25]

Mill's minority supposedly transcends interest, but any appeal to proportional representation is evidently a direct recognition of interest, quickly brings the idea of a "personal representation" (a phrase Mill also uses) to which different minorities might aspire: "every minority in the whole nation, consisting of a sufficiently large number to be, on principles of equal justice, entitled to a representative."[26] On what constitutes a sufficiently large number and as to what the principles of justice are, Mill is here vague; potentially there are an infinite number of categories in respect of which likeness can be affirmed and representation demanded. In reality, there is a political struggle for the social definition of relevant areas for likeness, for the recognition and expression of specific identities; as today with racial or sexual minorities, which are then too open to the contradictions of different identities, struggles of other minorities within them (think of lesbian women in relation to the general representation of women and then of S/M lesbians in relation to both). The result has been a challenge to the classical idea of representation and its institutions, even while idea and institutions have necessarily often provided the immediate terms and objectives for the particular movements out of which the challenge comes (it can be important at once to gain representation and to call into question the very assumptions of that in a given society). At the same time, psychoanalysis especially—undermining with its account of the subject any simple possibility of "representing oneself"—and modernism generally—stressing representation as construction, not reflection, as order of language—have offered a further challenge to any stable ground for the representative.

Television shifts representation into economic terms (even in Western European public service televisions prior to the breaking of state mono-polies, ratings and interchannel competition were important for advertising when this was allowed and for justification of the spending of license money when it was not): the consumer majority (Mill no doubt would have iden-tified this mass culture as collective mediocrity) and then the targeted con-sumer minorities (a kind of economic version of Mill's "personal representation"). Experiments within television which give viewers the vote through the interactive possibilities of cable symptomatically repeat these terms. Thus Warner's QUBE system in Columbus, Ohio, opened in De-cember 1977 with voting on what to call a just-born baby girl (43% for Elizabeth) and then rapidly harnessed interaction to commercial prospec-tion (for example, survey advertising asking which of several holiday spots viewers would most like information on) and data gathering (even though not making a profit from subscriptions, the system produced very sub-stantial and precise marketing information). Shifting representation into economic terms, furthermore, tying it to the movement of market forces from moment to moment, television has participated decisively in a logic of late capitalism: that of the coming together of commodity and image in a constitutive interdependence, with the image "the final form of com-modity reification"[27] and, indeed, the supreme commodity-reality. The full alignment of representation with commodification and the solicitation of consumer desire is finally the loss of the sense of representation (its sense as in any way representative *of*). The answer to the question as to what television represents, in other words, becomes television itself: it "repre-sents" the reality it produces and imitates (this gives those common feelings of television as source of reality, things existing only by virtue of being on television, events losing any specific singularity of eventfulness and having always already happened as they happen on television which is precisely where they happen—events now are television events, but then the only event is television).

Reactions to television in these terms, unsurprisingly, are often in one form or another the reassertion of representation, of grounds of identity. Thus the debates around cultural literacy that periodically recur (their recurrence over a longer period of mass cultural production should not lead us to ignore their particular occurrence in the today of television) are concerned with an identified decline of culture as value and increasingly with an identified decline of national cultural identity—witness the recent spate of books on the closing of the American mind and on what every American does not but should know. With no cultural identity, there is no representation for and of the American as subject and citizen, no stability from which representation could operate politically (no nationhood) or socially (only the dissolution of "the American mainstream"). Television can be directly blamed for this (it is all television's fault), or half blamed (television is damaging, but some amount of television is beneficially acculturative for some groups), or indirectly blamed (the schools are really responsible, including for excessive television watching). Even when not directly blamed, however, television is liable to be effectively dismissed from the conception of the cultural identity that should hold (E. D. Hirsch, for example, in his "list of cultural literacy," "What Literate Americans Know," includes "telescope" but not "television," and beyond the figure of Archie Bunker finds virtually no place for any television names: literate Americans should not know Lucille Ball, say, or even Walter Cronkite).[28] Thus the debates around what can be called political literacy, where television is seen as bound up with a demobilization of social identities and terms of struggle, an alienation of needs and aspirations—in Enzensberger's words, a "present depraved form" of the media works through "the falsification and exploitation of quite real and legitimate needs."[29] Television, that is, is *mis*representation; politically, the collapsing of identity into mass, social group into serialized conglomerate, a disenabling of agency and vision.

Such accounts are involved in an overall perception of the nature and effects of television, and the account given here so far is parallel with them in that (and some of the issues they raise will also be taken up later on), insisting on the necessity for a recognition of the institution of television, the functioning, as it were, of television itself. This is not, however, here at least, to foreclose thereby the reality too of the play between television and the particularity of its realizations at any given moment: the institution is overall, but that is not to say that television is then a simply homogeneous totality.

There is, of course, a way of thinking about and expressing this that has an official existence within the institution, part of the ideology of its self-presentation, namely that of *pluralism*. The pluralism of society, of its democracy, is reflected in the pluralism of what gets shown on television, which is then itself the democratic medium of the transmission of the social multiplicity and its freedom. The truth in this, the facts of variety and difference, need not be denied in order to stress nevertheless, simultaneously, that any pluralism exists only within the governing terms of plurality (pluralism is not defined naturally but within a system), terms in this case that are firmly political and economic: what constitutes the recognized spectrum of "opinion," holding television to a consensual center that it endlessly recreates, and what constitutes the recognized spectrum of economically viable programming, holding television to the market and its version of audiences (with the two potentially at odds but—and—with a series of accommodations of the former to the latter that differ from country to country). Pluralism is so many orders of television, as the latter's programs are so many orders of variety and difference.

There is another side to the reference to pluralism, its proposal with regard to a plurality of positions of reception: television is watched differently by different people with different histories that produce different experiences of the television offered—it is not television that controls but people who control television in their watching. It is possible too now in this respect to adduce new technological developments as confirming this, as allowing the viewer to increase pluralization: thus VCRs give the possibility of selectively multiplying viewing and of viewing in different ways, with different times (repeats, freezes, and so on); thus remote controls permit rapid movement in and out of programs, across channels, each viewer able to create his or her own absolutely unique viewing experience. Again, the point is not to deny this but to accept it only within limits, the limits of television, the institution.

Television is a construction of pluralism; the viewer participates in that construction. What is at stake is a determined consensuality, at once in the sense that television is determined by dominant social terms and that it itself is a powerful creation-articulation of those terms. "Dominant social terms" here should be taken to refer not to some single expression of a ruling class—though there is such expression—but much more to the hegemonic social ground that includes those specifically class forms at the same time that their inclusion is within the process of a general sociality which goes beyond them, accommodating a whole number of potentially disparate meanings, values, and practices in an extensively available, more or less cohesive space of social discourse, precisely the pluralism. The idea of democracy is a prime theme and figure of this space, with the more or less cohesion ("more or less" indicates the spectrum, the limits) focused around what constitutes it, what can and cannot be said, what is representative and what can be represented, what like is like. But then, as has been emphasized, television's own dominance and the nature of the economic realization of the medium also shift pluralism and consensus from old notions of representation to the new conditions of multiplication and indifference: the maximum number of heterogeneous images in the maximum homogenization, the saturation of signs and messages which is the reduction—the neutralization—of meaning, of representation (the heterogeneity is anyway above all quantitative: more and more images). The democratic now is interminable pluralization, not a set of representable positions (although these are also around in television, ever more archaic to it) but a fading of positions in the flow of the images and the assemblages created from their reception (the audience as representations of that). Television does not control, certainly, but then again it does, defining and encompassing, including us in its reality whether or not we watch—can anyone in our societies be outside television, beyond its compulsions? We can note, moreover, that the technological developments mentioned above are realized much more as continuations of the given television than as challenges to it: VCRs are used vis-à-vis television largely to watch more of it in perfectly conventional ways, in one's own time but as much in its; remote controls allow the picking and choosing of this or that and the making up of unique individualized sequences, bits from here and there, yet of course within the constraints of what is proposed by television in the first place—and, in fact, the phenomenon of zapping can be seen mostly as a kind of lateralization, a side-stepping through images that effects an insignificant—nonnarrative, nonhistorical—temporality which runs into and mirrors television's own performance of time.

Versions of pluralism have been and are important to television studies. In the elaboration of a sociological theory of the media, a sociology of mass communications, attention was typically focused initially on the effects of television as influence (investigations of the relations between violence on screen and violence in society and so on) and on "ritualized" viewing modes, the social roles of television and the kinds of viewer behavior induced by it. Subsequently, in reaction against this more passive conception of the viewer, a "uses and gratifications" approach was developed which envisaged the relation to television as one of selection according to prior dispositions, people manipulating rather than being manipulated by it. The prior dispositions, however, are not evidently separable from television, are formed within a social process in which television has a strong and constitutive part; something that the "uses and gratifications" approach did not often manage adequately to take into account. A left parallel to this sociology-of-mass-communications movement is to be found in the switch from the critique of "the culture industry" and its degraded products, with attendant ideas of something amounting to brainwashing (consumer pacification plus political orientation: Althusser talked of television "cramming" people "with daily doses of nationalism, chauvinism, liberalism, moralism, etc."),[30] to the insistence on viewers as actively judging and deciding subjects producing their own critical readings in function of their lived experience and on the need to understand the popular values of the programs so massively watched, which are thus not to be dismissed from what is then identified as an "elitist" position.

This latter emphasis is especially attractive now in television studies where the call to attend to "the popular" and to "pleasure" is increasingly strong. The necessary response to the failings of structuralism and the Althusserian account of ideology, with an analysis of subject and subject-positioning suggesting mere passivity, functioning acquiescence ("les sujets 'marchent' "),[31] can be acknowledged; but it can also be seen in some of its current developments as implicated in a damaging crisis in theory, falling into an equally demobilizing mirror-image version of mere activity. The thinking through of the nature of culture and cultural production today and of the difficult relations between mass culture and popular culture is often collapsed into the assumption of something of the latter in the former, "popular" quickly simply dependent on and guaranteed by the fact of being well liked by many people (but then what is and what are the conditions of this "liking," this pleasure?), and with evaluation too elided in that same fact. Pluralism then enters the argument, as it were, in addition, on the side of the viewers, a plurality of readings even granted the problems of mass culture: bad television turns into good audiences—and into good television studies. The pursuit of plural readings mostly just leaves television intact, unthought, including again in its role in the reality in and from which those readings are given: no one comes simply from outside television with a reading, from some authentic experience that is entirely television-free. At its worst, television studies uses this idea of viewers' plurality of readings to justify its own academic proliferation of readings, the demonstration of some alternative reading, often dubbed "resistance," taken as the demonstration of television and its reception in a falsely humble gesture of identification with "people" or even "the people," whose potential as readers-resistants we must not underrate—a view of things as patronizing as its passivity opposite. Which should make it clear that the point is not that people, we as viewers, do not at many or fewer times read plurally and critically and differently but that the active/passive, dupe/not-dupe dichotomy is an impasse that needs to be broken.

Something of this too can be followed through in the current fortunes of "the everyday," to return to that. The grand narratives and systems having failed, politically and theoretically, as is said in an indiscriminate gesture (*all* those narratives and systems), the day-to-day in its local activities and concerns is so much the more real, the site of a valorized particularity over against what is then to be seen only as reductive totalizing abstraction. The importance of the everyday can again at once be stressed: politics and theory should not be at the expense of everyday life—this after all the realm of the lived experience of actual men and women—which it is the aim of socialist politics and theory at any rate precisely to know, value, and transform. Moreover, the specific attention to the everyday, its bringing into political and theoretical focus, has been in some of its manifestations a crucial grasping of areas of life that have been typically ignored or marginalized, areas where oppression and struggles against it together with traditions of the creation of values have to be recognized and taken up in any valid vision of change: there is a politics of the everyday, that is, to be recovered, made, turned into action. Thus the editors of a recent *Yale French Studies* issue on the topic comment that "everyday life has always weighed heavily on the shoulders of women," and Michèle Mattelart writes of that: "Everyday life. Day-to-day life. These represent a specific idea of time within which women's social and economic role is carried out. It is in the everyday time of domestic life that the fundamental discrimination of sex roles is expressed, the separation between public and private, production and reproduction."[32] To reclaim this everyday of women's lives, to bring back its reality, is to demonstrate the oppression and to explore the potential from which transformation can come, a resiting of politics exactly.

The recourse to everyday life in other of its examples, however, can be a quite contrary retreat from any such radical-political conception. The transforming dialectic of appraisal and critique gives way to the smoothing out of the everyday into a good object, good by simple virtue of the everydayness, the beginning and the end of politics; with the latter now cast at best into the micromovements of "molecular revolution" ("underground," "transversal," "a kind of infinite swarming of desiring machines"),[33] at worst into the quietism of the interminable appreciation of ordinariness, a fetishism of the day-to-day. The academic realization of this last, the new production of everyday life as object of study, finds its apotheosis round television. Television and its programs (and this approach sees nothing but programs) are projected as value—as to be valued—because of their everydayness and their popularity (which is here the same thing) in a circle in which the mass existence of something is proof of that value and proof of the validity of its acceptance in the name of the everyday. I can drop critique and talk about my favorite TV programs with all the guarantee of political correctness, nonelitism, and requisite responsiveness to pleasure that "everyday life" has been constructed to provide. But then the fetishizing of everyday life as "everyday life" is not a politics of the former, nonelitism turns out to mean the refusal to negotiate terms of judgment and value that for any socialism cannot but transcend (which is not at all the same as deny or denigrate) the everyday, and pleasure is now become the automatism of an answer to everything and nothing—"we have to look at people's pleasure, the problem of pleasure," we are incessantly told, but "people's" usually screens the academic analyst's and the problem never comes, pleasure just left as an evidence, an effectively essentialized faculty, as inevitable and unquestionable as breathing.

Critical attention to the everyday comes with the insight that, however degraded, the latter contains within it something of the possibility of its own transformation: thus if mass culture is alienating, it is also expressive of needs, potentialities, contradictory forces—"the wishing is genuine," as Ernst Bloch once put it.[34] A particular—"postmodern"—account of the everyday of television is currently taking over a previous pessimism as regards mass culture, seen solely as degradation and manipulation, and switching it from negative to positive. It is not so much, in this account, that television is not a form of alienation; it is that in the reality of television and its world, alienation no longer has any great meaning, is now without any relevance. The work of Baudrillard has been more than influential here, setting out a description of television, its world, that cannot be avoided in discussion of this question of representing television today.

"Happily . . . the social will not take place," to which can be added the formulation of another of Baudrillard's constant themes: "There is only simulation."[35] What we are living now is the end of the social, the end of the political with any social meaning; this conjunction—the social-political—being in fact a creation of the eighteenth and nineteenth centuries.

Marxism supremely makes the political the representation of a social reality, but there no longer is any such social reality, no social referent as classically defined ("a people, a class, a proletariat, objective conditions").[36] In our world of simulacra and simulation, everything is always already and only model, image, spectacle, *television*; and reality is there in those determinations, not in some reality of a social being with an analyzable rationality, a determining history: "the media cause the disappearance of the event, the object, the referential" and "quite simply, there is no longer any social signified to give force to a political signifier."[37]

What Baudrillard offers is mass culture with a vengeance. In the scenario of total simulation which is our contemporary reality, the only actor is "the mass" or "the masses," the Baudrillard subject-object of postmodernism (but "subject" and "object" do not fit either): a kind of sheer force of insignificance, outside of any meaning, resistant to all reason, the derision of party or movement—of politics. Opaque to the order of representation (it has no representable existence), the mass is a creation of the régime of simulation, the imaginary referent of the opinion poll or the television network, at the same time that it is the point of the permanent attrition of that régime, an unfathomable inertia, sending back simulation for simulation in an ironic circularity: the mass "capable of refracting all models and reversing them by hypersimulation."[38]

Television is central, "the ultimate and perfect object for this new era."[39] Hence it is the prime focus of Baudrillard's McLuhanesque attention as condition of the world of simulation: "dissolution of TV into life, dissolution of life into TV."[40] "The medium is the message," indeed must be pushed to the limit at which the very notion of the medium itself gives way: "implosion of *the medium and the real*, in a sort of hyperreal nebula, where even the definition and the specific action of the medium are no longer distinguishable"; no longer any dialectic, any mediation from one reality to another, only "the total circularity of the model."[41] As medium and real implode, so the social implodes in the mass, the end of any such meaningful perspective: "the media are effectors not of socialization but, quite the contrary, of the implosion of the social in the masses."[42] With no existence other than in simulation, on the circle of media effects, the masses are the ruin of representation: "the masses swallow up the political, insofar as it implies will and representation."[43]

Baudrillard is scornful of a critical theory "that can only operate on the presupposition of the naivety and stupidity of the masses."[44] At the same time, the whole of his account depends on a continual characterization of the masses in ways which have the familiar ring of just such theory: "the masses remain scandalously resistant to the imperative of rational communication; they are offered meaning when what they want is spectacle."[45] The intellectual includes himself in "the screen stage"—"we are in the screen stage . . . one is no longer in a state to judge, one no longer has the potential to reflect"[46]—and in the very moment of that self-inclusion indicates his own judgment and reflection, while turning too to welcome the mass in these his terms by virtue of its absence from judgment, reflection, representation, any political sense. The masses become the heroes of history, except that there are no heroes, is no history, and the masses themselves are merely a black hole in the media, simulation for simulation in an endless disappearing act.

The conjunction of masses and media gives rise to what Baudrillard himself sometimes notes as a paradox: is it the media which neutralize meanings and produce the mass, or the mass which resists the media with its inert absorption of the meanings proposed? "Are the mass-media on the side of power in the manipulation of the masses or are they on the side of the masses in the liquidation of meaning, in the violence done to meaning and in fascination? Is it the media which induce the masses to fascination or is it the masses which divert the media into the spectacular?"[47] "Today when critical radicalness is useless,"[48] the response is clear: such either/or questions are unanswerable, irrelevant to the immixtion of media and mass; which means in practice that political analysis is dropped as outmoded. The strategic terrain is not any more that of "the liberating claims of the subject" but that of the radical inaction of the mass, "the refusal of meaning and the refusal of speech—or the hyperconformist simulation of the very mechanisms of the system, which is a form of refusal": "All movements which stake their all on the liberation, emancipation, resurrection of a subject of history, of a group, or speech in some gaining of consciousness, of unconsciousness even, by subjects and masses, do not see that they are going along with the system, whose goal at the present time is precisely the overproduction and regeneration of meaning and speech."[49] The logic of which is that those who vote for Le Pen and the *Front National* are resisting the system, hyperconformist simulation; those who join and work for *SOS-Racisme* are confirming it, old-style liberation of subjects. . . . [50]

Alienation has gone, the very term is contemptuous in its suggestion of a perspective of something better; there is anyway no perspective, no depth, no reality in relation to which alienation could be conceived. Cultural pessimism is tipped over into cultural celebration, the better is simply more of the same: more simulation, more repetition of what Baudrillard calls "the system," more mass (the mass *is* the repetition of the system). It is then no surprise that simulation is exactly the description of Baudrillard's own work. With social analysis out of the question, dependent as it would be on some rational notion of behavior, interests, goals, on some idea of representation, the point can only be to mimic—hyperconformism again— the new era, the media-real implosion. "The mass," in fact, is Baudrillard's term for this: it produces the unity the argument needs, the closure—the enclosure—into simulation. To read Baudrillard is to feel a closeness to aspects of the modern world that goes along with a failure to encounter anything specific, no particularity of contradiction, no real—which, of course, is the reality of his world of simulation. The mass is the theory of/screen for this nonencounter, and we can pause here on the interchangeableness of "the mass" and "the masses": the mass eliminates the masses who reappear only as its synonym, as the mass of the simulation mass culture, of television, with no possible social-political definition. Hence the brilliant immobility of Baudrillard's work, the fine mix of modern and conservative elements, precisely its "postmodernism."

For Baudrillard, then, the mass that television creates is the agent of its derision but equally itself the very fact of the media-real implosion. The institution and effects of television turn into the totality of the social which then disappears, implodes indeed. The recognition that television dissolves into life and life into television is falsely converted into an account in which life becomes simply television, nothing but simulation, the totalization that the intellectual can only celebrate, mimic, exacerbate ("what theory can do is to challenge it to be more so").[51] That it is necessary to recognize and follow through the nature and extensiveness of television has been part of the argument here, was part of the discussion earlier of representation: television is a mass, global phenomenon that does indeed change things, is not to be piously held to given modes of explanation. Which is not the same, however, as accepting its terms: the needed sensibility to mass culture is not some required acquiescence to that culture and some fascinated identification with its mass; the redefinitions and archaicizations that television operates in and catches up from the world in which we live today are not the sole facts of that world; the size of television is not the end of any more reality than itself.

Let us reinsert the more reality, the contradictions, the political: the mass as alienation. Mass culture works with a subject as constituted by the exchange and consumption of commodities, and supremely then as constituted by television, the ultimate commodity *form*. Television is a spectacular deflection: not false needs, even less empty simulation, but real needs, taken over in a version of the social and the social-individual which is nonreciprocal, atomizing and not representing the individuals it contains as mass as they receive back meanings that have been appropriated and constructed from their own signifying activities as groups, from their own lives. Television is effective, functions, insofar as we find in it some matter of our actual or virtual human-individual-collective experience, of our reality (thus Raymond Williams talks of a popular culture clearly persisting in television: "its direct energies and enjoyments are still irrepressibly active, even after they have been incorporated as diversions or mimed as commercials or steered into conformist ideologies").[52] The crux is that experience, reality are not separate from but are also determined by television which is a fundamental part of them, and increasingly so (the whole extension of television). This is not to say that media and real implode, end of the social, but that experience, reality are complexly defined, mediated, realized in new ways in which the power of the media is crucial. The assertion of the former, of the end of the social, with the media then some more or less total determination, is exactly a prime demonstration of the alienation of television, mass culture, and current postmodern theories—nothing but television and its terms.

The new ways need new ways of understanding and so a critical attention to the available concepts and modes of analysis which are not merely to be carried over and on; but which are neither to be merely jettisoned, as though critical attention could be just to assent to television's terms and effects, its archaicizations or whatever. Ideology provides the necessary example here, a concept that is now much less used than it was a decade or so ago and that has, indeed, fallen into discredit; this at once because of its supposed dismissiveness of other people's beliefs and pleasures and because of its supposed theoretical inconsistencies now that "we know" that there is no grounding of any discourse, only more of the same, an endless proliferation of discourses that leaves the conceptual framework of ideology—for instance, any paradigm of real/ideological—without object. Thus there is absolutely no need for Lyotard in his pamphlet explaining the postmodern to children to tell them anything whatsoever about ideology; all we have are "billions of little and less little stories, the weft of everyday life."[53] Everyday life here is once again an alternative to political, ideological analysis, with notions such as "complexification" replacing ideology and with room then only for "minimal resistance." In the mainstream of television studies, ideology is likewise dissolving away, both, as in film studies, in response to academic routinization and in response to the desire positively to value programs (remember the asserted nonelitist concern with mass culture mentioned above).

Ideology has, however, to be brought back into the understanding of television, recredited, as it were, but this is not to be done in any single, unified way. Television serves to mediate ideologies in the classic sense of defined expressions of class and interest (so many messages communicated) and is simultaneously indifferent to any such mediation, beyond it: the investment is in the universalization of reception and the circulation of capital, not in particular meanings—or not in the first instance in meanings other than those of that circulation (so that commercials are the meanings of television, programs merely the filling in of the gaps between them). Television is involved in Althusser's cramming *and* is not at all the simple expression of class, *at the same time that* it is fundamental in the elaboration of a ruling culture, the whole social-cultural grounds of reality, *and that* it inevitabilizes over and over again a basic economic order.

Clearly analysis needs to pose questions of ideology, of what kinds of necessity it has and how it is to be understood, at different levels: from this or that particular program through to the fact of television in its overall institution as medium.[54] In respect of this latter, we can come back to the sense of a loss of the ideological, its discredit, for one of the things to which television crucially contributes is a certain *erasure* of ideology. Take the importance of talk already described: the interminabilization of talk, its teletrivialization (talk all the time, all over the place from this topic to that, in all directions without reference to particular structures of address and response—just chat *shows* precisely), is the wearing away of speech, elaborated discourses of representation (what counts is the performance of talk, not its sense). More generally, the cultural saturation to which Jameson refers and to which television first and foremost tends gives the constant difficulty of separating out and identifying ideological effects: ideology is overloaded with culture which is television (and in reverse: television is culture is ideology which disappears in the saturation, in the social extension of television). But then when ideology drops out of the analysis of television, it is as blind spot to this overloading, to this erasure that is exactly part of the ideological work of television: its dissolution of positions into the event of the medium, its continual production of a temporality that goes against history and utopia (television holds past and future to its own perpetual present), its recasting of representation into circulation (of receivers, meanings, objects, capital).

Incorporation is a more appropriate concept here than indoctrination (although, stressing the complexity of levels and particular realizations that has always to be recognized, the latter is not to be lost sight of, can have its appropriateness too). We have our distances but we cannot escape television, and we move easily, naturally in its world, on its terms. What is at stake is television's colonization of everyday life which it becomes and defines, its possession of social time and space as we watch and read the *TV Guide* and have the commuter-train conversation and put the set in this room or that and plug into the network and . . . (there is a whole television geography to be described: the new multinational regions created by the development of satellite distribution, the specific territories—commercial, local, and so on—that can be produced with cable, the electronic transformation of space into network). The saturation of signs and messages is now the fact of television's dominance culturally, and that fact is the neutralization of signs and messages, their erasure into television (this is to agree with Baudrillard: the medium is more than medium, cannot just be identified as such). Television has an exclusive-inclusive functioning: exclusion straightforwardly (positions simply not seen/heard: the PLO on US networks: but then also less organized groups: there is opposition to military service in France, but conscientious objectors are never on television); exclusion quantitatively (gays get to appear with gay viewpoints now and then on the US networks but as a drop in the ocean of heterosexism); exclusion-inclusion (from the positive censorship of filling the screen, making up the world and keeping it *these* images, not all those possible others, and of constructing the terms of debate, the range of "points of view," to the saturation and the dissolution of everything into television, hence television as everything); and it is in this range of its functioning that television works affirmatively and persuasively, with the persuasion first and foremost to itself, not to this or that, to itself as capital investment and cultural production, as vital part of the economic order and as crucial elaboration of culture, the two together.

To talk of alienation in this context is not to refer to some loss of essence or to indicate some permanent condition of individuals today, an exhaustive fact of their existence, but to acknowledge the reality of the constant production of the individual in this television culture, its occupation of him or her in these politically neutralizing terms (the vice-president of a French advertising agency commented recently on a colleague who has run publicity election campaigns for both right and left: "Jacques has worked fantastically to depoliticize political communication";[55] which is exactly the description of television's work). As I watch *The Newlywed Game* or one of its European carbon copies (say, *Les Mariés de l'A2*) or *Wheel of Fortune* or one of its such copies (say, to stay with France, *La Roue de la Fortune*), I am being asked to assent not to anything in particular beyond television itself, to its energy of meaning-time-entertainment (the first sense of which is occupation); indeed, *I* am not being asked, there is no address, no identity of representation, it suffices that we switch on to these and all the other games, that I become part of the network, the circulation that game programs so excessively enact, with their incessant permutation of people and prizes in a never-ending present of self-congratulatory demonstration that television exists, that it works. Of course, game shows, along with the others, are in tune with the capitalist societies of their origin (they do not, after all, express or support socialism), but they are primarily in tune with television, expressive and supportive of that, which is also their origin—hence the ease of their international circulation, the carbon copies, the degree of indifference to the specificity of any actual society. We can see this, we have to, as the divergence between the political order of the nation-state and the economic force of multinational investment and development, with television more and more object and agent of the latter, and then as the combination of the most powerful realization of that economic force, the United States still (France buys and copies programs from the US, not vice versa; European programs that are sold to the US are often from an old version of culture, "quality television," as with BBC adaptations of literary works); but we can also see it, at the same time and in consequence, as the fact of a certain automony of television in its reality as saturation of signs and messages, as cultural occupation: the political-social is elided between the economic order and a massive cultural production which is itself part of that order and which offers a totalizing fragmentation, the television coherence of a moment-by-moment flow that relativizes any and every identity, meaning—and relative to television and its circulation, to the network (pluralism, to come back to that, can now be seen as a concept from an older style television inasmuch as it can suggest a certain political-social coherence, so many identifiable and valid points of view; relativism recognizes a different television: anything equals anything else, saturation, overloading, neutralization—what counts is television, which is the reality of this economic-and-cultural movement).

To recognize this is to recognize that television cannot be grasped as "subject-system," by which is meant here a system tending to construct and gather its effects on some unitary model of human being.[56] Systems of this kind are bound up specifically for us with the history of technology from the seventeenth century on, and their characteristic conceptualization is in terms of some extension-of-the-human-body perfection of "man," what Habermas calls the projection of "the elementary components of the behavioral system of purposive-rational action . . . primarily rooted in the human organism."[57] The success of film theory in the 1970s was related to the possibility of holding the institution of cinema to just such a subject-system (eye, gaze, imaginary signifier, all-perceiving subject). The difficulty of television is then the impossibility of simply doing likewise: it and electronic information/communication media more generally are changing the history. Developing his account of the idea of the projection of the human organism, Habermas writes: "At first the functions of the motor apparatus (hands and legs) were augmented and replaced, followed by energy production (of the human body), the functions of the sensory apparatus (eyes, ears and skin), and finally by the functions of the governing centre (the brain)."[58] That "finally" marks the close and the change: electronic media can be grasped as augmentations and extensions of the brain, but they also shift the terms of this history of man and mastery in which technology can be understood anthropomorphically rather than socially, rather than historically indeed; technology given a natural development and a certain autonomy thereby, following the body as it does in a steady and inevitable progress. The progress may then bring difficulties of control, machines versus men, mastery threatened, but not difficulties of reason, of the identity of the subject (the technologies are predicated on that identity, subject-systems, even when they challenge it).

From the perspective of that history, however, the electronic information/communication media displace the very assumptions of subject, reason, and the image of technology in their terms. When Lyotard stresses in his account of "the postmodern condition" that we must "anticipate a heavy externalization of knowledge in relation to the knower,"[59] he asserts precisely this displacement: "the governing center" is no longer within or augmented from the brain, and knowledge is in the capacity and speed of the information/communication circuits, those circuits in which the individual is now an element, a function, a point of transition and circulation. But the truth of the displacement is not convertible into a new form of determinism where the fascinated imagination of an overarching computer and communicational network takes over reality, takes over *as* reality. Which then again, however, does not mean that it can be pulled back into some sole determinism by and from the economic sphere, a reflection of the world-system of contemporary multinational capitalism, for instance. The latter envisaged thus is itself not easily distinguishable from the network imagination of which it can equally seem the reflection, and its reality is anyway bound up with the new reality of the information/communication media in ways that give the fact of a unity (economic-informational) that is not available for anaylsis according to old models of the economic base, of production, and so on.

Television, to return to that, is evidently, technologically-economically, part of this electronic information/communication media conglomerate, within which it represents a specific area of investment and development. Its institution as "television," TV, has a potentially subordinate existence in all this; symptomatically enough, the television screen is increasingly occupied by something other than TV, from video games to elaborate information display systems (for example, British Ceefax), not to mention rented movies, home video material, and so on (and we should mention, too, the other screens now competing with the television screen—for example, those of the home computer or of systems akin to that of the French Minitel). This potentially subordinate existence is entirely compatible with television's simultaneous dominance, which is cultural and cultural-economic (the production and circulation of images-commodities). It is as though television has its place within a crucial and ever-expanding sphere of economic activity that vastly exceeds it and that is transforming social life in ways that are diverse and not easily predictable (think only of the range of possibilities opened up by the "personalization" of computers, even though that can be understood at once in relation to basic forms of capitalist profit-maximalization strategies—expansion of market for sale of machines, realization of new facilities for the transmission of information regarding goods and services and of new modes of buying and selling and the whole range of financial transactions) while also serving as the overall expression of the new imagination of network, social link-up, as the institution of the society of that: universalization of reception and saturation of messages and signs.

Making up and figuring the network, television offers the coherence of its visibility (its mass) and the homogenization of its time-space (its neutralization). It runs exhaustively across the variety of given modes and energies, capitalizes and recycles them in an effect of randomness that is quantitative—the size of television, its insatiable demand for material to fill the screen and create audiences—and from there qualitative—this equals that in the interminable flow and its endless present, the extraordinary repetition of television. Television gives a *content* to the network of which it is a part but which it also precedes (its institution, after all, is now quite old, a little dated in its modernity nevertheless); *in between*, it negotiates the breakdown of the subject-system unity through the assembly of meanings, voices, sights, viewer-moments into the continuum of its functioning (that as "unity") and negotiates the radical future, the world today in its contradictions and transformations, including those of the social development and consequences and possibilities of the new information/communication media, through the continual recasting of assembly into old forms, old unities, all its repetition (there is always a basic television in television, its same stock TV). Television is paradoxically conservative (the "in between" again): reworking a hegemonic ground of social intelligibility—of culture—while relating simultaneously a fragmentation that goes against any hegemony understood as coherent world-view beyond that of the imagination of media and network—no world-view but television which is today ground and knowledge; but then too while having its economic place in an order that it equally reflects and figures, supports and enacts, saying that over and over again.

The mass swallows up the political insofar as it implies will and representation. Or, the as always necessary redirection of such formulations, television makes a mass in those terms, pulls away from representation and the political. Baudrillard eliminates the subject, will; the mass is nonsubject, nonwill (involved in no calculations), "is" only in simulation. As opposed to which can be put assertions of the subject as initial given, whether alienated by television from authentic being (a degraded mass culture) or not (a mass culture that takes up the components of a popular culture to which it contributes and that can be received in their own ways by individuals and groups). Television, ungraspable as subject-system, offers no choice between these assertions or between them and Baudrillard's elimination; it participates in all three, any of which might then need to be privileged—but never exclusively—in the analysis at this or that moment, and each of which must be understood and followed through in respect of the emphases that have been given here as to representing television. Alienation is produced as the occupation of the political as mass, the erasure of ideological struggle, the neutralization of representation, but this occupation and erasure and neutralization are not the sole reality even if they do have large and determining effects. The masses of people in our societies, all of us, are implicated in a mass culture, a television, that they, we, traverse in ways that are continually similar and different. The cultural occupation of television, its saturation, works and does not just work, and in complex formations, complex interlockings, with a particularity for such and such an individual or group. The coverage (to use television's word for this saturation) includes from the material it picks up fundamental asymmetries (class, racial, gender differences) which then come back as the *figures* of the culture, of the mass, produced and reproduced, appearing as so many images in the rhetoric of commodification (note immediately the assurance with which commercials mobilize asymmetry as consumer desire), as so many inevitable components of the world television makes and monitors and molds (these figures come back too in the world, which is to say again that there is no simple separation between television and some other reality of social life).

It is for a critical television studies to break the fact and assumption and effect of television. The attention to televisions in the world is necessary here, other televisions than television (thus the study of the varying articulations of resistance to external control, complicity of common interest between national and transnational forces, political debate around State and access and participation, initiation of cultural production in, say, the development of television in different African countries). So too is the attention to video that thinking about television so often leaves aside, in the image of the latter's institution (Jameson has argued for the study of video as the crucial hold on television, the point from which to work through a valid account).[60] In neither case, evidently, is it a matter of "alternatives": other televisions, video are at grips with television, and it is just this struggle, this process of conflict and contradiction, that is important, allowing of critical reflection. Equally, though, the break is to be achieved directly within the study of television, the institution we know. The task is to go against the normalization of the media, of television— something of what has been at stake here in the insistence on the terms of television, of television itself. Particular readings of particular programs can indeed be valuable, but they can also contribute to the very normalization that needs to be countered, to the extension of television, taken for granted and continued. There is a necessary struggle for meaning, but that struggle has effectively to take up television, cannot proceed as though it were just a question of more texts to be read, deconstructed, revealed in their radical contradictions; the unity of the program after all is precisely a unity—a term—of television, which latter needs then to be as much (and more) in the analysis as it is in the program.

Nothing is more depressing in academic discourse today, indeed, than the word "interesting" in television studies as these are now developing: this or that and every other program is "interesting," meaning usually that *I* can "do a reading" of it. What is then being avoided and replaced, however, is *evaluation*. The readings done are quickly indistinguishable, because their sole demonstration is of a complexity and multiplicity common to any program (they can all be made interesting, opened to plurality) or—but the two can as well go together—because their impetus is the commitment to the necessary value of any program as genuinely popular (they are all interesting, offer authentic experiences). But the requisite sensibility to mass culture mentioned earlier, to television, is not a required acquiescence, even less the mimicking of its forms and the celebration of its effects. Nor is it just the reverse: an automatic negation, a blind rejection that recognizes only degradation. And yet that reverse is not without *some* necessity. In one of the pieces shown in the first Deep Dish TV series (Deep Dish is a public-access satellite network), Flo Kennedy, who is perhaps best known to readers of this piece for her appearance in Lizzie Borden's film *Born in Flames* (itself, among other things, a political statement about the media), refers to television as one of "the most racist, sexist, exclusivist" institutions in the US, and this is something we cannot afford to forget. Evaluation is not exhausted in that not-forgetting, but it has also to depend on it: the task is to make the critical distance that television continually erodes in its extension, its availability, its proximity—all of which is played out on its screen from show to show in the endless flow. The struggle for meaning is here, and it is a struggle of *and for* political criticism; not against television in the old global terms, but not in defense of it either, outside of any such impasse: a criticism that is responsive to the heterogeneity of television and to the overall determinations of its specific institution within which—at times in contradiction with which—that heterogeneity manifests itself, that responds to the reality of television today in—as—late capitalism and to the complexity of its social functioning.

Television is an occupation, in both senses: it takes up our time, employs us, and it holds the ground, defines the terrain; television works as over-representation, again in two senses at once: it goes to excess, over any stable representing, and it multiplies sounds and images, over and over, the cultural saturation. To make critical distance is not to reduce television to ideology: it is to recognize it at any moment as in ideological process. Much of television, our experience of it, is *also* not ideological, not to be brought down to the production-reproduction of oppressive social relations and their validation—occupation here is wider than such production-reproduction, television is not just in essence the agency of the latter; we watch and react in different ways to a multitude of things, and the extent of those things, television's extension, its "everything" (its proposal of life as on screen), goes beyond any possibility of its being read off according to some single functionalization of it as ideological transmitter (the heterogeneity, there are more logics to television than ideology). Simply, we have to take the "also" seriously (this is the appropriate criterion for "serious discussion"): television is always at the same time bound up in our societies in the work of ideology, the expression of given ideologies and, exactly and specifically, the saturation of signs and messages and the erasure of the ideological—struggle for meaning—into fragmentation as the world in action, the indifferences of merely differences, the perpetual flow of a constant present without any hope beyond its repetition. Occupation is ideological operation, the generation of an all-embracing cultural space-time as unity and sense of reality, the holding definition of the existing and the possible, versus the conflict of groups and classes, the forging of political meanings, contradictions of representation.

"Everyday life defeats the representative institution," comments Lyotard.[61] Certainly. Inasmuch as the representation of parliamentary liberalism, the crucial historical establishment of democracy, is challenged by—and often, necessarily, on the basis of an appeal to that very tradition of representation—the forces that it marginalizes, denies, excludes in its forms of power, decision, majority, with a professionalization of "politics" and "representatives" that derides any active democracy. "A screen does not represent anything," writes Baudrillard; to think the contrary is the illogical projection of "an operational, statistical, informational, simulational system" into the terms of "a system of representation, will and opinion."[62] Certainly. Inasmuch as television in its institution is effectively involved in the occupation and erasure described. Yet, it has to be repeated, television is not the beginning and end of reality, whatever its symbiosis with a late capitalism—a multinational world-system—that it mirrors and creates in a totality that is powerful, yes, but not totally powerful; and which is anyway pervious to the oppositional interests and values with which it must always negotiate (part of ideological process, the work of constructing unity, trying to resolve contradictions), as the democracies of its institution are open to counterforces to the given consolidation of power, to representations that require more or less accommodation. Everyday life defeats the representative institution, and "everyday life" in this conception is itself quickly defeat, assent to the system, the totality which becomes precisely its definition; everyday life, television, and the postmodern condition fuse into an inescapable destiny that does then, indeed, archaicize political terms, social(ist) values—the future is here now in the technology, the network, the system as the fact of a society in which these terms and values have come to an end.

So the fight is against any such end; not against television but against the institution of that ending. So the fight is for, let us still say, representation but in new forms; forms that are bound up more with participation than delegation, dependent on significant associations of people rather than recorded majorities, moving toward the development of a nonrepresentative representation: the achievement of modes of presentation and imaging and entertainment and argument that are realizations of collective desires, group aspirations, common projects, shared experience at the same time that they refuse all ideas—all expression—of standing in for and subsuming the heterogeneous individual-sociality/social-individuality of the actual lives of actual men and women. The pressures today from the contradictions of different identities, and in movement (not static givens), across the individual as well as the society (the individual no one identity either), challenge the old conceptions of and faith in representation with its assumptions of the representative, x for y, like and in place of, a democracy of substitutes in which the social is never ours. A nonrepresentative representation will be as good as its moments of use, its particularity at any time in this or that context; with no claims to be representative beyond those moments, guaranteed not by some prior settled referent but by the reference it finds in its production in use, needing an institution not of representatives but of representings (exactly that production in use as opposed to the repeated generalization of fixed identifications), and specifically here a representing television. Something of which is suggested by

the versions now being developed of the operation of television as publishing house, with mobile and participatory access, plus freedom from the
institutional norms of "good television," rather than the—nevertheless valuable—more limited and traditional openings of "public television" (that
very label is indicative). Deep Dish TV, mentioned earlier, is one such
developing version; with nothing utopian about it, it exists and works, and
everything utopian, bringing back alternative values to "television" and
envisaging the radical future that the latter makes up and figures as its
present, utopia already here in technology and capital, that end of the
political, the social. . . . Deep Dish TV is about the renewal of representation, is involved in the idea of a fundamental redemocratization, is concerned with the reclaiming of literacy as an issue and a project.[63]

Literacy, that is, is more than a theme from the right, a worry about the
loss of the mainstream of the nation and the proposal of some fixed standard of an oppressive culture; as it is more than just another anachronism
in a world of everything as culture, the false equality of a relativism that
is quickly itself a disarming conservatism, an anything-goes confirmation
of the existing system hymned as liberation (often informed by and informing the accounts of the technology-network-circulation utopia). What
must be worked for is literacy as a culture that is truly equal to all, differ-
ential (aware of and articulated from differences) and inclusive (for each
of us and offering the basis on and in relation to which differences can be
created, perceived, and lived nonoppressively), without coercion and
shared, about identities and identity. As regards television, this as issue and
project is now urgent. Alongside those institutions which have been historically and are crucially the sites of the production of hegemony (religion,
law, education, and so on), television, interacting with and relaying these,
is also today this occupation, this screening of intelligibility as cultural saturation: contemporary hegemonic social ground as neutralization, literacy
as that, the adherence of our viewing, television's terms; for which the
accounts of "the postmodern" give us the familiarizing theory and of which
Baudrillard spells out in complementary fashion the political sense, "the
end of the social." But the social has not ended, as real struggle and future
imagination: to reclaim literacy is to say that and to strive for new relations
of representations, new possibilities. The importance of television studies,
its role, will surely be there, questioning television in that struggle and
imagination, toward a politics of representing television.

NOTES

1. See Raymond Williams, *Television: Technology and Cultural Form* (London: Fontana, 1974).
2. Herbert I. Schiller, "Electronic Information Flows: New Basis for Global

Domination?" in *Television in Transition,* ed. Phillip Drummond and Richard Paterson (London: BFI, 1985), p. 19.

3. Cited in *TV Quarterly* Fall 1979:17.

4. For a detailed account of the economics of programs/ratings, see David Atkins and Barry Litman, "Network TV Programming: Economics, Audiences, and the Ratings Game, 1971–1986," *Journal of Communication* 36.3 (Summer 1986):32–50.

5. Arthur C. Nielsen, Jr., and Theodore Berland, "Nielsen Defends His Ratings," in *Television Today,* ed. Barry Cole (New York: Oxford University Press, 1981), pp. 194–95.

6. Fredric Jameson, "Reification and Utopia in Mass Culture," *Social Text* 1 (Winter 1979):139.

7. Claude Lévi-Strauss, *Anthropologie structurale* (Paris: Plon, 1958), p. 95; C. Jacobsen and B. Grundfest Schoepf, trans., *Structural Anthropology* (New York: Basic, 1963), p. 83.

8. Jonathan Culler, *On Deconstruction: Theory and Criticism after Structuralism* (London: Routledge, 1983), p. 153.

9. Stuart Hall, "Theories of Mass Culture," paper to the International Conference on Mass Culture, Center for Twentieth Century Studies, University of Wisconsin-Milwaukee, 25 April 1984.

10. Vladimir Popov, cited in Terry Doyle, "Truth at Ten? Some Questions of Soviet Television," *Sight and Sound* Spring 1984:108.

11. Jürgen Habermas, *Jürgen Habermas, Autonomy, and Solidarity: Interviews,* ed. Peter Dews (London: Verso, 1986), p. 201.

12. Jean Baudrillard, *A l'ombre des majorités silencieuses* (Paris: Denoël, 1982), p. 115.

13. Maurice Blanchot, *L'Entretien infini* (Paris: Gallimard, 1969), p. 364. Susan Hanson, trans., "Everyday Speech," *Yale French Studies* 73 (1987):18–19.

14. Blanchot, pp. 361, 364; Hanson, pp. 16, 18.

15. Stanley Cavell also draws attention to the talking-meeting reality of television in his "The Fact of Television," in *Themes out of School* (San Francisco: North Point, 1984), pp. 235–68.

16. Eduard Zimmermann, cited in Claus Dieter-Rath, "The Invisible Network," ed. Drummond and Paterson, p. 201.

17. Nick Ross and Sue Cook, *Crimewatch UK* (London: Hodder & Stoughton, 1987), p. 115. (Ross and Cook are the presenters of the *Crimewatch UK* program.)

18. Ibid., p. 29.

19. See Gilles Deleuze, "Trois questions sur 'Six fois deux,' " *Cahiers du cinéma* 271 (Nov. 1976):8.

20. Earl Hamner, interviewed in Horace Newcomb and Robert S. Alley, *The Producer's Medium: Conversations with Creators of American TV* (New York: Oxford University Press, 1983), p. 164.

21. Fredric Jameson, "Postmodernism and Consumer Society," in *The Anti-aesthetic: Essays on Post-modern Culture,* ed. Hal Foster (Port Townsend, Wash.: Bay Press, 1983), p. 125.

22. For discussion of the issues raised around representation and identity in the debates over women's suffrage in Britain, see Denise Riley, *"Am I That Name?"* (London: Macmillan, 1988), pp. 67–95.

23. John Stuart Mill, *Considerations on Representative Government* (1861), *Collected Works,* vol. 19 (Toronto: University of Toronto Press, 1977), p. 457.

24. Ibid.

25. Ibid., pp. 476–79.

26. Ibid., p. 455.

27. Guy Debord, cited in Fredric Jameson, "Postmodernism or the Cultural Logic of Late Capitalism," *New Left Review* 146 (July-Aug. 1984):60.

28. E. D. Hirsch, Jr., *Cultural Literacy: What Every American Needs to Know* (New York: Vintage, 1988). For a recent example of the "so much so good/so bad" account of television, see Diane Ravitch and Chester E. Finn, *What Do Our Seventeen Year Olds Know?* (New York: Harper, 1988).

29. Hans Magnus Enzensberger, "Constituents of a Theory of the Media," in *Society of Mass Communications,* ed. D. McQuail (Harmondsworth: Penguin, 1972), p. 113.

30. Louis Althusser, "Idéologie et appareils idéologiques d'État," in *Positions* (Paris: Éditions sociales, 1976), p. 94; Ben Brewster, trans., "Ideology and Ideological State Apparatuses," in *Lenin and Philosophy and Other Essays* (London: New Left Books, 1971), p. 154.

31. Althusser, p. 121; Brewster, p. 187. For discussion and critique of Althusser's account of ideology and the subject, see Stephen Heath, "The Turn of the Subject," *Cinétracts* 7–8 (1979):32–48.

32. Alice Kaplan and Kristin Ross, "Introduction," *Yale French Studies* 73 (1987):3; Michèle Mattelart, *Women, Media, Crisis* (London: Comedia, 1986), p. 7.

33. Félix Guattari, *La Révolution moléculaire* (Paris: Recherches, 1977), pp. 241–90 ("Pour une micro-politique du désir") and passim.

34. Ernst Bloch, *Das Prinzip Hoffnung* (Berlin: Aufbau, 1960), p. 367.

35. Jean Baudrillard, *Amérique* (Paris: Grasset, 1986), p. 84.

36. Baudrillard, *A l'ombre,* p. 24.

37. Ibid., pp. 24–25.

38. Ibid., *A l'ombre,* p. 45.

39. Jean Baudrillard, "The Ecstasy of Communication," in Foster, p. 127.

40. Jean Baudrillard, *Simulacres et simulation* (Paris: Galilée, 1981), p. 54.

41. Ibid., pp. 126–27.

42. Ibid., p. 125.

43. Baudrillard, *A l'ombre,* p. 28.

44. Baudrillard, *Simulacres,* p. 124.

45. Baudrillard, *A l'ombre,* p. 15.

46. Jean Baudrillard, interview (1984), cited in André Frankovits, ed., *Seduced and Abandoned: The Baudrillard Scene* (Glebe, NSW: Stonemoss, 1984), p. 48.

47. Baudrillard, *Simulacres,* p. 129.

48. Jean Baudrillard, *Les Stratégies fatales* (Paris: Grasset, 1983), p. 272.

49. Baudrillard, *Simulacres,* pp. 130–31.

50. Baudrillard indeed sees in "the Le Pen effect" an event born of the indifference of the mass, with no ideology behind it, "not a fascist movement"; *La Gauche divine* (Paris: Grasset, 1985), pp. 118, 130. This book is devoted to an account of the French Socialist government of 1981 onwards and its "rehabilitation of a tired social history" (87).

51. Jean Baudrillard, *L'Autre par lui-même* (Paris: Galilée, 1987), p. 86.

52. Raymond Williams, *Towards 2000* (London: Chatto and Windus, 1983), p. 146.

53. Jean-François Lyotard, *Le Postmoderne expliqué aux enfants* (Paris: Galilée, 1986), p. 40.

54. For an initial attempt at developing a television analysis through consideration of a particular program, see Stephen Heath and Gillian Skirrow, "Television: A World in Action," *Screen* 18.2 (Summer 1977):7–77.

55. Bernard Roux, interview, *Le Nouvel Observateur* 1239 (5/11 Aug. 1988):45.

56. The term "subject-system" is adapted from Lyotard who uses it somewhat differently in his account of "the postmodern condition"; see Jean-François Lyotard, *La Condition postmoderne* (Paris: Minuit, 1979), p. 67.

57. Jürgen Habermas, "Technology and Science as 'Ideology,'" in *Towards a Rational Society* (London: Heinemann, 1971), p. 87.

58. Ibid.

59. Lyotard, *La Condition postmoderne*, p. 14.

60. Fredric Jameson, "Reading without Interpretation: Postmodernism and the Video-Text," in *The Linguistics of Writing*, ed. Nigel Fabb et al. (Manchester: Manchester University Press, 1987), pp. 199–223 ("Thinking anything adequate about commercial television may well involve ignoring it and thinking about something else: in the instance experimental video" [202]).

61. Lyotard, *Le Postmoderne expliqué*, p. 53.

62. Baudrillard, *Les Stratégies fatales*, pp. 124–25.

63. Deep Dish TV, 339 Lafayette Street, New York, NY 10012.

Contributors

WILLIAM BODDY is Assistant Professor of Speech at Baruch College, City University of New York. He has published articles in *Media, Culture, and Society, Cinema Journal,* and *Screen,* and is the author of *From the Golden Age to the Vast Wasteland: Television in the Fifties* (forthcoming from the University of Illinois Press).

CHARLOTTE BRUNSDON is Lecturer in Film Studies at Warwick University. She has written on soap opera and popular television and is the coauthor with David Morley of *Everyday Television Nationwide* (1978) and editor of the collection *Film for Women* (1986).

JOHN CAUGHIE is Senior Lecturer in Film and Television Studies at the University of Glasgow and Codirector of the John Logie Baird Centre for Research in Television and Film. He has contributed articles on television to *Screen* and other journals.

MARY ANN DOANE is Associate Professor of Modern Culture and Media and English at Brown University. She is the author of *The Desire to Desire: The Woman's Film of the 1940s* (1987), and of articles in *Screen, October, Yale French Studies, Discourse,* and *Wide Angle.*

JANE GAINES is Assistant Professor of English at Duke University. She recently coedited the collection *Fabrications: Costume and the Female Body,* and has contributed a chapter to a forthcoming book entitled *The Likeness: Image Properties in the Industrial Age.*

STEPHEN HEATH, Fellow of Jesus College, Cambridge, is the author of *The Nouveau Roman* (1972), *Questions of Cinema* (1981), and *The Sexual Fix* (1984). His book on Flaubert's *Madame Bovary* is forthcoming from Cambridge University Press.

LYNNE JOYRICH is Assistant Professor of English at the University of Wisconsin-Milwaukee. She is the author of "All That Television Allows: TV Melodrama, Postmodernism, and Consumer Culture," published in *Camera Obscura.*

EILEEN R. MEEHAN is Assistant Professor of Media Arts at the University of Arizona. She is the author of articles in *Journal of Communication Inquiry, Critical Studies in Mass Communication, Media, Culture, and Society,* and *Journal of Broadcasting.* She has also contributed a chapter to *Political Economy of Information* (1988).

PATRICIA MELLENCAMP is Associate Professor of Art History at the University of Wisconsin-Milwaukee. She is coeditor of three books on cinema, author of articles in *Screen, Afterimage, Wide Angle, Discourse,* and *Framework,* and author of *Indiscretions: Avant Garde Film, Video, and Feminism* (forthcoming from Indiana University Press).

MEAGHAN MORRIS is the author of *The Pirate's Fiancée: Feminism, Reading, Postmodernism* (1988) and *Upward Mobility* (forthcoming from Indiana University Press). She has also coedited two anthologies: *Language, Sexuality, and Subversion* (1978) and *Michel Foucault: Power, Truth, Strategy* (1980).

MARGARET MORSE is Assistant Professor in the School of Cinema-Television at the University of Southern California. She is the author of articles in *Afterimage, Discourse, Screen, Fabula,* and *Studies in GDR Culture and Society.*

ANDREW ROSS, Assistant Professor of English at Princeton University, is the author of *The Failure of Modernism: Symptoms of American Poetry* (1986) and *No Respect: In-*

tellectuals and Popular Culture (1989), and the editor of *Universal Abandon? The Politics of Postmodernism* (1988).

LYNN SPIGEL is Assistant Professor in the Department of Communication Arts at the Universtiy of Wisconsin-Madison. She is Associate Editor of *Camera Obscura*, coeditor of a special issue entitled "Television and the Female Consumer" (Winter 1988), and the author of articles in *Quarterly Review of Film Studies, Camera Obscura,* and *Critical Studies in Mass Communications*.

Name Index

Althusser, Louis: 19, 22, 284, 290

Baby Jessica (Jessica McClure): 11, 249–50, 252, 258
Bakhtin, Mikhail: 198, 250; chronotope, 194, 214, 216n.3, 217n.15
Ball, Lucille: 1, 3, 15–16, 21, 258, 261
Barnouw, Erik: 108, 112
Barthes, Roland: 8, 12, 31; *Camera Lucida*, 222, 242; "Myth Today," 203
Baudrillard, Jean: 6, 7, 8, 196, 205, 212, 244, 258, 279, 286–89, 291, 295, 298–99; banality and fatality, 14, 18–20, 25–26, 31–35, 40; *Simulations*, 145, 157, 159–61, 164–65. *See also* Simulation
Benjamin, Walter: 4, 8, 194, 201, 211, 216n.3, 227, 229, 233, 241–46, 253–54, 261
Bennett, Tony: 66, 179
Bloch, Ernst: 222, 237, 286
Bourdieu, Pierre: 44, 61, 69
Brodsly, David: 197, 199, 200, 203

Challenger disaster: 11, 17, 229–32, 235, 246, 253, 255–57
Chambers, Iain: 23–24, 25, 32
Crosby, John: 86, 99, 103, 108, 111
Culler, Jonathan: 227, 273

DC Comics: 174–75, 179–80, 183, 185–87
de Certeau, Michel: 7, 8, 26–39 *passim*, 53, 56, 194–95, 212
Derrida, Jacques: 31, 161, 244, 273
Doane, Mary Ann: 160, 259

Eco, Umberto: 178–79, 181
Ellis, John: 62, 159, 182, 183, 199, 205

Federal Communications Commission: 3, 82, 99, 102, 107–08, 110–12, 139
Feuer, Jane: 54, 65, 155n.19, 227
Fiske, John: 14, 22–23, 24–25, 33, 34, 56, 158–59
Foucault, Michel: 209
Flitterman, Sandy: 166, 207
Frankfurt School: 25, 26, 154n.13, 275
Freud, Sigmund: 12, 27, 35, 236, 241–61 *passim; Beyond the Pleasure Principle*, 243, 258; *Jokes and Their Relation to the Unconscious*, 257–58; *Inhibitions, Symptoms, and Anxiety*, 243, 246–51

Habermas, Jürgen: 274, 293
Hall, Stuart: 24, 173
Hartley, John: 158–59
Heath, Stephen: 227, 234, 237
Hebdige, Dick: 60, 62, 64
Huyssen, Andreas: 19, 23, 86, 157, 161

Jameson, Fredric: 273, 279, 291, 296

Kennedy assassination: 235, 242, 253–56 *passim*; Zapruder film of, 246, 248, 253
Kowinski, William Severini: 197, 198, 203, 211

Lanham Act: 174, 178, 186, 188
Lyotard, Jean-Francois: 35, 234, 290, 293, 297

MacAuliffe, Christa: 11, 255–57, 259
McLuhan, Marshall: 3, 146, 151, 158, 160, 215n.2, 216n.6, 287
Marchand, Roland: 75, 77, 78
Mattelart, Michèle: 66, 285
Modleski, Tania: 23, 157, 161
Morse, Margaret: 166, 225, 229

Petro, Patrice: 23, 24

Radio Corporation of America (RCA): 83, 111, 119–20
Reagan, Nancy: 46, 232, 249–50
Reagan, Ronald: 10, 29, 232, 250

Schivelbusch, Wolfgang: 230, 231, 236
Skirrow, Gillian: 227, 234
Sloterdijk, Peter: 44, 52
Spivak, Gayatri: 57
Stanton, Frank: 100, 107, 117

Thom, René: 234, 244–45, 252, 255, 259, 261

Van Doren, Charles: 7, 98, 99, 102, 105–07
Venturi, Robert: 44, 211

Weber, Samuel: 254, 255, 259, 260
Williams, Raymond: 2, 8, 24, 62, 64, 194, 206, 208, 216n.3, 240, 289
Wollacott, Janet: 66, 179

Zizek, Slavoj: 235–36

Subject Index